Remember all those renowned generations,
They left their bodies to fatten the wolves,
They left their homesteads to fatten the foxes,
Fled to far countries, or sheltered themselves
In cavern, crevice or hole.
Defending Ireland's soul...
Remember all those renowned generations,
Remember all that have sunk in their blood,
Remember all that have died on the scaffold,
Remember all that have fled, that have stood,
Stood, took death like a tune
On an old tambourine.

> W.B. Yeats, "Three Marching Songs,"
> in W.B. Yeats, The Poems, New Edition,
> ed. by Richard J. Finneran
> (New York: Macmillan, 1983), 333.

The way in which the earthly and the heavenly city interpenetrate each other can be recognized only by faith; indeed, it remains a mystery of human history, that is, of a history always troubled by sin until the glory of the Son of God is fully revealed.

> Vatican Council II, Pastoral Constitution on the
> Church in the Modern World, 40

See everything, overlook a great deal, correct a little.

> Pope St. John XXIII

If anyone wishes to be first, he shall be the last of all and the servant of all.

*Mark* 9:35

The Church is not afraid of history. On the contrary, she loves it, and desires to love it more and better, as God loves it.

Pope Francis, "On the Opening of the Vatican
Secret Archives of Pius XII," March 4, 2019

The more particular you make something, the more universal it becomes.

Greta Gerwig
quoted in Eloise Bondiau, "Lady Bird is a Rallying Cry for
Catholic Schoolgirls Everywhere," *America*, Nov. 13, 2017, 54.

Duty then is the sublimest [sic] word in our language. Do your duty in all things. You cannot do more. You should never wish to do less."

Robert E. Lee
Letter of Resignation from the U.S. Army
April 20, 1861

Give heed, my people, to my teaching; Turn your ear to the words of my mouth, I will open my mouth in a parable and reveal the hidden lessons of the past. The things we have heard and understood, the things our fathers have told us, these we will not hide from their children, but will tell them to the next generation.

*Psalm* 78:1-4
<u>The Grail</u> Translation

# JOHN MOORE

*Catholic Pastoral Leadership
During Florida's First Boom,
1877–1901*

Michael J. McNally

DIOCESE OF
St Augustine

**2020**

Library of Congress Control Number: 2020901484

John Moore: Catholic Pastoral Leadership during Florida's First Boom, 1877-1901

By Michael J. McNally

Published by the Diocese of St. Augustine

Book and cover design by Lilla Ross

ISBN: 978-1-64764-642-4 print
ISBN: 978-1-64764-658-5 e-pub

## Dedication

To my brother diocesan priest, mentor, and friend,

### Father Peter Dolan

Born April 25, 1931, Leitrim County, Ireland

Received his priestly formation at St. John's College, Waterford. Ordained June 17, 1954, at Holy Trinity Cathedral, Waterford, for the Diocese of St. Augustine

In the Diocese of St. Augustine from 1954 to 1968, he was assigned to Tallahassee, Miami, St. Petersburg, Orlando, Winter Garden, Palm Bay, and Melbourne, both in parish ministry and in high school work.

In the Diocese of Orlando from 1968 to 1984, he was pastor of Our Lady of Lourdes, Melbourne, founding pastor of St. Mark the Evangelist, Fort Pierce (1972-1979), and pastor of St. Lucie, Port St. Lucie, while serving in several diocesan level roles.

In the Diocese of Palm Beach from 1984, he continued as pastor of St. Lucie, and was also named the Vicar of Personnel and diocesan Consultor in the new diocese. On September 19, 1996, he retired as Pastor *Emeritus*, while residing in Fort Pierce and helping out at St. Mark the Evangelist.

# CONTENTS

# Acknowledgments

I am grateful to these two institutions that provided me financial support during the archival research portion of this project: St. Charles Borromeo Seminary, Philadelphia, for a Sabbatical Grant - Spring 2003 and the Cushwa Center for the Study of American Catholicism at the University of Notre Dame for a Cushwa Center Research Grant - Spring 2003.

The Poor Clare Nuns, Fort Myers Beach, offered me a prayerful, peaceful place and commodious space to write.

Bishop Felipe J. Estévez, Bishop of the Diocese of St. Augustine, was of inestimable value as an encouraging friend and promoter of the history of Catholicism in Florida; he assisted with considerable financial support in the production and publication of this book. Stephen Bell, CEO, of the Diocese of St. Augustine ably facilitated my various requests for assistance. Kathleen Bagg, Director of Communications of the Diocese of St. Augustine, Lilla Ross, literary agent for the Diocese of St. Augustine, and Brandon Duncan, Coordinator for Creative & Digital Services for the Diocese of St. Augustine, also lent their expertise to the project.

Father Thomas Willis, rector of the Cathedral/Basilica of St. Augustine, was a gracious and supportive host to me during the times I stayed in St. Augustine.

Father Peter Dolan and Gretta Connell shared with me some Irish archival materials. Father Dolan also showed ongoing interest and encouragement in the completion of this book. He afforded me gracious hospitality when I needed a break from writing.

Numerous archivists aided me when I did the majority of my archival research in the Spring of 2003, and afterwards. Their guidance at the repositories was very helpful, hospitable, and professional. I am especially grateful to Sister Thomas Joseph McGoldrick, SSJ, and Sister Catherine Bitzer, SSJ, who were of tremendous help during my research in St. Augustine; to Tricia T. Pyne of the Associated Archives at St. Mary's University and Seminary (Baltimore); to Wendy Clauson Schlereth, Ph.D., and to William Kevin Cawley of the Archives of the University of Notre Dame; and to Brian Fahey of the Archives of the Diocese of Charleston.

Cynthia Crawford Westaway carefully read the manuscript, providing me with many helpful suggestions. Msgr. Christopher J. Schreck did some of the Latin translations and made helpful suggestions about the manuscript. Chris Lissner and Sister Mary Frances Fortin, OSC, provided technical support.

Father Frank Giuffre, of the ArchDiocese of Philadelphia, provided some research assistance while he was a student-priest in Rome.

Father Timothy Lindensfelder of the Diocese of St. Augustine shared with me his private collection of historical photos.

# Illustrations – List of Sources

# *Foreword*

It is a blessed coincidence that, as the mother diocese of the State of Florida is about to celebrate the Sesquicentennial of its beginning, the most prominent historian of the Church in Florida, Father Michael McNally, who has a Ph.D. in history from the University of Notre Dame, was writing about our second bishop, John Moore. Bishop Moore was kept in obscurity even by the Encyclopedia of American Catholic History which surprisingly does not include his name. This book reveals the irony of Nazareth; the potential of greatness is often hidden in obscurity.

Father McNally, who had already published books on the history of Southern and Western Florida Catholicism, took the challenge of digging into this obscure Irish-born prelate to show how this significant and influential leader impacted both church and state in Florida at the end of the nineteenth century.

The modern reader could easily bypass the difficult challenge this research entails because the sources available to reconstruct "Silent John" in a rural society, which reflected a world where no photocopiers, typewriters, telephones, and the social media outreach we enjoy today existed. Moore left no personal diaries or interviews or even personal correspondence to discover. It took the cleverness of a persistent inquirer and the tenacity of an extremely hard-working researcher to make this book available for us. "Silent John" is silent no longer.

Without this book, Moore would have been long forgotten by succeeding generations, in spite of an existing high school in the College Park neighborhood in Orlando, Florida. The "Hornets" may carry his name and the school blog may show six lines of his legacy, but I wonder if there is a single student or teacher or administrator who could answer a few questions about what Moore did in Florida. The outstanding accomplishment of Father McNally is that he took this obscure bishop and literally brought him to life in the twenty-first century.

*The Letter to the Hebrews* states that, "Jesus Christ the same, yesterday, today and forever"(13:8), which is an inspiration for disciples of all times. A closer look at this leader of the faith in the ever-growing State of Florida reveals how, in a totally other context than our own, we find the same vitality flowing from the unique source, Jesus Christ, who is born again and again for and in us.

+ V. J. Estévez

The Most Reverend Felipe J. Estévez
Bishop of the Diocese of St. Augustine
September 24, 2019

# *Why Moore?*

I first met John Moore in the summer of 1980. I heard his voice in his letters and discovered something of his character in his deeds. He was dead almost eighty years that summer when I was traveling, doing research on my doctoral dissertation on the history of Catholicism in South Florida, my homeland. But since my work covered 100 years, from 1868 to 1968, Moore was just one figure of many in the story. A decade later during a sabbatical, while researching a book on Catholic parish life on Florida's West Coast from 1860 to 1968, I encountered Moore again. This time I spent more time with him, since he was instrumental in the development of Catholic parish life in that region of Florida. His complex character, his competence, his pathos began to intrigue me. When I was given the opportunity for a second sabbatical in 2003, I decided to devote it to plunging into the depths of Moore. That immersion took me into deeper, murkier waters than I had initially imagined.

In life and in death, Moore was not a readily cooperative subject of study. Because of his taciturn unassuming demeanor, he was the quintessential Irish "Quiet Man." In death, of all the bishops of Florida, he left the least in the diocesan archives — only six document boxes. Almost 90 percent of what is there is from other correspondents or financial accounts recorded in Moore's hand in formal books and on scraps of paper. He rarely kept copies of the letters he sent, virtually all of which were handwritten. Virtually all of his correspondence rests in archives found elsewhere (I accessed thirty-two in researching this book). Moore left only one interview of himself,[1] no articles in journals, no personal diary, and precious little personal correspondence. For example, we have no letters from his family in Charleston, SC. If he kept any family letters during his life, he may have destroyed them and any other personal papers before he died or he just did not keep them at all. Much of his communication was done verbally, in person, for which there is little or no evidence.

Not only is Moore an elusive person to study due to difficulty of finding documentation, but also he lived in a society vastly different from our own. During his time as a priest and bishop, he had no electricity, no automobile, no typewriter, no indoor plumbing, no telephone, no computer, and no internet. Transportation was propelled by the horse, or by train, or by steamboat. The newspaper was the only mass media of the day, while interpersonal communication was only done in person or by letter. The telegraph was available, but rarely used because of its expense. He lived in a world of odors: from animal manure scattered in the city streets or on the farm, from human sweat that was not washed off but about once a week, if that often, and from ubiquitous outhouses. If you wished to stay up after the sunset, you had only gas lighting or oil lamps to illumine the darkness. His was a society much quieter than today, especially on the farm, where 90 percent of Floridians lived up to 1890. His era was also slower-paced than today; technology of his day did not provide instant results, responses, and communication. But not only was Moore's world materially different from our own, he lived in a vastly different social and cultural world. People's roles in that society were clearly delineated, for better or for worse. Authority figures, whether parents, or civic leaders, or bishops, or pastors were rarely, if ever, challenged and respected, for the most part. Social roles were much more static than today and much more segregated — blacks from whites, rich from poor, educated from illiterate, native from the immigrant. A person's formal attire, as well as where they lived and worked, as well as with whom they associated, demarcated their social status. It is a challenge for us to understand Moore in his social context, since in many ways that context is so different from ours.

Yet Moore's actions, as do ours, reveal both character and leadership, no matter how our social contexts may differ.

Moore wore what John Keegan calls "the Mask of Command," the public face and the hidden inner character.

> Heroic leadership — any leadership —
> is ... a matter of externals almost as much as
> internalities ... The leader of men in warfare
> can show himself to his followers only through
> a mask, a mask that he must make for himself,
> but a mask made in such form as will make him
> to men of his time and place as the leader they
> want and need.[2]

In Moore, the man behind the mask of command can be known by his deeds, as much as by his written words.

But why bother to know him at all? After all, he is a virtually unknown prelate in the historiography of Catholic America's late nineteenth century. Even among Catholics of Florida, he lacks name recognition. More than one graduate of Bishop Moore High School in Orlando told me that they never knew for whom the school was named. Precious little is in print about him, except for mention I have made of him in previous works[3] and in brief tangential comments about him made by other authors.[4]

Yet, he is arguably one of the most important Florida bishops and leaders, since it was he that guided ecclesiastical affairs during what might be called Florida's First Great Boom from 1877 to 1901, when the state's economy shifted from cotton and cattle, to tourism and citrus. With the coming of the railroads, of winter visitors, of urbanization, and of the rise of Florida's population, new developments in Catholic parish life unfolded. Catholicism shifted from the frontier rural church of scattered small pockets of Catholics, to a more complex concentrated church, with immigrants from Italy, Spain and Cuba, as well as migrants from the Northern states.[5] In response, Moore instituted an annual parish report. He invited Benedictines and Jesuits to establish parishes and missions throughout South Florida. From Ireland he recruited men for the diocesan priesthood and women for the Sisters of St. Joseph of St. Augustine. To support his missionary diocese and to rebuild his Cathedral after it was consumed by a fire in 1887, Moore took to traveling frequently to beg money from Northeast and the Midwest parishes. In the late 1900s, when Jim Crow ruled the South and nativism permeated the minds of many, he was particularly solicitous for those on the margins of society — the Latins of Tampa and Key West, as well as the African-Americans. He also oversaw the establishment of nine new parishes, seventeen new mission churches, and nine new schools for both blacks and whites, Catholics and non-Catholics, while increasing priests to serve them from nine to thirty-two.

But Moore's interests and involvements extended beyond the borders to Florida. He addressed and was sometimes personally engaged in the major ecclesiastical issues of his day. He negotiated Rome's approval of the decrees of the III Plenary Council of Baltimore and worked quietly yet tirelessly for the reconciliation of his excommunicated friend, Father Edward McGlynn of New York.

Throughout the book we examine Moore in the context of American history, in the context of Florida history, in the context of American Catholic history in the late nineteenth century. The first part of this book is organized chronologically, covering the early period of Moore's life (Chapter 1 through 3). The remainder, from Reconstruction in Charleston through his episcopacy in Florida, is organized topically, in order to better understand the various challenges that Moore encountered. However, those topical chapters are not meant to be hermetically sealed off from one another. Some of the contents in one chapter spill over into another; they are not air-tight compartments. For example, a discussion of Moore's concern for the outcast also relates to earlier discussions about religious women and their ministry in Catholic education.

This study not only discusses what challenges he faced and his response to them, but also we try to take the measure of the man — through his words and actions we learn something about Moore the leader — his personality and character.

Many of his contemporaries respected him as an unassuming leader of character and integrity. His priests nicknamed him "Silent John" because of his quiet, thoughtful, unassuming demeanor and because he did not wear his thoughts and opinions on his shirt sleeve. In the early 1930s a priest of the Diocese of St. Augustine described Moore as "a self-sacrificing bishop of an obscure diocese ... Simple, studious, diffident, yet approachable, he proved a successful administrator."[6]

In a time of war and terrorism worldwide, in a time when corporate, military, political, and ecclesiastical leadership is being questioned at home in America, coming to know Moore invites us to re-examine the nature of pastoral leadership, as well as issues of the Church in the late nineteenth century, not from the perspective of the powerful and famous, but from the perspective of "a self-sacrificing bishop of an obscure diocese ..." It is my hope that such an examination will not disappoint, but enrich, encourage, and ennoble us in our own troubled times.

John Moore

# *The Formative Years, 1835-1860*

CHAPTER ONE

# *Ireland, Famine, and Diaspora*

As far back as anybody could remember the Moores lived in Westmeath, but the clan was not originally from there. The *Ua Mórda* (the O'Mores), an early name for the Moore family, were part of the Irish aristocracy whose traditional territory was in the area now known as County Laois.

The O'Mores founded Abbeyleix, a Cistercian monastery, where the last of the O'More chieftains, Malichi O'More, is buried. A succession of men named Rory O'More, allied with the O'Neills, fought against English invaders.

The O'More stronghold was the Rock and Fortress of Dunamase, whose ninth century ruins can be seen today, an indication of the strength and importance of the Sept. After the English victory at the Siege and Battle of Kinsale in December 1601, Rory O'More and other Irish aristocrats were finished as leaders and as a force against English occupation. Soon afterwards, some of the O'Mores relocated to Westmeath, where they were known as the Moores.

*1.1 Moore family heraldry. Source: IrishGathering.ie*

In Westmeath the Moores were now landless. Catholic land ownership in Ireland was 59 percent in 1641, then 22 percent in 1688, then 14 percent in 1703, and a mere 5 percent by the 1770s, due to the effects of the penal laws, which were more designed to reduce Irish Catholics to penury rather than simply suppress their faith. They were successful at the former aim, but ineffective with the latter. The penal laws not only excluded Irish Catholics from ownership of property, but from the professions and from membership in Parliament. Additionally, all former Catholic churches were confiscated by the Church of Ireland (Anglican), meanwhile Irish Catholics were too poor to provide income for priests or money to build and maintain churches.[1]

Carved out of County Meath in 1541, Westmeath comprises 679 square miles. It has grassland which can support the raising of livestock, oats, barley, and potatoes. By the time of John's birth, Westmeath was an English-speaking region, since in 1851 less than 5 percent of county's population were Irish-speakers. In the 1840s Mass attendance for the Irish Catholics ran between 25.1 percent and 31.7 percent. In the English-speaking areas, Mass attendance was slightly higher and in the cities it was between 40 and 60 percent. Delvin, that area of northern Westmeath in which John Moore was raised, is also called Delvin-More, so identified is the family with the region.[2]

Born June 27, 1835, in Sheepstown Townland, near Rosmead, Delvin Barrony, County Westmeath, he was the son of William Moore and Mary O'Farrill. John was the second youngest of five children. The family must have been prosperous enough, since John was sent to elementary school, which would have demanded tuition, but was nothing more than a tiny bare-floor cabin school in Rosmead. Upon completing his studies there at age twelve, he did not go on to the secondary school. Perhaps his parents could not afford the tuition. Instead, young Moore went to Clonyn Castle, home of the British landlord, where he worked as a butler's boy until his family left Ireland when he was thirteen.[3]

The Ireland into which John Moore was born was decidedly rural. Westmeath had no town over 5,000, including Mulligar, its principal city. The people of Westmeath, as in the whole of Ireland, were heavily dependent on one foodstuff — the potato. So successful was the potato in nourishing the Irish that the country's population grew by 172 percent between 1779 and 1841. In 1840 Ireland was peopled by about eight million; in 1850 six and one-half million; today

IRELAND
in the 1840s

*1.2 Ireland 1840 Source: Colm Tobin and Diarmaid Ferriter, The Irish Famine (1999), front piece.*

the entire island has about five million. An acre and one-half of land planted in potatoes supported a family of six for a year. So dominant was the potato as a basic foodstuff that baking was virtually unknown in Ireland.

Early September 1845, the first signs of the potato blight disease (the fungus *Phytophthora infestans*) were reported in Ireland, a month before the October harvest. This was the beginning of the Great Potato Famine, which lasted from 1845 through 1855, which took between a million to 1.5 million Irish lives by starvation or disease, forcing over 1.5 million to emigrate to the U.S. alone. After the crop failure of 1848, the Moores, like many farmers, became convinced that the situation in Ireland was hopeless and joined the lower classes in flight. Between 1841 and 1851, the barony in which the Moores lived, Delvin, lost between 20 to 59 percent of its inhabitants either to death or emigration, even though the people's diets there were supplemented by oats and barley. Westmeath was the sixth greatest consumer of oatmeal of all Irish counties.[4]

The Irish Potato Famine made an indelible mark, a definitive line of demarcation on Irish history, culture, and memory, most especially upon those who survived it, including young John Moore.

But it was more than just famine conditions that drove the Moores out of Ireland. When John was thirteen, William, his father, passed away. Later, in 1880, as an expression of filial devotion, Moore returned to Ireland to erect a headstone on his father's grave, which tells us that William Moore died on June 24, 1848, in his 66th year. The fever (of several types), *marasmus* (a protein deficiency), smallpox, measles, or consumption took more lives at the time than starvation.[5] Whatever the exact cause of her husband's death, Mrs. Mary Moore decided to leave Ireland with her family to start life anew in America. Since the family was landless, they were not encumbered with liquidating their real estate.

The forty-eight-year-old widow and her five children, ages nine to twenty, probably traveled by cart twenty miles to Mullingar, then on by barge or coach or cart to Dublin, some sixty miles away. From there the family took a steam ferry to Liverpool, a 24-hour trip at one shilling per head. Steamers that crossed the Irish Sea were notorious for their overcrowded conditions and poor sanitation. After a short stay in Liverpool, the great cotton port for the Southern U.S., packet boats sailed directly to Charleston, SC, in about fifty days (passage in steerage cost about $20 per person). Depending on conditions on board, some passengers died in transit, as many as one-quarter of a ship's complement of about 100 to 500 passengers. Nevertheless, Mrs. Mary Moore and her five children survived and disembarked at Charleston in October 1848.[6]

Thirteen-year-old John Moore experienced emotional trauma with the potato famine, the death of his father, the separation from his homeland and kin, the terrible conditions on the ferry across the Irish Sea to Liverpool, and the awful rite of passage across the Atlantic. Never, during or after these horrendous experiences, did John record anything about the trauma of his leaving Ireland and being an exile in America. Although never forgotten, it was not something one cared to write and talk about, especially someone with a quiet temperament like John Moore.

In October 1848 the Moores arrived in Charleston, where most probably they had relatives and where an established Irish community already existed. In 1670 the first permanent settlement

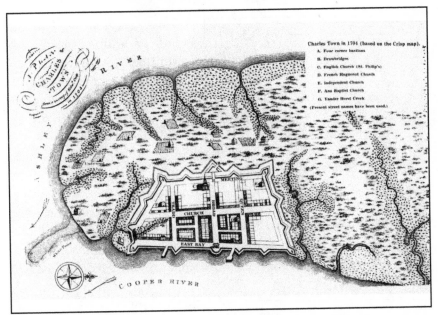

*1.3 Charleston, 1704 Source: Junior League of Charleston, <u>Historic Charleston Guidebook</u>, 1975 p. 2*

at Charleston was founded and comprised of both English and Irish colonists. In August 1669 three ships left England for the Carolinas. They stopped at Kinsale, Ireland, on September 1 to gather colonists, then picked up more at the overpopulated island of Barbados, where Oliver Cromwell had transported a large number of Irish in 1655. The captain of one of the ships, *The Carolina*, was Florence O'Sullivan, whose name is perpetuated by the name of Sullivan's Island in Charleston Harbor. Several of the Irish had land grants — the Sullivans, the Daltons, the Logans, and the McLaughlins. There were also Irish servants as part of the original colony — Philip O'Neill and Michael Moran among them.

By 1685, James Moore, the son of the Irish chieftain, Rory O'More, who was at the Siege of Kinsale, and who was one of the leaders of the Irish Rising of 1641 (which continued until 1653 after Cromwell's invasion), arrived in Charleston. By 1685 James Moore was a member of the Council for South Carolina, then in 1700 he was appointed Governor and Chief Justice. In 1703 he was Chief Justice. His three sons, James, Maurice, and Roger, also held prominent positions in the colony.

*1.4 Charleston 1855 Source: John H. Colton, New York, 1855*

Irish Catholics in Colonial South Carolina were not permitted to practice their religion nor were priests allowed to reside there. Consequently, the names of prominent Irish colonists appear in the rolls of Charleston's St. Philip's Anglican Church in the eighteenth century. Throughout that century, Charleston continued to welcome colonists from Ireland. St. Patrick's Day was celebrated with banquets and merriment by Charleston's Irish community, with the earliest description dating from 1771. The St. Patrick's Club was organized in 1773, but was disbanded during the American Revolution. Several of Charleston's Patriot volunteer companies of cavalry and foot soldiers had Irish members. After the war, in November 1786, a new Irish society was formed, the Friendly Brothers of Ireland, "to assist the distressed, to inculcate by precept and example obedience to the laws of state and adherence to moral principles." After the failure of the Irish Rebellion of 1798, a new wave of Irish refugees came to South Carolina. As a result, Charleston's Hibernian Society was created, comprised of Protestant and Catholic Irish. The seven founding members were members of the Society of United Irishmen, one of whom was elected president, the Catholic priest Father Simon F. Gallagher, who was well-liked among Charlestonians of all faiths.[7]

When Gallagher immigrated to Charleston in 1793 from Dublin, he found a Catholic parish already gathered. The Trustees of the Roman Catholic Church of Charleston (St. Mary's Parish) incorporated in 1791. Father Thomas Keating of Philadelphia was the pastor from 1791 to 1793 and oversaw the construction of the first church. Gallagher took over as pastor in 1793. A graduate of the University of Paris, the cultivated and articulate Gallagher joined the staff of the newly formed College of Charleston upon his arrival. When South Carolina established free schools in 1811, Gallagher was named Chairman of the Board of School Commissioners. However, Gallagher was a problematic person, intemperate in drink and impulsive in language, who came into conflict with the Trustees of St. Mary's Parish, with America's first Roman Catholic Bishop, John Carroll, and later with Charleston's first bishop in 1820, John England.[8]

So when the Moore family arrived in Charleston in late 1848, there was already an established Catholic community, comprised of largely Irish congregants. According to the 1850 Census, the Moore household in the St. Philip District consisted of six persons: Mary, age fifty; Catherine, age eleven (later Mrs. Rodden, then Mrs. Levy); James, age twenty, a laborer (later a Charleston businessman); John, age 16; Anna, age twenty (later Sister Alphonsa, OLM). Also listed in the household were Thomas, age twenty-two, a carpenter; Anna Quinn, age forty-six; George Quinn, age thirty-four, a laborer. Thomas and the Quinns were probably relatives of the Moores, as were some others in the city, such as William Moore, Martin Moore, Patrick Moore, and Maurice Moore. The Moore household had at least three wage earners. It seems that James' prospects improved quickly, because by late 1851 he is listed in the City Directory as a clerk. Although the 1850 Census does not indicate it, the Moore's address was most probably 16 Spring Street, which is north of the city (an area called "Charleston Neck") in St. Patrick's Parish, considered the "Irish Parish" of the time.

But two Moore children were not listed as part of the household: Anna age twenty-one and John age fifteen. In 1849 John had enrolled in Charleston's seminary, St. John the Baptist, and Anna entered the Sisters of Charity of Our Lady of Mercy in Charleston in April 1850, taking the name of Sister Alphonsa.[9]

Undoubtedly, his family, the "domestic church," had a profound influence upon the formation of John's quiet yet firm personality. The faith of his mother, who was called "pious" in her obituary, undoubtedly shaped faith life and his desire to be a priest.[10] But then, so did the extraordinary experiences of his youth that brought him to Charleston. Yet, never in any of his extant writings does he mention his life in Ireland, the Famine, his passage to America, or his reception in Charleston. He is silent about it all. Often a man's character is forged and tempered on the anvil of personal suffering. Just as often, the only response to the awesome mystery of suffering is silence. As St. Paul writes: "... affliction produces endurance, and endurance, proven character, and proven character, hope..." (*Romans 5: 3-4* -Revised New American Bible).

CHAPTER TWO

# *Education*

Not long after arriving in Charleston, young John Moore went back to school. Having completed his elementary schooling in Ireland, John was prepared to continue his studies and entered the Charleston seminary sometime in 1849.

St. John the Baptist Seminary was established in 1822, just two years after the founding bishop, Irishman John England, arrived in Charleston. Besides Moore, the three other seminarians there in 1850 ranged from seventeen to twenty-three years of age.

Characteristic of American seminaries of the day, the seminary was connected with a college, which in 1848 had 114 students. During the period that Moore attended the seminary, from age fourteen to sixteen, the faculty consisted of Bishop Ignatius Reynolds, Fathers James A. Corcoran, Patrick N. Lynch, Felix J. Carr, Timothy J. Sullivan, and Leon Fillion. These priests served the seminary, the college, and the Cathedral of St. Finbar, which had two missions and three stations.

Typical of other such institutions at the time, discipline at the Charleston seminary was strict. Its <u>Regulations</u> comprised a long list of do's and don'ts. For example: 1) "No seminarian shall go into the room of another without special leave of

**The Horarium of St. John the Baptist Seminary, Charleston, S.C., circa 1850**

**5:30 a.m.** Rise
**5:50 a.m.** Morning prayer and meditation, ending with the Angelus
**6:30 a.m.** Community Mass, followed by short study period
**7:30 a.m.** Breakfast in silence with the reading of "Following Christ," after which conversation was allowed.
**7:50 a.m.** Recreation (conversation)
**8:30 a.m.** Classes begin
**2:00 p.m.** Dinner (Scriptures read in Latin while students stood, then the martyrology was read. After dinner, recreation.
**3:45 p.m.** Rosary recited with a few moments spent before the Blessed Sacrament
**4:00 p.m.** Study period and some classes
**7:00 p.m.** Supper in silence with reading
**7:30 p.m.** Recreation (indoor conversation)
**7:45 p.m.** Study period
**9:30 p.m.** Spiritual reading, night prayers and reading of next day's meditation
**10:30 p.m.** Lights out

2.1 Horarium of St. John the Baptist Seminary, 1850
Source: ADSA

the Superior;" 2) "No seminarian is to enter into conversation with his room companion;"3) "Seminarians shall be extremely careful to avoid meddling with the book, property or furniture of the other;" 4) "No seminarian shall go outside the premises, without special leave."

On a daily, even hourly basis, it was believed that the strict *Horarium* (daily schedule) conformed the seminarian to values and habits desired in a future priest — discipline, obedience, prayer, learning, generosity, and faithfulness to the Western ecclesiastical tradition. The Regulations and the *Horarium* were the primary instruments of formation in the priesthood at the time. "You keep the Rule and the Rule will keep you" was a dictum in seminaries until the reforms of Vatican Council II.

The academic program extended over three years. Courses included the following: English (grammar, composition, rhetoric, and literature; French (grammar and books on the Liturgy); Latin (grammar, Cicero, Virgil, and both

Horace's <u>Odes</u> and <u>The Art of Poetry</u>); Greek (grammar, prose composition, and the New Testament); History (U.S. History and World History); Mathematics (Arithmetic, Algebra, Conic Sections, and Analytical Geometry); Natural Philosophy (astronomy and chemistry).[2] The academic program was a classic education in the humanities, with an emphasis on the mastery of ancient and modern languages. Moore excelled in the latter.

Nevertheless, by the end of June 1851, Bishop Ignatius A. Reynolds decided to close Charleston's seminary. Reynolds, Bishop of Charleston since 1843, laid the cornerstone of St. Finbar's Cathedral on July 30, 1850. In attendance were nine priests and the four seminarians "in cassocks," one of whom was John.

Then as now, seminarians were trotted out for special ecclesiastical occasions. But, by September 1851 it was clear that the Cathedral's construction was not going well. There were unexpected cost overruns — with the foundation, with higher freight rates, with higher labor costs, with other financial miscalculations. The building was supposed to cost $41,000. Now it would take $64,000 to complete. Reynolds needed money, and he needed to raise it fast.

On November 2, 1851, the bishop called an emergency meeting of "All Catholics of Charleston." He announced that he required $7,000 immediately and a further $13,000 to complete the project. As a way to husband his cash resources, Reynolds decided to close the seminary and divert its expenses to finish the Cathedral construction. The college already closed the year before. In April of 1854 St. Finbar's Cathedral was dedicated, however not by Reynolds, but by the founding Bishop of Savannah, Francis X. Gartland. Ill at the time of the dedication, Reynolds died almost a year later on March 6, 1855, at the age of fifty-six.[3]

By then John Moore was no longer in Charleston. With St. John the Baptist Seminary's closure in 1851, Reynolds sent Moore to France to continue his preparation for the priesthood.

In the fall of 1851, Moore studied the liberal arts and

*2.2 College at Combrée, France Source: https.amicalecombree.fr*

philosophy at Combrée, France, [where he would remain for the next four and a half years].[4] Why was Moore sent to a relatively obscure French seminary at Combrée? Most probably Reynolds sent him there because of Father Leon Fillion, professor at the Charleston seminary from 1849 to 1851, was a native of Angers, France, and was a priest of that diocese when he was recruited by Reynolds on a visit to France in 1849. Fillion attended the seminary at Combrée and had connections there. So, at the age of sixteen, John Moore was wrenched from his family and friends, and his new found home of Charleston, to matriculate in a seminary at Combrée, near Segré, in the Department of Maine et Loire, in the Diocese of Angers. His classes were in French (liberal arts) and Latin (philosophy), as were his conversations. In Charleston he had taken only one course in French grammar, so Moore the young man most certainly suffered from loneliness and his share of headaches from immersion in a foreign language and culture, that is, from what today is called "culture shock."[5]

Moore's regimen at the College of Combrée was similar to the one he underwent in Charleston. Discipline, a devotional spirituality, and academics were core to formation, all shaped daily by the rigorous *Horarium* and all designed to mold a strong, obedient, and generous character.

Reading, writing, and the mastery of French, Latin, and Greek formed a major part of the curriculum. At the end of his studies in philosophy, the student was expected to write a philosophical "dissertation" in both French and Latin, an assignment designed to demonstrate the student's command of both languages, as much as his mastery of philosophy or his readiness for the study of theology. Because of his experiences at the College of Combrée, Moore spoke, read, and wrote French and Latin fluently. Later in life, he felt fondly enough about his days at the College of Combrée to visit the campus while in Europe in 1885.[6]

With the termination of his courses in France, Moore returned to Charleston in mid-1855, but then was assigned to complete his seminary formation at Rome, Italy, by Patrick N. Lynch, soon to be the Reynold's successor as the Bishop of Charleston. Moore traveled to Baltimore where he boarded the schooner *Samuel* which departed for Italy on September 17, 1855. Moore was not the only seminarian destined for Rome on board. He sailed with Thomas Becker, a convert who eventually studied for the Diocese of Richmond, and William Augustine Williams, a black convert studying for the Diocese of Cleveland.

After four weeks at sea, the trio landed in Palermo, then went on to Rome, where they met Father Bernard Smith, OSB, an Irish Benedictine who received all American students to Rome. Smith accompanied them to the Irish College, where they were introduced to Archbishop Paul Cullen, Archbishop of Dublin. The next day Smith took them to a large stone building on the Piazza di Spagna which housed the Urban College of the Congregation of the Propagation of the Faith, which would be Moore's residence and place of study for the next five years.[7]

In 1627 Pope Urban VIII established the Pontifical Roman College of the Propagation of the Faith (soon called the Urban College). Housed in the administrative building of the Congregation of the Propagation of the Faith, near the Spanish Steps, this theological seminary was founded to supply clergy for missionary countries and to provide a quality

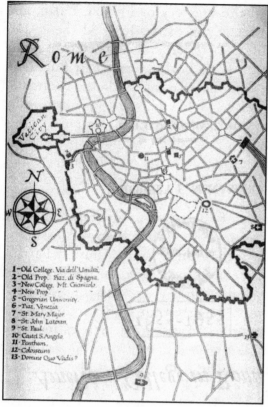

1-Old College. Via dell'Umiltà.
2-Old Prop. Piaz. di Spagna.
3-New College. Mt. Gianicolo.
4-New Prop.
5-Gregorian University.
6-Piaz. Venezia.
7-St. Mary Major.
8-St. John Lateran.
9-St. Paul.
10-Castel S. Angelo.
11-Pantheon.
12-Colosseum.
13-Domine Quo Vadis?

*2.3 Rome 1850s Source: Robert F. McNamara*

priestly formation to indigenous clergy from throughout the world. Martin J. Spalding, later Archbishop of Baltimore, was the first American to get his Doctorate in Theology there in 1834. Patrick N. Lynch and James A. Corcoran, both of the Diocese of Charleston and both later associated with John the Baptist Seminary, arrived at the Urban College in 1834. Lynch had attained his doctorate from there in 1840, while Corcoran received the same degree afterwards in 1843.[8]

What was the quality of the academic program in Rome in Moore's time? John H. Newman arrived in the Urban College in late 1846 as a mature man of forty-five. He was shocked at the state of academic life, for neither Aristotle nor Saint Thomas Aquinas was in favor in Rome. Philosophy there was an eclectic hodgepodge, cobbled together from various scholastic authors. Newman confided this to a friend in 1847: "You will not, cannot, get education here."[9]

Reports like Newman's were common enough long after he left the Urban College. Englishman Lord Acton wrote to a friend in 1862: "... the Romanists, [are] lovers of Authority [sic], fearing knowledge as such, progress more, freedom most, and essentially unhistoric [sic] and scientific."[10]

A priest alumni of the Urban College, Dr. Manahan, felt that the school taught too much Canon Law, an emphasis which was exacerbated for Americans, said Manahan, by the fact that most of Canon Law did not pertain to the U.S.[11] In the 1870s Irishman Canon William Barry complained about his professors at that Roman College who seemed "completely unaffected by any modern influence."[12]

Even the Ultramontane German historian, Johannes Janssen, was scandalized by Rome's complete indifference to scientific methodology and the disorganization which typified Roman libraries and archives. He quoted an Italian acquaintance who summed it all up by saying: "Here studies are dead. The only thing that counts here is getting ahead."[13] Rome was not Tübingen! By 1850, some Roman Ultramontane theologians began to view historical and Biblical criticism as a danger undermining the ecclesiastical fortress besieged by the political and ideological forces unleashed by the French Revolution and the Italian Resorgimento. As a defensive response, they rejected modern historical methodology and literary criticism. At the same time, they embraced scholasticism as timeless, changeless, and metaphysical. Italian neo-Thomism, soon to be the antidote to modernity, only became a force in Catholic thought in Rome in the 1860s, after Moore had finished his studies.[14]

Despite these contemporary criticisms of the state of theology at the Roman colleges and later criticisms by some of his contemporaries,[15] Moore liked the Urban College and did well academically. His linguistic abilities were appreciated and admired there.

The chief administrators of the Urban College were Filippo Tancioni, Rector from 1855 to 1859, and Giovanni Bottoni, the Spiritual Director. Faculty members were stable throughout the period and included the following: Bernard Smith, OSB, in Hebrew and Dogma; Agostino Accoramboni in archeology and liturgy; Aloysius Galimberti in Dogma; Pio Delicati in Church History; Vincenzo Tuzzi in Sacraments; Giovanni Sottovia and Giusepe de Camillus in Dogma; Achilles Rinaldini in Moral Theology; Filippo Arcangeli in

---

**The Horarium of Urban College circa 1856**

**5:30 a.m.** Prefect awakens students with "Benedicamus Domino to which the awakened students replied "Deo Gratias"
**5:45 a.m.** Te Deum and Angelus said in the hall in the corridor
**6:00 a.m.** Meditation
**6:30 a.m.** Mass
**7:00 a.m.** Light breakfast, coffee and pagnotti (hard rolls) in silence
**8:00 a.m.** Classes begin
**10:00 a.m.** Study period
**11:15 a.m.** Examen
**11:30 a.m.** Dinner (always with meat and wine, with public reading)
**Noon** Recreation, siesta, study period
**3:00 p.m.** Class
**5:00 p.m.** Walk
**6:30 p.m.** Study period
**7:30 p.m.** Spiritual reading
**7:45 p.m.** Rosary and Litany (all prayers in common were in Latin)
**8:00 p.m.** Supper (light soup, meat, plenty of wine and fruit, along with a public reading)
**8:30 p.m.** Recreation (conversation)
**9:30 p.m.** Examen
**10:00 p.m.** Retire

---

*2.4 Urban College Horarium, 1856 Source: Robert F. McNamara*

Sacred Scripture; Luigi Lazzarini in Canon Law. Texts used by the professors were Latin manuals written by Perrone, Devotis, Palmas, and Gury.[16]

Classes were held in large lecture room where desks were hard and benches were even harder. Courses were cycled in large classrooms and lectures were delivered in Latin, with annual end of the year oral exams also in Latin.

During his four years of study, Moore took four courses in Dogma, four in Church History, two in Moral Theology, and one each in Scripture, Hebrew, and Liturgy & Sacred Archeology. Additional classes were mandatory in Italian, chant, Canon Law, Liturgy, and sacred eloquence. In all his courses he received the highest grades, except in one, Church History, in which he received the grade of "average."

At Concursus, or end of the year academic awards in August, Moore, over the span of five years, received

*2.5 Urban College, 1850s Source: "Propaganda"* <u>The Catholic Encyclopedia</u>, 1911 ed., 459.

several first and second prizes in various disciplines. Given that the Urban College had about 130 students in Moore's time, receiving academic awards made him stand out among his peers.

At the conclusion of his studies, he was one of five in his class to undergo doctoral comprehensive exams in Theology on May 18, 1860. These exams took five hours and comprised a written defense in Latin on some chosen fifty to one hundred theses. In addition to the written portion, a verbal public defense was conducted in Latin in the college's aula before professors of the Urban College and some Cardinals. Moore passed, as did his classmate from New York, Edward McGlynn. Both received the Pontifical Degree of D.D, Doctor of Divinity (comparable to the modern S.T.D.). In a ceremony later, Moore received his doctoral ring, a four-peaked biretta, and the title "Doctor" (a title which others used to refer to him up until the time he became a bishop). A month before, Moore was ordained a priest for the Diocese of Charleston in Rome on April 9, 1860. According to custom, he returned to the Urban College the next day to celebrate Mass for the students.[17]

Life at the Urban College in Moore's time was not just classes and exams, but also the interaction among the seminarians. The Urban College had students from forty nations who spoke about thirty languages. Of a student body of 130, only sixteen were Americans. The regimen was less strict than that which Moore had been accustomed previously and less strict than other Roman Colleges at the time. As with the other seminaries that Moore attended, the tightly organized *Horarium* provided the discipline, the human development, as well as the spiritual and academic formation thought essential.[18]

While the *Horarium* regulated the daily rhythm of a student's waking time, the physical living situation regulated his comfort levels. Accommodations for students at the Urban College were relatively comfortable by nineteenth century standards, but the rooms had no heat, as was true most everywhere in Rome.

Each student was supplied with a wool double-breasted cassock, a red sash, a *soprana* (a broad-brimmed three-cornered felt hat worn in public), and two liturgical apparel — a *zimarra* and *biretta*. The student was also outfitted with boots, linen knickerbockers, long black stockings, a long-sleeve linen shirt, and soft white linen collars. Each week the student got a linen towel and three handkerchiefs (two of which were supposed to be used to take snuff, which the Americans did not use). Weekly laundering was provided at no charge. All expenses were paid by Propaganda, except for small luxuries and books.

But when it came to food, things were decidedly more comforting. Although breakfast comprised only coffee and hard rolls, lunch was the main meal of the day and a magnificent one at that, especially for a young person who escaped the Irish Famine only eight years before. There were several courses — soup, salad or pasta, one or two meats, several kinds of vegetables, a small bottle of wine per person, and fruit. A siesta followed then one or two afternoon classes. Supper was at 8 p.m. and although lighter than the main meal, still it was substantial enough: soup, meat, potatoes, and wine. Being in Italy had its culinary advantages for the international seminarians at the Urban College.[19]

The *camerata* was the basic unit of student organization and discipline in Roman colleges since the seventeenth century. Comprising ten to twelve members, the *camerata* was presided over by a prefect (that is, an upperclassman chosen by seminary officials), who provided peer evaluation, supervision,

*2.6 Pope Pius IX Source: beweb.chiesacattolica. it/benistorici/bene/6587257*

and discipline. Members of a *camerata* lived in an assigned area and normally did not associate with students from other *cameratae*, except at the garden recreation, at the noon meal, and at feast days. Otherwise, the camerata ate together, slept in the same dormitory, sat together at chapel exercises, took daily walks together, as well as the lengthier ones on Thursday. International in composition, *camerata* members spoke to one another in Latin or Italian, which gave Moore further opportunity to hone his linguistic skills.[20]

A popular saying among American seminarians in the late 1960s and early 1970s was the phrase: "Don't let your classes get in the way of your education." Moore's education in Rome in the late 1850s was much more than classroom lectures or exams. Extracurricular events also played a crucial educative role.

Students attended Papal ceremonies and regularly met Pope Pius IX, who visited the college several times a year. At these events the Pope rehearsed his favorite motifs — religious revival in Europe, missionary zeal, devotional piety, and the centrality of the Papacy in the Church. All of these themes were capsulated by a Papal event that must have impressed itself on the mind of Moore, as well as all those who attended. After an absence from Rome of four months, the Pope returned on September 5, 1857. On September 8, at the *Piazza di Spagna* near the Urban College, the Pope blessed a monument to the Immaculate Conception, which he commissioned in 1855, the year after he proclaimed the dogma of the Immaculate Conception. Urban College students attended this event.

Yet even beyond exposure to the Papacy and the personal charisma of Pius IX, the frequent walks taken in *camerata* were a significant extracurricular activity which exposed Moore to Rome's history and culture. Moreover, when classes were suspended for the summer, Urban College students moved to the school's summer Villa in Tivoli, from which trips to ancient Roman sites were organized.[21]

Surely the most memorable extracurricular event happened when Moore was completing his studies. Archbishop Gaetano Bedini, then Nuncio to Brazil, visited the United States from July 1853 to February 1854. One point in Bedini's report to Rome was that American seminaries needed strengthening. The "single most important thing," he wrote, was to erect an American college in Rome. In 1856 Bedini was appointed to the influential position of Secretary of the Sacred Congregation of Propaganda, where he advanced his pet project, the establishment of an American College in Rome. Meanwhile, American bishops, most especially John J. Hughes of New York and Francis P. Kenrick of Baltimore, collected about $48,000 for the proposed college. A former Visitation Sisters' Convent on *Via dell' Umilta* was purchased and renovated. On December 8, 1859, a procession of 130 students from the Urban College began there and ended at the new North American College. Twelve of their numbers were to become the first residents. A professor of Dogma at the Urban College, Irishman Bernard Smith, OSB, was appointed the pro-rector.

He was replaced in March 1860 by William G.

*2.7 First students of North American College in Rome, 1859 Source: Henry A. Brann*

McCloskey, an Urban College graduate ordained in 1852 for the Archdiocese of New York. Initially Moore's classmate, Edward McGlynn, also of New York, was appointed the Prefect. With Smith being absent most of the time from the college, McGlynn actually oversaw the day-to-day operations of his twelve charges, one of whom was Michael J. Corrigan, later Archbishop of New York. When McGlynn graduated from the Urban College in July 1860, he was nominated to be the Vice-Rector of North American College, but McCloskey rejected that nomination, on the grounds that he did not know McGlynn. The North American College adapted the Urban College cassock and the *Horarium*, but only U.S. citizens could attend. But, North American College was not established in time for Moore to reside there nor was he yet an American citizen.[22]

Living in Rome in the late 1850s also revealed to Moore the vicissitudes of international politics and revolution, as he wrote Bishop Lynch in July 1860: "The political aspect of Italy is very threatening at the present moment. Rome is almost the only tranquil spot on the whole peninsula. Naples is on the high road to revolution . . ." Rome was surrounded by revolutionary liberals of the Italian Risorgimento movement. Moore did not know it, but soon he would pass from a nation-forging war in Italy to nation-forging war in his own country.[23]

Yet the most important of extracurricular events related to his family, Moore was unable to attend. On November 22, 1856, his sister Catherine married Jossue Redden at St. Patrick Parish, Charleston. Even more telling, he was not informed of the funeral of his mother in Charleston until after it took place. Mrs. Mary Moore was sixty years of age when she died on April 15, 1857. Father James Corcoran, former professor of Moore's at the Charleston seminary and editor of the *U.S. Catholic Miscellany* wrote this about Mrs. Moore: "Her steadfast adherence to the precepts and practices of our Holy Church, endeared her to a large circle of friends and acquaintances." He called her "a pious Catholic mother." Her piety certainly influenced her son. Yet far away in Rome, he could only pray for his deceased Mother. "Silent John" left no extant record of his response to the mystery of suffering, separation, and sorrow he endured in 1857.[24]

The seminary formation experience, especially in a foreign country, forged bonds of friendship, some of which for John lasted a lifetime. Moore befriended the best and the brightest, such as Thomas Becker, Richard Burtsell, and his classmate, Edward McGlynn, who was the most brilliant and respected American student at the Urban College at the time. Ascetic, athletic, and academic, McGlynn was ordained a couple of weeks before Moore, on March 24, 1860.

McGlynn and Moore had an affinity for each other because of their mutual interest in learning, because of their similar demeanor of silence and gravity, because of their Celtic heritage, and because of their considerable talent and promise.[25] Later, the lives of Moore, Burtsell, and McGlynn would be inextricably intertwined in controversy and intrigue on a national and international level.

At the age of twenty-five, Moore officially completed his sz at the Urban College on June 30, 1860. Administrators there recommended him highly in a letter to Bishop Lynch: "He is a person of exemplary conduct." Moore viewed his years in Rome as a wonderful opportunity. He wrote his bishop that "I leave here content and happy," even though during those years he admitted that he was at times in dire financial straits. His family was poor and so was his diocese. When he departed from Rome July 11 he was uncertain of how he would defray his expenses to return home.[26] Uncertainty of another kind would greet him soon after his arrival in Charleston — the ravages of war.

John Moore

# Pastoral Care in War and Reconstruction, Charleston, 1861-1877

CHAPTER THREE

# *War & Pastoral Care*

U nlike the practice in priestly formation today, field education was unheard of in the seminaries of Moore's day. Instead, he received his pastoral training "on the job" as a newly ordained priest in Charleston. On July 7, 1860, Moore left Rome to return home, but stopped several times along the way to visit friends and family in France, Ireland, New York, Philadelphia, Baltimore, and Wilmington, NC.

On October 30, 1860, he finally arrived at Charleston, where he was assigned as an assistant at St. John the Baptist and St. Finbar's Cathedral and secretary to Bishop Patrick N. Lynch. At the time, his diocese, which comprised all of North Carolina and South Carolina, had, with Moore's arrival, a total of sixteen priests, eight of whom resided in the City of Charleston, which had three Catholic parishes, five missions, and as many stations. The other eight priests were scattered among the other thirteen churches and thirty-five stations outside the City of Charleston.[1]

Moore returned to a Charleston and to a country rapidly being torn apart by sectionalism, secession, and eventually war. With the Secession of South Carolina on December 20, 1860 (the first state to do so), events unfolded rapidly. The Confederate States of America formed on February 1, 1861. The bombardment of Fort Sumter began April 12, 1861, with the Union garrison surrendering thirty-four hours later. President Lincoln promptly called for 75, 000 volunteers to put down what he termed the "insurrection" in the South. Then, on April 19 he called for a Union blockade of all Southern ports from South Carolina to Texas. Sixteen Federal ships were in and around Charleston Harbor by December 19.[2]

Through combined operations of the Union Navy and Army, gradually islands around Charleston were occupied. On August 21, 1863, Maj. Gen. Quincy A. Gillmore, U.S.A., ordered the bombardment of the city by batteries located four miles away.

Thus, the Siege of Charleston began and did not cease for 587 days. No one city in Europe in either World War I or World War II was continuously bombarded for so long of a period. Gillmore stated that he expected no military results from the bombardment; rather it was "an experiment." In fact, it was an experiment in terror, in reprisal upon the city which spawned secession and war, and in a new Union policy of "total war," later perfected by General William T. Sherman. Charleston's civilian population lived with the "experiment," which created constant anxiety, fear, and terror. Would the shells come today or not? How many — one or 100? What or who would be hit? Although only about eighty people died during the siege, citizens and civilian property were the targets of indiscriminate and erratic destruction.

By early fall 1863, Charleston's glittering social life was no more. Funerals and deprivation replaced dances and parties. Entire sections of the city were vacant. Schools were closed, as were most churches. With house slaves disappearing daily, Charleston's upper class women, who never before washed any clothing or mopped any floors, were forced to learn the rudiments of housekeeping. The blockade and the bombardment also created shortages. Ordinary articles dis-

*3.1 Cathedral of St. John and St. Finbar, Charleston, SC, after the Great Fire of December 1861. Photo by George N. Bernard in April 1865.*

appeared from stores. Meat, butter, and salt were the scarcest of commodities. For example, in the Spring of 1863 a pound of bacon sold for one dollar; by the Spring of 1864 bacon was five dollars a pound. Altar wine, when it could be had through blockade runners, was ten dollars a gallon by 1864. Scarcity and inflation went hand in hand because of the blockade. In late November 1861 Charleston priests were unable to secure from Baltimore or New York an Ordo for 1862, the book of ritual which designates the dates and order of liturgical rites for the coming year, so Bishop Augustin Verot of Savannah felt it necessary to publish one for distribution throughout the South.[4]

After Sherman took Savannah on December 21, 1864, he then marched on Columbia, SC, not on Charleston. On Feb. 17-18, 1865, the C.S.A. troops abandoned Charleston.

The siege officially ended after twenty-two months. Union troops occupied Charleston on Feb. 18, 1865, which commenced months of looting by the occupiers. Sidney Andrews, a Northern reporter, toured the South at the end of the war in 1865 and wrote these impressions of Charleston: "'A city of ruins, of vacant houses, of widowed women, of rotting wharves, of deserted warehouses, of weed-wild gardens, of miles of grass grown streets, of acres of pitiful and awful barrenness — that is Charleston, wherein Rebellion loftily reared its head five years ago.'"[5]

In the midst of these wartime conditions, Father Moore underwent his "field education," as he exercised his ministry in Charleston from 1861 to 1865.

Moore's priesthood in Charleston started out on October 30, 1860, in the most ordinary of ways. He was stationed at St. John and St. Finbar's Cathedral, as an assistant, along with Bishop Patrick Lynch, Fathers T. S. Sullivan, J. A. Corcoran, Leon Fillion, and Felix Carr. The Cathedral had five missions attached, including Walterboro, Sullivan's Island, and Beaufort, SC, as well as five stations. The two other parishes in Charleston were St. Mary's with R. S. Baker as pastor and Patrick Ryan, D.D., as assistant, and St. Patrick's with Patrick O'Neill as pastor. Charleston's population was about 48,000 (27,000 whites, 17,500 slaves, and 3,700 free blacks). Moore would serve each segment of the city population during the course of the war.[6]

March of 1861 was a busy time of contrasts for Moore, since during that month he celebrated his first St. Patrick's Day and his first Holy Week as a priest in Charleston. On St. Patrick's Day, a big day of celebratory pride for Charleston's Irish community, High Mass was sung at the Cathedral by Father Fillion, with the sermon delivered by the Rev. Dr. Moore. St. Patrick's Benevolent Society was present "in full costume." Bishop Lynch was out of town in New York on a speaking tour. A Mass and a sermon were also celebrated at St. Patrick's Parish, Charleston's Irish parish, and at the mission on Sullivan's Island for the Meagher Guards on duty at the batteries there. But the next week, the tone of joyous celebration shifted to the somber realities of Holy Week. At the Cathedral, special services were held every day of the week. Confessions were heard for six hours every day of Holy Week. *Tenebrae* service was held on Wednesday, Thursday, and Friday. All in all, it must have been an exhausting couple of weeks for the newly-ordained Moore.[7]

But the rhythm of life at the Cathedral was about to change abruptly. On December 11, 1861, Charleston was devastated by a fire, unrelated to the War, which destroyed a third of the city, or some 540 acres. Gen. Robert E. Lee, C.S.A., at the time assigned to inspect the city's defenses, stood on the second floor balcony of the Mills House Hotel watching the fire. Over 600 homes, businesses and public buildings were destroyed, including four churches. Among the casualties were several Catholic institutions, including the bishop's residence, the hall of the Catholic Institute, the seminary library, St. Mary's Free School. The orphanage was saved, but was inhabitable. St. John and Finbar's Cathedral lost its roof and interior. The Cathedral congregation met for Mass at the Hibernian Hall, until the bombardment of 1863. The Cathedral congregation was unable to gather again until the Pro-Cathedral was dedicated in September 1866. A final casualty of the fire was the diocesan newspaper, the *U.S. Catholic Miscellany*, whose last edition of December 14, 1861, reported on the fire (it became the *Charleston Catholic Miscellany*). The deprivations due to the War also contributed significantly to the paper's demise.[8]

As an alumnus of the Urban College, Moore was obliged to write an annual letter to the Congregation of the Propagation for the Faith, explaining his present ministry. In July 1862 he sent a guarded missive to the Congregation, fearful that his letter might be intercepted by the Federal blockade and published in some Northern newspaper. At the time he was the Administrator of St. Joseph's Parish in the absence of its pastor, Father Fillion, who was assigned to the Bahamas by Bishop Lynch until Lent 1863. He mentions that before the War, his salary was $150 a year. Since the fire, he received no salary, only a few Mass stipends. He recently

*3.2 Bishop Patrick N. Lynch in Paris, 1864*
*Source: ADC*

had occasion to seek the aid of a doctor, but had difficulty finding one, since most of them had left town. "The city is being deserted everyday more and more." While lamenting the lack of Catholic schools in Charleston, he instructs white kids in their Catechism on Sunday mornings and free people of color after Sunday Vespers. He also conducts a night Catechism class twice a week for older slave children who are ashamed to come on Sunday's with the younger children and who work for their masters during the day. He also prepares children for First Communion. But the Cathedral fire interrupted all of these instructions, since there is now no place to hold class. Moore hears four or five hours of Confessions every Saturday. On Sundays he says two Masses, one at a mission, the other in Charleston. He also attends the sick and wounded in Charleston's two Confederate military hospitals and visits the city jail, where he was able to convert three prisoners before they were condemned to death. Regarding the hospitals, they are under the direction of Protestants and in some instances he is prohibited from visiting patients in them, even though a number of those patients are Catholic. Moore says he has to be diplomatic with hospital officials in order to be allowed to make his hospital rounds.[9]

Christmas 1863 was unlike any ever celebrated in Charleston or any other American city. Just after midnight Christmas morning 1863, five guns on Morris Island opened up a severe bombardment. Some shells were as large as 300 pounds. Before Christmas Day was over, firebombs from 134 rounds rained on the city causing several fires to break out. Later, in the month of January 1864, 1,500 shells were fired into Charleston in nine days. Because of the bombardment, Bishop Lynch and his secretary, Moore, moved to St. Joseph Church in the northern part of the city at the beginning of the New Year. When St. Joseph's Church was hit by shells in January of 1864, they moved again, this time to St. Patrick's, just out of range of the guns.[10]

3.3 *Archbishop Martin Spalding of Baltimore* Source: *findagrave. com/memorial/9180933*

In March 1864, Bishop Lynch accepted the appointment by President Davis as Special Commissioner for the C.S.A. to seek Vatican and European recognition for the Confederate government. Before departing for Rome, he named two Vicar Generals: Father James A. Corcoran, the pastor at St. Thomas the Apostle, Wilmington, NC, in charge of matters outside of Charleston; and Father Leon Fillion in charge of Charleston and its missions. Fillion asked Lynch that Moore oversee diocesan financial affairs for him. Escaping by a fast blockade-runner out of Wilmington, NC, on April 11, Lynch reached Rome on June 26 and stayed over a year. His mission to Rome and European leaders was ultimately unsuccessful. He did not return to Charleston until November 1865 and that only after a special Presidential Pardon by Andrew Johnson on August 5, 1865.[11]

Meanwhile, Father Patrick O'Neill, the pastor of St. Patrick's, died of pneumonia on February 10, 1865, at age fifty-five. Immediately, Fillion appointed Moore as pastor of St. Patrick's. On February 21, Father Fillion, the Vicar General in Charleston, died at age forty-five of typhoid fever, contracted while visiting Union prisoners of war incarcerated at Florence, SC. With Fillion's death, the Archbishop of Baltimore, Martin Spalding, appointed Moore the Vicar General of the Charleston region of the diocese. By now only two priests remained in the city, fifty-nine year old Robert S. Baker, pastor of St. Mary's, and thirty year old Moore, pastor of St. Patrick's.[12]

There was one other priest in Charleston at the time, Union Chaplain Father Thomas Brady of Buffalo. Moore reported to Archbishop Spalding that Brady taught in the public schools and did "many queer things," but never attended the Federal military hospital in Charleston, as Moore did. He said he let Brady preach once at St. Patrick's, but never again. Worse still, Brady tried to organize a chapter of Fenians in Charleston, an action that drove "Silent John" to speak out from the pulpit, warning Catholics against joining the revolutionary group for Irish independence. Moore's intervention was successful. The Fenians never got established in Charleston and Brady, a priestly rabble-rouser and independent operator, left the city by April 21.[13]

By April 1865, Moore was at the end of his rope. He begs Archbishop Spalding in a letter to send a priest to Charleston. People are now returning to the city with the bombardment over. The city hospital, jail, and workhouse are reopened. The Federal military hospital also needs tending, as do the stations on Mount Pleasant and Sullivan's Island. St. Mary's Church, having been struck by shells several times during the siege, is now repaired and opened. St. Patrick's is functioning, but in very dilapidated condition. "I never saw such distress in the city," wrote Moore, yet he adds, "I will stand my post."[14]

The pastor of St. Patrick's was at his lowest ebb by May 1865. He felt isolated and wearied. Moore had not heard from Bishop Lynch in months. Father Patrick Ryan left the city in January to care for refugees in the interior and Moore was unaware of his whereabouts. Finally, in mid-September Ryan returned to Charleston. However, Ryan's return was not a blessing, for Moore reports to Spalding in early October that Ryan "soon gave scandal as he has previously done on former occasions." Although he does not specify it in his letter, the scandal was most probably drunkenness. Although Moore wanted to suspend him, he refrained from doing so, since he believed that Bishop Lynch would be returning home soon and it would best to remit the matter to him. Father Baker's health is failing and is unable to say Sunday Mass. Moore is now the only functioning priest left in Charleston. He is relieved that Bishop Augustin Verot of Savannah promised to station a priest in Hilton Head and did. He eagerly awaits to receive Holy Oils from Verot. But he still works alone in Charleston, where every Catholic church building was damaged by shelling, except dilapidated St. Patrick's. Months earlier, in Columbia, the Ursuline Convent School was torched, St. Mary's College was pillaged, then burned, and Columbia's only parish church, St. Peter's, was ransacked, its rectory burned, all by Sherman's troops.[15] Writing to Lynch, he uncharacteristically moans:

> A little money would suffice, but our people haven't even a little ... They are not paid for their work and the very life's blood is given out of them for taxes ...What will become of us all? ... Your bank is in immense trouble ... Write soon, and often, and come home yourself, as soon as possible ... I am already discouraged and fear I cannot long be able to hold out.[16]

Although Archbishop Spalding sympathized with Moore's plight, he was only able to send one priest, a New Orleans Jesuit, the forty-eight year old Louis-Hippolyte Gache, Confederate Chaplain to the 10th Louisiana Regiment and a recently paroled prisoner of war at Richmond (on April 14, 1865). Gache arrived in Charleston on a June 1, "not a day too soon," wrote Moore, who was overwhelmed by the multiplicity of pastoral demands placed upon him in the city. He used the Jesuit as a pastoral "utility infielder." In August Gache departed Charleston for Columbia to give the Ursuline Sisters there a retreat. He returned to Charleston, but had to leave for good on October 5. Moore was impressed with the Jesuit, writing Spalding that Gache "has edified me very much by his piety, his regularity, his zeal for the salvation of souls." Later in 1888 when he found himself in another personnel crisis while bishop in Florida, Moore would have cause to remember the New Orleans Jesuits and previous services of Father Gache in Charleston in 1865.[17]

Even though Father Charles Croghan, a Confederate Chaplain, returned to Charleston as pastor of St. Joseph's in early July and despite the happy presence of Father Gache, as the summer of 1865 passed into the fall, Moore's responsibilities only increased. From late May, Father Baker was totally incapacitated with the whooping cough. Father Corcoran took ill in Wilmington, and left his post under what he said was "doctor's orders." With Corcoran's absence, Spalding appointed Moore the Vicar General of the entire diocese.[18]

By late August, Moore was beside himself with the frustrating problems of the financial and personnel shortages he faced alone. Moore begins to see that Lynch's leadership style, especially his absence from the diocese, is at the core of many of these problems, as he explains to Spalding:

> The finances of this diocese are, I may say, in a hopeless condition. The Bishop's creditors are anxiously awaiting his return ... Bishop Lynch is a great deal to blame for this spirit of insubordination which has grown up among his clergy... The dissatisfaction of the priests, which drives them to extremes, is caused chiefly by the bishop's neglect of them... If he ever not come back to us a changed man, we had better no bishop at all.[19]

Moore writes Spalding again in mid-September repeating that he hopes that Lynch comes back a changed man. If only Lynch would "cease to be a digger of artesian wells, a railroad engineer, an architect ... a diplomatist, a politician, a banker, etc. and be a bishop." Moore predicts that Lynch may be very popular with Protestants in the South upon his return, but "He is not popular with Catholics, because they have some

*3.4 The ruins of Charleston, S.C., from the Civil War, 1865, by Mathew Brady. Source: Library of Congress*

knowledge of what a bishop should be."[20]  Moore's dissatisfaction with his bishop began from this point and continued to grow in the years to come.

Nor was Moore enamored with Charleston now being occupied by Federal forces.  After all, it was the Union forces whose bombardment of Charleston damaged churches and other Catholic institutions.  He had to beg Gen. Quincy A. Gillmore, U.S.A., the chief commander, not to let the city's Catholic churches be confiscated and used as theaters or hospitals or as Abolitionist schools for blacks.  To this end, Moore solicited Archbishop Spalding's help.  Spalding wrote Gen. Gillmore: "That none of the Catholic churches or schools of Charleston be seized on this score. I am sending priests to his [Moore's] assistance and our churches will be imperatively needed for Catholic use." No Catholic institutions were confiscated, except the school in Beaufort.[21]

U.S. military officials pressured Moore to take an oath of allegiance to the Union, but the pastor of St. Patrick's refused to do so. As a result, his mail was held up and thoroughly inspected by Union occupying authorities. Much later, a priest friend said Moore, like Lynch, "was a stout Confederate," who had "aggressive Southern sympathies." Little wonder he never became a U.S. citizen until 1873![22] David T. Gleeson demonstrates how the Irish in the South identified with Southern nationalism because of their previous experience of British colonialism and frustrated national aspirations, as well as their perception of the Democratic Party as the sole protector of their rights in America, especially States Rights.[23] Therefore, Moore's "stout" Confederate sympathies were not singular. He personally experienced the Irish Famine, which many blamed on British Colonialism, he certainly followed the troubles in Ireland, he witnessed the Italian revolutionary liberals' invasion of the Papal States. These experiences provided an interpretive lens for his seeing the present troubles in Charleston being the product of Northern aggression, colonialism, and social radicalism (Abolitionists and Radical Reconstructionists), while at the same time allowing him to identify with the Southern quest for independence.

Moore's financial and personnel worries were relieved somewhat by mid-October 1865. In late August, Moore informed Archbishop Spalding that the Federal commander had appealed to the U.S. government for funds to rebuild the OLM (Mercy) Sisters convent, which was destroyed by the U.S. shelling during the siege. In October Spalding conducted a special collection for Southern dioceses. The $12,263 collected in the Archdiocese of Baltimore were distributed to Bishop Verot of St. Augustine/Savannah, Bishop Elder of Natchez, Father Thomas Becker of Richmond, and Father Moore. Moore received a check for $1,600 and was able to "sell" the check for $1,584 in cash-poor Charleston. Moore gave $400 to the Sisters of Mercy, $200 for the missions of Columbia, $200 to J.J. O'Connell, pastor of St. Peter's in Columbia, specifically for the neediest of the city "without distinction to creed." The remaining $784 went to the Sisters of Mercy in Charleston to distribute to the urban poor. Moore earmarked $984 of the total amount Spalding gave him, that is 62 percent, for the poor. Although Father Baker was still sick, a Father Shadler arrived by mid-October from Rome via the Archdiocese of New York to provide some help. Moore continued to be anxious for the arrival of Lynch from Europe, so that he might be relieved of his diocesan burdens. Moore again confided to Spalding that he hoped Lynch would return a changed man, no longer engaged in matters Moore felt were extraneous to his episcopal office.[24]

While Bishop Lynch was still in Rome, he wrote a long begging letter in September 7, 1865, to the missionary Society the Propagation of the Faith in France, giving an assessment of his diocese (even though he had not been there since April of 1864!). He estimated the diocese's losses to be at $316,500. When Lynch did return to Charleston in late November 1865, he inspected matters for himself and was both shocked and crestfallen. In January 1866 he wrote to the Archbishop of New York, John McCloskey:

> Was your Grace ever in Pompeii? Columbia is more like that than any other city in America. I am like Marius, amid the ruins of Carthage. There are ruins on every side of me, architectural, ecclesiastical, industrial, religious and social. But I trust in God things will come straight. But I have a very gigantic work before me. Part of it however I will have to leave to my successor.[5]

## CHAPTER FOUR

# Pastor of St. Patrick's, Charleston

With the return of Bishop Patrick Lynch to Charleston at the end of November 1865, Catholicism in the diocese began the huge undertaking of reconstructing the faith — a financial, physical, and spiritual undertaking. The War did not just destroy or damage Catholic institutions; it also undermined moral and spiritual values. Bishop Lynch was the chief orchestrator of the reconstruction and Father John Moore was his main cooperator, as pastor of the most vital parish in Charleston during the period. Yet both men had differing views as to how best to build up the Church and differing styles of leadership.

Even before Lynch returned to Charleston, Moore was the pastor of St. Patrick's, appointed so in February 1865, while Lynch was in Europe. By the time that Moore became its pastor, the parish was already twenty-eight years old. Bishop John England bought a lot facing St. Philip Street and Radcliff Street on November 25, 1828, for $2,900. Since it was outside the city limits in the Charleston Neck area, he intended that the property become a Catholic cemetery and a parish. In January 1837 England appointed Father

John Fielding as the parish's first pastor, who initially said Mass in the home of a parishioner. In October 1837 Father Patrick O'Neill was named pastor. In January 1838 the parish trustees were elected and on St. Patrick's Day 1838 the cornerstone of the church, located on the northeast corner of St. Philip and Radcliff Streets, was laid. Blessed by Bishop England on December 23, 1838, the 50 feet by 36 feet wood-frame structure cost $4,319.22 and had a choir loft on its west end, an altar on the east end, and galleries on each side, the northern one for African-Americans and the southern one for whites. From the beginning the parish was biracial, although most parishioners were Irish immigrants, hence it was named St. Patrick's.[1]

4.1 *Father Patrick O'Neill*
*Source: ADC, "St. Patrick's Parish," 1937, p 12*

Patrick O'Neill was born in Thomaston, Kilkenny, March 17, 1810. He studied for the priesthood at St. Patrick's Missionary College, Carlow, (where John England had attended also) and volunteered to serve the Diocese of Charleston. He completed his priestly studies at St. John the Baptist Seminary, Charleston, and was ordained in 1836. Just over a year later, he was named the pastor of St. Patrick's. With a fair complexion, medium height, and strawberry blond hair, O'Neill was a tireless worker, neither eloquent nor learned nor bothered by administrative details, he was a much sought after Confessor to bishops, priests, seminarians. With no assistant priest, he taught in the parochial day-school, made sick calls, buried the dead, said the parish Masses, preached at the Sunday High (sung) Mass and led Vespers on Sunday. He was available to those in need day or night, beloved and venerated by Charleston's Catholics, Protestants, and Jews of all classes whom he met often while walking the streets of Charleston. Dressed in his well-worn faded cassock, he was particularly solicitous of the poor and destitute, whatever their creed or race. He was rivaled in respect and esteem in Charleston only by Bishop England. His

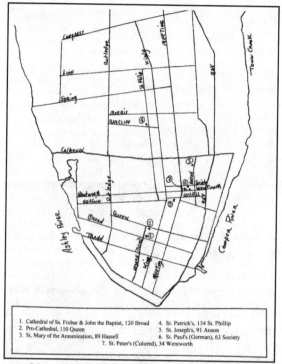

1. Cathedral of Ss. Finbar & John the Baptist, 120 Broad
2. Pro-Cathedral, 110 Queen
3. St. Mary of the Annunciation, 89 Hassell
4. St. Patrick's, 134 St. Phillip
5. St. Joseph's, 91 Anson
6. St. Paul's (German), 63 Society
7. St. Peter's (Colored), 34 Wentworth

*4.2 Charleston's Catholic Churches, 1865-77*
*Source: Author*

temperament was calm, patient, and generous, governed always by common sense. In the 1850s he began collecting money to build a new brick church, but during the war his nest egg evaporated due to depreciation of his investments and inflation. The War bankrupted the parish and the church fell into disrepair. O'Neill caught pneumonia while attending the sick at the age of fifty-five and died on January 10, 1865. Immediately, John Moore was named his successor.[2]

When Moore took over the parish in January of 1865, the War was still raging. Although it was the only one of the four remaining churches in Charleston undamaged by shells from the bombardment, it was by Moore's own admission "dilapidated." As pastor in a war-torn city he had many problems to deal with and needed the support, advice, and consent of his bishop, but he continued to be frustrated with Lynch's inaccessibility, even when he was in town. In February 1866 he writes Lynch, "I ... needed to speak to you about many things but you were too preoccupied with other thoughts when I was with you yesterday."[3] Moore was faced with reconstructing St. Patrick's — physically, administratively, and spiritually.

As two Catholic boys were about to be forced into the Protestant orphanage in April 1866, some men of St. Patrick's proposed founding a Catholic boy's orphanage. Moore encouraged them. He told Lynch that this notion was initially started by some Fenians in the parish, so he felt he could put their energies to good use for this cause. The "St. Patrick's Male Orphan Society" was established to raise money for the proposed institution. Although this idea started as a parish initiative, with only $36 in hand in early May, Moore asked Lynch permission to mount a citywide fund-raising campaign, since the orphanage would serve the entire citizenry. It is unclear from the extant correspondence if such permission was given.[4]

Meanwhile, in the spring of 1866 Moore announced to his parishioners that he was resolved to establish a parish school for boys. On January 12, 1866, the nine priests in Charleston met at the behest of the absent Bishop Lynch at St. Joseph's Parish under the chairmanship of the Vicar General, Timothy Bermingham. The gathered clergy recognized "the necessity of establishing at the earliest possible opportunity Catholic parochial schools." Charleston as yet had none. Moore, who felt a parochial school was essential to preserve and pass on the faith to the next generation, sought to be the first to implement the episcopal and clergy mandate. To this end, in early March 1866 he informed Lynch that the Lutheran Church on Morris Street between St. Philip and King Street was for sale for $4,700 and would serve well as a parochial school. On May 30 Moore organized a fair held in Hibernian Hall to support the proposed St. Patrick's Parish School. Around the end of June, Moore reminded Lynch that he wrote him at the end of May about "other matters which I really did consider worthy of your attention and about which I expected a word in reply, but I have waited in vain."[5] Moore continued to be frustrated by Lynch's leadership style and those frustrations would only worsen.

In early November Moore wrote Lynch complaining about his present predicament. Parishioners were asking him why the parochial school was not open and what happened to the $4,400 dollars which the May 30th Fair collected for the school. Moore says he would like to put in the paper the reason the parish school has not opened and "hopes the bishop will not place any obstacles" in his way. Despite his threat, Moore published nothing in the newspaper, despite the fact that Lynch had confiscated the money for the parish school and appropriated the sum for his own purposes, namely a new boy's Catholic orphan asylum.[6]

All of Moore's energetic pastoral efforts and frustrations during and immediately after the War took its toll, so much so that his health broke down in the fall of 1866. He was physically and mentally exhausted. From the end of September to mid-October he was mostly bed-ridden with an undisclosed ailment. On the second Sunday in October, St. Patrick's had no Sunday Mass since Moore and his assistant priest, John Schachte, were both incapacitated. With Lynch's permission, Moore took a brief sabbatical, taking a ship in mid-November from Charleston to New York, where he visited his classmate, Edward McGlynn.[7]

Staying at St. Stephen's Parish with McGlynn improved Moore's health, so much so that by the end of November he preached at St. Stephens. But beyond his physical healing, Moore had an opportunity to unburden himself among his Urban College friends. He confided to McGlynn that he found Lynch "selfish and lazy." Not only did the bishop force Moore to hand over the $4,400 collected at the fair for the parochial school, but also he refuses to give an account of the money collected during his various begging trips in Northern parishes. Meanwhile, Lynch "has bought a house on speculation, instead of a church for his people." Moore refers here to the purchase of the new bishop's house at 114 Broad Street and the fact that there is no building erected to replace the cathedral destroyed in the fire of 1861. Finally, he tells McGlynn that Lynch is never willing to take advice about diocesan matters and "is disliked by the clergy and the laity."[8] Perhaps "Silent" John felt disinclined to express his pentup feelings about Lynch in Charleston, but not so the first time he is away from the diocese with trusted friends.

In early December, Moore attended a parish fair and had dinner at St. Stephen's where he met Fathers Richard Burtsell, Henry Brann, and Patrick McSweeney, all graduates of the Urban College. At the dinner the subjects of the temporal power of the Pope and the Latin language in the Liturgy were discussed. This was the first in a series of dinners and discussions that Moore had with his fellow "Romans" while in New York. Just before Christmas, Moore writes Lynch that his "health is greatly improved." He feels that in one or two months more his health "will return completely," since he is getting good nourishment at the rectory of "my good friend Dr. McGlynn." Moore attended the consecration of St. Stephen's Church at the end of December. All these activities and discussions did Moore good, moreover, McGlynn promised Moore that he would give him a collection from St. Stephen's for his proposed parochial school.[9]

At the orchestral High Mass Christmas Day at St. Stephen's Moore preached. It is one of the few of his homilies that we have of him, at least in outline form, thanks to Richard Burtsell, who attended the ceremony and recorded some of his classmate's address. Moore spoke of instances in the Old Testament where mankind feared God: in *Genesis* after the Fall, in Exodus when the Hebrews asked God not to speak to them lest they die, in Judges when Samson's parent's say "We shall certainly die because we have seen God." In the Old Testament men feared more than loved God. But with the birth of Christ, men learned to trust God's mercy. Jesus became poor, humbly entering into a suffering world to give us confidence, lest we fear His majesty, and to teach us not to love the world's riches, to bear suffering, to be fearless in ignominy. After Mass, the clergy had dinner with seven laity, and then Burtsell, Moore and McGlynn took a walk in Central Park, discussing Inspiration of Scripture. Yet in this, as well as in other of the theological discussions that Moore participated while in New York, Burtsell, our only witness to these events, never mentions any of Moore's views on these topics. However, on the occasion, Moore does share Lynch's views on the temporal power of the Papacy, namely, the loss of it "will do no harm." Whether Moore agreed or disagreed with this position is unknown.[10]

Moore also attended meetings of what Burtsell called an "Ecclesiastical Society." This theological discussion group was the second founded in New York. The first was called the "*Accademia*," but it was disbanded since ecclesiastical authorities felt that it was comprised exclusively of Roman graduates. The "Ecclesiastical Society" was supposed to be more inclusive, though in fact its membership and purposes were similar to the first group. At the founding of the second organization on November 20, 1866, Burtsell reported that "The Abolition-Roman priests met to organize an Ecclesiastical Society." Burtsell was present, along with McGlynn, Thomas McLoughlin, Isaac Hecker, James Nilan and Thomas Farrell. Nilan was appointed by the chair, forty-year old Thomas McLoughlin, to draft a constitution for the new organization.

*4.3 Rectory of St. Patrick's Catholic Church, Charleston, SC, purchased in 1866, circa 1937. Source: ADC*

Others were undoubtedly present, but it is unclear whether Moore was there, especially since he surely was not an "Abolitionist-Roman priest." Moore did attend some of the meetings of the Society in January. He encouraged Burtsell to publish a paper he had delivered at one of the meetings on the liturgical languages in the Church. Father Hecker was willing to publish it in the *Catholic World*, as it was a "wedge for the change of the language of the Liturgy" into the vernacular, a position which Moore must have found appealing, since he encouraged Burtsell's publication of the position. However, either Hecker or Burtsell must have thought better of it, because the article never was published in the *Catholic World*.[11]

By the end of January 1867 Moore was preparing to return to Charleston, since by his own admission his health was "very much improved." Moore wrote Lynch saying that the assistant priest at St. Patrick's, Father Schachte, is doing well running the parish in Moore's absence. Moore hopes that Lynch will keep Schachte at St. Patrick's since there is plenty of work there for two and good priests are hard to find. Moore will begin a journey on January 29 which will take him to Philadelphia, Baltimore and Washington, then back to New York City. He has free boat passage back to Charleston and hopes to arrive by the First Sunday of Lent. Moore reminds Lynch to thank McGlynn for the money he sent to the diocese. Moore is particularly grateful to McGlynn, for "nothing can equal

Dr. McGlynn's kindness to me."[12]

Moore never forgot McGlynn's hospitality, understanding, comradeship, and generosity. Not only was Moore's New York sabbatical restorative, but it further cemented the bond of friendship among himself and McGlynn and Burtsell, bonds which in twenty years would be tested in ways they never imagined.

Moore returned to Charleston in late February 1867 reinvigorated and full of pastoral plans. He found the general health of his parish good. It had about 2,000 parishioners and retained Schachte as the assistant priest. Although Moore would have liked to establish a parochial school, Lynch's 1866 confiscation of the Fair money for that purpose forced Moore to take on other construction projects instead. He contracted a builder in May 1867 to renovate the building he bought earlier in 1866 as a rectory. By the summer of 1867, it was ready for occupancy.

A parochial school was founded in Charleston, but it was not in his parish. Charleston's first free parochial school opened in the fall of 1869 on the site of the former Cathedral Rectory. Feeling the need for a larger church building due to the crowded conditions, he repaired and enlarged St. Patrick's wooden church, doubling its capacity. It was rededicated in September 1868. He had to borrow over $3,500 to realize his plans, thus creating debt.[13]

The times were not propitious for raising money for building projects. Unemployment in Charleston was high in June 1867 and there was almost a famine in the city, observed Moore. He received 150 bushels of corn to distribute to the poor since he "is besieged at the church by an army of beggars." He tells Lynch, who was presently in Rome, that "My thoughts are in Rome a good part of this day [the Feast of SS. Peter and Paul] and I have often wished I were there." Such a nostalgic reminiscence of his student days was small comfort amidst the hard realities of being a pastor of Charleston's largest parish during financial hard times.[14]

Moore looked not only to his own parishioners, but also to Northern friends for funds. Desperate for capital by March 1868, Moore begged Lynch, who was in New York, to call upon McGlynn to ask for a loan of $2,000 he promised Moore. "If you don't get it for me ... I do not know what I shall do," wrote Moore. In November 1872 Moore was still struggling with loans and debts. McGlynn gave Moore a grace period on his $2,000 for a loan which was due in January. Meanwhile, St. Patrick's pastor informs Lynch that the past summer was the very worst since the War for farmers "to whom I have been looking for liberal contributions."[15] Yet through it all, Moore learned how to manage debt and finance it, skills which he would need later as bishop in Florida. For the rest of his life, debt and how to resolve it would be his daily companion.

Besides building, remodeling, and financing, Moore was reconstructing St. Patrick's Parish in other ways. He was, of course, engaged in the routine spiritual ministrations of a parish priest: celebrating the Eucharist, preaching and holding Vespers on Sundays, hearing Confessions, making sick calls (some of these to outlying areas could take hours or days), visiting the sick in hospitals, overseeing the assistant priest, saying Mass at Catholic institutions and visiting attached missions and stations. In early 1873 St. Michael's Mission, Beaufort, was no longer being tended, nor was the station at Ferebeeville, so Moore stepped into the ministerial vacuum and traveled to those places for Mass until April 1875.[16]

Moore also had two Catholic orphanages within the territory of the parish, but not run directly by the parish. He visited both regularly. In 1869 the boys' institution was one-quarter mile from the church, while the girls' residences were three-quarters of a mile away. Summer and winter, rain or shine, these children were marched from their respective buildings for Mass at the parish church.[17]

As part of a revival of religious instruction in the parish, in the spring of 1868 Moore dedicated the 9 a.m. Sunday Mass for the Sunday School Catechism children, who were now more numerous than ever. All pews were reserved for them and their teachers exclusively. Pew-holders were asked to vacate their pews, to the consternation of some, who had paid for pews they were now told they could not occupy. Moore asked them to sit in the side aisles or the galleries. When some parishioners complained about the new policy, Moore responded that he wished to give no offence, but he felt he must do his duty toward the youth of the parish. He was characteristically polite but firm.[18] This policy demonstrates how committed Moore was to the Catholic education of youth. He was even willing to alienate the pew-holders in order to do what he considered a priority — the religious education of the young people of the parish. With no possibility of having a parochial school, which would have been his preference, he tried to make his Sunday School the best possible means of religious instruction. In 1870 he joined with the pastors of three other Charleston parishes (the Cathedral, St. Mary's, and St. Joseph's) to found the Catholic Sunday School Union, a body comprised of seventy laity and four pastors. A superintendent and assistant were elected from each parish. The Union was composed also of members of various parish societies who supplied teachers who aided pastors in their task of religiously educating youth. In many places at the time only the priest conducted Sunday School, but in Charleston members of the laity were engaged in the task also.[19]

Not only did Moore have the largest Sunday School of any denomination in Charleston, he also had a city hospital to visit as of 1867. Yet these responsibilities did not prevent him from pouring out his energies to build up his parish in other ways. He organized a parish Total Abstinence Society (Temperance Society) in 1870. Moore was a life-long temperance advocate, as was John Ireland, later Archbishop of St. Paul, and Thomas Becker, his contemporary in Rome. The Catholic temperance movement began in Ireland under the auspices of Father Theobald Mathew, who visited the U. S. in 1849. Parish temperance societies were a common feature of Irish-American parishes from the 1840s, but by 1870 the Catholic temperance movement was being reinvigorated. During the parish mission held at St. Patrick's Parish in June of 1870, the Jesuit who conducted the mission urged the congregation to form a temperance society. After the mission was over, Father Moore, strong on temperance, was more than happy to organize such a society in his parish. The Catholic Total Abstinence Union was founded in 1872, a national confederation of parish societies. Later as a bishop, Moore would attend a few of their meetings.[20]

In March of 1866 Moore informed Bishop Lynch that he had forty-three First Communions and that Vespers were well attended every Sunday evening. He knew he had the largest parish in Charleston, but he did not know exactly how many people were in his parish. In the spring of 1869 Moore sought to remedy this ignorance by undertaking a parish census, which he personally did himself by walking from residence to residence, knocking on each of his parishioner's door. Either because of sickness or recalcitrance, Schachte did not help Moore in the task. The pastor commented that his assistant was not fit for duty. Besides counting heads during these visitations, Moore asked for a donation forty to fifty cents per person to help ameliorate the parish debt. He thought he had about 1,000 parishioners, but discovered almost double that number, most of who were of Irish descent. In Ireland parishioners were familiar with an annual home visitation by the pastor during which a special donation to the parish was expected.[21]

An important part of the spiritual revitalization of parish life in the South during Reconstruction was the introduction of the parish mission, which was a Tridentine method of graphic, dramatic, and emotive preaching for about a week in a parish designed to bring people back to the Sacraments, especially Confession, and devotional life. Parish missions were introduced into some parts of the South in the 1850s. In Charleston in 1857 the Redemptorists conducted a rousing parish mission at St. Finbar's Cathedral, hearing 3,000 Confessions and making twenty converts. These parish missions had particular relevance in Southern parishes especially right after the defeat on the Confederacy. Parish missions, what Jay Dolan calls, "Catholic Revivalism," were guided by Paulist, Jesuit, and Redemptorist priests. In 1868, 1869, and 1873 parish missions were conducted in parishes in Florida, Georgia, and South Carolina. In January of 1869 the Redemptorists came to the Cathedral and St. Patrick's in Charleston. A special mission was also conducted for African-Americans at St. Peter's Church. Jesuits led a mission at St. Patrick's again in 1870; one of its fruits was the establishment of St. Patrick's Temperance Society. At the end of May 1873 the Jesuits from the New Orleans Province came to Charleston once more. With a concern for the next generation, they conducted a three-day mission for children from ages seven to fifteen, which was judged a big success. On June 8 a mission for adults was held with a large attendance. Over 1,600 received Holy Communion, which meant they all went to Confession beforehand. One of the Jesuits lectured at the Charleston Academy of Music to a packed audience of mostly Protestants. The 1873 parish mission especially was considered a "grand success." These parish missions were considered an essential element in the "Spiritual Reconstruction" of Charleston in particular and the South in general.[22]

Although the average number of baptisms was somewhat lower under Moore's pastorate than under O'Neill's, more African-Americans were baptized by Moore. From 1850 through 1864, O'Neill baptized an average of 152.5 persons per year. During those years, only fourteen persons baptized were black (two of whom were slaves), that is, blacks represented only 0.6 percent of the total of baptisms of those years. From 1865 through 1876, during Moore's pastorate, on average 107.8 persons were baptized yearly, but 144 were African-American, or 11.1 percent of the baptisms of the period. Although the larger number of black baptisms after 1865 can to some extent be attributed to emancipation, one might also conclude that Moore's own ministerial sensitivity to the black community is also an important factor. Additionally, in 1876 a vast majority of those baptized had parents who were either born in Charleston (45.5 percent) or Ireland (36.6 percent). That last year of Moore's pastorate, about 70 percent of the parents of infants baptized were Irish or Irish-American.[23]

Moore had a gift for organization and administration. When one compares the entries in the Baptism registers, Moore's are much more legible and exact than O'Neill's. Moore also is careful to distinguish "colored" from "white," but in the same record book, not in two separate books as was done in some parishes in the South. In January 1871 Moore introduced a new printed Baptism Record Book. Whereas before entries were written on blank pages of paper in English, following a mandate of Charleston's first bishop, Bishop England, henceforth the entries were now standardized forms and written in Latin, as mandated by the 10th Provincial Council of Baltimore(1869). Also, in 1871, Moore introduced a printed book for the St. Lawrence Cemetery Burial Records. He was in charge of the diocesan cemetery as part of being the pastor of St. Patrick's. These initiatives not only followed ecclesiastical law, but also reflected new standardized accounting procedures of the American business community, resulting in more accurate and legible accounts.[24]

Moore's "blessed rage for order"[25] was also reflected in his liturgical concerns. In June 1867 Moore wrote Lynch that he had staged "grand Vespers Roman style for a couple of Sundays and [with] large attendance." He had a procession of the Blessed

Sacrament outside the church for Corpus Christi which included all elements of the parish, including the catechism kids who were "nicely dressed."[26] Being Roman trained, he took pride in properly performing the rites of the Church following Roman models and regulations.

As pastor, Moore acquired not only the admiration of his parishioners, but the respect of the entire Charlestonian community. The local Charleston newspaper summarized his contribution to the city as he concluded his pastorate at St. Patrick's:

> His patient industry, purity of character and unobtrusive learning endeared him to the Catholic congregation and caused him to be esteemed and admired by all who were brought into contact with him.[27]

As pastor of St. Patrick's, Moore had an opportunity to share the joys and sorrows of his local family and relatives, something he had missed during his years away. In August 1871 Moore traveled to Sweet Chalybeate Springs in Virginia to reinvigorate his health. He took with him his sister, Sister Alphonsa, OLM. She was accompanied by Sister DeSales Brennan, OLM. Both Sisters also were in poor health at the time and their conditions improved at the spa. Sister DeSales was stationed at nearby White Sulphur Springs, Virginia, (the Greenbrier Resort) during the War as a nurse in a Confederate hospital.[28] Earlier in August 1866, he baptized his niece, Mary Ann, daughter of his brother Thomas Moore and his wife Bridget Ryan. In September 1872 he christened a nephew, Charles James, and in July 1873 another niece, Anna Immaculate, both from the same parents, Thomas and Bridget.[29] Little Mary Ann Moore died at age two years, eleven months, on July 24, 1869. Father Moore secured a 13' x 16' plot for the infant at St. Lawrence Cemetery. Less than a decade later the same plot would be used again. Little Mary Ann's father, Thomas Moore, died of "hydrothorax" at age of fifty on January 28, 1877. He was a carpenter and lived at 16 Spring Street, the same residence the Moore's settled in as a family when they arrived from Ireland in 1848. Although John Moore did use his influence to acquire a burial plot for his niece in 1869, the same one later used by his brother in 1877, neither he nor his brother's widow could afford to pay for the plot. Even though the matter would have been forgotten when Moore left to become the Bishop of St. Augustine, Moore's sense of duty motivated him as Bishop of St. Augustine to pay for the plot with $80 in cash in February 1878.[30]

## Moore's Reflections on His Pastoral Situation

As mentioned in the previous chapter, any alumnus of the Urban College was required to write every other year a letter to the head of the Congregation of the Propagation of the Faith in Rome to describe the experience of his priestly ministry. These letters, written in Italian, served several purposes. On the one hand, they allowed the writer to candidly express his own experiences in a forum that was unique. On the other hand, for the reader far way in Rome they provided some insight into the realities of the local Church. Letters from Moore and other alumni in missionary countries throughout the world gave those in the Congregation insight and information about those various countries which they would not otherwise have. The Congregation governed the churches in various missionary countries throughout the world, yet rarely if ever visited those countries personally. Therefore, information from their "agents" abroad helped them assess those places, which sometimes they had to make decisions about from their offices in Rome. Also, since Rome always acknowledged these letters and also added some comments, they provided a source of affirmation and encouragement for their alumni far away in a missionary land. Through these letters, the alumnus felt connected to Rome. He was not just a priest from a particular diocese or country, but a churchman, whose concerns and connections were larger than his local church. Moreover, they kept the man tethered to Rome in mind and spirit. He was not just a native priest, but a Roman. He was not just a priest of his particular diocese, but a priest of the Church universal.

Moore's letters followed a certain formula. He began by discussing his current health, then his priestly duties, and finally his spiritual life. Both his salutation and his conclusion were formal and formulaic. Yet beyond their basic structure, they are surprisingly frank and personally revelatory, not only for a quiet man like Moore, but also for in general for men of the late nineteenth century. During the Reconstruction Period, Moore wrote seven of these letters.

In April 1866 Moore refers back to the letter he sent to Propaganda in April 1864 which he gave to Bishop Lynch to deliver when he arrived in Rome. Apparently, Lynch did not deliver this letter, which created yet another aggravation for Moore in his relationship with Lynch. Consequently, Moore reviews events of 1864 and 1865, including his appointment as Vicar General by Archbishop Spalding. He then discusses his present circumstances. His parish of St. Patrick's involves more work than any parish in the diocese. He says the tasks would be more than enough for two priests, although he is presently alone. Despite the pastoral burdens, he writes that "I trust in God's help and the mercy of God [that] I'll be able to fulfill my responsibilities." Although he feels he is not lacking in any temporal needs, he is in need of spiritual sustenance. Because of the War and his present pressing obligations, he has not been able to take an annual retreat. What he failed to mention was his physical and emotional exhaustion. His sabbatical, which he took later in 1866, would give him the physical, emotional, and spiritual rejuvenation he so desperately needed.[31]

In April two years later he writes to Rome again. He mentions that he has 2,000 parishioners at St. Patrick's, whose territory extends several miles outside the city. This means that in the heat of summer, which is a time of increased sickness both inside and outside the city, he is required to make extended sick calls which take "a good deal of energy on my part." He mentions that his own health broke down in September of 1866, which necessitated his four month sabbatical up North on doctor's orders and with Lynch's permission. When Moore returned to Charleston, he said his bishop gave him an assistant. Actually John Schachte was his assistant before he left and during his absence. Moore's real point here, though he does not express it, is that Lynch did not take away Schachte from the parish, as Moore thought would happen when he returned. He admits that since his return as pastor he has become more involved in temporal affairs than ever before because he had to build a rectory, but "has not been able to pay for all the expenses, so great is the poverty of the people in these parts." He adds, "This situation gives me a lot of worries." Then he reveals his deeper pastoral and personal concerns.

But a greater sadness for me is the spiritual destitution that I see in this diocese. We are far

from the houses of religious orders and the Fathers
[religious order priests] have not been invited to give
us a retreat. I feel greatly in need of encouragement.

This latter remark is an indirect dig at Bishop Lynch, since it is
he who would have to arrange for an annual retreat for his priests.
He failed to do so=. Moreover, it is clear that in 1868 Moore is
overwhelmed by his pastoral and temporal responsibilities.[32] But
having been weaned as a young pastor with debt and financial
burdens, he would learn to cope, a skill he acquired and that
acquisition would serve him well later as a bishop.

Like clockwork, Moore dutifully writes Rome again in April
1870. He mentions that his health has generally been good, though
"from time to time I'm unable to do my duties, although in the last
six months now I enjoy good health." With now 2,500 souls to
minister to in his parish, he often feels physically and spiritually
spent. He hungers for a deeper spiritual life, but feels frustrated in
his desire.

> While I work for others, I believe that instead of
> growing in the priestly spirit that I brought back from
> the Propagation of the Faith, I have lost much. My
> experience of about ten years of priestly service on
> the mission has convinced me that it is very difficult
> to be a good priest for a long time in this diocese.
> Here we live in a perfect spiritual desert! In this
> diocese the opportunity for priests to make a retreat
> has not been offered in twenty-five years and nobody
> even thinks about it!

Here we see that Moore's greatest critique of Bishop Lynch
hinges on what Moore perceives as a lack of spirituality. While
recognizing that Lynch has many fine qualities, he adds:

> ...But he absolutely has no devotion, no missionary
> zeal, and the priests and people have become just like
> him! He loves being out of the diocese too much and
> it was always this way. Priests and people complain
> of this for years. In truth, it would be better for us not
> to have a bishop at all: then everyone could think and
> act for himself. As a consequence of our situation, I
> fear greatly for my soul.[33]

At the root of Moore's dissatisfaction with Lynch was that he felt his bishop did not share with him his own desire for things spiritual and for the nourishment of a priestly spirituality.

Just a year after Moore wrote his letter to Rome as an alumnus of the Urban College, Bishop Lynch, also an alumnus, wrote to Propaganda. His tone is less personal, less spiritual, less emotional, less revealing than Moore's, while at the same time more self-serving. To demonstrate his allegiance to the Holy Father, he reminds the reader that he just made the third offering within nine months to the Holy Father, namely forty *lira*. He mentions that he has given talks twenty times on the topic of the situation of the Pope in Italy. This past December 11 Catholics of Charleston joined in a public protest of the Papacy's treatment by the Italians, which was reported in the papers. Not a single voice in Charleston supports the actions of the Italian army. "We all pray that the war in France is finished and that Catholics in France and Europe will restore to the Holy Father what has been taken away from him."

Changing the subject, Lynch says that he is still working to restore the damage to the diocese created as a result of the Civil War. He hopes to restore everything in three more years, except for the Cathedral. His view of the state of the clergy is quite different from Moore's. He feels that his priests are zealous and good. Presently he has not one problem priest. Father James A. Corcoran has moved to Philadelphia to teach theology at St. Charles Borromeo Seminary, after Archbishop James Wood of Philadelphia and Bishop William O'Hara of Scranton begged him for three years to come. Lynch agreed to Corcoran's move, while keeping him a priest of the Diocese, since the Bishop of Charleston said, " ... considering his obesity, he can do very little work in the care of souls and would be a very capable professor." Lynch then mentions some Roman alumni. John Moore and Augustus McNeal are both working with zeal and profit. Lynch thanks the Congregation of Propaganda for Simon Carew, a recent alumnus. He works "with zeal, good behavior, and is loved by all."[34] As we shall see, Carew is an example of Lynch's poor judgment of character. But what we also see is that Lynch, at least formally in his letter to Rome, has a high regard for Moore as a pastor.

In March 1872 Moore wrote Rome again. He repeats themes

in his previous letters. With the summer heat he often feels weak and listless. Previously in July and August of 1871, with his bishop's permission, he traveled to the mountains of Virginia for the sake of his health. His parish is flourishing, increasing in piety by their Mass attendance, their attentiveness to preaching, and their frequent reception of the Sacraments. He admits that unfortunately he cannot give such a good spiritual report card to himself. He feels his devotional life is lessening from what it was when he was a student in Rome. He blames himself for not better responding to God's graces, but once again he blames his bishop, for "the lack of zeal and devotion for which Lynch is notorious reacts harmfully on the clerics and religious of this diocese."[35] Part of Moore's disappointments with his own spiritual life is about the disjunction between the kind of devotional and spiritual routine given at the seminary and the practical realities of a pastor in a missionary diocese. That is, the spiritual training given him in formation was not adaptable to the active apostolic life that he was leading and he consequently felt deprived spiritually. The need for a specific spiritual life, separate from monastic, or religious, or lay spirituality, which is adapted to the practical needs of the diocesan priest is a topic that only recently has come to light.[36] But in any case, Moore valued a lively spiritual life and desired to have a closer relationship with his God. "Silent John's" more introspective, contemplative side was being starved in the pastoral world of activity, financial worries, and the various demands on his time and energy.

Dutiful as always, Moore writes Rome again in March 1874. He begins by saying that for the last two years he has enjoyed good health. This is a first for him. He mentions traveling into the countryside to visit Catholics "who too rarely have the chance to hear Mass and receive the Sacraments." He has an assistant priest, but he is not in good health. Moore can scarcely trust to leave him alone. What he doesn't mention is that this priest is an alcoholic. Once again, he puts in his all too familiar stab at his bishop. Lynch is now away from the diocese "the greater part of the time." He also expresses his desire to be faithful to his priestly duties. "It's true that sometimes I face difficulties that almost make me lose heart, but up to now I've been able to overcome them, with the help of God."[37]

When he wrote his June 1876 letter to Rome, he had no idea that it would be the last of his alumnus letters. He begins by commenting on his good health over the last two years, even though he admits that "I am not of a strong constitution." He estimates his parish has at least 2,000 souls, maybe more. He admits that his most laborious duty, especially in the heat of summer, is making sick calls, since some of his parishioners live as far as six miles from the rectory. St. Patrick's is once again a single-man parish, since Moore's assistant died last March 17. He says he is doing the best he can under the circumstances. For the first time, he makes no references to Bishop Lynch. Perhaps he is now reconciled to the bishop's personality and leadership style, or perhaps his own responsibilities have emotionally distanced him from any dependence on his absentee bishop. On a personal note he adds, "although sometimes I feel saddened with many things and almost discouraged, I hope that God will help me again, as in the past." As a pastor, Moore depended on God's aid to help him face pastoral challenges and the burdens of his office.[38] This spiritual attitude will remain with him for the rest of his life.

CHAPTER FIVE

# *Vicar General of Charleston*

**M**oore saw himself as not simply the pastor of the circumscribed geographical territory of St. Patrick's, but a priest of Charleston and appointed Vicar General of the diocese again in 1872. Therefore, his involvements often took him beyond his parish responsibilities. With Bishop Lynch absent from the diocese a large part of the time during Reconstruction begging for money, aspects of the administration of the diocese needed tending. Among others, Lynch called upon the pastor of St. Patrick's Parish to assist him in a number of diocesan affairs. Charleston had the largest concentration of Catholics, Catholic personnel, and Catholic institutions in the diocese. In 1866 the city had five parishes and nine priests, while in 1876 there were the same number of parishes and eight priests. During the period, the Sisters of Our Lady of Mercy ran the diocesan girls' and boys' orphanages, an academy on Meeting Street (from 1870), and the Cathedral Free School (from 1869). Charleston's Catholic personnel and institutions commanded the attention of Lynch's delegates.

St. Patrick's Day in Charleston combined civic, ethnic, and religious dimensions, as was the case in every major city where it was celebrated both before and after the War. Charleston's newspapers covered the annual preparations that led up to March 17th. Events in 1873 were particularly elaborate. That year St. Patrick's Day fell on a Friday and those celebrating had no thought of working that day. In February the papers began reporting about various Irish societies

*5.1 Msgr. D.J. Quigley, 1886. Source: ADC*

preparations. There were five such organizations: the St. Patrick's Benevolent Society, the Irish Rifle Club, the Irish Volunteer Rifle Club, the Irish Volunteers, the St. Joseph Total Abstinence Society. On Feb. 30 all the Irish organizations met at the Hibernian Hall and elected Capt. James Armstrong of the Irish Rifle Club as the Grand Marshal, along with Lt. D. J. Erwins of the Irish Volunteer Rifle Club and James Cosgrave of the St. Patrick's Benevolent Society as his assistants. At the core of the day's events was the Charleston Ancient Order of Hibernians, founded in 1801. The parade, or "the procession" as the newspaper called it, formed about eight a.m. on March 17th in front of the Hibernian Hall at 105 Meeting Street. They would then proceed up Queen Street to the Cathedral where Bishop Ignatius Persico of Savannah would deliver the sermon and Father D. J. Quigley, rector of the Cathedral, would celebrate High Mass. During the Eucharist, some of the Sisters of Mercy presented a banner which they fashioned for the St. Patrick's Benevolent Society. After Mass, the "procession" marched through King and Broad Streets to East Bay, then through Market and Meeting to Line Street, then back down King and Queen to the Hibernian Hall. Each Irish organization marched in their own unique uniform, accompanied by various brass bands, such as the St. Patrick' Brass Band and the U.S. Post Office Band. A member of the Irish Rifle Club carried the American Flag, the Irish Rifle Club's Dominick

Spellman, who fought in over 100 battles in Virginia during the late War. After the parade, each organization gathered in a different rented hall for "a substantial lunch" and the annual election of new officers. The Hibernians met in their building on Meeting Street for a banquet at 7 p.m. As one newspaper wrote, this "national festival represents the fondest hopes and noblest aspirations of a people who love their native land."[2]

Of the five Irish organizations represented in the "procession," the one most closely allied to the Church was the St. Patrick's Benevolent Society. It was also the group with the smallest treasury; consequently they had their dinner in the hall over the Byrne and Fogarty Grocery Store on King Street. Besides food and drink, Irish music accompanied the festivities, which also included seven toasts, each followed by a response. The first toast was to Christianity and Father John Moore was the responder, though we have no record as to what he said. The other toasts followed in this order: to Ireland, to South Carolina, to the City of Charleston, to the press, to womanhood, to the Sisters of Mercy.[3] The toasts celebrated localism, regionalism, and the Victorian cult of womanhood, both themes that would have resonated with Southern sensibilities both before and after the War. At a time when the Radical Reconstruction sought to reform the South's social and political life, and when Federal troops were still occupying the South, to toast things local was a strong political statement. Needless to say, there were no toasts to the federal government in Washington. Moore, the temperance man, must have toasted a glass of milk, along with other Catholic temperance men; however, many others present would have charged their glasses with more potent liquids.

St. Patrick's Day celebrated the dignity of a minority, which was climbing the social ladder and becoming more accepted in Charleston. It celebrated a religious heritage once despised and pushed to the margins of society. And in the South, it also served to ennoble the Lost Cause, to embrace the Irish as an important part of the community, and even to express Americanism, symbolized by the Irish Confederate veteran marching with the American Flag. Besides Charleston, other Southern cities also had similar St. Patrick's Day events: Atlanta, Augusta, Richmond, Wilmington, N.C., Columbia, Savannah, Mobile, and New Orleans.

Moore was an active member of the St. Patrick's Benevolent Society, founded in 1817 as a city-wide Irish-American fraternal organization "to cultivate a spirit of brotherly love among its members and to assist each other against unforeseen casualties of life." As was mentioned earlier, among all of the several fraternal organizations associated with Charleston's annual St. Patrick Day celebration, this one was one closest to the church. Many, if not most, of the membership were male parishioners of St. Patrick's Parish, even though technically it was not a parish organization. Its elected presidents were both laymen and priests. Fathers Richard Baker and C. J. Croghan served as president, as did the Rev. Dr. Moore from 1875 to 1877. Members were males of good character from ages eighteen to fifty. As a mutual aid society, the initiation fee and monthly dues went towards paying for relief of sick or disabled members and for their funerals. On St. Patrick's Day the members attended Mass at St. Patrick's Church, marched in the annual parade with their fraternal badges in prominence, then retired to a rented hall for refreshments and the annual election of officers. As president, Moore presided over two St. Patrick's Day celebrations. On March 17, 1877, he gave a "lengthy address" to the membership and was re-elected president. Moore resigned the office in April, since he was to become a bishop. In May the organization voted on a resolution which stated "the profound respect and devotion we bear him for his constant manifestations of interest in our body, shown in his rare good judgment in the management of its affairs." They had collected $14.50 and with it purchased a gold-headed cane as an ordination gift.[4]

## A Public Controversy

"Silent John" did something quite uncharacteristic in early 1873. He entered into public controversy for the first and only time in his life. At the February 18, 1873, meeting of the Charleston City Council, the Mayor reviewed the state of public administration, enumerating "the discouraging legacy of public debt, demoralized public institutions, dilapidated public buildings, ruined streets and pavements, choked drains." He and his new administration wished to change all this. He was particularly concerned "to prevent any waste or imprudent extravagance in public expenditures." As an example, he pointed out the reduction in appropriations to the city orphan house. In 1871 $28,680.80 was appropriated, while in 1872 $22,707.67 was given. He proposed that this year the city orphan house receive $20,000. The Mayor also recommended that the Catholic Sisters' boys and girls orphanages be appropriated the same amount as last year, that is $6,000, pointing out that Bishop Lynch had sent to him a detailed annual financial report of each orphanage and it is clear that the public funds sent there was well used.[5]

At the following month's City Council Meeting, Alderman Alva Gage of Ward 3 stood to explain his opposition to the proposed appropriation to the Sisters of Mercy whom, he was quick to point out, "he respected very highly." Although as an individual, he was "ready to assist this noble order of women," but as a publicly elected official he listed four reasons he opposes any appropriation to the Sisters' orphanages. First, since the present Council is committed to reform of expenditures, it is not right for one-third of all grants to orphanages go to the Sisters of Mercy. The city orphanage is open to all, which is not the case with the Sisters' institutions. Second, the appropriation is a dangerous precedent and "will be fatal to the liberties of the people and destructive to the principles of our government." Third, the appropriation "is illegal and very unjust to all taxpayers belonging to other denominations in the city." Fourth, such an appropriation would destroy "the bulwark of our Republican government" and our much prized free public schools.[6]

In the March 7th edition of the *Charleston Daily Courier* contained a letter to the editor signed by "A Catholic," that is, Dr. John Moore. Alderman Gage's objection "seems to be the protest of a mind laboring under some strange hallucination," began Moore's combative letter. The previous administration of Mayor Gilbert Pillbury (1869-1871) viewed the Sisters' appropriation as a just claim, as had the present administration of Mayor John A. Wagener for the past two years, with the single exception of Councilman Gage. Moore continued: "Catholics were beginning to believe that an era of justice and fair dealing had dawned upon them," as a result of the City Council's previous deliberations supporting the Catholic orphanages. The arguments used to grant the appropriation in the past still hold. We Catholics, wrote Moore, "want nothing done in a corner, but everything in true American style, in the broad light of day." In other words, Moore believes in American principles as much as Gage and welcomes the public debate which precludes any secret deliberations about or hidden appropriations for the Catholic orphanages. Moore "emphatically denies" Gage's assertion that the principles of government are endangered by a $6,000 appropriation. "Catholics of this community have proved themselves in the past to be law-abiding citizens and firm conscientious upholders of the principles of government." The appropriation to the Sisters is not unjust to anyone, nor is it illegal, for if it were so why has Alderman Gage remained silent about it for the past two years? Playing on the Southern sympathies of the paper's readers, who remain under military occupation and who still are being dominated by Northerners, Moore strikes a raw nerve of Charlestonians when he adds: "We have the gravest objection to the system of public schools as now established in the country, which are not of Southern origin, but an exotic transplanted into our land from New England, whence many other evils have come to us." This was particularly poignant slam on New England's creation public schools and its fostering of Abolitionists, since Gage was from New England! Moore writes that Gage accuses the Sisters' orphanage of being a sectarian, but "we are not more so than the public orphanage," since it is influenced by the Protestant ethos. The Catholic community is not inclined to disturb the peace or agitate religious controversy, "yet we will not shrink from it when it is forced upon us." Moore concludes his letter with a rousing appeal to American justice and democratic values by stating that Catholics "are convinced that they can make their claims good to even-handed justice in all matters that concern the community in which they live. They ask no more, and they will never be satisfied with less."[7]

Moore wrote Lynch, who was out of town, on March 7, informing him that the City Council appropriated $6,000 for the orphanages, although Gage dissented and had his dissent published in the paper. Moore said that he responded to Gage and his letter signed "A Catholic" was printed in the newspaper. He hoped that the episode was now over. Moore adds that he wants to write a long article for the newspaper or produce a pamphlet on the issue, "unless you advise me differently." Unbeknownst to Moore, Lynch was getting advice and information from another source, Sister DeSales Brennan, OLM. She states she lacks confidence in Moore and wishes Lynch were in Charleston to moderate the controversy. She includes a clipping of Moore's letter to the editor, and mentions that he has addressed a second article to the newspaper.[8]

Unaware of Sister DeSales' correspondence, Moore informed Lynch on March 11, about becoming a U.S. citizen, taking his certificate of citizenship that very day from Judge Ryan in the U.S. Court, and then about the state of the controversy. He enclosed the newspaper article of Gage's protest about the appropriation to the Catholic orphanages and included a copy of his letter to the editor, which he signed "A Catholic." He also mentions that two laymen, M. P. O'Connor ("Vindex") and Bernard O'Neill ("Civis" and "Taxpayer") also wrote letters to the editor. T. J. Mackey penned a long article, but the newspaper refused to publish it. Moore felt that at this point the issue is closed, unless Gage provokes him further. Apparently, he had as yet not read the letters to the editor in the newspaper of the day before in which Gage responded specifically to the letter by "A Catholic." Gage said that he and two other commissioners had visited both the girls' and boys' Catholic orphanages in February 1869, when the Sisters had received no city appropriations. He found the children well attended from the resources of the Catholic community alone. He pointed out that this year the Sisters reported 110 charges in both institutions, forty-two more than they had when they received no aid. Gage argued that even if there was an appropriation the Sister's orphanages, it should be only $2,056.32, not $6,000, since that would be the cost of caring for the extra forty-two kids in the orphanage since 1869, when the Catholic community was able to support its own institution without government money. Gage, however, was careful not to discredit the Sisters or their good works, which he said every citizen would gladly contribute to freely. He admits that this Sisters' charity is not sectarian, that is not just for Catholics, but for all people. But for him the real issue here is not economizing on the city's treasury, but sectarianism. Tax money should not be used to support sectarian education in any orphanage or school. Gage says the author of the letter signed "A Catholic" fulminates "religious bigotry and intolerance... religious animosity and hate." Gage will not employ an argument about the usefulness of Catholic Schools verse public schools, however he says that the place of his birth, "so flippantly alluded to by your correspondent," is not pertinent to this present discussion. "Having given your correspondent all the attention he can reasonably ask of me, I bid a final adieu to the subject."[9]

Gage had provoked Moore and so it was not "adieu" for him. "A Catholic" wrote a rejoinder to Gage, published on March 11. Moore minces no words by saying that the reasoning that Gage applies regarding the cost of supporting the Catholic orphanages "is based on a sophism." He analyses the actual per orphan costs of the city orphanage at $106.28 per child per year, although Gage said it was $48.96, which leaves a large sum of $10,000 appropriated but unaccounted for by Gage's figures. Surely he does not "suggest that this money has been misapplied, and far be it from me to insinuate in the slightest degree any conclusion so uncharitable and unjust." Rather, the problem is with Gage's calculations which use the base of costs from twelve years ago. Moreover, "The Catholics of this city assert their right to an appropriation for the maintenance of their orphans. They themselves are taxed equally for all the children in the City Orphan House." Finally, Moore is unwilling to back off from his point about Gage's place of birth and training. Moore believes Gage's personal background accounts for "his prejudice and unjust charges" against the Catholics of Charleston. This final epistolary salvo ended the public controversy. The Catholic Orphanages did receive their subsidy from the city government and the issue remained dormant for the rest of the 1870s.[10]

Why was it that Moore jumped out of his quiet reserved character to enter into public controversy in 1873? Largely, it was due to his sense of duty and responsibility. In early June 1872 Timothy Bermingham, Rector of the Pro-Cathedral and Vicar General, died. In the summer of 1872, Lynch made Moore the new Vicar General, to oversee certain matters delegated by the bishop due to his frequent absences from the diocese. It seems that Moore was charged with supervising personnel matters both in regards to the priests and the Sisters of Our Lady of Mercy. Yet many of the other aspects of diocesan life, especially matters financial, were delegated to Daniel J. Quigley, Rector of the Pro-Cathedral beginning in 1872. Quigley was an Irishman born in Scotland. In June 1864 when Lynch was in Rome, he met Quigley at the Irish College and poached him for the Diocese of Charleston. Quigley was transferred to the North American College and was ordained in 1866. During Lynch's many absences, it was Quigley with whom he corresponded about diocesan finances, not so much Moore, his Vicar General. Moore had a title, but Quigley had much of the power and trust of the bishop. Lynch only designated Quigley as his Vicar General when Moore left the diocese in 1877.[11]

So when Moore entered into the public epistolary exchange with Gage, it was not in his role as pastor of St. Patrick's, but as the Vicar General of the diocese, at a time when the bishop was out of town. At risk was the city's allotment to the orphanages, institutions near and dear to Moore. Also at stake was the work of the Sisters, whom Moore was deputed to oversee. In addition, money which the poor Diocese of Charleston desperately needed to maintain their two orphanages was at jeopardy. With no one else to enter the fray to protect the Church's interests, Moore felt it his duty to do so, even if to do so meant acting in a manner not accord with his natural reticent character. In Moore's mind, duty came before personal preference.

Besides his sense of duty and social justice, another factor was at work influencing his actions. Alva Gage was born in New London, New Hampshire in 1820. He was a businessman who came to Charleston in 1853. During Reconstruction, he rose in local prominence. He was Director of the People's National Bank and of Lockhart Mills, Vice-President of the Associated Charities Society, Second Vice-President the Society for the Prevention of Cruelty to Animals, and member of the New England Society of Charleston since 1855. He was elected from the Third Ward, an affluent part of town at the time, as part of the new Wagener Democratic city government in 1871. He was also a member of the Unitarian Church, who named the parish house after him when he died in 1896. In short, Gage was everything that a Southern Catholic like Moore found distasteful about Reconstruction and the military occupation, which only formally ended in March 1877 when 686 Federal troops withdrew from Charleston and nine other posts in South Carolina.[12] This is why Moore was insistent on making the point twice about Gage's New England background and how his prejudices from there were getting in the way of his judgments. Moore implied that Gage's problem with the Catholic orphanage allotment was a two-fold prejudice — against Catholics and against Southern institutions. Moore's rejoinders to Gage reflected his identity as a Catholic, as a Southerner, and as a newly minted American.

## Priest Personnel

The largest portion of Moore's extra-parochial energy was not spent in public controversy, but on responding to behind-the-scenes personnel problems. It seems that Lynch had deputed to Moore some deliberative power over personnel, even before he made him his Vicar General. As early as October 1866, Moore had headaches handling some of the clergy.

Father Patrick Walsh, a clerical vagabond of the type who sometimes found their way to the priest-poor South in the nineteenth century, came to Charleston in 1866. Moore warned Lynch that he was a drinker, but the bishop accepted him anyway. Not long after arriving, Walsh had the police arrest Mrs. McNeal and her daughter, along with a black woman. Mr. Dotage, a German Catholic and proprietor of a grocery store, tried to prevent the arrest, but Walsh had the police incarcerate Dotage too! The women were not detained and Mr. Dotage got out on bail. The next day Walsh and Mrs. McNeal were to appear before the Mayor's Court, but the Mayor refused to hear the case. Walsh then sent a letter of protest to the Mayor, and to the newspaper, who printed it. When Moore confronted the priest about the incident, Walsh had a seven-barrelled revolver in his hand. When asked what he was doing with the gun, Walsh said he needed it since he had received threats against him on account of a sermon he delivered. Moore telegraphed the bishop on October 8 asking that the priest be suspended, that is to deprive him of his priestly functions, something only a bishop or his delegate can do. On October 10 Lynch assented to Moore's request. Moore suspended Walsh "since his conduct was outrageous." Walsh responded by threatening to beat up Moore, but fortunately Father Schachte intervened and ordered him to leave the rectory. Walsh's erratic behavior reflected his addiction to alcohol. All this drama happened while Moore was laid up sick in bed for most of the time.[13]

At the end of October, Walsh, who was in Kinston, N.C., wrote Bishop Lynch asking "not to be cast out into the world penniless [sic] and friendless." He says has no desire to minister in Charleston any longer, but hopes that Lynch will allow him to work as a priest in North Carolina, which was still in the Diocese of Charleston at the time. Apparently Lynch did not see it that way. Walsh is next heard from in January 1867 when he writes Lynch from Our Lady of Gethsemani Abbey in Kentucky, the first permanent Trappist monastery in the United States. "There are some other priests here on the penitential chair with me," wrote Walsh. From the Middle Ages, monasteries were used as places of penance for priests who got themselves into trouble of one sort or another. Apparently Lynch sent Walsh to the abbey to "dry him out" from his heavy drinking and bring about an interior spiritual cure to his alcoholism. Walsh thanks Lynch for all his kindness and asks the bishop to forward his trunks.[14]

Continuing his vagabond ways, Walsh cut a deal late April 1867 with the Bishop of Louisville, who was willing to take him in to teach in the seminary for two or three years. But one month later he is in Pittsburgh, at St. Paul's Cathedral. Following year he asks for a letter from Lynch so as to be accepted into the Diocese of Dubuque. Whether he stopped his vagabond ways or was ever cured of alcoholism is unknown.[15]

But not all of Charleston's problem priests came from outside the Diocese. In 1870 Moore lost his assistant, John O'Neill Schachte, which left Moore the sole priest at St. Patrick's for the next year. Schachte, who was a Charlestonian, born October 26, 1840, graduated from St. John's College, Fordham, New York, in 1861, whereupon was sent to the North American College, Rome, where he was ordained May 1866. His first assignment was at St. Patrick's with Moore, but it seems that Schachte was removed from St. Patrick's for disciplinary reasons, since he was reassigned to the Cathedral in 1870, where the rector, Bermingham, states in September 1871, "he is not at all needed." Bermingham inquires of the bishop whether Schachte will remain "one of your family of priests," that is whether he is suspended or not. Apparently Lynch did not suspend him, because in late 1872 Schachte is reassigned as an assistant at St. Mary's, Charleston, under Claudian Northrop, pastor.

But his performance there was less than satisfactory. Moore, now the Vicar General, writes Lynch in August of 1872 that Schachte "is out of the house [St. Mary's Rectory] all the time and is hardly ever at hand when he is needed."[16]

In early 1873 Schachte attracts Moore's attention once again. Moore observed that Schachte was not visiting the hospitals as he was supposed to and concerns were raised over the content of his sermons at St. Mary's. He preached that "it was useless" to attend Mass or Vespers or Benediction or pray to the Saints if one was in mortal sin. To do so would only bring malediction on the one who did so. Initially, no formal complaint was made about these statements by either the pastor or parishioners, but if this were to happen, Moore tells Lynch, that "I would feel my position to be a very painful one." After all, it was Schachte who had been an assistant at St. Patrick's and who had done such a fine job when Moore was on his sabbatical in New York. Moore asks Lynch's guidance about what he should do about this matter of the content of Schachte's preaching. In March, Moore asked Schachte to make a public retraction of his erroneous doctrines to a Sunday congregation at St. Mary's. The priest did so, but Moore added that "It was scarcely more orthodox than the first preaching."[17] Other personnel problems which Moore faced were not always solved as easily.

The case of Father Simon Carew is one such example. Ordained in Rome in the summer of 1871, as an alumnus of the Urban College, Carew's first assignment was as Moore's assistant pastor at St. Patrick's in 1871. Soon thereafter, in the fall of 1872, Edward Kedney, a graduate of All Hallows Missionary Seminary, Ireland, was assigned there also. Suddenly, Moore went from having no assistant to having two. He also went from having no personnel problems in his rectory, to having two.

In November 1871 the newly ordained Carew wrote that everything was going very well for him and that there is "not the slightest thing that I can complain about." However, others perceptions of him were not as sanguine. As early as September 1871 Timothy Bermingham, the Vicar General, wrote Lynch that Carew was unpredictably moody, "Alternately up and down."[18] By the spring of 1873 Carew's actions began generating controversy.

It seems that young Father Carew was spending a bit too much time visiting the home of two young sisters, Elizabeth and Maggie Wynne of 12 St. Mary Street. These visits became known by some. On May 26, 1873, Sister DeSales Brennan, OLM, (director of the Boys' Catholic Orphanage) and Sister Agnes, OLM, marched up to the Wynne house and knocked on the front door. They were a two-woman vigilante committee in search of Father Carew, whom they believed to be concealed presently in the Wynne house. Elizabeth responded that Father Carew was not in the building. Sister DeSales asserted that he was indeed concealed somewhere in the house and that she had "positive information" that this was the case. Elizabeth was indignant and told the Sisters to come in and search the house if they wanted. The religious women backed off and returned to their convent. Meanwhile, both Wynne sisters proceeded to St. Patrick's Rectory to confront the pastor. Elizabeth asked Moore if it was he who sent the Sisters. She said at first he refused to answer, and then added that he knew about their actions since he had given them the information about Carew being at the Wynne's. Just then Carew came downstairs and vehemently denied that he had recently been at the Wynne's. Moore asked him when the last time he was at the Wynne house and he replied "not in two months." Five days later Elizabeth wrote Bishop Lynch complaining about Moore, reporting that he "has done us a great personal injury, subjecting us to great scandal and reproach in the parish." She added that Moore neglected to apologize to the women or to make any reparation to them.[19]

We have no record of Moore's side of the story or of Carew's for that matter. It seems that Carew had caused scandal and concern in his overly solicitous attention to the Wynne Sisters, but that was not the root of his problem. Alcoholism was the source of Carew's mounting unacceptable behaviors. Lynch got the particulars of the case from Moore and sent a telegram at the end of May instructing his Vicar General to act on the case. By this time Carew had left the rectory and was in desperate shape in a drunken stupor. Sister DeSales and Sister Agnes suggested to Moore that they accompany Father Carew to Baltimore, where he could be treated at St. Agnes Hospital. "Oh, what a time we had with him — he was very sick on the train," wrote Sister DeSales, a nurse during the War. In mid-June Carew wrote Lynch from St. Agnes Hospital saying that he feels better than when he left Charleston, thanks to the kindness of Sisters DeSales and Agnes. The Sisters at the hospital are giving him good care also. He intends to write Dr. Moore soon.[20] Whether he did or not, we have no extant record.

Carew penned Lynch again a month later to report that his health "is very much improved." He thought he would be able to relocate in Baltimore, but asked for Lynch's advice on this matter. It is clear that after what happened, Lynch would not take him back to Charleston. At the same time a Sister Nurse at the Baltimore hospital wrote Lynch saying that Carew "has gotten quite well." "I feel sure this will be a warning to him as long as he lives," she wrote confidently. Apparently he had taken "the cure," which is to say he had "dried out" from the alcohol and was feeling remorse for his actions. She added that he spent lots of time in the chapel in prayer and would benefit from a letter from Lynch. The Bishop of Charleston wrote Carew at the end of July, encouraging him to pursue a position in the Archdiocese of Baltimore. However, the Archbishop declined to see him and refused to grant him faculties to minister in the archdiocese. By mid-September Carew was still languishing in St. Agnes Hospital not knowing what to do next. "I feel so unhappy and out of place and at a perfect loss as to how to act," he wrote Lynch, pleading for advice and direction. A month later he informed Lynch that he felt "in the way at the hospital." He would try to be accepted by Bishop Thomas Becker of Wilmington, Delaware, and if not by him then by Bishop O'Hara of Scranton. Yet by June 1874, he was in Iowa. After trying Chicago and Nebraska, he was given hospitality by a pastor of St. Francis Xavier's, Council Bluffs, Iowa, and faculties for the Diocese of Dubuque. He said he was happy "to have a chance to redeem myself." He asked Lynch to use his influence to get him accepted by the Diocese of Dubuque. But he did not stay there. By 1877 he was no longer in Iowa. His whereabouts cannot be determined precisely. In 1885 he reappeared as an assistant at St. Vibiana Cathedral, Los Angeles, California. Two years later, he moved to Exultation of the Holy Cross Parish, Santa Cruz, California, in the Diocese of Monterey-Los Angeles. He died at the age of fifty-four on August 11, 1888, at St. Mary's Hospital, San Francisco.[21]

Carew was just one of several priestly personnel headaches that Moore had to address. Alcoholism and physical sickness continued to be the chief maladies of the clergy. Moore lost one assistant pastor, Carew, to alcoholism in the summer of 1873. His other assistant, Father Kedney, was also turning into an alcoholic. By early 1875 Moore says that Kedney is constantly "under the weather" and can't be counted on "for anything." By the end of September Moore reveals to Lynch the personal cost of living with an alcoholic. "Dear Bishop, my spirit is well nigh broken and I feel more than ever the need of your prayers." He elaborates upon his frustrations.

> He [Kedney] has done nothing for me all summer but say the 7 a.m. Mass on Sundays. For over two months he has every week made himself sick for the great part of the day, or two, or longer; talking to him or advising him is useless. At last I went to his room last week and took away the liquor from him. He had drunk the great part of a gallon of corn whiskey in less than twenty-four hours. I cannot bear with him much longer.

But Moore did bear with him a little longer. Less than a year later Kedney died on March 17, 1876, a victim of the self-destructive disease which addicted him to alcohol.[22] Moore's dealing with alcoholics in the priesthood only confirmed him further in his own temperance stand.

Bishop Lynch, with his many begging tours to New York and other Northern cities, sometimes would charm priests to come to the South to help out. Often his judgment about these men's character was flawed. These clerical "carpetbaggers" who came to the Diocese of Charleston were oftentimes an additional personnel problem for Moore to handle in Lynch's absence. Recruited by Lynch, Father Hanon traveled to Charleston where was assigned to St. Patrick's for a short time. He then went back to New York for a visit, and then returned to South Carolina. He got roaring drunk on the *South Carolina* on his sea voyage from New York to Charleston. He became "really crazy" and cried out "Fire! Fire!" — to the consternation of both crew and passengers. Although Lynch had reassigned Hanon to the single-man parish of St. Peter's in Columbia, Moore felt that, given Hanon's behavior shipboard, he should not be trusted to be alone in Columbia. He recommended that Hanon be assigned to Charleston instead, but not to his parish, since he was already there for a short time previously. "I beg that you will not send him to me. I have had enough of him and I am getting on better without out him." Sometimes the best help is no help, especially when the help is a difficult person. After dealing with Carew and now Kedney, Moore confided to Lynch that "I am becoming very much disheartened — If I had been alone all along, I would have St. Patrick's in better condition now."[23]

It was clear that Moore did not look kindly upon Lynch's informal "recruitment program" in the North. But he was not the only one. Father Quigley, rector of the Pro-Cathedral and chief financial agent for the bishop *in absentia*, wrote Lynch in November 1874 that Father McEvoy of New York was shipped back from whence he came. "I hope you will spare me in the future by your selection of priests a repetition of these scandalous occurrences. This last case was the most satiable drunkard I have ever met." Last Tuesday, reported Quigley, McEvoy "was tottering around from bar-room to bar-room until yesterday." McEvoy admitted that he had lost his last position in New York for the same reason — alcoholism. "For God's sake, bishop, leave these men where they are. Our Catholic schools will furnish us all the candidates [to the priesthood] you want." A little over a week later Moore wrote Lynch on the same topic. Probably these letters were part of a concerted effort on the part of the two most influential clergymen of the diocese to curtail one of Lynch's behavior patterns. Moore was working in concert with Quigley using the McEvoy case to drive home the point that Lynch should discontinue admitting priestly vagabonds like McEvoy. "I hope, dear Bishop, that under no circumstance will you again admit a rambling priest into your diocese." Moore reiterates Quigley's point that sufficient vocations from the priesthood will come from "youth of the diocese, if you make an effort to encourage and cultivate vocations to the priesthood among them."[24]

To the consternation of both Quigley and himself, often Lynch's discernment in choosing priests to come to Charleston while on begging trips up North was imperfect at best. Another source of exasperation for Moore was waiting for orders from the absent Lynch. It is clear from the correspondence that Moore as Vicar

General had to consult and usually get permission from Lynch before taking action on any personnel matters. Lynch did not delegate, nor did most of his contemporary bishops. Moore had to wait for a reply from his bishop from wherever he was by mail. In matters of urgency, on rare occasions Lynch would telegraph his instructions.

Poor health was another cause for concern for Moore in his role as Vicar General. Father Charles Croghan, pastor of St. Joseph's Parish (founded in 1866), took ill in early February 1875. So sick was he that Moore administered to him the "Last Sacraments" - Penance, Anointing of the Sick, and Viaticum (Holy Communion before death). Meanwhile, Father Schachte, an assistant at St. Mary's, was stricken with pneumonia. Croghan recovered, but got sick again in September 1875. Father J. Gore, pastor of St. Peter's Colored Church, which was founded Charleston in 1866, took ill with "gastric fever" and died in late November 1876. Informing Lynch that Gore's body was being taken back for interment in Baltimore, where Gore was from, he added that all the other priests are well and that "I have not a single sick person to attend for the last ten days."[25]

## Women Religious Personnel

The other aspect of personnel management that Moore oversaw was as the bishop's delegate to the Sisters of Our Lady of Mercy, the diocesan community of religious women.

When Father Timothy Bermingham died at St. Vincent Hospital in New York City on June 4, 1872, he was the rector of the Pro-Cathedral and Vicar General. Lynch immediately appointed Moore the new Vicar General with charge over priest personnel matters and with the title of the Ecclesiastical Superior of the Sisters of Our Lady of Mercy. In early August he presided at the election of Sister Superior, Sister Teresa Barry. Moore arranged for Bishop Ignatius Persico of Savannah to preach a retreat for the Sisters prior to the election. At the end of August Moore and the Sisters Council approved the independence of the Sisters in Wilmington, who since 1868 were no longer part of the Diocese of Charleston, but in the newly-formed Vicariate Apostolic of North Carolina, and who had petitioned for their independence from Charleston.[26]

Just as with the clergy, Moore had to monitor the transfer of Sisters, as well as their health. By the end of October 1873, Moore wrote Lynch that he was unable to respond to Lynch's previous letter because he just returned from Beaufort attending the mission church there. Moore then reports on the health of the Sisters, who numbered about twenty professed Sisters at that time. Sister DeSales Brennan was very sick for three weeks, but is now on the mend. "The other Sisters complain that they are breaking down ..." Their work as teachers in the Cathedral's parochial school, in the two Catholic orphanages, and in Our Lady of Mercy Academy on Meeting Street (opened in 1869) was laborious. The stress was not just physical or mental, it was also financial. In 1873 a national economic depression gripped the country called the Panic of 1873. In the South the effects of this financial downturn lasted the rest of the decade. Moore mentions that cotton now sells for thirteen cents, but "there is no money to buy it." Moore admits to Lynch that: "My own health is very good but I am discontented and unhappy."[27] He had a lot on his plate as pastor, as overseer of the clergy (recall that two of his assistant priests were alcoholics), as Superior of the Sisters of Mercy. Needless to say, not all of the religious women were pleased with Moore's oversight.

One of Moore's chief critics was Sister Mary DeSales Brennan, OLM. Born on August 3, 1827, near Clones, County Monaghan, Ireland, she most probably emigrated to Charleston during the Great Famine. Her people knew the Lynch family in Ireland, therefore she always felt a sense of kinship with Bishop Lynch. She kept in constant contact with him during her life and he was protective of her. She entered Charleston's Mercy Sisters' Convent in 1847 and was professed on March 25, 1849. Showing promise, she was named Treasurer of the community in 1856.[28]

In December 1861 when Bishop John McGill of Richmond asked Bishop Patrick Lynch for Sisters to serve as nurses in a newly established Confederate Hospital at the Greenbrier Hotel at White Sulphur Springs, Lynch and Mother Teresa Barry, Superior of the Mercy Sisters, chose five Sisters for the work, one of whom was Sister Mary DeSales Brennan. Mother Teresa accompanied the five on their journey to Virginia, along with Father Lawrence O'Connell as their chaplain, who held the rank of Major in the Confederate Army as a chaplain. They arrived at the Greenbrier just after Christmas 1861 and went immediately to work caring for about 150 patients. They were less than enthused when they learned that they were placed under the supervision of Miss Emily Mason, a Protestant laywoman. On March 30, 1862, Miss Mason was transferred from the Greenbrier to the Confederate hospital in Charlottesville, which left the Sisters in complete control of the nursing services, an arrangement they preferred.

When Mother Teresa returned to Charleston in March 1862, she left Sister DeSales in charge of the nursing Sisters, who dressed wounds, distributed medicines, assisted at operations, and supervised the kitchen and linen department. The prevailing diseases treated at the hospital were typhoid, pneumonia, and measles. Two months later, Bishop Lynch visited the Sisters at the Greenbrier to recover his health. When the Union Army captured Lewisburg just ten miles from the Greenbrier on May 16, 1862, the Confederate hospital and the Sisters from Charleston moved farther south to Montgomery White Sulphur Springs, six miles from Christianburg, where they remained for the duration of the War. In the summer of 1862 that hospital had over 400 patients. By the end of September of that year, with the hospital census on the rise, two other Sisters arrived from Charleston in October, one of whom was the sister of John Moore, Sister Mary Alphonsa Moore. Father O'Connell left Montgomery Hospital on March 18, 1863, his health and spirits broken. It was six weeks before Lynch could send another priest to replace O'Connell. Father Charles Croghan, already commissioned a Confederate chaplain, arrived at Montgomery Hospital in June. The Sisters saw their most and worst cases of wounded soldiers from September to December 1863. During that period, they served 2,831 patients, between 600 and 900 at any given time. Eighteen different individual Charleston Mercy Sisters served the Virginia Confederate hospital during the course of the War, which was over 80 percent of the total members in the community at the time, the largest percent of any religious community serving as nurses on either side of the conflict. Except for the initial $100 the government in Richmond gave to them for transportation from Charleston to Virginia and also for the purchase of warm clothing, the Sisters never received any further compensation for their services during the entire War, not even for food. Only Bishop Lynch supplied for their needs. When the hospital closed in May 1865, the Sisters and their hospital chaplain, Father Croghan, had no money for the return trip to Charleston. Croghan went to parishes in Washington and New York City to beg funds for the ship passage home.[29]

It was three months after the war's end before the nursing Sisters of Montgomery Hospital returned to Charleston on July 9, 1865. Father Croghan accompanied them on their way home. Croghan was appointed pastor of St. Joseph's by Moore, who was delighted to have another functioning priest in the city besides himself.[30] The horrors of war had taken their toll on Sister DeSales, although she was unaware of it. Curiously, in none of her letters during or after the War does she refer to the presence or treatment of wounded men in the hospital. The part of her job, the horrors of war, she refused to acknowledge, when it was happening and after, but this denial took its toll on her and would haunt her the rest of her life. Sister DeSales did not return to Charleston the same woman as when she left. Not all the casualties of war are soldiers on the battlefield. War generates "collateral damage" to the human mind and spirit which remains long after physical wounds are healed.

During their time in the military hospital, not only did Sister DeSales and the other Sisters deal with soldiers who were dying or recovering from wounds or disease, but they also were faced with infighting among the doctors, nurses and staff. In April 1864 Dr. J. Lewis Woodville, the surgeon in charge of the Montgomery Hospital and an admirer of the Sisters' contributions as nurses, was brought before a Court Martial Trial. The charges were embezzlement of military stores, keeping three slaves on the hospital payroll, even though they were of no use to the hospital, and the failure to enforce quarantine regulations. Sister DeSales was one of fifteen witnesses for the prosecution. Dr. Woodville was acquitted.[31] The working relationship between Woodville and the Sisters had to have been strained due to Sister DeSales testimony against him at the Court Martial.

In April 1867 Sister DeSales and Sister Xavier Dunne journeyed to Washington to add their weight to an appeal to Congress for Federal money for the orphanage wrecked by the Siege of Charleston. Later in 1871 the government did appropriate $12,000 to the Sisters for the ruined orphanage. Not waiting for the Federal appropriation, in June 1867 Bishop Lynch reopened the boy's orphanage damaged during the War, although at a different location at 77 Cannon Street. Without consulting Mother Teresa or her Councilors, Lynch appointed Sister DeSales the director of the orphanage at 77 Cannon Street and asked Mother Teresa to send Sisters to the new institution to aide Sister DeSales. The Sisters at the Motherhouse were not happy with the bishop's unilateral decision, especially since they knew that Sister DeSales was in no shape to take on those responsibilities.[32]

It did not take long for problems to surface among the Sisters assigned at the orphanage, problems which had Sister DeSales at the center. She wrote to Bishop Lynch at the end of August 1868 complaining about "a spirit of insubordination" among the Sisters at the orphanage. She names the perpetrators. Sister de Chantal is "insubordinate and intolerable ... she has a most violent temper." Sister Aloysius "has been doing her utmost to provoke me ... she passes me in the hall with a look of contempt." Sister DeSales says she is humiliated by all of this, especially since she knows that Sister de Chantal is supported by Mother Teresa, to whom she constantly makes reports. "My health is given way under the continual worry." Sister DeSales knows that she is not feeling well, but blames it on the people around her. In fact, her mental health was deteriorating, so much so that in the summers of 1870 and 1871 Bishop Lynch allowed her to take water treatments and relaxation at the spa near Montgomery White Sulphur Springs, site of the military hospital where she worked during the War, accompanied by Sister Alphonsa. In the summer of 1871 John Moore accompanied his sister and Sister DeSales to Virginia. In early August Moore writes Lynch that Sister DeSales had "two very severe nervous spells." Ironically, Dr. J. Lewis Woodville, the one she testified against during the War, was treating her and told Father Moore that "her condition was critical." Dr. Moore returned to Charleston, but the two Sisters stayed on into the fall. On October 15 in a very shaky hand Sister DeSales wrote Lynch that she had just received the Last Sacraments. The next day Sister Alphonsa telegraphed Lynch to come or send someone to take Sister DeSales back to Charleston. "Her mind is impaired," added Sister Alphonsa.[33]   Her wartime demons were not exorcized nor would they be.

Sister DeSales returned to her duties as director of the Boy's Orphanage, assisted by Sister Alphonsa and Sister Agnes Gallagher. But Sister DeSales' paranoia tried their patience to the breaking point, so much so that in March 1874 they literally walked out on her in the orphanage and returned to the Motherhouse, precipitated by the Director's refusal to allow Sister Agnes to talk to Bishop Lynch about matters at the orphanage. After this episode, Lynch finally acted. Sister DeSales was dispensed from her vows and left the community, yet she continued to write Lynch as she traveled to San Antonio (Texas), New Orleans, Pittsburgh, Baltimore, and Montreal, to find another religious community that might suit her. As a religious vagabond searching for a new home and for a new self, she never seems to have found either. Her last letter to Lynch was from Boloeil, Canada, on February 11, 1882. Fifteen days later Lynch died. In him she lost her best friend, protector, and supporter her even after her departure from Charleston.[34]

It was from the time that Bishop Lynch visited the Greenbrier in May 1862 that Sister DeSales came to know Lynch, and it was from that time that she felt a personal connection with him. From that time she begins to correspond with him. Unilaterally, she assumes the role as an unsolicited self-appointed informant and advisor on personnel matters of the Diocese of Charleston. Not only does she opine on matters concerning persons in her religious community, but she also shares her views with Lynch on various priests of the diocese. It should be noted that any remarks she made about Moore, or anybody else for that matter, must be put in the context of her mental instability. Moreover, her fierce loyalty to Lynch made her suspicious of anyone she perceived to be a threat to him.

John Moore occasionally appears in her "reports." She coyly remarks to Bishop Lynch just four days after Moore was appointed Vicar General that "Dr. Moore seems to wear his new dignity with considerable grace and pleasure." She disagrees with Moore's opposition to buying a piece of property for a new Boy's Orphanage in June 1873. The property was purchased and Moore asked if Sister DeSales was behind it, but she denied it. She expressed her dissatisfaction with Moore to Lynch: "Dr. Moore loves and indulges his self-ease a little too much, is fearful of having another block to walk occasionally to say Mass, to which he has already given expression." Her negative feelings about Moore remained. In April 1877 when she heard about Moore's appointment as bishop, she sarcastically commented to Lynch: "The country seems surprised at Dr. Moore being appointed Bishop of Florida. Truly this is The Age of Wonders!"[35]

Undoubtedly, Sister DeSales was aware of Moore's impatience with Lynch's constant absences from the diocese and his erratic leadership style. Out of loyalty to Lynch, Sister DeSales may have been over critical of Moore. She also may have seen Moore as a talented rival of Lynch. In an action characteristic of someone with a fierce loyalty, she sought to "cut the head off" of someone like Moore who was sticking his head up too far above the crowd.

## Moore's Relationship with Lynch and Lynch's Leadership Task

In discussing Sister DeSales, we return to the theme Moore's relationship with his bishop. During his visit to a New York in 1866 and with Father Quigley in 1874, Moore expressed his unhappiness with Lynch as a bishop, a discouragement that began in his expressions to Archbishop Spalding of Baltimore as early as the summer of 1865. Moore's complaints about Lynch were that he was constantly absent from the diocese both during the War and during Reconstruction, that he appropriated funds for his own purposes (such as Moore's funds for a parochial school at St. Patrick's Parish), that he did not really delegate when he was absent from the diocese and consequently it sometimes took considerable time for his decisions to be communicated, and that on his various trips up North he recruited priests for Charleston who often turned out to be problems. Although Moore's litany of Lynch's faults are factual, they also contain an emotional content, a disappointment with, an exasperation over, even a resentment towards Lynch that goes beyond the mere facts. Moore lost his father at the age of fourteen and Lynch as bishop symbolized the father that he no longer had. But as with many father-son relationships, the father does not measure up to the son's expectations and vice versa. So it was with Moore's relationship with his spiritual father, Bishop Lynch. As time went on, their relationship became more and more formalized and emotionally distant. For example, Moore asked Lynch to preside at Epiphany Vespers at St. Patrick's in early 1877, offering to send him a carriage to pick him up, if needed. The note sent is formal and terse, even though it could have been communicated verbally since Lynch was in town.[36] Yet, to be fair, Lynch on his part faced what appeared as insurmountable odds during his entire episcopacy.

Patrick Neison Lynch was born in Clones, County Monaghan, Ireland March 10, 1817. Two years later his family immigrated to the United States, settling in Cheraw, South Carolina. At the age of twelve he entered St. John the Baptist Seminary in Charleston. Discerning the intelligence of the young man, Bishop John England sent Lynch to study in Rome in 1834, along with James A. Corcoran. Ordained in April 1840, Lynch received

*5.2 Bishop Patrick Lynch, 1880. Source: Library of Congress*

a doctorate of Divinity (today called a doctorate in Sacred Theology) that September. Twenty years later Moore would receive the same degree from the same institution. Upon his return to Charleston, he became the secretary to the bishop and editor of the *U.S. Catholic Miscellany* until 1845, when he was appointed the rector of the Cathedral and taught in the seminary until its closure in 1851. As rector of the Cathedral, he supervised the completion of the stone Cathedral of St. Finbar and St. John the Baptist. When Bishop Ignatius Reynolds, the man that succeeded Bishop England in 1844, died on March 9, 1855, Lynch was named the administrator of the diocese, and then consecrated the Bishop of Charleston in 1858.

Like John England before him, Lynch quickly became involved in civic issues. He was active in the Charleston's Hibernian Society, he established the St. John's Savings Association (a bank for immigrants), engaged Protestant divines in polemical debates in the secular press, and accepted the appointment as a Special Commission for the Confederate States of America in early 1864, whereby he became a diplomat in Europe for the C.S.A. from 1864 to 1865. An ardent Southern patriot and agent of the C.S.A., Lynch had to receive a special pardon from President Andrew Johnson to return home to the U.S. from Europe after the War. The bishop did not reappear in Charleston until late November 1865.[37]

Upon his return, he found his diocese in very desperate shape, physically and spiritually. As with Moore, Sister DeSales, and others, the effects of the War impressed themselves upon Lynch. War changes everyone it touches.

Before the War began, Lynch was making progress building up the Church of Charleston. In early May 1861 St. Joseph's Church on Anson Street was dedicated. In mid-May 1861 St. Paul's German Catholic Church on Society Street was established. The building was constructed in 1838 as the home of the Charleston Philharmonic Society, who conveyed it to the Second Presbyterian Church in 1856. A year later the structure was converted for the Sisters of Our Lady of Mercy and renamed St. Mary's Free School for Girls, but that institution then moved to a new building on Queen Street in 1860. St. Paul's closed from 1863-65 due to the War, but reopened in January 1866, until it closed for good in October 1869, as a result of internal wrangling and a lack of congregants (around forty parishioners). The building was remade into St. Peter's Catholic School for blacks.[38] By War's end all but one of the four remaining Catholic churches of City of Charleston were either destroyed or unusable, namely St. Patrick's.

Even before he returned to Charleston, Lynch sent a detailed begging letter to the missionary society in Lyons, France. He calls the present condition of the Diocese of Charleston "truly desolate." He rehearses a litany of loses. First, as a result of the fire of December 1861, the following buildings were lost: the Cathedral, the episcopal residence, the diocesan seminary and library, the boy's orphanage, a free school for girls. Besides these losses, the Motherhouse of the Sisters of Mercy, their academy, and the girl's orphanage, three out of four of Charleston's Catholic Churches were severely damaged, as a result of the bombardment of Charleston. In the interior of the diocese "a chapel for Negroes" was ruined, another church was damaged, a third church was appropriated for military usage. In Columbia the Ursuline Convent and Academy, the rectory, and a school for boys were all destroyed by Sherman's marauding army. The building damages he estimates to be at $252,500. Lynch has no financial reserves since the diocese's Confederate stocks, securities, and monetary reserves are now worthless. The total losses to the diocese he estimates to be $316,500. Lynch goes on to state that he has a "load of debt" from construction projects begun before the War, which he estimates to be an additional $49,000. Upon returning to Charleston, Lynch must repair the damaged churches and institutions, pay for operating expenses of those same places, respond to the ongoing demands of charity for the poor, reply to the needs of "the newly emancipated Negroes." He feels that separate black Catholic schools, churches, orphanages, and old folks' homes are needed for that group. He concludes his begging letter with a final *fervorito*.

> The work immediately before me is so great that my heart would sink, were it allowed to a Bishop [sic] to yield to despair. 'God chose the weak of this world so that He might confound us all.' It is His work to which I devote myself.[39]

Although Lynch's frequent absences from the diocese aggravated and exasperated Moore, Lynch saw his constant begging and speaking tours as an absolute financial necessity to rebuild his diocese and to devote himself to what he considered was God's work for him to accomplish. He did receive annual allotments from the Society of the Propagation of the Faith at Lyons, France, throughout Reconstruction. From 1865 to 1870 he accepted from them the largest amount sent to any Southern diocese. In addition he journeyed to parishes in New England, Philadelphia, and most especially New York, where the people and clergy were notably generous. He was especially welcome at St. Stephen's in New York where its pastors, first,

*5.3 Exterior of Pro-Cathedral in Charleston, SC. 1957*
*Source: ADC*

Father Jeremiah Cummings, then Edward McGlynn provided hospitality at their sprawling Irish immigrant parish.[40]

Of course, begging and grubbing for money is not much fun, and constantly living out of suitcase was wearying, at times even discouraging. He could never raise enough money for the pressing needs of his diocese. Even in the summer of 1876, he confessed to "Bishop James R. Bayley of Baltimore that his diocese was so heavily in debt that he must continue to borrow money "and I must pay or go to jail or be disgraced or bankrupted."" He wrote Father D. J. Quigley in November 1876 from New York that "My health is good. But I am rather downhearted." He had some rebuffs from pastors whom he had to ask for permission to preach a begging sermon at their parish and many postponements. Two engagements were canceled completely. Again in New York in March 1877 he writes Quigley:

> I'm dodging in and out of New York... Collections
> up here are bad, very bad. There's so much poverty.
> It is disheartening to work hard, travel, coax, preach
> again and again — and see the result in a weighty
> pile of pennies and five cent and ten cent pieces
> — the whole coming to only fifty or eighty dollars
> sometimes — but every little [bit] helps.[41]

Moore must have intellectually grasped what Lynch was doing while on his begging trips and why he was doing it; yet, on a personal and emotional level he resented Lynch for his continued absence from the diocese. Ironically, when Moore becomes a bishop he will be forced into the same position of having to beg up North for his

*5.4 Interior of Pro-Cathedral in Charleston, SC, 1877. Source: ADC*

poor diocese. Yet Moore was not alone in his criticism of Lynch's prolonged absences. As early as May 1869, Archbishop Martin J. Spalding took Lynch to task for not being present enough in his diocese. Lynch defended himself by saying that although he found the begging work disagreeable; he felt he did it without neglecting his pastoral responsibilities. If he was forced to cease these begging trips, he would seriously consider resigning his See. He maintained that he was fulfilling his duties, since in the year 1869 he visited "every priest in my diocese and have visited every church but two … so I really do not think that I have failed in substance." Was it not Moore's complaints about Lynch, beginning in 1865, that spurred the archbishop later in 1869 to inquire about the Bishop of Charleston's frequent absences from the diocese and did Lynch know that Moore was the informant? If so, this fact could not have improved their relationship.[42]

Earlier in June 1866, Lynch purchased the Pinckney House at 114 Broad Street for $18,000. Father Bermingham, the Vicar General, whom the bishop had sent to New Orleans to beg, wrote from the Crescent City to register his dissatisfaction with Lynch's purchase.

I suppose the 'Pinckney House' is your recent purchase on Broad Street. If so, allow me to say that I did not rejoice at the purchase. And I would advise you, if you can honorably get out the purchase, in God's name and for the benefit of his church in Charleston, to get clear of it.

Bermingham suggested that the bishop could purchase St. Andrew's Hall, next to the Cathedral, as an episcopal residence. We can only guess Moore's views on the house purchase were also negative, but we have no record of his opinion. Despite the negative reaction of his priests, Lynch did not "get clear of it" and purchased the house, which remains to this day the episcopal residence of the Bishop of Charleston.[43]

A second expenditure of Lynch's for 1866 was the completion of the Pro-Cathedral on Queen Street, which was dedicated on September 30. Since the Fire of 1861 which destroyed SS. Finbar and John the Baptist Cathedral, its congregation had no permanent place to worship. Built at a cost of $17,000, its interior was plain, with three aisles, and spacious, since it could seat 1,000. Located at 105 Queen Street, its exterior was rectangular in shape, well-built with bricks. It served as the Pro-Cathedral until the older building, destroyed in 1861, was finally reconstructed and rededicated in April 1907.[44]

Lynch had an abiding concern for the newly freed African-Americans and did whatever his limited means would allow. Before the War, in parishes like St. Patrick's, blacks and whites worshiped in the same church, although blacks were designated a separate portion of the church. At St. Patrick's they occupied the gallery. After the War, Lynch along with most other U.S. bishops felt that blacks needed their own separate black churches. Separate black churches, reasoned Lynch in 1865, would provide for special preaching and instruction aimed "at their capacity." He felt the pomp of Catholic ceremony, processions, novenas, would draw many of them "from the cold services of Protestant worship." Of course he was referring to white Protestant services. During the post-war period, separate black Protestant churches were being founded throughout the South. Their worship services could hardly be characterized as "cold."

In late December 1866, the bishop bought a synagogue on Wentworth Street. The black parish, named St. Peter's, began on January 12, 1867, led by Father Louis Aloysius Folchi, SJ, pastor. Lynch met Folchi in Rome and invited him to the diocese to work with Italians and blacks. Despite everyone's good intentions, Folchi's broken English made his preaching to the black Catholic community practically incomprehensible. Yet, the Italian Jesuit worked hard at being a good pastor. By 1870 he operated a black Catholic school with about fifty kids and reported that by that year he had baptized 218 persons. Later, in February 1875, the Mill Hill Fathers, an English missionary society who specialized in working in Africa, took over the parish at the behest of Bishop Lynch.[45]

Lynch took a more experimental approach in a second effort to serve the needs of the black community. Earlier in 1866, Lynch proposed to Bishop Martin Spalding of Baltimore to found a "Paraguay Colony" on an island, modeled after the seventeenth and eighteenth century Jesuit Reductions of Paraguay. Adapting the reduction design to the plight of the newly freed slaves, Lynch wrote to Gen. O.O. Howard, Chief Commissioner of the Freedmen's Bureau, to sanction the project, since South Carolina was under occupation and governance of the U.S. military at the time. The general approved the project. Lynch planned to purchase a Sea Island with a design to form a religious-based community of 5,000 black Catholics. Yet the plan proved too costly, both financially and in terms of the personnel needed to staff it, so nothing became of it. However, it was not an altogether fanciful concept. In 1875 Bishop William Gross of Savannah did implement a similar plan as Lynch's reduction with two Benedictines from Subiaco, Italy, on the Isle of Hope, near Savannah. However, a year into the project, it was abandoned due to the three Benedictine leaders dying of yellow fever.[46]

Undaunted by the collapse of his idea for a black reduction, Lynch secured the services of two European Capuchins, Lewis Nuccetelli and Patrick Knaresboro, to serve black Catholics in and around Beaufort. The two missionaries arrived there in early 1869. Nuccetelli reported that "the colored people of the city and adjoining islands have entered different religious sects since their emancipation." He also said that on Hutchinson Island he found only 300 blacks, only 120 of whom claimed to be Catholic, all of whom had not seen a priest in eight years. A small chapel was built on the island in the spring of 1869, but by April 1870 the two missionaries withdrew from the area, convinced that their work with blacks there had no future, so strong were the black Protestant churches.[47]

Bishop Lynch's relentless begging trips and speaking engagements provided the fuel for running his physical and spiritual reconstruction of the diocese. By the fall of 1869, Lynch had renovated St. Mary's and St. Joseph's Parishes. Three orphanages were reopened in the diocese, two of which were in the territory of St. Patrick's Parish. The Cathedral boasted of having the diocese's first parochial school in 1869, while the Sisters of Mercy began a girl's academy on Meeting Street in 1870. Lynch also arranged to have parish missions conducted in Charleston in 1869, 1870, 1873, as has been previously discussed in Moore's pastorate. When Lynch died on February 26, 1882, he had reduced the diocese's debts to just $10,000, an extraordinary accomplishment. After Lynch died, Moore returned to Charleston to deliver Lynch's funeral eulogy. It is unclear whether Lynch had requested this himself or whether it was decided by the living.[48]

One striking aspect of Moore's relationship with Lynch is that in a number of ways they were more alike than dissimilar. Both were Irish-born, both were trained in Rome at the Urban College, both had an intellectual bent; both were energetic creative pastoral leaders. Yet Moore seems to be more introspective, less prone to take the stage of public discourse, more attracted to the contemplative aspects of the spiritual life. The real irony in their relationship is that in a number of ways Moore as bishop ends up doing exactly what he criticized Lynch for, being absent from his diocese for a considerable amount of time due to the necessity of begging trips up North.

## Called to the Episcopacy

In July 1876 Lynch wrote Bishop J. Roosevelt Bayley of Baltimore in response to an inquiry from him. Bishop Augustin Verot, the first Bishop of St. Augustine, died on June 10, 1876. Bayley inquired of

Lynch for some suggestions as to who might succeed Verot. Lynch wrote that he knows of no priest candidate in the diocese of St. Augustine; therefore, it will be necessary to seek a candidate from outside that diocese. He thinks it is best to put a priest from the North in the position, since "Florida will rise, if at all, by settlers from the North." He offers two suggestions. Father Clowry, pastor of St. Gabriel's Church in New York City. Lynch calls him "a most worthy priest ... [he is] strong, vigorous, courageous, a fair preacher — an excellent manager." About the age of fifty-two, he has both prudence and ability, says Lynch, so much so that the Cardinal of New York even considered him as his Vicar General. Lynch admits that for years he has seen him as a bishop, especially of a missionary diocese such as is St. Augustine. Lynch also recommends Francis Farrelly, pastor of St. James, Baltimore. Lynch is leaving Charleston for St. Augustine on the Fourth of July in order to attend the Month's Mind Mass for Verot, then he will be off to the North to beg. He promises to stop to see Bayley on his way up to report on whatever he may have learned while in St. Augustine.[49] It is curious whom Lynch does not mention as a candidate — his Vicar General, John Moore.

The bishops of the Province of Baltimore, which included the entire Southeast, met in early October 1876 and produced a *terna*, three suggested names, for the See of St. Augustine. The nominees were: Paul LaRoque, a Canadian who was the pastor of St. Mary, Star of the Sea, Key West, Florida; John Moore; and William Wayrich, CSSR, of Baltimore. This provincial terna designates no favorite candidate, so the order of listing has no significance.[50]

At the end of January 1877, the Congregation of the Propagation of the Faith produced its own *terna*. As customary, the order of preference was given. Also, more information was included about each candidate. First in order of preference was Paul LaRoque, a priest of the diocese of St. Hyacinth, Canada, who has worked, with the permission of his bishop, for several years in the Diocese of St. Augustine as the pastor of St. Mary, Star of the Sea. Born in October, 1846, he studied with distinction in the Seminary of St. Hyacinth and St. Teresa in Canada. Ordained on May 9, 1869, he spoke English, French, and Spanish.

Second on the list was John Moore. His *curriculum vitae* is given, along with this description of his character, namely, he is *tenax* ("firm, steady, tenacious"), devoted to learning, and of conspicuous piety."

The third candidate was William Wayrich, CSSR, who is a native of Baltimore, forty-one years old, and "eloquent, zealous, pious, learned, strong." Of the three, Moore was the oldest, the only Irishman, the only graduate of a Roman College.[51] The Sacred Congregation of the Propagation of the Faith met, and among the three candidates, they chose Moore. Their recommendation was sent to Pope Pius IX on February 4, 1877, who approved Moore as the new Bishop of St. Augustine on March 8, 1877.[52] Moore got the news in Charleston by mail from Bayley, with the Papal documents enclosed. He responds to Bayley:

> Had I been allowed to have my own choice, I would have elected to remain as I am and where I am, as I told Bishop Lynch when he spoke to me on the subject, but now you have imposed on me the burden [written in Latin, "Men enter in where angels fear to tread"], and your decision in a matter wherein the interests of God's Church are so sacredly involved I consider it my duty to regard as the expression of God's own will. His grace will accompany the obligation; I hope I shall have the wisdom and strength to correspond to it.[53]

Moore accepts his new appointment with a strong sense of duty, of obligation, and of trust in the power of grace. These are not concepts that we use often today. Perhaps some in the twenty-first century might find his response as a bit of a cliché, formulaic, even stilted to our ears. But, there is no reason to doubt that it was a sincere expression of a Victorian man of faith's view of his situation and his responsibilities. His response is consistent with his character before and after this event.

Moore chose May 13 as the day of his episcopal consecration. Although Bayley and Lynch recommended that the ceremony be held in St. Augustine, Moore preferred Charleston. The chief reason was that the hotels in St. Augustine shut down at the end of April (the end of the winter visitor season), making it impossible for guests to be accommodated or entertained. Such was not the case in Charleston. Moore wanted Bayley, not Lynch, to be his chief consecrator, but the archbishop was going to be out of the country in Europe at the time. In just over a month, Moore tied up loose ends in St. Patrick's Parish and the Diocese of Charleston, took a retreat at Frederick, Maryland, and packed for the move south.[54]

We have no list of persons that Moore invited to his ceremony, but we do know that he asked Bishop James Gibbons, a fellow Irishman and recently appointed Bishop of Richmond, to preach the sermon. At Charleston Pro-Cathedral were seven bishops: Patrick Lynch of Charleston (the chief consecrator), Thomas Becker of Wilmington (the senior assistant consecrator and a contemporary of Moore's at the Urban College), William Gross of Savannah (the junior assistant consecrator), James Gibbons of Richmond (the preacher), John Quinlan of Mobile, Dominic Manucy of Brownsville (a native of St. Augustine), and John Kain of West Virginia. Also present was Boniface Wimmer (the abbot of St. Vincent's Archabbey, Latrobe Pa.). Fifteen priests attended, including Msgr. Robert Seton of Newark (an Urban College alumnus), Peter Dufau, (the administrator of the Diocese of St. Augustine and the only priest from Florida present) and Father F. J. Shadler of New York (the Master of Ceremonies). Also present were Charleston's civic leaders.

Gibbon's sermon began with Biblical verse *Mark* 16:14, "Finally, as they were at table, Jesus was revealed to the Eleven. He took them to task for their disbelief and their stubbornness, since they had put no faith in those who had seen him after he had been raised." His theme was the power that Christianity has to influence society. He alludes to the missionary situation where a bishop must "labor in poverty and privation" amidst "perils in the wilderness." Gibbons invited both the Florida clergy and laity to cooperate with "your zealous and active bishop" who will soon be laboring among you." The new Bishop of St. Augustine will soon "build up and repair" the Church of Florida "with a small band of missionaries." He suggested that Moore had just the proper qualities for such a challenge because of "your solid leaning, your patient labor, your unflagging zeal, your personal piety."

Music at the Mass was provided by the Fifth Artillery Band and Mozart's 12th Mass was sung by the Cathedral choir. After the Consecration Mass, dinner was served for invited guests at the Episcopal Residence, the former Pinckney House on Broad Street. At the dinner layman M.P. O'Connor, who rehearsed Moore's accomplishments as a priest and pastor of Charleston's largest parish, St. Patrick's, said: "The considerable but firm manner in which you have always exercised your [pastorate]... removes all doubt that the graver responsibilities with which you are now clothed will be met with true

5.5 *Bishop John Moore's episcopal ordination, age 42, in 1877. Source: ADC, "St. Patrick's Parish," (1937) p. 13*

Christian valor and be faithfully discharged."

Emotionally moved by O'Connor's words, Moore responded humbly that he feared "that his labors have been over estimated," but whatever he may have previously accomplished, he always endeavored "to perform conscientiously and zealously."[55]

Of course, Gibbons and no one present knew what lay ahead for Moore, but he was going to need all of those qualities Gibbons outlined, plus plenty of *tenax* to face the challenges that were waiting for him in Florida.

On Saturday, May 18 Moore was greeted at the St. Augustine train depot by a committee of local dignitaries, civic and ecclesiastic, then taken by carriage from there to the Cathedral Rectory, where refreshments were served. The entire population of St. Augustine lined the streets to catch a glimpse of the new bishop. The next day Moore was installed at 10:30 a.m. Mass at the Cathedral. The procession was led by Father Dufau, while Bishop Becker walked in front of Moore. Various diocesan priests, a few religious order priests were present, along with some of the Sisters of St. Joseph and several benevolent societies of laity. The church was packed. The sermon was delivered by Bishop Becker, who used *Acts* 2: 1-12 as his sermon text. Observers called the sermon "eloquent." Becker paid tribute to Moore's virtues, namely, his "learning and excellent administrative abilities." The preacher augured from these leadership qualities that "the dawn of a new era of future prosperity for the diocese" had arrived with Moore's episcopacy. This proved to be true, not only because of Moore's talent, but also because of social and economic change that would unfold in Florida during Moore's episcopacy.

Moore addressed the congregation at the conclusion of the ceremony. He spoke of his desire to fulfill his duty among the people of the diocese and pledged to do all "for the greater glory of God and to increase faith and good will among men." Then Moore spoke in touching terms of his predecessor, whom he said he had known personally over many years. He is sent to fill the place so well-filled by Bishop Verot, whom Moore perceived as "a man of true piety, of solid and varied learning, who always faithfully performed his duties." Moore adds that he, like Verot, "is willing to spend himself and be spent, to learn to be a father and spiritual guide," since his reward will be in heaven, not here on earth. He invites the priests, Sisters, and people to cooperate with his future leadership initiatives. The newspaper account comments that the congregation at once liked Moore, as did those present from other denominations — "his appearance being impressive... full of goodness and amiability."[56]

*The Shepherd of the Diocese of St. Augustine,*
*1877–1901*

CHAPTER SIX

# *The Context:*
# *A People and A Place*

L eadership is not simply the imposition of one's will upon others, but always takes shape in a context (historical, social, economic, political) and in a dialogue with others. It is effectively expressed by creatively responding to needs which result from circumstances, often not of one's making. This is true not only for military and business leaders, but equally true for leaders of ecclesiastical communities. In this chapter we will look at the context of Moore's Episcopacy, and then the chapters that follow will explore how Moore responded to the needs as they surfaced.

## Background to Catholicism in Florida

When Moore arrived in Florida in 1877, he came to a region, parts of which had been settled for centuries. When the first Spanish encountered native peoples in 1513 near Charlotte Bay, Juan Ponce de León and his men encountered the indigenous Calusa, a population of about 7,000 people who lived in about fifty villages scattered along Florida's West Coast. The Calusa were just one of eight major native cultural groups and eleven language groups who resided throughout the state. Their ancestors lived in Florida, stretching back 12,000 years. The first permanent European settlement, not only in Florida, but in all that would become the United States, was established in St. Augustine on September 8, 1565, where the first parish was also founded at the same time. The following year the first Catholic mission for native peoples was launched. After the Jesuits pulled out of the colony in 1572 as missionaries to the indigenous peoples, the next year the first band of Franciscan missionaries arrived and organized a system of missions among the native Floridians which reached their peak from 1606 to 1675, when there were about thirty-five missions and at least 50,000 Christian Indians. John Hann reckons that a total of 128 missions were established during the entire Spanish colonial period. But, colonial expressions of Queen Anne's War (1702-08) between Britain and Spain destroyed the missions. The remaining three-hundred Christian Indians huddled around St. Augustine. The eighty-nine who remained in St. Augustine in 1763 were removed to Cuba when the Spanish handed over their colony to the British.[1]

By the time Moore came to St. Augustine, the Native-American missions were long gone, as were the Spanish colonists, but not native Americans (both black and white) and not Hispanics, as we shall soon see. Lower Creeks from Georgia and Alabama began moving into northwest Florida in the early 1700s, later encouraged by Spanish, and later British officials. Gradually they became independent from their origins in the Creek Confederacy. By the 1760s they became known as the Seminoles, from the Spanish word cimarrones or "runaways." By 1820 about 5,000 Creeks and Seminoles lived as far South as Tampa Bay, but after the Second Seminole War (1835-42) only 200-300 remained in the swamps and Everglades on the southern tip of the state. By 1900 the U.S. Census counted 358 native Americans in Florida.[2]

Florida became a U.S. Territory in 1821 and a State in 1845. It was a thoroughly southern state politically and economically, dominated by cotton production and a plantation system centered in four North Florida counties. In 1850 the state population was 87,445, 39,310 of whom were slaves. In 1860 it had 140,500 residents, 61,750 of whom were slaves. That year in all of Florida, only two persons owned more than 200 slaves, 808 owned from twenty to 199, while 863 owned just one. Also by 1860, there were 400 Florida plantations which had more thirty slaves. But most Floridians neither needed nor could afford slaves. They lived as self-sufficient farming families on the Florida frontier, making the State decidedly rural not urban.[3]

With sympathies for the Confederacy, Florida seceded from the Union on January 10, 1861, the third state to do so. On the periphery of the Confederacy and the War, Florida had only one major military engagement during the War, the Battle of Olustee in February 1864. The federal blockade, imposed early in the War, successfully shut down southern ports. Union forces raided and occupied Florida coastal ports at will. Key West was held by Union forces at the War's commencement. From the beginning of the war, Union forces held Fort Pickens near Pensacola. Fernandina and St. Augustine were occupied from March 1862 and Tampa was occupied for a month in 1864. Jacksonville suffered the worst damage, being invaded and occupied four times, with a fire destroying one-third of the city during the third occupation. Of the 15,000 Floridian men who entered into Confederate service, over one-third lost their lives in battle or from disease.[4]

After the Confederate defeat and the end of the War, the small and scattered Church of Florida and throughout the South needed reconstruction, physically and spiritually. What might be termed the Catholic Spiritual Reconstruction went on throughout the South from 1865 through the 1870s. Frenchman Augustin Verot, Vicar Apostolic of Florida from 1858 and also the Bishop of Savannah from 1862, orchestrated a Catholic Reconstruction in Florida and Georgia, which included both material and spiritual elements.

In 1860 the Vicar Apostolic of Florida had six churches and chapels, four schools, but only three priests. As a consequence of the War, three of his churches were either destroyed or severely ransacked. At St. Michael's, Fernandina, the church was ransacked. The chapel at St. John's Bar (Mayport, east of Jacksonville) was razed and pillaged by Union forces, who also carried sacred vessels and vestments in an anti-Catholic parade, mocking both priests and Catholicism. Another senseless act of bigotry took place at Jacksonville when Immaculate Conception Church and rectory were sacked and burned by invading Union forces in 1863. In addition, Florida Catholics at the time were poor and had no means to rebuild. As a result, Verot became a beggar. He received some money from Archbishop Martin J. Spalding and the people of Baltimore. He also obtained annual financial assistance from the Society of the Propagation of the Faith in France. But he needed more money to rebuild; consequently, he went on begging tours of parishes in New York, Pennsylvania, Rhode Island, and Connecticut. Through Verot's strenuous efforts, by 1870, when the new Diocese

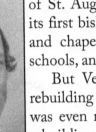

of St. Augustine was created, with Verot as its first bishop, there were nineteen churches and chapels (parishes and missions), seven schools, and twelve priests.[5]

But Verot understood that the spiritual rebuilding of the People of God in Florida was even more important than the material rebuilding. He used some of the money he collected to fund the Spiritual Reconstruction of Florida. From June to August 1865 he traveled to Europe securing finances and teachers for a creative idea he conceived — the establishment of free Catholic schools for the newly freed blacks. In early July, Verot

*6.1 Bishop Augustin Verot of St. Augustine, 1870*
*Source: ADSA*

visited his hometown of Le Puy, France, where the mother house of the Sisters of St. Joseph was located. He presented to the Sisters the desperate situation of the newly freed slaves and his desire to establish free Catholic schools for them. The Superior General of the Sisters of St. Joseph asked for volunteers. Sixty responded, but Verot could only afford to take eight. These Sisters arrived at St. Augustine at the end of August 1866. Although they had started studying English before they left France in early August, the Sisters got a crash course in it from Verot when he returned to the diocese in October from attending the Second Plenary Council of Baltimore. On February 9, 1867, with only a rudimentary knowledge of English and with thick French accents, they opened a school for blacks in St. Augustine, where about one-half of the black population was Catholic. In 1867 and 1868 more Sisters came from Le Puy. Black Catholic schools were opened by them in Savannah (1867), Jacksonville (1868), Fernandina (1877). In 1868 Verot invited the Sisters of the Holy Names of Jesus and Mary of Montreal to establish Catholic education at Key West. He also wanted them to establish a school for blacks there too, which they did in 1876 (St. Francis Xavier School). Before Verot's death in June 1876, black Catholic schools were also established in Palatka and Mandarin, as well as Key West. Following the admonitions of the Second Plenary Council of Baltimore of 1866, attempts were made to establish African-American Catholic schools throughout the South, especially in Louisiana, but most failed due to lack of funds and personnel. Verot's experiment was the most successful of any Southern bishop's. By 1876 he had six black Catholic schools in Florida, with about 300 pupils in them.[6]

As was true in Charleston when Moore was pastor of St. Patrick's, the parish mission was seen as the chief means for spiritual renewal for Catholics in the South during Reconstruction. Verot used some of his "begging money" to sponsor four Redemptorists, who conducted three months of parish missions in early 1868 in Georgia and Florida. Jacksonville and St. Augustine were the two locations selected in Florida, even though only a temporary wooden church was available in Jacksonville. These parish missions attracted large crowds and were considered a success. Verot invited the Redemptorists to return again in early 1869. That year seven priests conducted missions in twenty-two churches in Florida and Georgia. Special missions were given to black communities in Savannah and Columbus, Georgia, and in St. Augustine and Jacksonville, Florida. In 1870 two Redemptorists conducted missions at Key West and at the federal prison at Dry Tortugas (where Dr. Samuel Mudd was incarcerated from 1865 to 1869).[7]

Verot not only begged money for his Catholic Spiritual Reconstruction, he also begged for personnel. He received three more Mercy Sisters from Providence, Rhode Island, for St. Mary's Academy in St. Augustine, more recruits from the Sisters of St. Joseph at Le Puy, the five Sisters of the Holy Names of Jesus and Mary from Montreal for Key West, as well as two Italian priests from Genoa and a French priest from Besançon, France. When St. Augustine was made the See for a new Florida diocese in 1870 with Verot as its first bishop, the diocese contained nineteen parishes and missions, seven schools, and twelve priests. Verot relinquished the Diocese of Savannah to fully devote himself to Florida.[8] Verot's considerable efforts did not go unrewarded.

## Moore Takes Over the Diocese of St. Augustine

Moore inherited a diocese not yet seven years old from a saintly energetic missionary bishop, Augustin Verot, who died on June 10, 1876, at the age of seventy-one.[9] When Moore arrived in St. Augustine to take over his diocese in May 1877, he was just forty-one years of age.

At the time of his installation, the diocese included all of Florida east of the Apalachicola River. Land to the west in Florida's panhandle was in the Diocese of Mobile (and would remain so until 1975). Florida was a frontier state throughout the late nineteenth century. In 1880 the entire state was populated by just fewer than 270,000, while 90.0 percent of its people lived in rural areas. In 1900, 80 percent

*6.2 Diocese of St. Augustine, 1870. Source: Author*

of Florida still resided in rural areas, although the state's population had increased to almost 530,000. The Federal Census defined a frontier technically as less than two residents per square mile. Much less populated than the northern part of the State, most of south and central Florida's residents lived on the frontier, since in 1880 the entire state's population per square mile averaged 4.9. By 1900 it was only 9.6. Until overtaken by Jacksonville in 1900, Key West was the largest city in the diocese in the nineteenth century. From 1880 to 1900, Key West, Jacksonville, and Tampa were the most urbanized areas. But even in 1900, Florida's largest city, Jacksonville, had only just over 28,000 citizens.[10] As we shall see in the next chapter, the fact that the Diocese of St. Augustine was largely a frontier affected parish life and the leadership style of John Moore.

The ethnicity of Florida's population did not precisely mirror either the United States or the South at the time. In 1880, Florida's population was 3.8 percent foreign-born, as compared to the U.S. which had 13.3 percent foreign-born. In 1890, Florida contained

## 6.3 Florida Statistics & Urban Centers, 1880-1900

| Year | Total Pop | % Chng | %Urban | %Rural |
|------|-----------|--------|--------|--------|
| 1880 | 269,493 | 43.5 | 10.0 | 90.0 |
| 1890 | 391,422 | 45.2 | 19.8 | 80.2 |
| 1900 | 528,542 | 35.0 | 20.3 | 79.7 |

### Florida's Largest Population Centers, 1880-1890

| City | 1880 | 1900 | % Growth |
|------|------|------|----------|
| Key West | 9,890 | 17,114 | 173% |
| Jacksonville | 7,650 | 28,429 | 372% |
| Tampa | 720 | 15,839 | 2,200% |

*6.3 Florida Statistic and Urban Centers, 1880-1900. Source: Anne H. Shermyen, ed., 1989 Florida Statistical Abstract.*

5.9 percent foreign-born, while the U.S. had 14.8, although the entire South Atlantic states had only 2.4 percent. In 1900, Florida's foreign-born persons were 4.5 percent of the population, while the entire U.S. had 13.6 percent, with only 2.1 percent in the South Atlantic states. In 1880 Florida had a total of 9,909 foreign-born persons, of these 2,170 were from Cuba, while 2,830 were other Hispanics from the Western Hemisphere and Spain, that is, all Hispanics represented 50.5 percent of the total foreign-born persons in the state. The other immigrants foremost places of origin were: Germany (978), England and Wales (897), and Ireland (652). Florida also had a higher percentage of non-whites than either the U.S. or the aggregate of the Southern states. In 1880, 47.1 percent, in 1890 42.5 percent, and in 1900 43.7 percent of Florida's population were African-Americans. These percentages were much higher than the national average of 13.5, 12.5, and 12.1 respectively. In southern states in 1880 the percentage of blacks was 36.1, in 1890 it was 34.1, and in 1900 it was 32.6 percent.[11] Both on the frontier and in the cities, Florida was a very ethnically diverse place, a fact which presented unique pastoral challenges for the Bishop of St.

Augustine. At the same time, no single ethnic group predominated, not even in ethnically rich and segregated Tampa.

When Moore arrived in St. Augustine in May 1877, he found a frontier diocese which had eight parishes, eleven missions and about seventy stations. Ten priests served the Catholics of the diocese, none of whom were an American-born. Three were French Canadians, three were Italians, and four were French. All had been recruited by Bishop Verot to serve his missionary territory. Although no free parochial schools existed, six private academies were run by religious women (five by the Sisters of St. Joseph and one by the Sisters of the Holy Names of Jesus) and six Catholic schools for blacks were maintained by those same groups (five by the Sisters of St. Joseph and one by the Sisters of the Holy Names of Jesus). The total Catholic population of the diocese in 1877 was estimated to be 10,000, but nobody knew exactly how many there were since no precise Catholic census of the diocese existed, nor were parish records, especially of finances, kept well or consistently.[12] Moore would soon remedy this lacunae by applying methods borrowed from the American business community and from the Archdioceses of New York and Baltimore to provide more exact statistics of the diocese.

## Developers and Developments

Up to the 1880s, Florida cities turned to the sea for commerce and used rivers for transportation inland. Other forms of inland transportation were rudimentary, including railroads. But the last two decades of the nineteenth century, the technology of the railroad introduced something that not only brought tourists and also enabled Florida farmers, citrus growers, and ranchers to get their product to northern markets. The railroads also enabled better faster communications and faster travel within Florida and beyond.

Two entrepreneurs brought the railroad to Florida. Henry Bradley Plant of Connecticut first arrived in Florida in 1853 as a thirty-four-year-old land speculator. After the War, he became the president and principal owner of the Southern Express Company, an amalgamation of several Georgia and South Carolina railroad lines. In early 1881 he extended a line from Savannah to Jacksonville. With a grant of 13,840 acres from the state government, Plant expanded his railroad to Tampa, reaching there in late January 1884. In 1885 he created the Port of Tampa, constructing a causeway and piers in deep water with the capacity for berthing twenty-six ocean-going ships. From there he inaugurated a steamship service to Key West and Cuba. In 1886 Plant convinced Vincente Martinez Ybor and Ignacio Haya to move their Key West cigar factories to Tampa. Soon, Ybor City developed as an extensive cigar-making center. Plant was a big Tampa booster, at the expense of Disston City on the Pinellas

*6.4 Henry Bradley Plant. Source: Florida Photographic Collection*

peninsula (later St. Petersburg). He tied his railroad expansion to a series of resort hotels in Tampa, Belleair (Clearwater), Punta Gorda , and Fort Myers. To attract wealthy tourists from the North, in early 1891 Plant completed construction of the Tampa Bay Hotel, a $3 million Moorish edifice designed for pampered luxury, a thousand-foot long brick building with silvered domes and minarets, with twenty acres of gardens on the bank of the Hillsborough River. By 1894, 20,000 well-heeled tourists visited Tampa annually. Before his death in June 1899 in New York, Plant planned to extend his Florida West Coast Railroad from Fort Myers, then across the Everglades to Miami.[13]

Henry Morrison Flagler built his railroad down Florida's East Coast. Even more than Plant, Flagler was a developer of and booster for Florida. Born in Hopewell, New York, in Ontario County, New York, on January 2, 1830, his father was a Presbyterian pastor, who moved his family to Toledo, Ohio, where his wife's relatives had a business. At the age of fourteen, Henry convinced his parents to allow him to leave home to make his way in the world and to save his impoverished parents from the burden of feeding and clothing him. After working as a freight handler on the Erie Canal, Henry returned to Toledo and began working there in a relative's store.[14]

From these modest beginnings, the entrepreneurial young man rose in several successful business ventures to become a captain of industry and a millionaire. During the Civil War, Flagler made a fortune producing salt in Saginaw, Michigan, but by 1866, with the salt industry in disarray, Flagler went bankrupt. Undeterred, he learned from this failure: the value of cooperation and combination rather than competition, and the advantage of monopoly, lessons that he would apply later in Standard Oil and in railroad building.[15]

Flagler moved to Cleveland to work with a grain merchandising firm. Soon he recouped his fortunes, buying out his grain partners. He also renewed ties with John D. Rockefeller, whom he first met in the 1850s while in the grain business in Bellview, Ohio, and who was now working full time in the fledgling oil business. Soon Flagler joined Rockefeller in the oil business. Rockefeller recognized Flagler's business genius, namely, his shrewdness in identifying new opportunities and then capitalizing on their potential. Quickly Flagler became Rockefeller's most trusted advisor and confidant.[16]

Flagler and Rockefeller incorporated the Standard Oil Company in 1870, in which they were the core decision-makers. Both agreed that success lay in eliminating competition. The organizational structure of Standard Oil was a combination between the older partnership concept and new concepts of management, such as committee organization. When the Standard Oil Trust was established in 1882, Flagler was one of the original nine trustees. The stockholders approved the creation of interlocking companies in various states. Flagler became the president of Standard Oil of New Jersey. But by the early 1900s, as a result of several court cases and increasing investigation of Standard Oil by the U.S. Congress which was concerned about its anti-trust violations, Flagler began to spend less time at Standard's New York headquarters, but he did maintain an office and a secretary on 40 Broadway for the rest of his life. Only in 1908 did he resign his position at Standard Oil of New Jersey, but still remained as a director of the holding company until its dissolution in 1911 as a result of a Supreme Court case. He held shares in the company until his death in 1913.[17]

Flagler's interests soon shifted to Florida and away from New York and Standard Oil, not simply for business reasons, but initially for personal ones. In late 1876, soon after moving to New York from

Cleveland, Flagler's wife Mary was diagnosed with tuberculosis. Physicians advised that she might benefit from a winter in Florida. Following doctor's orders, in the winter of 1876-77 Flagler moved himself, Mary, his daughter Jennie Louise and her husband, John, and his seven-year-old son Harry to Jacksonville. The Flagler's traveled by train to Savannah, and then took a steamboat to Jacksonville. The hotels of the city were primitive and there was nothing to do. Flagler moved his family to St. Augustine, which had 2,300 residents, about a third as many as Jacksonville. The accommodations there were poor and most of the guests were consumptive. Although he was fascinated with the natural beauty of Florida, Flagler's first impression of the region was decidedly negative.[18]

Mary died in May 1881. Ida Alice Shourds was the thirty-five year old nurse of Mary's whom Henry married in June 1883. Flagler was fifty-three and had a net worth of $20 million. They spent their honeymoon in December 1883 in Jacksonville and St. Augustine, returning to New York in March 1884. But in February 1885, he was back in Florida with his wife. An hour after arriving at the San Marco Hotel in St. Augustine, Flagler visited Villa Zorayda, winter home of Boston architect, Franklin W. Smith, and one of the first cast-in-place concrete buildings in the U.S. The Spanish-styled building impressed him. After the visit, Flagler decided that he would build a Spanish-styled luxury hotel in St. Augustine using Smith's concrete technique. Flagler struck up a friendship with a local land owner and politician, Dr. Andrew Anderson, with whom he shared his idea of building a hotel. He also told Anderson that St. Augustine would need city improvements, such as sewers and paved streets, before such a hotel could be built. Before departing on April 1, 1885, Flagler purchased several acres of Anderson's Markland groves as site for his proposed hotel, making Anderson his agent in St. Augustine. In November 1885 Flagler wrote Anderson "I believe... we can make St. Augustine the Newport of the South." Thus began Henry Flagler's development of Florida.[19]

The Ponce de Leon Hotel was completed in May 1887, but it did not open until January 10, 1888. At a cost $2.5 million, the luxury hotel had 540 rooms, electric lights, and a gourmet restaurant. Its architecture was Moorish-Spanish and its building technique was poured concrete with coquina rock. The rates for the hotel were

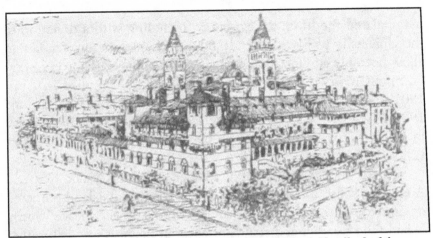

*6.5 Ponce de Leon Hotel in St. Augustine, 1890. Source: <u>King's Handbook of the United States</u>, p. 177*

such that only the very rich could be guests. Across the street from the Ponce de Leon and built in a similar style, Flagler opened a smaller luxury hotel, the Alcazar, for guests not quite so wealthy. The quality of the amenities and service in these hotels was equal to those in Chicago or New York, to the amazement of the press.[20] In 1887 Flagler shared with a reporter the reason for his building hotels in St. Augustine.

> For the last fourteen or fifteen years I have devoted my time exclusively to business and now I am pleasing myself. I want something [the Ponce de Leon Hotel] to last [for] all time to come... I would hate to think that I am investing money that will not bring a return in the future. I will, however, have a hotel that suits me in every respect and one that I can thoroughly enjoy, cost what it may." [21]

Although an extraordinarily successful businessman, Flagler's personal life was peppered with tragedy. He lost his first wife, Mary, in 1881. In 1889 Flagler's only daughter, thirty-one year old Jennie Louise, died in childbirth. Flagler was devastated. As a memorial to her, he built in St. Augustine the Venetian-domed Memorial Presbyterian Church, completed in 1890. Later, his first wife, Mary, and he would be interred there. Beginning in 1893, Flagler's second wife, Ida Alice, began showing signs of mental illness. She was permanently institutionalized in 1897, but lived until 1930. Flagler manipulated the Florida Legislature, including with a donation to the University of Florida of $10,000, to change the divorce law to allow not only adultery but insanity as grounds for divorce, so that he might marry a third time. The legislature complied in April 1901, and the governor signed the bill, passing it into law. In June 1901, Flagler, age 72, received a declaration of divorce from a judge in Miami. Two months later he married thirty-six year old Mary Lily Kenan in North Carolina.[22]

In late 1888 or early 1889 Flagler sailed his yacht from St. Augustine south to an eighteen mile slender sandy island bordered on one side by the Atlantic Ocean and on the other by Lake Worth. It had mild weather and stands of coconut palms, along with other palm trees. Perhaps a dozen people lived on the island at the time, most of whom were African-Americans. Flagler returned in the summer of 1892 with the intention of buying land for a hotel there.[23]

With Flagler projecting to build a series of resort hotels down the East Coast of Florida, he realized he also needed to build a railroad to connect and supply them. By the late 1880s he decided to go into the railroad business. By 1884, Florida had a few railroads, but those had different gauges. Cargo and passengers had to be unloaded and loaded traveling from one line to another. While the Ponce de Leon Hotel was being built, Flagler purchased the Jacksonville, St. Augustine, & Halifax River Railroad, widening its track to standard gauge. He also had a bridge constructed across the St. John's River so that St. Augustine could be connected to this line. He bought up two other lines, converting them also to standard gauge, giving him access to Ormond Beach and Daytona Beach. At Ormond Beach, Flagler purchased a wooden hotel built in 1875 and remodeled it. There John D. Rockefeller built his winter home, The Casements, right across the street from Flagler's Hotel. In 1887 Flagler brought his first train to Daytona Beach, then pressing the line further south. Residents of Rockledge, eighty miles south of Daytona Beach, petitioned Flagler to extend his railroad down to them, with the enticement of free land. He made it happen. Now halfway down the peninsula, Flagler decided that he would drive his line 400 miles further south, all the way to Key West.[24]

One of Flagler's most profitable ventures was land acquisition and sale. After he began his railroad construction, he claimed

*6.6 Royal Ponciana Hotel in Palm Beach, Florida, c 1920. Source: Postcard published by C. T. American Art for J. F. Kirkton, Palm Beach*

from the state 8,000 acres per mile of track laid. His total claims eventually totaled 2.04 million acres. To oversee these real estate holdings, he established a real estate department as part of his Jacksonville, St. Augustine, and Indian River Railway Company (which became in 1895 the Florida East Coast Railroad Company). Soon this department became a separate organization, the Model Land Company. In October 1892 Flagler hired Henry Plant's star employee, James E. Ingraham, to run the Model Land Company. Part of Ingraham's job was to advertise East Coast land sales to Northerners, enticing them to come on down. This real estate was sold at a relatively modest $1.50 to $5.00 per acre. Many settlements grew up along the railroad as a result. Flagler employees even planned the street grid for these new towns. Flagler realized the importance of getting new settlers to come to Florida, since their freight and passenger traffic helped his railroad. He once said that each new resident was worth $300 to him since his railroad brought everything in and out of Florida's East Coast.[25]

Meanwhile, Flagler continued to push his rails south. By November 1894 his line reached West Palm Beach. A year-and-a-half before he began construction of the wooden Royal Poinciana Hotel on Palm Beach, with 1,000 men working on the project, including Flagler's contractors Joseph A. McDonald and James A McGuire (both Catholics). With no housing on the island, the workers were quartered across Lake Worth in what would be called West Palm Beach. The Royal Poinciana was the largest wooden hotel of its time, with 1,200 guest rooms and a dining room which seated 1,600. In 1895, he built another wooden hotel on the beach directly east of the Royal Poinciana, the Breakers. To further boost business, Flagler imported Col. Edward Bradley to operate a gambling casino, the Beach Club. Bradley was born in Johnstown, Pennsylvania, in

1859. He eventually bred horses in Lexington, Kentucky, at Idle Hour Farm, which produced four winners of the Kentucky Derby. Bradley and his brother John opened gambling houses at resorts in New York and New Jersey. Flagler recruited them to operate the Bacchus Club in St. Augustine just after the Ponce de Leon Hotel was built; later he operated the Beach Club, which became one of the most famous casinos in the world. Bradley was a Catholic and became an important benefactor of Catholicism in the Palm Beaches.[26]

*6.7 Edward R. Bradley, circa 1930*
*Source: Historical Society of Palm*
*Beach County*

In April 1896 the railroad reached Miami and the next year Flagler opened the Royal Palm Hotel on Biscayne Bay and the northern bank of the Miami River, on land given him by Julia Tuttle, an early Miami settler. From Miami, Flagler extended his line further south to Homestead. From there in 1905 he began his push to reach Key West, after some major engineering feats. He personally arrived on the first train to Key West on January 22, 1912.[27]

By the turn-of-the-century Flagler had invested $12 million in hotels and $18 million in railroads on Florida's East Coast. His Florida investments were not made primarily to increase his fortune. His hotels, railroad, and land sales created Southeast Florida as a desirable place to work as a resident or play as a wealthy tourist. To those who came to settle, he saw himself as a paternal benefactor. "'I

*6.8 Bradley's Beach Club in Palm Beach, opened in 1898. Source: Historical Society of Palm Beach County*

feel that these people [the residents of Florida] are wards of mine and have a special claim on me.'"[28]

Another developer of the period neither built railroads nor hotels; rather he was interested in land development. Born in Philadelphia in 1844, Hamilton Disston headed Keystone Saw, Tool, Steel and File Works of Philadelphia at the age of thirty-six. He first visited Florida in 1877 as a tourist and sportsman. Its undeveloped lands in the southern part of the state attracted his attention. He envisioned turning the Everglades into an agricultural sugar empire. In February 1881 he struck a deal with the State of Florida, which was at the time at the brink of bankruptcy. Disston offered the State $1 million for four million acres of South Florida wetlands and the cash-poor State took the offer. His was the first Northern investment in Florida since before the Civil War, but he had one major problem — most of the land he bought was under water. He set up the Atlantic and Gulf Coast Canal Company to drain the land and established several different land companies to sell it. He was eventually able to wrest 1.6 million acres from his Everglades drainage operations from his original 4 million acre purchase. These dredging, canal-building, and channel construction operations were centered north and west of Lake Okeechobee, from the Caloosahatchee River to the

Kissimmee River. By 1885 steamboat passage was now possible from the Kissimmee River to the Gulf of Mexico, by way of Lake Okeechobee and the Caloosahatchee River. Disston sold some land packages to other developers, while he promoted some developments himself, such as Disston City (Gulfport on the Pinellas peninsula), Tarpon Springs, and Lake Constance near Orlando, where he sold 250 families twenty to eighty acre plots for $1.25 to $5.00 per acre. The Panic of 1893 brought these land sales to a screeching halt, as did Disston's early death at the age of fifty-two in 1896. But, Disston's

6.9 *Henry Flagler, c. 1890. Source: The National Cyclopaedia of American Biography, Vol. XV, 1916 no page*

efforts opened up a large portion of South Florida for further development, although he himself lost a good part of his fortune through his Florida investments.[29]

Not all important developments in Florida in the late nineteenth century were due to intrepid developers or to well-heeled tourists who stayed in the luxury hotels built by Flagler and Plant. Some winter visitors were attracted to Florida for its mild winters, natural beauty, hunting, and sports fishing. These types of tourists preferred not to lounge in salons designed for the rich, but rather in the smaller hotels which catered to the naturalists, hunters, and sports fishermen (both men and women).

Sometime in the 1870s Sen. Matthew Quay of Philadelphia and his son Richard wintered in an area that would become St. Lucie Village on Florida's East Coast, just north of modern-day Fort Pierce.

Originally, Quay, with his entourage of family, servants and political friends, boarded at the home of Judge James Paine on the St. Lucie River for $3 a night or $15 a week, but by 1875 the Senator built a large home nearby in which family and friends wintered. Eventually, the Florida East Coast Railroad built a spur off their tracks nearby to accommodate Quay's private railroad car. Built between 1897 and 1902, the St. Lucie Club was erected near Quay's home by a group of Philadelphian Republican politicians for their annual winter visits.

There they indulged in sports fishing and hunting. Most assuredly they also indulged in some whiskey drinking, poker, and politicking, besides fishing and hunting. Quay, who died in 1904, particularly loved tarpon fishing.[30]

The first tarpon of record was caught in March 1885 by New York architect William Halsey Wood. This was quite a feat, since the lining of the mouth of a tarpon is steel-like and well-nigh impossible to hook. To catch a tarpon one must snag the gills or go all the way down to the gut. Wood used a bamboo rod and a large cod "O-hook." Instead of immediately pulling back on the rod and line when the fish struck, he let it run with the mullet bait for about 250 feet, giving the fish time to gnaw on the bait before planting the hook in the gill or stomach. To prove his technique worked, he caught four more tarpon in six days. Although tarpon are a great sport fish, they are virtually inedible; nevertheless news of Wood's technique spread, attracting men and women anglers, both on the Southwest and Southeast Coasts. These tourists did not stay in luxury hotels, but in small fishing camps, boardinghouses, or modest hotels, nearby where tarpon and other game fish were known to swim. The same year Wood caught the first tarpon, commercial fishermen in Pensacola discovered red snapper as a commercial fish.[31]

## Patterns and Centers of Settlement

When Moore arrived in St. Augustine in 1877, Florida was still largely a frontier. In 1880, 90 percent of Floridians lived in rural areas. Even in 1900, 80 percent of Florida's citizens were rural residents. However, Disston's drainage-canal project and most especially the coming of the railroad going down both the East and West Coast of Florida encouraged the settlement of cities, either in places where there was one already started or at brand new locations. Jacksonville, Tampa, St. Petersburg, West Palm Beach, and Miami all developed in what amounted to Florida's first land boom from 1880 to 1900.

*6.10 Florida East Coast Railway Depot in Fort Pierce, circa 1900. Source: State Library and Archives, Florida*

But one important city was unaffected by the railroads up to 1912, that is Key West.

From 1880 until almost 1900, Key West was Florida's largest city with a population reaching just over 18,000 in 1890. As a naval port and fueling station, it benefitted from in influx of federal money. It was also a center for fishing, sponge-diving, shipbuilding, and marine salvaging. But most of all, Key West in the 1880s was a center for cigar-making, with 8,000 workers producing over 60 million cigars a year in about 200 factories. From the incorporation of Key West in 1828, Cubans emigrated there. But the Ten Years War (1868-1878) forced even larger numbers to emigrate from Cuba to nearby Key West for political and economic reasons. As more Cubans and Spaniards came to Key West, more cigar factories opened on the island. Thus, the Catholic population on the island swelled.[32]

Jacksonville was another area of development. It had a port, open to ocean-going ships. Situated on the St. Johns River, it was a terminal for steamboat travel going north and south. In 1830 the steamer *George Washington* plied the St. Johns River. By 1861 six boats ran regularly between Palatka, Jacksonville, and Charleston, South Carolina. After the War, steamboat lines ran from Jacksonville to Savannah, Charleston, Palatka, Sanford, and Green Cove Springs, carrying passengers and freight, such as the oranges planted south of Jacksonville.[33]

Even before Plant and Flagler's lines, railroads passed through it heading north, south, and west. In 1875 a ticket from Jacksonville to New York City cost $36.75 ($833.40 in 2017 dollars). The trip took between seventy-five to ninety hours because of train transfers from one line to another and from broad gauge (on southern railroads) to standard gauge (on northern railroads). By 1880 this same trip took twelve hours less, due to improved railroad organization. In 1888 southern railroads switched from a broad gauge to a standard gauge. Now passengers could travel from Jacksonville to New York in twenty-nine hours and thirty minutes. The speed for freight shipments also improved. Meanwhile, Henry B. Plant connected Savannah and Jacksonville by rail in 1881. By 1884 Plant's line connected Tampa to Jacksonville through Sanford and Palatka. That same year Flagler began his Florida railroad venture by buying the narrow gauge Jacksonville, St. Augustine, and Halifax River Railroad, rebuilding the Jacksonville to St. Augustine line to standard gauge. All roads led to and from Jacksonville. Its population increased as a result of its being a transportation hub. In 1850 the city had 1,045 people, in 1860 it had 2,018, but as a result of the railroad developments, in 1890 it had 17,201, an increase of almost 10,000 from ten years before. By 1900 Jacksonville was the most populous city in the state, with 57,699 residents. In March 1895 electric lights illumined parts of downtown for the first time, with electric lines extended in 1898 and 1901. The entire downtown was lit by electric lights by 1915.[34]

The Tampa area grew faster and had the most varied population than any other place in Florida. In 1880 Tampa had but 720 residents. The majority hailed from southern states, especially Georgia, with a minority from the North, especially New York. Foreign-born residents came from England, Ireland, the Bahamas, Canada, Germany, France, Spain, and Cuba.[35] With the coming of the railroad, Tampa's population spiked to 5,532 in 1890, and to 15,839 in 1900. It was rapidly transformed from a backwater frontier town to the third largest city in Florida in just twenty years. In addition, Ybor City, two miles northeast of Tampa, was founded in 1886 by Vincente Martínez Ybor and Ignatio Haya, cigar makers originally from Cuba, but since 1869 operating cigar factories in Key West. Don Vincente attracted other cigar manufacturers by offers of free land, new factories, and newly constructed worker's homes in what amounted to a company town. Because of the cigar industry, by 1890 one-half of greater Tampa's population was immigrants. It had five distinct ethnic groups: whites (mostly Southerners), Cubans, Spaniards, Italians (mostly Sicilians), and African-

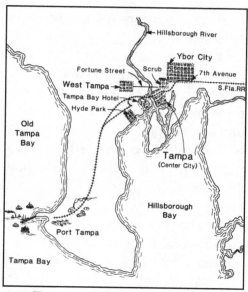

6.11 Tampa and vicinity, c. 1900. Source: Morimo and Pozzetta, *Immigrant World*.

Americans. By 1890, Tampa was the most ethnically diverse city in Florida, with 29.5 percent persons being blacks, 43.8 percent Cubans, 4.2 percent Spaniards, while 1.0 percent being Italians. By 1900 three-fourths of Tampa was first or second generation immigrants or African-Americans. Most of Tampa's Latin immigrants were segregated into enclaves in Ybor City and West Tampa (founded 1892), who's *lingua franca* was Spanish.[36]

Tampa, chartered in 1834, became an urban center rapidly in the 1880s, beginning with the construction of Plant's South Florida Railroad in 1883, which connected Tampa with lines to Jacksonville. Tampa had streetcars in 1885, an electric company in 1887, a water works, sewers, and street paving in 1889. A telephone service started in 1890. In 1888 Plant extended his railroad ten miles to Port Tampa and developed extensive docking, shipping, and storage facilities there.[37]

Across Tampa Bay on the Pinellas Peninsula was St. Petersburg, whose population was much smaller and more homogeneous than Tampa's. In 1888 when the Orange Belt Railroad reached the Peninsula, St. Petersburg had fifty residents; by 1890 the town had 273 persons, largely due to the exclusionary tactics of Henry

Plant. Incorporated in 1892, St. Petersburg had one-tenth of Tampa's population throughout the 1890s. By 1900, the number of its residents rose only to 1,575. Unlike Tampa, it was tourism, not industry or transportation, which was its economic base. By 1890 the city had two hotels, the Detroit and the Paxton House, as well as a pier and bathing house. In 1897 the city possessed its first power plant. A year later its first telephones. City water and sewers began functioning in 1899.[38]

Flagler founded West Palm Beach and reshaped sleepy Miami. More than any other city, West Palm Beach was the town that Flagler built. In 1873 four families lived on the island of Palm Beach. In 1893 he purchased several hundred acres of land and laid out the mainland town site of West Palm Beach, which grew rapidly. Tearing down the first temporary structures, he built more permanent ones, including a Catholic Church and rectory in 1896 (St. Ann's), which served many of his workers, including his contractor, Joseph McDonald, as well as winter visitors staying in his hotels. Flagler used his political influence in Tallahassee to separate Palm Beach County from Dade County in 1894. When the railroad reached West Palm Beach in 1894, West Palm Beach had about 1,000 residents, mostly those associated with the construction of the Royal Poinciana or The Breakers Hotels or with their ongoing operations. Flagler's agents were already selling lots to future residents in the plotted and planned West Palm Beach. Besides high-end tourism, he promoted agriculture in the area to keep his freight trains busy. He also manipulated the City Council from its inception in 1894. With the coming of the railroad to Miami in 1896, that community awoke from its doldrums. Incorporated in 1896 by its 343 voters, out of an estimated population of 1,500, Miami had its first newspaper, *The Miami Metropolis*, also that same year.[39]

Given these patterns of settlement in the Diocese of St. Augustine from 1880 to 1900, it is not surprising that much of John Moore's pastoral attentions were focused on Tampa. Yet, a great number of Floridians of the period experienced their lives not in the cities of Tampa, or Jacksonville, or Key West, but in the rural areas, where 80 percent of Floridians lived as late as 1900.

Most children in Florida's rural areas had to walk considerable distances to wood clap-board one-room schools. If the children had shoes, they would often carry them tied together over their shoulders while walking to school to keep the leather from getting wet and mildew. They would then put them on when they entered the classroom. One teacher, almost always a female, taught from ten to twenty-five children of different ages and skill levels. Although it opened in early September, often children did not attend school until the end of October when all the crops were harvested and left school in April to help with the planting, even though school remained open until June. Because of the demands of farming and family life, a considerable number of children never graduated from the eighth grade, but left by the fourth, fifth or sixth grade, especially the boys.[40]

Although most Catholic schools (virtually all of them were private academies run by the Sisters of the Holy Names of Jesus and Mary or the Sisters of St. Joseph of St. Augustine) were in urban areas, with only a few were in rural places. St. Anthony Parish was an exception. In the fall of 1883, Mrs. Marie Cecile Morse of San Antonio, a mother of six, began teaching fourteen children in her home. In April 1884, she moved her school into the parish church, St. Anthony's. By that fall a 12 feet by 24 feet wooden school house was constructed adjacent to the church. By the spring of 1885, she had thirty-five students, most of who were of French, German, or Irish descent. She taught reading, writing, arithmetic, as well as Bible history, the Catechism, and Catholic moral values, all without maps, a globe, or a blackboard. In March 1889 the Benedictine Sisters of Allegheny, Pennsylvania, took over the administration of St. Anthony's Catholic School.[41]

Mrs. Morse's school was an extension of the domestic church which every conscientious Catholic family had as part of their home life. With infrequent visits by priests into rural areas either to missions or stations (family homes), it was up to parents to provide a Catholic atmosphere and religious instruction (by personal example, family devotions, and the Catechism) in the home so that the Faith might be passed onto the next generation. Mothers played an important role in the domestic church by teaching the children prayers, the Catechism, providing meatless Fridays, preparing special meals at Christmas and Easter, by decorating the home with Catholic images and symbols.[42]

Life on the frontier was hard. Farm work was backbreaking, monotonous, and unrelenting from dawn to dusk. The cows had to be milked, the pigs fed, the corn shucked, the bread baked. Before electricity and labor-saving devices, every task was manual, time consuming, and physically demanding. On the farm women worked as hard as men and the children were expected to do their part to help with the family business of farming. In Florida the heat and humidity for at least six months of the year was oppressive, especially in the days before fans or air conditioning. Before refrigeration, people live in rustic simplicity eating picked beef, salt pork, bacon, ham, dried beef and fish, garden vegetables, and dairy products. There was nothing romantic about life in rural Florida in the late nineteenth century.[43]

Moore's pastoral approach was concerned both with Catholic urbanites, as well as with those living in the rural areas.

## Natural and Man-Made Events

Disston, Plant, Flagler, and Vincente Ybor were modern businessmen of the late nineteenth century. They believed that progress could be achieved by human effort, rational planning, organization, massive capital, and talent. The forces of nature of the draining of the Everglades and canal-building, for example, could be tamed and the frontier could be civilized by the railroads, hotels, retail businesses, and housing developments. They also believed that what was good for their interests (i.e., profit) was good for the larger population. For them, the Florida frontier could be conquered and tamed for human ends. The ends justified the means. Naturally, they took a beneficent view of their activities and a paternalistic attitude toward their charges, their workers and those they recruited to settle their developments. However, not even these "prime movers" of the Florida Boom of the late nineteenth century could control everything and everyone. Many greater forces of nature were at work which were much older and much more powerful than any of the "titans of capitalism."

Then as now, natural phenomena, as well as man-made events affected all Floridians.

Of all the natural phenomena, the potentially most destructive were hurricanes. During Moore's episcopate, a total of ten hurricanes affected the people throughout his diocese. The years of 1878, 1880, 1885, 1886, 1888, 1893, 1894, 1896, 1898, 1899 all brought hurricanes to Florida.

Barely one year after Moore arrived in Florida, on September 7, 1878, a major storm just missed Key West, making its way north up the center of Florida. It returned to the Atlantic near St. Augustine on September 11. Although the path of the 1878 hurricane covered mostly unpopulated areas, those areas that were populated suffered bridge and railway washouts, downed trees and telegraph lines, flooded farmlands and homesteads, and wrecked ships. So severe was the August 23-24, 1885, hurricane that after it grazed the Central East Coast of Florida further settlement in that area was discouraged, since the storm surge pushed ocean waves over the ten foot high barrier islands, completely flooding out homesteaders there. The beach near the Canaveral Light House suffered serious erosion, so much so that Congress allotted funds to move the tower one mile west. On September 16, 1888, a major storm made landfall near Miami, crossing the state to Fort Myers and into the Gulf of Mexico. At Miami the storm's surge was fourteen feet. Although storm damage was extensive, human habitation along the Southeast Coast was sparse at the time. The storm's effects were felt as far north as the Sebastian Inlet where seventy-five miles per hour winds were recorded, where trees and telegraph poles were downed, where boats were blown ashore, where orange groves sustained severe damage into the thousands of dollars. This reminds us of the most damaging aspect of hurricanes, water damage and flooding. Given the overwhelming agricultural nature of the economy and lifestyle of Floridians in the late nineteenth century, farming and citrus crops were ruined by the deluge of a hurricane, wrecking not only produce but livelihoods.

The hurricane season of 1893 was one of the most tragic ones for the Caribbean and the United States. Six hurricanes made landfalls in the U.S., each killing over 2,000 persons. An October storm that year tracked along Florida's Atlantic Coast, creating a storm surge of several feet from Palm Beach to Jacksonville. In St. Augustine the streets were deep in water. Winds at the Sebastian Inlet were recorded at 90 m.p.h. The cyclone eventually made landfall near Charleston, S.C. Both South Carolina and Florida lost twenty-eight persons due to the storm. An 1894 hurricane pelted Key West on September 25 at 104 m.p.h., then headed northward, hitting shore near Clermont, where 12.5 inches of rain was recorded in one twenty-four hour period. The storm came out into the Atlantic near St. Augustine, where water and debris smothered the city streets. The terrific wind and rain produced great damage to houses and railroads, as well as orange and vegetable crops.[44]

The weather played unexpected havoc in Florida in other ways, not just by tropical storms, but unseasonably freezes. The most famous of these happened in the winter of 1894-95. Beginning on Christmas Eve 1894, most of Florida was hit with a series of freezes that winter. In February of 1895 orange groves, truck farms, nurseries, gardens, and pineapple fields froze from Jacksonville to as far south as Palm Beach. Losses were in the millions. Thousands abandoned their homesteads and worked themselves back north. In St. Augustine the water pipes at the Ponce de Leon Hotel burst, oranges froze solid on trees, vegetables were ruined, tropical foliage perished. Perceiving the threat to his investments and drawing from his paternalistic nature, Henry Flagler issued free seeds to farmers, hauled fertilizer and other farm materials free on his railroad, and sent one of his agents into the affected areas with a whopping $100,000 in cash ($2,988,857.76 in 2017 dollars) with these instructions: "Use it as necessary. I would rather lose it all, and more, than have one man, woman, or child starve." However, the Miami area was untouched by the freeze, a fact which helped persuade Flagler to continue his railroad south past West Palm Beach to Miami. The offer of free land in Miami by Julia Tuttle and William Brickell sealed the deal for Flagler, not only to extend the railroad, but also to build a luxury hotel on the Miami River. Flagler's railroad reached Julia Tuttle's front door by February 1896. Ironically, supposedly frost-proof Miami was not immune from freezing temperatures. A second major freeze hit Florida in early February 1897, which reached down even as south as Miami and resulted in virtually 100 percent losses in the orange and vegetable crops throughout the State. Having built the railroad to Miami with the promise of a frost-proof farming area, Flagler could hardly pick up the rails he extended to Miami.

Instead, he told his agents to order supplies and seeds to be handed out free. Also as before fertilizer and crated agricultural equipment would be shipped free on his railroad.[45]

Disease is another expression of a natural disaster. Port cities of the South were frequently visited by disease throughout the nineteenth century, especially in the summer and early fall months. For example, in 1875 in Key West 268 persons died of various diseases, thirty-five of whom expired from yellow fever, the greatest cause of death from disease. In 1878 yellow fever broke out in 100 U.S. cities, with 120,000 victims and 20,000 deaths. The most serious flare-up of yellow fever in Florida was in late summer 1887. St. Augustine and Jacksonville were quarantined, including not only persons, but also the mail. Florida's tourist industry was adversely affected. Only in the winter of 1890 did Flagler's hotels return to their normal level of elegant society. Later, we will see the devastating effect yellow fever epidemic of 1887-88 had on Moore and his clergy.

An attack of yellow fever was characterized on the outset with headache, dizziness, rapid rise of fever, backache, nausea, and vomiting. This first stage lasts two or three days and may be followed by a brief remission lasting another day or two. In severe cases another stage sets in with high fever, jaundice (a yellow pallor to the skin), collapse, and death on the sixth or seventh day of the illness. But only a small proportion of those infected die. Recovered cases have no after-effects and retain a lifelong immunity from the disease. No specific treatment existed at the time.

Worse still, nobody in the nineteenth century knew what caused the disease. Some thought it was contracted as the result of poor sanitation, from inhaling infected air, from a parasite germ or seed. It was observed that survival from it produced immunity and that it was not contracted from others, as was an infectious disease. Between 1877 and 1880 the theory that the *Culex* mosquito was the agent of yellow fever was floated by two British physicians, Patrick Manson and Ronald Ross. Experiments by Dr. Walter Reed in Cuba during the Spanish American War focused the mosquito theory. Finally, it was proved conclusively in August 1900 by the Cuban physician, Carlos Finlay.[46]

But not all disasters were natural. Some were created by human instrumentality. In 1893 America encountered hard times, the deepest economic depression ever to hit the United States up to that date commenced. In the Northeast thousands were unemployed. Strikes and labor violence spilled out into city streets. Even the wealthy were affected. Winter tourists to Florida, especially at the Flagler Hotels, diminished.[47]

Another form of local disaster was labor union unrest resulting in social upheaval, violence, and sometimes personal tragedy. Labor unions were largely unheard of in Florida, except for the workers in the cigar factories. Florida's first labor strike was among cigar workers in Key West in 1875. The Key West cigar workers strike of August 1885 was so severe that it convinced cigar factory owners, such as Vincente Ybor, to relocate to Tampa, where Henry Plant and the city fathers of Tampa were offering business incentives and real estate enticements, in order to create a separate factory town near Tampa, soon to be called Ybor City. Lectors, paid and elected by the factory workers, read proletariat literature while workers rolled cigars. This mostly European socialist literature gave workers sophisticated economic and social ideas, fanning the flames of "class struggle" and grievances about real and perceived injustice. In Ybor City tensions between the mostly Spanish owners of the cigar factories and their Cuban and Italian workers erupted with Tampa's first labor strike in 1887. Allied with the Spanish cigar factory owners were Tampa's political and business elites, especially the Tampa Board of Trade, which used both legal means and vigilante methods to suppress the strike. This alliance and its use of violence, including lynching, characterized the Tampa power clique's response to the subsequent cigar industry strikes of 1899, 1901, 1910, 1916, 1920, 1921, and 1931. Vigilante committees of "respectable citizens," allied with the factory owners, unified to break striking cigar workers' unions. Tampa's law enforcement officers were conveniently absent when vigilantes struck. They never investigated nor took legal action against the perpetrators of the anti-labor union violence, nor did state or federal authorities. Although Tampa's cigar workers never won a strike after 1899, Tampa's Latins never lost their sense of justice, dignity, and solidarity, concepts which were grounded not only in the socialist literature they heard read in the factories, but also in their Catholic cultural and theological heritage.[48]

John Moore

*16.2 Immaculate Conception Catholic Church in Jacksonville after the Great Fire of 1901. Source: ADSA*

Urban conflagration was another form of localized disaster. Fire was an ever-present danger to nineteenth century urban residents, mainly because of the mostly wood construction of buildings and the still primitive state of firefighting in America. A devastating fire in Key West in March 1886 reinforced the decision of cigar factory owners there to relocate to Tampa. On Christmas of 1896 fire practically leveled the fledgling community of Miami, although Flagler's almost completed wooden Royal Palm Hotel remained unscathed. The conflagration there destroyed twenty-eight buildings, many of them commercial establishments, and killed one person. Commerce in Miami came to a screeching halt. With little money available to replace what was lost, especially since Miami's sole bank was in cinders, hundreds were out of work. Joseph McDonald, in Miami to oversee the construction of the Royal Palm Hotel, persuaded Flagler to authorize the construction of cottages in downtown Miami to provide some work and housing for its residents. Flagler also ordered the dredging of a shipping channel from the ocean into Biscayne Bay, another source of income for local workers. Of course these actions by Flagler weren't precisely charity since he later not only sold the houses, but also profited from Miami being made into a deep water port. On January 15, 1896, the 350 room Royal Palm Hotel opened, with its electric generator which provided electricity for the hotel and the residents of Miami.

Prospects for the fledgling city seemed more promising than even before the fire.[49]

The most devastating fire of the period happened in Jacksonville in 1901. On May 3 at 12:30 p.m. sparks from a nearby shanty ignited fiber laid outside at the Cleveland Fibre [sic] Factory at Beaver and Davis Streets. Fragments of the highly flammable material blew into the factory's interior. By the time the firemen arrived with their horse-drawn pumper, the factory was already doomed. The building's roof collapsed, scattering burning particles of fiber which rained down upon nearby wooden roofs. With a strong west-northwest wind blowing, by 1 p.m. Hansontown, a suburb of Jacksonville, was ablaze, the wooden shingles of its pine shanties were sent aloft by the brisk wind, spreading the fire into the city proper. Only when the wind died at 7:30 p.m., was the fire brought under control. Besides numerous residences, the city's largest hotel, the Windsor, was lost, as were the St. James Hotel and the armory. The fire also took a heavy toll on Jacksonville's Catholic community structures. Immaculate Conception Catholic Church, along with its rectory, school, orphanage, and convent were immolated, a loss estimated of at least $200,000 ($5,997,715.52 in 2017 dollars). All told, 146 city blocks were incinerated and 2,368 buildings were destroyed. Every public structure, except the US Government Building, was totaled, along with twenty-three churches and ten hotels. Total property damage was estimated at $15 million, $4 million of which was uninsured. It was the largest fire in any Southern city up to that time.

The day after the fire, Jacksonville's citizens assembled in the U.S. Government Building to consider relief measures. They organized the Jacksonville Relief Association, which coordinated the distribution of daily rations to the needy and formed 113 teams assigned to clean up and remove the dead animals (mostly horses) and other noxious substances from the city's twenty-two miles of streets. An appeal was sent out to the entire U.S. for free-will offerings. Altogether, $224,913.72 was collected, along with about $200,000 worth of supplies. Flagler's railroad and other transport companies hauled supplies free of charge. In an age of limited government, the Federal administration confined its aid to the issuance of over 200,000 rations and of 12,000 tents.[50]

One event was not a disaster for Florida, but could have been — the Spanish-American War. Even before the U.S. declaration of war against Spain on April 25, 1898, Floridians were anxious about the possibility of an invasion by Spanish forces, and for good reason. Not only was Florida close to the Spanish possessions of Cuba and Puerto Rico from whence an invasion fleet could be launched, not only was the Florida peninsula indefensible with a coastline of 472 miles on the Atlantic and 674 miles on the Gulf of Mexico, but also it was a source of Cuban Revolutionary fervor and contraband goods for the Cuban Revolution. In 1891 Cuban patriots José Martí and Tomás Estrada Palma reorganized junta in New York City to raise sympathy and aid in the U.S. for the revolution they planned for Cuba. Of the 200 Cuban patriotic clubs they founded in the U.S., seventy-six were in Florida — sixty-one in Key West and fifteen in Tampa. Martí visited Ybor City frequently, where he was well received among cigar workers, many of whom pledged 10 percent of their earnings to the cause. Much of the money went to the purchase in Florida of arms and ammunition for the insurgents in Cuba. With the connivance of Florida firms and local officials, the illicit traffic departed on boats (called "filibustering") from Jacksonville, Fernandina, Cedar Key, Tampa, and Key West. In 1896, seventy-one such "filibustering" expeditions embarked from Florida, although due to the dangers of the enterprise, only thirty-two of them succeeded in their mission. One of the most famous such boats was the "Three Friends" out of Jacksonville, captained by Napoleon Bonaparte Broward, who was elected governor of Florida later in 1905, due to the popularity of his exploits.[51]

The War of Independence in Cuba began in earnest on February 24, 1895. When this news reached Tampa, 1,000 Cuban cigar workers danced in the streets of Ybor City. In May 1895 crowds in Ybor City became hysterical on the news of José Martí's death on the battlefield. Cuban exiles fed American journalists with a steady stream of propaganda against the Spanish in Cuba. Northern newspapers demanded U.S. intervention, but Florida's newspapers up to the end of 1897 gave little heed to "yellow journalism," largely due to Florida's vulnerability to attack by Spain.[52]

With the destruction of the U.S. battleship *Maine* in Havana Harbor on February 15, 1898, and the subsequent loss of 260

American lives, which was erroneously blamed on the Spanish, America began preparations for war with Spain in earnest. On April 5, the War Department announced the installation of new shore artillery batteries at Jacksonville, Fernandina, St. Augustine, and Miami. On April 16 the base for American supplies and troops was Tampa. War with Spain was declared by the U.S. on April 25.[53]

In late April 1898, a vanguard of military officers and journalists arrived in Tampa, where Brig. Gen. William Shafter, commander of the Fifth Corps, established his headquarters at Henry Plant's Tampa Bay Hotel. Visiting journalists were uncomplimentary about Tampa, one of whom described it as a town loaded with "derelict wooden houses, drifting on a sea of sand."

By May 19 about 7,000 infantrymen bivouacked at Tampa Heights, 3,000 cavalrymen were encamped west of the hotel, and 6,000 were scattered in other camps. By May 25, Tampa hosted 23,000 U.S. officers and men. These numbers put a severe strain on the facilities of the port. The vast amount of equipment and supplies accompanying the troops created monumental congestion in a town unprepared for such a massive influx. Both the Plant and Flagler railroads did a whirlwind business. Merchants gouged soldiers, the railroad overcharged the Army, profiteering became a way of life. Local businesses strained to keep their shelves stocked. Early in the afternoon of June 7 thirty-five transports began loading troops, supplies, and equipment, including 2,300 horses and mules. Thirty-one hours later, all the ships were loaded with about 16,000 soldiers. Due to a lack of room on the transports, Shafter had to leave with 12,000 troops still in their military encampments and the cavalry (including Teddy Roosevelt's Rough Riders) was forced to leave their horses behind. By the end of the month, the soldiers encamped in Tampa swelled to 18,000. By July 20, about 25,000 soldiers bivouacked in Tampa. Well before that time, it was clear that troops had to be moved to other camps throughout Florida.[54]

On June 4 Gen. Fitzhugh Lee (nephew of Robert E. Lee) designated Jacksonville as headquarters for the 7th Army Corps, establishing a tent city called Camp *Cuba Libre*. On June 13 Jacksonville was designated as a commissary depot for the 7th Army Corps. Jacksonville hosted its peak number of soldiers, 31,000 volunteers in September, at which time the soldiers began leaving the city. In early August a convalescent hospital was established at nearby Pablo Beach. In the five months the Army was at Jacksonville, over $2 million in salaries was disbursed, most of which was spent locally. Even though liquor was plentiful in Jacksonville and drunkenness among the troops was common, the relationship between the local residents and soldiers was generally good. Irish-born assistant-pastor of Immaculate Conception Catholic Church, Patrick Barry, ordained in 1895, served as chaplain to the U.S. troops stationed in Jacksonville during the summer of 1898. Later in 1922, Barry became the fifth Bishop of St. Augustine. Camp *Cuba Libre* was dismantled finally on January 11, 1899, but when the city burned in 1901, many expressions of sympathy and contributions to the relief fund came from former servicemen stationed there during the War of 1898.[55]

Fernandina and Miami also got troops, but the experience there was not positive for the residents or the soldiers stationed there. Volunteers from Alabama, Louisiana and Texas reached Miami at the end of June, some 7,500 men. The plan for the camp in Miami was poorly conceived. Sanitation problems caused typhoid among the troops. The men stationed there were unhappy from the outset, complaining that the drill field was a mile from the camp, that proper sanitation was severely lacking, that the city offered nothing for the troops, who described the city as being the luxury Royal Palm Hotel and barren wilderness. In a month the troops in Miami were transferred to Jacksonville.

Fernandina, the terminus of the Florida Central and Pacific Railroad, had a good harbor and a population of 3,500 citizens. Soldiers of the Fourth Corps, 7,200 by the end of July, were encamped on the site of old Fort Clinch. But on August 22 they were ordered to Huntsville, Alabama, headquarters for the Fourth Corps.[56]

Naval activity was crucial for the U.S. during the Spanish-American War, with Key West was the base for ships of the Atlantic Squadron. When war was declared, three battleships, seven cruisers, and nineteen other naval craft anchored at Key West. But storage space and reserve coal supplies were lacking. For minor repairs, tools and mechanics from the Philadelphia Naval Shipyard were transferred to Key West. Over 1,000 journalists descended upon island at the start of the war. The water supply at Key West was always problematic. In 1898 the island had a drought, so cisterns were of no avail. The U.S. Navy obtained 50,000 gallons a day from a newly improved expansion of a sea water distillation plant built during the Civil War. Water was also hauled by ship from Tampa. The Sisters of the Holy Names, who ran Catholic schools at Key West, offered their convent and academy building as a hospital. Twenty-three of the sisters served as nurses in what became a 500-bed hospital.[57]

Hostilities between Spain and the United States ended on August 12, 1898, with America receiving from Spain its former possessions of Puerto Rico, Cuba, and the Philippines. During what Ambassador John Hay called "the splendid little war," the health record in the military camps in Florida during the war damaged the state's reputation as a health resort. A poor water supply and the humid weather were blamed for diseases, especially typhoid fever, which adversely affected the troops encamped nearby Florida cities. The State's hot humid summer months affected comfort more than health, especially in Miami, which got the worst reputation of any Florida city due to the war. The Jacksonville camp was the best administered and enjoyed the best reputation of all other camps. Although Tampa suffered from over-crowding, as well as a lack of planning and coordination, yet it became better known as a result of journalists being based there during the War. After the Spanish-American War, some soldiers returned to live in the Tampa Bay area. Port Tampa was enlarged by Congressional appropriations in 1899, 1905, and 1910, as a result of the war-time experience, making it a major deep water port by World War I.[58]

Not only did the Sisters of the Holy Names in Key West volunteer their facilities and their talent as nurses to the U.S. forces during the war, but their fellow Sisters in Tampa, who also ran an academy, showed patriotic fervor. They made scapulars and three Sisters distributed them among the soldiers encamped around Tampa, a gesture unthinkable during peacetime, since the Sisters were cloistered, except for their teaching duties. When the 69th Regiment of New York, comprised of mostly Irish Catholics, arrived in Tampa on June 6 tired and hungry with neither provisions nor money, they walked from the train station to the Sisters Academy to beg for a cup of coffee. Upon seeing them, the Sisters gave them not only coffee, but also would not let them leave without providing them with breakfast. News of their hospitality and charity spread throughout the camp, so that from 6 a.m. to 8 p.m. on June 7 the Sisters fed over 600 men, while also passing out rosaries, scapulars, and medals. By July 31, the Sisters had fed 3,500 men. That same day, the Army contracted for the use of the Sisters Academy as a hospital for six weeks for $400.[59]

In early July 1898, the Bishop of St. Augustine, John Moore, received a letter from Archbishop Michael Corrigan of New York inquiring about the status of chaplains to the Army in Florida and offering to lend some volunteer priests as chaplains in Florida. This was quite a remarkable gesture, given, as we shall see in Chapter 13, the undoubtedly strained relations between Corrigan and Moore over the McGlynn case. Moore, who replied from Buffalo, N.Y., said that the soldiers are well attended by priests in Miami, Jacksonville (Father Patrick Barry was a full-time chaplain there), Tampa, Key West, and Fernandina. Moore said that he will forward Corrigan's letter to Father William Kenny, the Vicar General and pastor of Immaculate Conception Parish, Jacksonville, who, "if he judges more help is needed, I will inform you and gladly accept the services of your priests." Then, Moore, ever practical, asks Corrigan rhetorically: "How would such priests, if they came, get their support?" Moore could not pay them out of the treasury of his poor diocese, the U.S military will not pay, nor will the State of Florida. On July 27 Moore writes Corrigan from Lockport, N.Y., stating that he has heard from Father Kenny. Apparently Father Barry "is showing signs of breaking down under the heavy labor and the heat." Moore asks Corrigan to send a New York priest to the camps at Jacksonville, and then adds "I would hope that some charitable person of New York could contribute to the priest's support. The priests in Florida can hardly live [on what they receive from parish collections], especially in the summer season [when there are no tourists]." With the War's cessation and the gradual dismantling of the camps throughout the fall, Corrigan did not have to send a priest nor find a New York benefactor for his support. Meanwhile, Father Barry held his own under the strain of the extra pastoral demands of the soldiers.[60]

CHAPTER SEVEN

# *Clergy*

**M**oore faced similar leadership challenges as the captains of industry of the Gilded Age, such as Plant and Flagler, except that Moore did not have the financial resources, the political power, the personnel, and the ability to make a profit. Moore inherited the state of the diocese from his predecessor and then had to give a dynamic, effective response to not only what he received, but what unfolded due to changing conditions. A key aspect to effective leadership is finding the appropriate response to unforeseen circumstances. One of the key resources he had was the clergy, an indispensable asset for him to fulfill his pastoral responsibilities. Pastors were in charge of a particular demarcated territory (the parish boundaries), responsible for leading their people in the parish spiritually and financially, leading parishioners in prayer the Liturgy in traditional devotions, dispensing the Sacraments, and passing on the living tradition of the Church to the people. They also shared in their people's lives, in sickness and in health, in sorrow and in joy, in birth and in death. They literally and figuratively lived with their people. Pastors were assigned and were accountable to their bishop. The bishop not only needed a sufficient quantity of priests to match the pastoral needs within his diocese, but he also needed collaborators and cooperators, men of quality and commitment. Unlike Plant or Flagler, who could search out and buy talent, Moore could only try to recruit future priests or beg priests from elsewhere to come to frontier Florida, where incentives were sparse and people were poor.

When Moore became bishop in the summer of 1877, he had ten priests in his diocese: three French Canadians; three Italians; four French. Note, there were neither Irishmen nor Americans. Moore reported after his first visitation of the diocese in August 1877 that all the clergy spoke English well, despite their being foreigners. The ten were stationed in Tampa, Palatka, Fernandina, Tallahassee, Key West (Florida's largest city), Jacksonville, and St. Augustine. Altogether there were seven parishes. From those bases priests visited Catholics at various missions (seventeen in number) and stations (seventy in number). Catholics gathered in a church building at a parish or mission, where no priest resided, whereas a station had no church, so Catholics met at the home of a prominent Catholic of the area. Some missions were visited weekly or monthly, whereas stations were visited less frequently. Every parish at the time had missions and stations attached, which meant that priests were sometimes not at the parish church, a situation that was particularly the case in the four parishes that had only one priest (Tampa, Palatka, Fernandina, and Tallahassee).[1]

One of Moore's chief preoccupations throughout his episcopacy was the recruitment of priests to serve the people of his diocese. As early as November 1877, Moore asked Gibbons for the two burses (scholarships) the Archdiocese of Baltimore had vacant at North American College in Rome. He ended up sending two Florida natives to Rome as a result, although only one was ordained. In the early days of his episcopate he thought he could get "plenty of vocations from Florida," since he was tired of refusing questionable applications from throughout the U.S. In 1879, he was in Baltimore visiting St. Mary's Seminary trying to entice seminarians for Florida. From 1877 to 1885 three priests died and three returned to their homeland, so his priest personnel situation was constantly changing and needed constant replenishment. By 1885, Moore had eleven priests: three French, two Italians, one German, three Irish or Irish-Americans, and one English-born Irishman. Also by that year he had seven seminarians in the pipeline, one of whom was the first native Floridian, Edward A. Pace from Starke, who was studying at the North American College, Rome.[2]

But Pace was an exception, in more ways than one. Moore could not depend on native Floridians as a source of priests for his diocese, not that he discouraged them, but except for Pace, they just were not forthcoming. The missionary Church in Florida had not yet reached a stage of development where native priestly vocations could arise. Bishop Verot sought clerical assistance from France, French-speaking Canada, and diocesan missionaries from Italy. Moore would look particularly to Ireland or to the Irish in America.

Bernard O'Reilly was ordained June 15, 1880, at St. Bonaventure Seminary in New York; Edward Clarke on June 11, 1881, in St. Augustine; Anthony F. J. Kilcoyne on June 30, 1882, at St. Vincent's Abbey, Pennsylvania. These men were sent to various American Seminaries where Moore got tuition *gratis,* since the diocese was too poor to support seminarians. Two burses (scholarships - a "burse" is from Medieval Latin *bursa,* meaning a bag or purse) were available for the Diocese of St. Augustine seminarians at St. Mary's Seminary, Baltimore.[3]

But by mid-1886, Moore became disenchanted with the quality of men trained in American seminaries. Writing to the rector of North American College in Rome, Denis O'Connell, he says: "Oh, the evil result from a superficial education and ignorance and pride of some of the priests who come out of our American seminaries." He goes on: "I must look to Ireland, chiefly, for my students and Rome for their education. One good priest from your college (North American College) or from the Jesuits is worth at least three of the riff-raff [sic] that comes out of many of American seminaries." However, Moore was not indiscriminate in his acceptance of even Irish seminarians, despite his desperate need for priests. As he wrote to O'Connell in February 1888 just after having lost two priests to yellow fever: "I cannot wait for my students to be ordained. So I am thinking about going to Ireland next summer for two or three [months]. I have a dread of accepting priests recommended merely by letter. It frequently happens that bishops will recommend priests whom they are glad to get rid of." Moore was not desperate enough to accept either a seminarian or a priest sight unseen and was aware that some bishops might want to "dump" a troublesome priest upon some unwary needy missionary bishop. He had already experienced this phenomenon earlier in Charleston.

Not only did Moore prefer Roman educated Irishmen as seminarians, but also the North American College and the Propagation of the Faith in Rome and in Paris paid for the education of his seminarians, because they were studying for a missionary diocese. Some bishops from Ireland also helped defray education costs for Irish seminarians in Rome studying for Moore. Still, Moore did have to pay some of educational expenses for some of his seminarians. In 1886 he had to refuse two seminarians who were offered to him because he could not afford to take them on.[4]

Moore was forever preoccupied with suppling priests for Florida. As he wrote to Bishop James Gibbons of Baltimore in 1883:

> I could not express to our Grace the anxiety I feel on account of the want of priests in this diocese. Catholics are coming to all the little towns that are now springing up so rapidly all over the southern part of the state, and I find everywhere I go the very bad distortions of our religion on the part of non-Catholics. Oh, if I only had priests to minister to them all!

But Moore was unwilling to compromise quantity for quality. He mentions in 1885 the difficulty of trying "to find good priests willing to work for God and not for money."[5]

Since Moore thought that Irishmen made the best missionaries and Rome the best place to educate them, he began reaping the fruits of his personnel investments in the 1890s with the ordinations of nine young Irishmen, namely: Patrick Barry, Michael Fox, James Nunan, Michael Maher, William Hughes, Patrick Lynch, John O'Brien, J. F. O'Boyle, James Veale. By 1900, of the fourteen diocesan priests Moore had, nine or 64 percent were Irish-born. This preponderance of Irish-born priests in Florida, a trend which Moore initiated, was a legacy which continued well into the 20th Century. As late as 1968, 65.4 percent of the priests of the Diocese of St. Augustine were Irish-born.[6]

# The Yellow Fever Crisis

John Moore was familiar with yellow fever since he had lived in Charleston, one of many Southern port cities exposed to the disease periodically during the nineteenth century. In fact, when his mother died in 1858 while he was studying in Rome, Charleston's population of 40,500 decreased by 717 or 1.8 percent, as a result of deaths due to the disease.[7]

Yellow fever is an air-born virus which is carried from victim to victim by *Aedes aegypti* mosquitoes. Frost or cold temperatures kills the mosquitoes, so the disease is tropical and appears in the hot humid summers and fall. *Aedes aegypti* breeds in freshwater, particularly in cisterns, puddles, buckets, etc, and prefers urban areas to swamps and lakes. In the nineteenth century the cause of the disease was unknown.

In its mild form it produces flu-like symptoms for a week or so. In its classic form it spawns chills, fever and muscle aches, followed by liver failure and jaundice. Blood clotting causes hemorrhage of gums, nose, and stomach. When vomited, the digested blood looks black. Renal failure is evidenced by a cessation of urine output, then in one or two days the patient dies. Mortality ranged from 10 to 60 percent of those infected. As one might well imagine, caring for yellow fever victims left long-enduring horrific memories with the care-giver. In the nineteenth century most believed that the lack of sanitation was the principal culprit in the spread of the disease.

Italians and the Irish were particular susceptible to the malady, while African-Americans were generally immune. The genetic pool of the former groups had no exposure to the disease, while the latter group had immunity going back to Africa. Yellow fever not only took a toll on human life, but also burdened Southern commerce, stopping trains and bottling up ports. City quarantines were imposed, sometimes for three or four months. Nothing and no one was allowed in or out, thus wrecking commerce. Quarantine was the chief defense against epidemics, as regulated by local, state, and later even federal public health officials.

By the 1870s most Southern doctors felt that the agent of yellow fever was a living germ of microscopic size which entered through the respiratory tract. Some felt this microbe was indigenous to the South, others did not.[8]

Moore encountered yellow fever soon after he arrived in St. Augustine. Bishop Gibbons invited Moore to Baltimore in early October 1877 for the celebration of Gibbon's receiving the pallium, a strip of wool hung around the neck given by the Pope as a sign that a prelate is a Metropolitan or Archbishop. Gibbons added that the occasion was an opportunity for Moore to meet the other bishops of the Province of Baltimore and join them in proposing episcopal nominations for the Diocese of Richmond. Moore declined the invitation. "I believe that nothing but absolute necessity would justify my absence even for a short time... if I should go away, I may find it impossible to return" wrote Moore. Yellow fever had hit Fernandina first, and then spread south to Jacksonville and St. Augustine by mid-November, putting the citizenry in a panic. The ever-dutiful Moore demurred from traveling to Baltimore for this reason.[9]

Ten years later, in May 1887, yellow fever reappeared in Key West; by that fall it reached Tampa. On October 7 Jacksonville was quarantined against anyone or anything from Tampa. Forty-three-year-old Father Charles Peterman, the much respected pastor of Tampa's St. Louis Church contracted the disease on October 24, 1887.[10]

Peterman came to the Diocese of St. Augustine after teaching as a professor of classics at St. Mary's College, San Francisco, for fifteen years. Then, as a seminarian for St. Augustine, he was sent to the seminary in Innsbruck, Austria. Upon ordination, his first assignment was to the Cathedral in the fall of 1880. In January 1883, he was named pastor of St. Louis Parish, Tampa, which was founded in 1860 and had three missions at Tarpon Springs, Bartow, and Bloomingdale. Considered the most learned priest in the diocese, Peterman brought with him to Tampa his extensive library. Unlike his predecessor, he was immediately popular among his parishioners, an esteemed preacher by both Protestants and Catholics. Also unlike his predecessor, he was able to get monetary support from his parishioners, so much so that by the Fall of 1883 he added two wings onto the wooden church, increasing its capacity from 120 to 200 persons. By 1887, Peterman developed plans to erect a new convent for the Sisters of the Holy Names and built a church for the Latins in Ybor City; however, these plans went unrealized because on October 27, 1887, he died, a victim of yellow fever.[11]

Upon hearing the news on October 24 of Peterman's illness, Moore sent the closest priest to Tampa, Father Felix P. Swembergh, the founding pastor of St. James Parish, Orlando, which was established in 1886. Swembergh was born in 1844 in Topeka, Kansas, and studied for the priesthood with the Jesuits at Woodstock, Maryland. He was ordained for the Vicar Apostolic of Kansas on June 7, 1884, but moved from the western frontier to the Florida frontier in 1885. Only four days after his arrival in Tampa, Swembergh too expired of yellow fever at the age of forty-three. Next Moore sent Frenchman Father Henry P. Clavreul, pastor St. Joseph's, Mandarin (near Jacksonville) to Tampa, arriving just before Swemburgh passed. Clavreul was an experienced Florida missionary, having been recruited from France by Bishop Verot in 1859, along with six others. Importantly, he was immune from yellow fever, since he had the disease in the past and survived. After burying Peterman and Swemburgh, as well as taking care of their personal effects, Clavreul advised Moore not to send another priest over to Tampa for the time being, since yellow fever is still present.[12]

Almost a year later, Clavreul was finally relieved in Tampa by Father Denis O'Sullivan, a young Irishman from the Diocese of Newark and a former missionary to Africa, who volunteered to serve in disease-ridden Florida. Moore sent him to Tampa, thinking that his service in Africa immunized him from tropical diseases. He was wrong. Arriving in Tampa on September 12, 1888, he was dead of yellow fever after only twelve days in Tampa. From September 24 to October 17, 1888, Tampa had no priest. In 1887 Moore had thirteen diocesan priests (and two religious order priests) to staff twelve parishes and a missionary center covering Volusia and Brevard counties; by the fall of 1888, death took 23 percent of his diocesan priests. Moore faced a crisis in pastoral care.[13]

If that was not enough, Moore caught yellow fever himself. By early August of 1888 the epidemic appeared in Jacksonville. It would only subside in December, with 430 deaths or 2 percent of the city's population. In early September the pastor of Immaculate

Conception Parish, Jacksonville, William J. Kenny, caught the fever. With no one to send, Moore went himself to Jacksonville to serve the parish for the stricken pastor. Earlier in August Moore came down with a light case of the fever in St. Augustine, but he was not worried since he was of the opinion that he was immune due to his time in Charleston. In late October in Jacksonville, Moore came down with the disease again, but it was a glancing blow, since he recovered by early November. He wrote in early December of his experience during the height of his illness: "I suffered from a great weakness of memory and even now I feel at times a great lassitude which almost incapacitates me for mental labor." Staying on in Jacksonville until mid-December, he commented: "I begin now to feel as if I were shut up in a prison." Father Kenny recovered after two weeks. Sister Mary Ann, SSJ, director of the orphanage, was in bed for two days due to over work after caring for the eight orphans who caught the disease, but who recovered. Three other SSJ Sisters came down with the fever; one died, Sister Rose de Lima, SSJ. While in Jacksonville, Moore was able to secure the temporary services of Father James Duffo, SJ, a New Orleans Jesuit who was stationed at Selma, AL.[14]

## The Jesuits

Even before the yellow fever crisis, Bishop Moore was trying to get the New Orleans Jesuits to come to work in Florida. Pressured by the developer of what he called "a Catholic Colony," which was located in the rolling hills near Lake Jovita and named San Antonio, Bishop Moore asked the New Orleans Jesuits in 1882 to serve the new settlement. The Jesuits refused the offer, for reasons stated by Bishop Moore: "The Jesuits are prevented from coming to us for the present because of the shortage of priests assigned to the Province of New Orleans."[15]

In 1888 Father John O'Shanahan, SJ, became the new superior of the New Orleans Jesuits. His perspective was different from his predecessor's. He saw Florida as an opportunity and his personnel sufficient for expansion. When he heard of the 1888 yellow fever epidemic in Jacksonville, he took the initiative of offering to send to Moore one of his men there to help out. The man that O'Shanahan sent to Jacksonville was Father James Duffo, SJ. He was French, a Jesuit since 1841, and came to the U.S. in 1848, along with many European Jesuits who arrived here because of political turmoil there. In the late nineteenth century, the New Orleans Jesuits had 76 percent of their membership of European origin. Of the 302 foreign-born New Orleans Jesuits who died before 1907, the largest national representations were as follows: eighty-seven French, seventy-seven Irish, thirty-seven German, and thirty-seven

*7. 1 Father Philippe de Carriere, SJ*
*Source: ANOPSJ*

Swiss. Duffo was immune to yellow fever because of his exposure to it in past postings. Though elderly, he was a perfect candidate to send to Jacksonville, where he labored for two months before returning to New Orleans in January 1889, when the health danger ceased. He was the first Jesuit to work in Florida since the Spanish Jesuits left in 1569, that is, in 319 years. He died on February 27, 1900.[16]

In early October 1888 Moore wrote a second letter the New Orleans Jesuits asking for temporary help in multilingual Ybor City (near Tampa), another place under siege by yellow fever. The day after receiving Moore's letter, Father John O'Shanahan, New Orleans Jesuit Superior, called into his room the sixty-three year-old French-born Father Philippe de Carriere, SJ.

Born in Toulouse on April 20, 1825, of an aristocratic family, de Carriere entered the Society of Jesus in 1844. He arrived at Spring Hill College (Alabama) in 1848 and was ordained in Mobile in 1857. O'Shanahan picked the Frenchman not only because of his Caribbean missionary experience and multilingual skills, but also because he thought him immune to yellow fever because of his many years laboring in the tropics. However, de Carriere knew differently. He had never contracted the disease and therefore could very well not be immune! He did not communicate this fact to his Superior and with typical Jesuit obedience "accepted willingly his Superior's 'invitation'" to the Tampa area. Given Tampa's disease-ridden reputation, he later wrote that he thought for sure he was going to his death: "I pledged my life for the sake of that mission."

The next day, Sunday, October 7, 1888, with prayers, alms, and provisions for the journey, de Carriere left new Orleans by rail for Tampa. Along the way he stopped to visit fellow Frenchman Father Joseph L. Hugon, a diocesan pastor of Blessed Sacrament Church, Tallahassee, whose church building was in ruins because of the poverty of his congregation. Instead, services were held in Hugon's parlor. After two days, de Carriere moved on to Orlando where he was received by Irishman Father J. J. Creed, pastor of St. James Church. Creed had no rectory, living instead in a hotel and boarding with a Catholic family. On October 17, de Carriere left Creed by train and arrived at Tampa at 10:30 p.m., when he discovered that Tampa was quarantined. "The city was almost deserted," he later wrote," I was the only minister dwelling in it." What struck de Carriere as most discouraging was what he called the "spiritual misery" of the people of Tampa. The French Jesuit asked friends in the South and in France to pray earnestly for the Tampa's residents. "In a word, heaven had been stormed in favor of Tampa and of Florida."[17]

Meanwhile, Moore sought a more permanent solution to the pastoral needs of Tampa and Ybor City.

In 1880 Tampa was a sleepy backwater Southern town of 720 residents, but that was to change on the West Coast due to the influx of new capital, new industry, new land development, and new people. This influx was prodded by the investments of Disston, Plant, and Martínez Ybor, whom we discussed in Chapter 6, but we visit again, this time in the context of the pastoral challenges their activities posed for Moore.

In 1881 the State of Florida teetered on the edge of bankruptcy. As a result, Gov. William B. Bloxham enticed financiers to invest in Florida by offering them as an incentive 15 million acres of state land, most of it under water. Hamilton Disston, the thirty-six year old heir of a Philadelphia tool and die works, struck a deal with the governor. Disston offered $1 million for 4 million acres of South Florida wetlands, an offer Bloxham could not refuse. Disston planned to reclaim the wetlands with a network of canals, to dredge the Kissimmee River to improve inland navigation, and to establish agricultural colonies. He packaged land parcels to sell to developers, while developing some places himself: Disston City (Gulfport), Tarpon Springs, Boca Ciega Bay, and a few other places. He also attempted to build a railroad connecting his developments with one another and to the outside, but he failed because of outstretched finances. Draining and developing South Florida's interior turned out to be much more costly than Disston anticipated.[18]

It was Henry B. Plant of Connecticut who brought the railroad to Florida's West Coast. During Reconstruction, Plant was the president and principal owner of the Southern Express Company, an amalgam of several lines in Georgia and South Carolina. By early 1881, he extended his railroad from Savannah to Jacksonville. Then he proposed to build from Kissimmee to Tampa. The state promised 13,840 acres for every mile laid (seventy-five miles were needed), but it had to completed by January 24, 1884, or the land give-away was off. Astoundingly, Plant's construction crew completed the link on January 22, sixty-three hours before the deadline! Not only did Plant's men beat what seemed an impossible challenge, but he also beat out Disston, who was also trying to build a railroad to Tampa at the same time. This was not the only Disston-Plant rivalry. Plant did everything to promote Tampa and everything to demote Disston City on the Pinellas Peninsula. His efforts were successful. Plant's railroad not only opened the West Coast and Florida to the shipment of agricultural products by rail, but also opened the area to tourism. Like Flagler on the East Coast, Plant built a series of luxury hotels to attract high-end tourism — at Tampa, Belleair (Clearwater), Punta Gorda, Fort Myers, and several central Florida cities. Before his death in 1899, he was planning to extend his line from Fort Myers to Miami across the Everglades.[19]

The coming of the railroad to Tampa, and to the rest of Florida, revolutionized time, communication, and transportation. As one newspaper reporter in Ocala wrote in 1881: "How the railroad kills time and space!" It brought capital, facilitated trade, encouraged development, expanded tourism, and added a much-needed transfusion of new people, one of whom was Don Vincente Martínez Ybor.

Born into a wealthy family in Valencia, Spain, in 1818, Ybor immigrated to Cuba, where he invested in modernizing the cigar industry in Havana. When the Cuban Revolution broke out in

Yara in 1868, Vincente supported the separatists for political and business reasons. To avoid arrest by the Spanish colonial authorities, he fled Cuba for Key West in 1869, establishing a cigar factory there. Following his lead, soon other Cuban cigar manufacturers joined him there, where by 1875 fifteen cigar factories operated, along with several hundred Cuban cigar workers and their Spanish plant managers. By the mid-1880s, irked by several devastating strikes and limited transportation options at Key West, Ybor decided to relocate once again.

Lured by the notion of creating a company town under his control and enticed by offers made by Plant and leaders of the Tampa business community, Ybor and another cigar manufacturer in Key West, Ignatio Haya, negotiated for a large parcel of land of uninhabited wetlands two miles northeast of downtown Tampa. As a further incentive, the Tampa Board of Trade paid almost half of the asking price of the property to facilitate the relocation of the two cigar industry leaders and their workers. In the Spring of 1886 the first group of Cuban cigar workers arrived in what was to be called Ybor City. Ybor, now a developer, attracted others cigar factory owners by offering free land, new factories built to their specifications, and worker's homes, a rare commodity in both Havana and Key West. Soon Ybor City became a company town run by Vincente and his fellow factory owners, populated by what Mormino and Pozzetta call an "ethnic paella" of various Latins —Cubans, Spaniards, and Sicilians (who already had arrived in Florida in the early 1880s to work in agriculture, on Disston's canals, and on Plant's railroad). Spanish was the *lingua franca* of the cigar factories and Ybor City.[20]

Ybor was the Spanish version of elite business magnates such as Flagler, Plant, and Disston already shaping the destiny of Florida, moving it from a frontier to a more urbanized environment. Moore had to find ways to respond to these changing environments which also affected pastoral care. By 1888, the bishop had a two-fold problem: 1) a shortage of priests, especially aggravated by the recent yellow fever epidemic; 2) a unique pastoral challenge in Tampa due to the presence of the Latin (Spanish, Cuban and Italian) cigar workers. He simply did not have the personnel resources to respond to either problem, let alone to both.

Although de Carriere was supposed to minister in Tampa temporarily, Moore could find no one to replace him, so the French Jesuit remained at his post there longer than either he or his superior anticipated. He was pastor of St. Louis Parish from October 17, 1888, until September 25, 1889.

With his back to the wall, Moore sought a permanent solution to the pastoral needs created by Tampa's rapid growth and soon to be the demographic growth of all of South Florida. Again he contacted the Jesuits, but not those in New Orleans. In March of 1889 he wrote to Father Louis Martín, SJ, Provincial of Castile, Spain, inviting them:

> To establish such houses and institutes of your society [sic] as you may judge best for obtaining the end in view in the counties of Hillsborough, Polk, DeSoto, Manatee, Osceola, with the exception of Kissimmee, Lee, Dade, and in time Monroe in the State of Florida... I will expect that the Fathers of the Society will take upon themselves the spiritual care of the souls that are found in the territory which is steadily acquiring great importance and promises in the near future to be the most important portion of the whole State of Florida.

Moore offered the Spanish Jesuits the pastoral care of the upper part of Southwest Florida, that is Tampa and its vicinity, which was the fastest growing part of his diocese. Martín refused the offer, stating two reasons: 1) he lacked sufficient personnel; 2) since English was Florida's chief language, he did not have a sufficient number of men who could speak it.

Unaware of the Spanish refusal, but upon getting wind of Moore's offer, probably through de Carriere, O'Shanahan, the New Orleans Jesuit Superior, rushed by rail to Tampa to visit de Carriere in order to have him convince Moore to invite his province to the West Coast, instead of the Castilians. Moore initially demurred O'Shanahan's overtures, after all the same group had rejected his offer in 1882. But with de Carriere's intercession, the bishop reconsidered, proffering them even more concessions than he had to the Spaniards.[21]

The Jesuits had come in 1837 to New Orleans from Lyon, France — four priests, two brothers, and one novice. In 1838 they opened St. Charles College at Grand Coteau, Louisiana, then in 1847 Immaculate Conception College, New Orleans. That year they also began operating Spring Hill College, Mobile, which initially opened as a diocesan institution in 1830. By 1880 they were an independent mission from Lyon and had fifty priests, thirty-seven brothers, and forty-eight scholastics. From their foundation, they benefitted from an influx of European Jesuits, refugees of the political turmoil on the Continent. By the 1880s the New Orleans Jesuits were in an expansion mode. In 1884

7.2 *Father John O'Shanahan, SJ*
Source: *ANOPSJ*

they accepted a parish and college in Galveston, Texas. In 1886 they purchased Pio Nono College, built in Macon, Ga., in 1874, and renamed it St. Stanislaus Novitiate, making it a center for Jesuit formation in the South.[22]

Moore wrote O'Shanahan on April 15, 1889, offering the New Orleans Jesuits pastoral care of all of South Florida, including Key West, with the exception of Pasco, Hernando, and Citrus counties, which were north of Tampa and as we shall soon see already under the care of the Benedictines. O'Shanahan replied on July 4 that the Jesuit General in Rome accepted the proposal, then on July 30 he was in St. Augustine meeting with Bishop Moore to propose that the diocese cede to the New Orleans Jesuits eight South Florida counties: Hillsborough, Polk, De Soto, Manatee, Osceola, Lee, Dade and Monroe, that is, one-third of the diocese of St. Augustine "in perpetuity." O'Shanahan drove a hard bargain, but Moore was desperately in need of the Jesuits' specialized skills and manpower, both of which were lacking in the present state of his diocesan clergy. The New Orleans Jesuits were a perfect fit for the growing and multilingual Tampa area, not only because of Moore's desperate clergy shortage, but also because of the Jesuit's linguistic skills. Most

Jesuits assigned on the South Florida Missions were foreign-born. In 1897 the Tampa Jesuits comprised seven nationalities and spoke five languages. Besides all this, Moore respected and admired the Jesuits from his Roman student days.

The next day Moore wrote the Congregation for the Propagation of the Faith in Rome requesting permission to implement the agreement. Up to 1908, the U.S. was considered a missionary country, therefore under the direct supervision of the Propagation of the Faith, part of the Roman Curia in charge of missionary lands. Giving away one-third of your diocese to the exclusive care of a religious community was considered a major undertaking which needed Roman permission. On August 30 Propaganda wrote Moore asking precisely why he was giving exclusive and perpetual possession of South Florida to the Jesuits. On October 15 he responded that O'Shanahan demanded it as a *sine qua non* of any agreement. Furthermore, Moore explained, O'Shanahan's demands were reasonable: 1) because the Jesuits felt they could not care for the missionary territory unless they had full liberty within it; 2) because the Jesuits were better equipped than diocesan priests to embrace the missionary enterprise of the territory; 3) because diocesan priests were linguistically incapable of responding to the pastoral needs of the over 10,000 Cubans in Key West and Tampa (Ybor City). Finally, Moore pointed out an important proviso in the agreement, namely, that the Jesuits agreed to hand back the missions of the territory to the diocese "when they [those missions] were in a condition of development to be staffed with secular priests."

Curiously, there is no record of any formal reply from Rome to Moore's October 15 letter. As a product of Roman training, Moore was always meticulous in following Church law and directions emanat-ing from Rome; however, the pastoral situation demanded that he forge ahead. Moore took for granted that the Roman permission would be forthcoming and believed that whatever difficulties might ensue between himself and the Jesuits could be worked out in a gen-tlemanly fashion between himself and O'Shanahan.

The formal agreement between the New Orleans Jesuits and the Diocese of St. Augustine was signed on September 3, 1891. It lasted for thirty years, with little or no disagreements between the parties over the three decades. But the actual implementation of the agreement happened before it was signed. On September 25, 1889, Irish-born Father John Quinlan, SJ, took over as pastor of St. Louis Parish, Tampa, replacing Father de Carriere and signaling the official beginning of the Jesuit Mission in South Florida.[23]

Before he left Tampa, Father de Carriere settled on the purchase of property for a church in Ybor City, negotiations that had already

commenced under Father Peterman. After some horse trading, Vincente Ybor agreed upon a purchase price of $5,000. The deal was concluded when railroad magnate Henry Flagler, a friend of Bishop Moore's, agreed to pay $1,000 as a down-payment for the property.

Father Quinlan said the first Mass in Ybor City in the home of Mr. Tissler of St. Louis on March 16, 1890, with thirty persons present. By April, the Jesuits initiated weekly service there. In September 1890 Ybor City had its first church, the wood-framed Our Lady of

7. 3 Jesuit territory in Florida
Source: Author

Mercy, named in honor of the nineteenth century Marian devotion of Cubans. It remained a mission of St. Louis Parish until 1911, when it was designated as a parish.[24]

When Father Quinlan took over as pastor of St. Louis Parish, de Carriere stayed on as his assistant. Quinlan described the parish as 260 miles long and 150 miles wide, comprised of twenty small settlements. He listed nineteen stations and missions, all which had been visited previously by de Carriere. It was clear that the Jesuits had a two-fold missionary enterprise: to respond to the needs of the urban Catholics in Tampa and its environs, but also to serve Catholics scattered in small settlements in the hinterlands. For reaching Catholics outside of urban areas, the Jesuits employed a three-staged missionary model used throughout the South and throughout the Diocese of St. Augustine.

First, a priest journeyed to gather Catholics of a particular locale, usually at the home of some prominent Catholic — saying Mass, administering the Sacraments, hearing the Catechism of the children. This locale was called a station. It was visited irregularly, sporadically, briefly, infrequently, and usually unannounced and never on a Sunday, since Mass had to be said at home base, the parish.

The second stage of development was the building of a church, but with no resident pastor. This stage was called a mission, where a priest would visit more regularly, often at a set time, once a month, or once a week.

The third stage was reached when the bishop appointed a resident pastor and erected the parish, most probably with missions and stations attached, which meant that the pastor was not always available to parishioners since he was traveling to various missions and stations, usually during the weekdays. Whereas a mission or station was hardly ever self-supporting, a parish was supposed to be. From 1889 to 1919 Jesuits exclusively tended Catholics at all three stages of development on both coasts of Florida. It is a tribute to their diligence that by 1919 more South Florida missions were ready to become parishes than there were Jesuits to staff them.[25]

*7.4 Father William Tyrell, SJ*
*Source: ANOPSJ*

Let us illustrate the life and challenges of the Jesuits in South Florida by looking at one outstanding missionary — William Tyrell. In July 1892, Father Quinlan was transferred and replaced by Tyrell, an Irishman born in Kings County in 1854. He entered the Jesuits in France in 1873 and was in the U.S. by 1876, where he taught at St. Charles College, Grand Coteau, LA, followed in 1877 with an assignment at Spring Hill College, where from 1891-92 he was the vice-president. Upon his arrival in Tampa in 1892, he was named pastor of St. Louis Parish and Jesuit Superior of the Florida Jesuit

Missions. When Tyrell arrived in Tampa, three other Jesuits were already there: Philippe de Carriere, assistant pastor and confessor to the Sisters of the Holy Names; Conrad Widman, *excurr.* (from the Latin verb *excurrere*, "to make an excursion or a sortie," that is a full-time missionary to the outlying areas); and Brother Joseph Leunda, builder.

During Tyrell's seven years as pastor/superior in Tampa, the pastoral care of the South Florida Jesuit Missions grew in complexity. Tyrell's energetic talents oversaw the construction of the following: the Sisters of St. Joseph Convent, Ybor City; the Young Men's Catholic Club on Twiggs Street, Tampa; St. Ignatius Church, Port Tampa; St. Peter Claver Chapel and School for African-Americans, Tampa; St. Francis Xavier Church, Fort Myers; Holy Name Church, Miami; and St. Ann's Church, West Palm Beach. Also during his tenure, St. Mary Star of the Sea Parish (founded in 1852) came under Jesuit jurisdiction on February 15, 1898, with Alexander Friend, SJ, as pastor, along with another Jesuit priest and brother. From the Jesuit perspective, Tyrell achieved the peak accomplishment when he opened the Jesuit College for Boys in Tampa on September 11, 1899. That very same day, Tyrell was transferred to Spring Hill College, soon to become its president. When he was transferred, he was in the process of fund-raising and building a new stone church in Tampa, a project completed finally on January 15, 1905, and called Sacred Heart Church. The Jesuits renamed St. Louis Parish for a devotion that they especially promulgated, the Sacred Heart of Jesus.

But Tyrell was more than a financier and builder, speaking Spanish, he often ministered to the Latins of Ybor City. His Irish convivial optimistic personality made him popular with Bishop Moore, with his fellow Jesuits, with his parishioners, and with the general population of the Tampa area. By the time Tyrell left in 1899, fifteen Jesuits were stationed in South Florida. Except the two who were assigned to Key West, the rest were based in Tampa, two of whom were Jesuit Brothers and three were full-time missionaries (*excurr.*) to the outlying areas, gathering Catholics on the frontier, in newly-developed towns, and tending to missions and stations.[26]

One other event that marked Tyrell's extraordinary pastorate was the Spanish-American War. On April 20, 1898, the 5th and 6th Regiments of the U.S. Army arrived in Tampa; four days later Father Tyrell went to their encampment to say Mass. On May 8 he initiated at St. Louis Church a Sunday 9:30 a.m. Mass especially for the soldiers; 300 soldiers attended, with fifty going to Holy Communion. Every day brought more soldiers to Tampa. Fortunately, three regular U.S. Army units had their own Catholic chaplains. The Jesuits undertook the pastoral care of the rest of the Catholics in Regular Army and volunteers. During that hot, crowded, anxiety-filled summer of 1898, approximately 30,000 soldiers encamped in the Tampa vicinity. Typical of his personality, Tyrell did not see this as a burden, but as an opportunity. He wrote: "Our Fathers immediately realized that no time should be lost. The harvest is great but the reapers were few, and besides the harvest was already ripe and in many cases only waiting for the sickle." Of the five Jesuits who assisted Tyrell with ministry to the military, one was the 74 year-old Philippe de Carriere. Tyrell noted: "Father de Carriere seemed to grow young again when he saw the soldiers flocking around him... his age did not diminish his ardor and zeal." Besides saying Mass for the soldiers, the Jesuits were kept busy with catechetical instruction and Confessions. Tyrell reported that nearly every Catholic soldier got to Confession and Holy Communion before embarking for Cuba. Dormant faith is often resuscitated in the face of possible death. Tyrell also mentioned performing quite a number of Baptisms, having several First Communions, and reclaiming some "wayward sons." As the Sisters were doing, the priests also handed out scapulars and religious medals, which were particularly popular among men about to go into battle. Finally, the Jesuits had extra funerals due to the number of victims of typhoid fever that summer in Tampa. Tyrell admitted that the pastoral work was intensely difficult during that summer of 1898, "but we did not mind since we had the consolation of seeing so many thousands of men approach the Sacraments." Army units began embarking for Cuba on July 9, but the process took much longer than expected due to inadequate port facilities. By August 20, all Army units pulled out of Tampa.[27]

The Jesuits spent much time and energy in their role of the *excurr.* In 1898 four out of the nine Jesuit priests in Tampa were assigned as full-time missionary circuit riders (*excurr.*) throughout South Florida. The most outstanding of these in Bishop Moore's time was Father Conrad Widman, who was born in 1833 in Bavaria, Germany, and became a Jesuit in 1851. Because of poor health, he was transferred to the Lyons Province, then to New Orleans in 1859, where the warmer climate might be beneficial to his health. In November 1890, he was sent to Tampa to take on the rigors of the South Florida Missions as an *excurr.* Before leaving Tampa in August 1894, he visited Catholics scattered throughout every county under Jesuit jurisdiction. He was the first Jesuit

*7.5 Father Conrad Widman, SJ*
Source: *ANOPSJ*

to say Mass in St. Petersburg on September 11, 1892 (at the San José Hotel with twenty in attendance). It was Widman who first contacted Catholics in South Central Florida and on the Southeast Coast. He took a ship from Tampa to Key West, then sailed on to Miami in late November and early December of 1892. The round-trip took him twenty-seven days. In January 1893, Widman was the first priest to visit Catholics along the Indian River and south to Lake Worth (around which Palm Beach and West Palm Beach would soon be founded). In March and April 1893, Widman contacted Catholics in St. Cloud, Haines City, Tarpon Springs, Fort Myers, and Naples. With his linguistic abilities, he traveled to Ocala to visit the Italian families residing there in April 1894. Widman's delicate health did not seem to deter his robust missionary travels to gather Catholics throughout South Florida's frontier towns and hinter-lands. After departing Florida in 1894, Widman died at the age of seventy-three on February 16, 1906.[28]

Bishop Moore was extremely attentive and supportive of the pastoral efforts of the Jesuits at Tampa and throughout South Florida, as well as to the endeavors of religious women working in Tampa's Catholic schools. The rapid growth taking place during Florida's First Boom was precisely in the area under Jesuit pastoral care. During this period, some South Florida towns, such as Tampa, were moving rapidly from sleepy frontier outposts, to bustling urban centers because of improvements in infrastructure, commerce, transportation, and development.

Moore maintained excellent relations with the Jesuits, as is indicated in a letter he wrote them in August 1895: "I would have your Fathers to be persuaded, and thoroughly persuaded, that I appreciated their services in Florida. The Mission is difficult, but with time and perseverance we may hope that matters will get into better shape." The feeling was mutual, as Father de Carriere wrote upon hearing of the bishop's death in 1901: "In him our Society lost a true friend and the Jesuit Fathers of the Mission of Florida their beloved founder, protector, and benefactor."

Like all bishops, then and now, Moore had a two-fold role: chief pastor and chief administrator of the diocese. When in Tampa, Moore said Mass, preached, administered the Sacrament of Confirmation, as well as overseeing personnel, land purchases, contracts, construction, and other financial matters, since as corporation sole he owned all diocesan properties not specifically possessed by the Jesuits. In July of 1895 he deeded over to the Jesuits the property of St. Louis Church, since they were planning to build a new stone church and rename the parish. Moore managed his diocese, not from behind a desk or from the confines of a chancery building with its large bureaucracy (which he never had), but from being continually on the road, making frequent pastoral visitations. This was particular true for Tampa. With decent rail connections from St. Augustine to Tampa, Moore's first recorded trip there was February 18-19, 1890. From 1890 to 1899 he traveled to Tampa an average of three times a year, Confirming young people at St. Louis Parish and Our Lady of Mercy in Ybor City every year, except 1898, 1900, 1901, the latter two were when Moore's health was in decline. Living in Italy for five years as a student and speaking English, Italian, French, and some Spanish, Moore would have felt comfortable among the Latins of Ybor City.[29]

## The Benedictines

Tampa was not the only place growing on Florida's West Coast in the 1880s. Edmund Dunne, former chief justice of Arizona Territory, was given 100,000 acres in Florida in return for legal services rendered to Hamilton Disston for his massive land purchase of 1881. For over twenty years Dunne dreamed of founding a Catholic colony and with the help of his cousin, former Union Capt. Hugh Dunne, picked a site in Florida for such a colony in 1882 from the land he had received from Disston. Edmond named the site San Antonio in honor of St. Anthony of Padua (although Dunne was unaware of it, this was the name given to the Jesuit parish for the Calusa tribe on an island in Estero Bay, which existed from 1567-69). Located in the rolling hills surrounding Lake Jovita, by the of 1882 San Antonio had forty settlers; by 1884, 256; by 1885, 500. During the colony's first six years, only Catholics could purchase property, but afterwards anyone could.

Besides the practical considerations of making the place economically viable through the harvesting oranges, Dunne was also concerned with the spiritual welfare of his fellow Catholics, seeking a pastor for the colony from Bishop Moore, who had no priest to spare. Moore first wrote the New Orleans Jesuits for help in 1882, but they said that they had no personnel available. Despite not yet having a priest, Dunne built on San Antonio's town square a wooden church, St. Anthony's, which Moore dedicated on June 13, 1883.

Fathers Lynch and Peterman occasionally visited from Tampa when they could. Other priests vacationing from the North stayed for short intervals, but the Catholic colony lacked a resident pastor. At last, Bishop Moore obtained in May 1884 Polish-born Father Emilius Stenzel of the Archdiocese of New York, but he resigned as pastor on September 15, 1884, stating that the community was unable to financially support him. Next, Moore sent a successor, Irishman John F. O'Boyle, who was recruited as a seminarian by Bishop Verot and became pastor of St. Michael's, Fernandina, in 1878. A graduate of St. Bonaventure Seminary, O'Boyle arrived at St. Anthony's on December 8, 1884. By early 1885, the largest ethnic group in the parish, the Germans, was clashing with their Irish pastor over the language of his sermons (English) and over the quality of his pastoral care for them. The parish also contained Americans, Irish, and French. In April 1885 the German-speaking Catholics broke from the parish and founded a separate community at St. Joseph, two-and-one-half miles north of San Antonio. They built a church, Sacred Heart, which opened in October 1888.

With O'Boyle not working out and with the German splinter group in mind, Moore invited in February 1886 the Benedictines from St. Vincent Abbey, Latrobe, Pa, founded in 1846 from Germany, to establish a monastery and take over the pastoral care of Pasco County, where Dunne's colony was located. The monks were multilingual, fitting the pastoral needs of Catholics there.[30]

Even before any formal agreement was signed by the Benedictines and at the specific request of Bishop Moore, Archabbot Boniface Wimmer, OSB, sent out one of his best men to San Antonio, fifty-four year-old Father Gerard Pilz, OSB, a native of Bavaria, who arrived at St. Anthony Parish on May 12, 1886. His bilingual skills and his personality helped calm the storm of ethnic tensions. Everyone seemed happy with Father Pilz, except the previous pastor, who was disgruntled about his reassignment as the priest-in-charge of the missions of Volusia and Brevard Counties, based at St. James Parish, Orlando, with fellow-Irishman Joseph J. Creed as pastor (only in 1891 was O'Boyle made pastor again, in Titusville). For O'Boyle, Moore's reassignment of him was an embarrassing demotion and the Germans' complaints about him drove him from a pastorate that was rightfully his. However, Moore was not going to put up with a pastor who created pastoral discord. From 1886 to 1889 the stubborn and disgruntled O'Boyle made periodic visits to San Antonio, each time stirring up the flames of discontent among some Irish parishioners against Father Pilz. Finally abandoning his war of attrition, O'Boyle handed over to Pilz the keys of the church on June 7, 1889. Even O'Boyle had to admit, despite years of his undermining techniques, that Pilz was well-liked by the vast majority of his parishioners.

The priest-poor Moore, with Vatican approval, gave over the pastoral care of Catholics of what became Hernando, Citrus and Pasco Counties to the Benedictines in perpetuity on June 1, 1887. This arrangement later became a model for Moore's later agreement with the New Orleans Jesuits. In 1888 the Benedictines transferred the pastoral care of the area to the recently-founded Mary help of Christians Abbey, Belmont, N.C., 500 miles closer to the Florida West Coast Missions than St. Vincent's. Father Pilz transferred his obedience to Belmont Abbey, which had at the time only eleven priests.[31]

*7.6 Benedictine Florida Mission Territory.*
*Source: Author*

Father Leo Haid, OSB, Abbot of Belmont Abbey (as Mary Help of Christians Abbey would be known), arrived in San Antonio on February 7, 1889, in order to pick a site for a new monastery and college. Developer Edmund Dunne proffered thirty-six acres on the south shore of Lake Jovita. One June 4, 1889, "The Order of Saint Benedict of Florida" was incorporated for two specific purposes: 1) "the education of youth"; 2) "the establishment of churches and conducting services therein." Abbot Leo ordered the erection of a college/monastery building, a three-story wood-frame structure, which was completed in 1890 at the cost of $10,000 ($ 276,890 in 2017 dollars), a debt which took the monks twelve years to pay off. The only Benedictine in the area during construction was Father Roman Kirchner, Father Pilz's successor as pastor of St. Anthony's since November 1889.[32]

During the summer of 1890, Haid picked four priests (including Kirchner) and two OSB brothers as St. Leo's founders. Their leader was twenty-seven-year-old Charles Mohr, an Ohio native, who led the enterprise until his death in 1931. This was a considerable investment of personnel for Haid. Mohr's youth indicated the challenging nature of the assignment, which demanded energy and talent. In August 1890 Mohr traveled to each of the fourteen parishes in the Diocese of St. Augustine to canvas for potential students for their boys' college scheduled to open in the fall.[33]

St. Leo College, named for three Leo's, namely, Pope Leo the Great (440-60), Pope Leo XIII (1878-1903), and Abbot Leo Haid, OSB (1885-1924), was dedicated on September 24, 1890. Thirty-two student boarders matriculated the first school year. Tuition and board was $200 per year ($5,538 in 2017 dollars). St. Leo called itself a "Military College" from 1890 to 1903, not because it trained students for a military career, but because it sought to instill military values of discipline, order, and respect for authority. The school uniforms were Confederate grey with blue caps, a concession to both the Confederacy and the Federal Union. By December 1890, St. Leo Abbey had three priests and seven brothers; the College comprised fifteen boarders and five day students. Father Mohr, commenting on the financial fragility of the enterprise, wrote "we make a living and nothing more." By 1897, St. Leo's Abbey had three priests, two scholastics, and ten lay Brothers; the College had thirty-four students, thirty-one were boarders, while three were day students. Of the student population, six were Protestants. In 1891 St. Leo was incorporated as a town, the same year the monks initiated the choral recitation of the Divine Office (the monastic communal prayer recited seven times a day), a sign of their maturation as a monastic community. With the help of Bishop Moore, in May 1894 St. Leo's became an independent priory with Charles Mohr as Prior. As a result, the OSB's connected with St. Leo's transferred their vows to St. Leo Priory from Belmont Abbey, that is Fathers Mohr, Roman Kirchner, Benedict Roth, James Schabacher, and Louis Panoch, with Brothers Thomas, Anthony, Gerard, and Leander. All were either from Germany or sons of German immigrants. Although Moore did not live to see it, on November 27, 1902, St. Leo's became an independent abbey, with Mohr as its first Abbot.[34]

As with the Jesuits, Bishop Moore was very supportive of the Benedictines, but not so much by frequent visitation, as was the case with the Jesuits. Moore spent much more time in Tampa, undoubtedly because of the rapid urbanization taking place and the complexity of the pastoral challenges there. The fact is there were just more Catholics to serve in Tampa than Pasco County. It also may be said that Moore liked the Jesuits, appreciated their pastoral work, respected their active spirituality and their intellectuality.[35]

Besides the monastery and boys' school, the monks had the pastoral care of the Catholics in their territory. In 1902, just after Moore's death, the monks served the 441 Catholics in Pasco, Hernando and Citrus counties (a 2,000-square-mile territory), with one parish (St. Anthony's), four missions and twenty-two stations. Sacred Heart Church in St. Joseph was called a "parish" by its 100 German-speaking parishioners, but was not erected as such by the bishop and did not have a resident pastor. It was technically a mission served from St. Leo's Abbey. St. Mary's Mission was dedicated in 1890 at St. Thomas, but was served only once a month by a priest from St. Leo's. St. Thomas also had an African-American mission which was the site of sporadic evangelization from 1894 through the turn-of-the-century. Inverness had a small mission chapel which seated twelve, but was visited only several times a year. The twenty-two stations (residential gathering places with no chapel) had from two to fifteen Catholics each and were visited no more than four times a year.[36]

Abbot Mohr wrote of the pastoral difficulties in the Benedictine missionary territory in 1902: "The gross receipts from all the parishes and missions amount to $500 *per annum*. I have four men looking after these missions. But the poverty of our missions and our own lack of means are great hindrances to successful work in this otherwise very promising field." With the exception of the pastor of St. Anthony's, the four monks cited by Mohr "looking after the missions" were not full time in parochial or missionary work, unlike the Jesuit excurr. From the 1890s to World War I, San Antonio and its environs was decidedly German in culture and language, so much so that in 1896 the *San Antonio Herald* changed its name to the *Florida Staats Zeitung*. St. Leo's German-speaking monks were invaluable in preserving the faith of German Catholics in the area. Yet the monks also spoke English, which was the language of both the Abbey and the boys' school.[37]

## Diocesan Clergy

Unlike the Benedictines or the Jesuits, diocesan priests of this period generally lived alone, worked alone, and prayed alone, except at the Cathedral and St. Mary, Star of the Sea, Key West. Although Key West was the largest city in Florida throughout most of Moore's tenure, it was an isolated outpost, accessible only by boat. Until 1898, with the founding of Holy Name Parish in Miami, Tampa was the closest parish to Key West. In addition to ministering to their parish, diocesan priests also had the responsibility to tend outlying missions and stations. If that was not enough, they were most often isolated from one another. They were expected to go to the Sacrament of Confession once a month, but that expectation was often impossible to fulfill because of distance, lack of time, lack of money for transportation, sometimes heaping a burden of guilt upon the lack of priestly companionship. Beginning in 1861, Bishop Verot called all of his priests together for an annual clergy retreat and meeting, an opportunity to renew and review one's life and to fraternize with fellow priests. Bishop Moore continued this tradition during his episcopacy.

Diocesan priests did not stay in the rectory (if they had one); rather, they were expected to seek out Catholics in the outlying missions and stations. There they would say Mass, administer the Sacraments, instruct adults and children, comfort the sick and the dying. Upon demand, they were expected to respond immediately to requests to visit the sick and dying. Sometimes these visitations took days to complete due to their considerable distance from the parish. Being a parish priest was physically, psychologically, and spiritually demanding, all of which sometimes took its toll on an individual priest, creating problems not only for the priest himself, but for parishioners and the bishop.[38]

Sometimes Moore was called upon to adjudicate disputes between parishioners and their pastor. Irishman Father Patrick Lynch arrived in St. Louis Parish, Tampa, in February 1879, after his predecessor resigned on the grounds of his poor health and because parishioners could not support him or the parish. When Lynch arrived, aware of the parsimonious reputation of Tampa Catholics, he took strong measures to remedy the situation, so much so that a committee of parishioners complained forcefully to the bishop. The committee reported that Lynch rented the church pews at $3 per month, "the money being paid at the door" before entering. Lynch was also brought to court and fined for shooting at some men. "He has lost confidence of the people in general and has caused much talk," reported the complaint committee, adding a petition signed by forty parishioners calling for Lynch's removal. They added that seven families refused to attend church for three weeks now because of Lynch. Moore presented these charges in writing to Lynch and asked for an explanation. Lynch defended himself. Regarding shots he fired at men, a group of male serenaders came to the rectory and mocked him through song. Shots were fired at them, but not by him. Lynch knew who fired the shots, but refused to disclose this in court, thinking that people might think that if he told he broke the seal of Confession. So, he was charged and fined. Regarding his new pew rent policy (renting pews was a common practice at the time), when he arrived only a few families contributed any pew rent, and that amounted to only $12 per month. His new policy was designed to increase giving and increase the amount of givers. He did announce that if they could not afford a whole pew, they could rent a part of one, or see him for an exception due to cause. Nobody came to see him about the matter. Lynch said that some parishioners responded by banding together and refusing to come to church. Parishioners at that time and place were not docile. For Lynch the issue was not just about their refusing to support the parish, but their challenging his authority.

To be fair, Tampa was not easy on its people or its priests. Since it was established in 1860 until Lynch arrived, St. Louis had five pastors up to 1880. The first stayed eleven months, the second seven months, the third six months, the fourth a few months, and the fifth three-and-a-half years. In between pastors there were times, once over six years, where no priest resided in the parish. Pastors in Tampa were poor, unhealthy, lonely, and isolated, especially before the coming of the railroad. On the other hand, parishioners were not used to having a pastor stay very long. Nor were they used to understanding his English, since all were either French or French-Canadian, with the exception of one Italian. So Lynch came into a difficult set of circumstances. He also brought with him from Ireland a set of authoritarian assumptions which clashed with the democratic egalitarian spirit of those living on the Florida frontier. Lynch expressed himself in this way:

> I would never yield a hair's breadth because they are the most unreasonable, ungrateful, and in-considerate people I have ever met. They regard the priest as their servant and one who is bound to do just as they please.[39]

Moore, as the "court of appeals," resolved the brouhaha in mid-November by sending a letter to the St. Louis Committee. He wrote that Father Lynch most likely misinterpreted the nature of the rectory serenaders as insulting, on the other hand it is the parishioner's duty, not the Bishop's nor the pastor's, of supporting the parish financially; all are obliged to contribute to the parish according to their means, no matter how small the offering. Then Moore lectured to the parishioners:

> ... the Catholics of Tampa, I regret to say, have the reputation of having shown in the past very little consideration for their pastors. This is the impression that prevails with the priests of the diocese, and I am satisfied that there is not one of them who would go to Tampa willingly. I could not easily find another priest who would be likely to stay in Tampa so long and put [up] with so much as Father Lynch, and I venture to express the hope that the Catholics of the place will show that they are capable of appreciating his services. I am doing as much for Tampa as any other mission of the diocese and I am willing to do more still, but I have a right to look for better evidence of a desire to help themselves on the part of the congregation.

Moore wanted St. Louis' parishioners to pause and reflect on their actions heretofore. To this end, Moore was sending a Franciscan priest to give a parish mission (a Catholic form of revivalism and parishioner renewal) in the hopes that Tampa Catholics would avail themselves of the Sacraments and be reconciled. Moore concluded his letter by stating that the next time he visited Tampa he expected all to be well.

Apparently the bishop's written intervention had its desired effect of reconciliation, because nothing further is heard of parish turmoil in Tampa. Moreover, no doubt due to Moore's persuasion, Lynch stayed on as pastor for another two years. When he was transferred as Rector of the Cathedral in early 1883 (a sign of Moore's appreciation for Lynch's efforts in Tampa), the Sisters of the Holy Names called him "our kind and devoted pastor." Lynch died in 1913 after serving several other Florida parishes.[40]

But Moore did not always sympathize with the pastor when it came to disputes between priest and people. His primary concern was judging fairly and providing the best possible pastoral care for the people. Recall the Father O'Boyle incident at San Antonio of 1885-86, previously mentioned. In this case, Moore ended up sending O'Boyle to a newly created post as head of the Florida

Missions in Central Florida, depriving him of a pastorate and sending a German-speaking Benedictine priest to replace him. For Moore, it was not the protection or blind defense of O'Boyle that was foremost, but the good pastoral care of the people. In Moore's judgment O'Boyle failed in his role as pastor and peacemaker, so there were consequences for O'Boyle. In the end, with a shortage of diocesan priests to meet the pastoral needs of the region, Moore reached out to the Benedictines at Latrobe, Pennsylvania, to provide pastoral care to the three counties north of Tampa. Yet, Moore's disciplinary action with O'Boyle, as necessary as it may have been, did not leave Moore unmoved. He wrote to Rome in his 1895 *Ad limina* (a bishop's ten-year report to the Vatican about the state of his diocese): "I feel this case with great pain." Moore added in 1897 in a letter to Rome that O'Boyle shows much energy and has given edification in his present ministry. So in the end, the disciplinary action which O'Boyle first found distasteful, resulted in his exposure to a new opportunity as missionary to Volusia and Brevard Counties, one which may have more suited his personality and talents.[41]

But Moore's supervision of his priests was not limited to adjudicating problems between them and their people. It also involved financial matters. Although pastors had the canonical authority to manage the parish finances and keep the parish fiscally self-sustaining, some pastors lacked the skills or inclination to fulfill these tasks.

St. James Parish in Orlando was established by Moore in 1886 with Father Felix Swembergh as its founding pastor. Father O'Boyle resided there at the time while he attended the missions of Volusia and Brevard. In 1887 Swembergh was transferred to St. Louis, Tampa, where he died of yellow fever only four days after arriving. Father Joseph J. Creed, newly ordained, replaced Swembergh in Orlando that same year. At the time, the parish had no rectory, so Creed lived in a hotel, taking his board at the home of a Catholic family.

In May 1891 Creed took out a promissory note for $500 at 10 percent interest for three months, not a very astute financial deal for the parish. In August, Creed paid off the loan by check, but it bounced! Moore had to cover for Creed, the parish, and the diocese by paying off the loan himself in February 1892. The bishop of a diocese is the corporation sole, meaning he is responsible for and owns all church property and debts. When Moore initiated a new policy of an annual parish financial and pastoral report in 1878, right after taking over as bishop, printed on the bottom of the annual form  was the message that priests of the diocese are not allowed to contract debts in the name of the parish without episcopal permission. Also, any expenses regarding church repairs or improvements over $100 needed episcopal approval in writing. Moore was serious about knowing both the spiritual, as well as the financial health of each parish.

In late July of 1891, Moore received a letter from an architect builder, William Cotter, stating that Father Creed had amassed unpaid debts amounting to $1,109.95 for utilities, labor, overdue loans, and land, largely for a new mission church in Sanford. The writer was shocked at the priest's financial irresponsibility, adding "Father Creed was in the eyes of the public acting as your agent or representative." The next month Cotter sent the bishop an itemized bill for working on the church in Sanford to the amount of $1,598.95 ($44,270.49 in 2017 dollars).

By early September, Creed had skipped town for New York. One of his creditors wrote the bishop, with a letter from Creed enclosed. In it Creed declared that he has made no arrangements to pay off the note of the creditor, adding that "the bishop will assume charge of the church debt. He should have paid you before this, as he promised..." We can assume that Moore was not pleased to hear this news. With Creed decamping, Moore got Father James Widman, SJ, the *excurr.* stationed in Tampa, to visit Orlando once a month.

Moore bemoaned to Archbishop Gibbons in November of 1891 that he is threatened with yet another lawsuit due to Creed's profligate ways. Moore told Gibbons that Creed's debts and loans were taken out on in the name of the Church "without my knowledge or consent," therefore he refused to acknowledge or pay the debts. Finally, Moore conveyed to his Metropolitan that he had withdrawn faculties for Creed and ordered him to spend two years on retreat at a religious house. Creed never acknowledged his letter. Moore adds: "I learn that he is now in Boston acting as a real estate agent for the sale of lands in Florida."

Earlier on November 4, 1892, young Irishman Father Michael Fox, a graduate from Propaganda's Seminary in Rome who arrived in the diocese exactly a year earlier, disembarked at Orlando as the new pastor of St. James, the unenviable successor of Creed. As always, Moore was concerned with the spiritual welfare of Catholics in the area after the mess created by Creed. Fox reports to the bishop in February 1893 that St. James and its mission in Sanford has a surplus of $25.93, after including income and expenditures from November 1892 until February 1893. Fox adds that he has not paid himself for four months. It was a rough start for the young priest.

This episcopal reaction to Creed's behavior was the strongest of any disciplinary actions against any of his priests. Creed had jeopardized the good name of the bishop and the diocese, creating an embarrassing public financial mess. This was a very serious offense that demanded a very serious response. Creed actually helped the situation by skipping town. Diocesan records do not indicate if Moore ever won the lawsuits resulting from Creed's actions or whether Moore ever paid the debts that Creed generated. Some diocesan priests, including Anthony Kilcoyne, pastor of St. Michael's, Fernandina, expressed sympathy with Moore and were embarrassed by Creed.[42]

One problem that Moore had with one of his priests was of the bishop's own making. Joseph Leon Hugon was Bishop Verot's nephew. On his way back from Rome after attending Vatican Council I, Verot spent several weeks in late July and early August 1870 in Le Puy, his hometown, made a retreat under the Jesuits, recruited a young Jesuit, Stephen Langlade, for Florida, and ordained his nephew, Joseph Hugon, who declared to his uncle that he wished to serve in the missions of the newly created Diocese of St. Augustine. Hugon, made pastor of Mater Dolorosa Church in Tallahassee in 1876, not only had an affinity for Verot as the first Bishop of St. Augustine, but also as his nephew. Verot had visited Tallahassee earlier in 1869, "repairing the house belonging to the Church and putting up a little chapel." The parish had its first resident pastor in 1871. When the Sisters of the Holy Names arrived in 1872, the church was decrepit due to slip-shod construction and Mass was being said in the convent chapel. In 1873 the Sisters left Tallahassee, saying they lacked the financial means to sustain themselves. By

1880, the parish had one mission (Ascension in Lake City) and five stations attached. When Hugon arrived as pastor four years earlier, he quickly discovered that the Catholic community of Tallahassee was small and poor. So much so, that they were unable to pay the pastor's salary of $200 per year ($4,675.80 in 2017 dollars). Father Dufau, Administrator of the diocese after Verot's death in June of 1876, pledged Hugon that the diocese would pay his annual salary. When Moore took over the diocese, he agreed to continue this arrangement, but ended it in 1890, likely because the bishop felt that the parish had matured enough to pay their pastor's salary. Also, Moore, up to his neck with bills for the Cathedral repair, had little money to spare.[43]

By the 1890s, Hugon's displeasure with the "new" Irish bishop was mounting. After Moore became bishop in 1877, he initiated better sacramental record-keeping and more financial accountability for pastors, through the annual *Notitiae*, along with a policy stating that nobody could contract debts in the name of the church, either for building, improvements, or repairs, for over $100 without first getting the bishop's express permission.[44] Some of the French priests recruited by Verot were unaccustomed to these new episcopal initiatives and chaffed under them. As a form of passive aggression, initially some of the French priests dragged their feet in submitting their annual *Notitiae* or submitted incomplete data on it. It was also clear that Moore was no longer recruiting French priests for the diocese as Verot had but Irish priests. Finally, there was the matter of the cessation of Hugon's annual salary in 1890.

In 1895 Hugon made a report to the bishop about the state of his parish in Tallahassee. In it he asks for part of the $1,000 from the sale of the old church in 1880 which the bishop was holding toward the building of a new church, so that the French pastor might apply some of that sum for the repair the old church building's roof. Hugon stated that the bishop told him that he had no money for any of the parishes or missions presently. So tight was the financial condition of the diocese, the bishop reported to Hugon that he was obliged to borrow money to travel to Rome for his *Ad limina* of 1895. In his letter Hugon stated that the convent which contained the chapel used by the parish and the quarters where he lives are both "unsafe and hardly habitable." Father Kenny, the Vicar General, visited Hugon, who was ill at the time, on behalf of the bishop and in response to the pastor's letter. Kenny concluded that the pastor was no longer well enough to visit the various missions and stations attached to the parish and consequently proffered him retirement with a $200 annual pension. Hugon refused the offer, since "as the diocese has no money and is in debt, I could not consider such a proposition as a serious one." In other words, Hugon does not trust the bishop to fulfill his pension promise, given his track record of not honoring the previous promise of the annual salary, which ceased in 1890. When Moore returned from Europe, Hugon wrote him again for money for the convent repairs, claiming that the bishop never answered his previous letter, but sent Kenny instead.[45]

Frustrated and admittedly discouraged, Hugon decided to make matters public in an "Open Letter" to the parish's building committee, dated February 7, 1897, with a copy sent to the bishop. In it he rehearses all that has previously transpired. In addition, he states that as of January 1, 1897, the diocese owes him $746.45 in back salary. Hugon writes that, although the bishop claims he has no money, the diocese sold the Quincy property (a mission of Mater Dolorosa's) for over $5,000 in early 1896. Hugon maintains that the bishop promised him verbally that he would give $4,000 toward the construction of a new church, but adds that promise was not put in writing. Hugon proclaims his commitment to the new church project, pledging personally $1 for every $10 parishioners raise, up to $1,000, as long as the bishop pledges $2,500 in cash to the new construction. Also, the pastor in Tallahassee will give back the salary of $746.45 to the project, as soon the bishop pays it to him. Finally, he proposes that he will build a new parsonage at his own expense. Apparently, Hugon was not without personal resources, including sixty-one acres of property worth $40 to $50 an acre.[46]

Undoubtedly with Hugon's encouragement, the Church Building Association of Tallahassee wrote a typed letter to Moore three days after Hugon's. In it they comment positively on their pastor's "Open Letter." "Such noble generosity touched the hearts of his little flock here deeply, for we all felt and appreciated the contents of his communication... What more could a pastor do for his people?" It is clear that Hugon had the full support of the building committee when he decided to battle the bishop indirectly through that body.[47]

Increasing the leverage on the bishop, Hugon wrote a second "Open Letter" to the Church Building Association on March 11, this time not forwarding a copy to Moore. The pastor states that the bishop has rejected Hugon's financial plan for the new church construction, quoting from the bishop's letter dated February 17 sent to him: "The conditions expressed by Father Hugon cannot be accepted." Frustrated by the bishop's disapproval of his entire financial plan, Hugon declares; "Therefore, I am no more bound to fulfill any of them. You now understand who must be blamed for the present condition in which we are." Here Hugon plays the people against their bishop, whom he quotes as writing to him in the February 17 letter: "I wish your Association every success in the efforts you intend to make to collect money for the building of a church in Tallahassee." Subtly, Moore throws the responsibility for building the new church back into the lap of the pastor and parishioners, feeling that the Mater Dolorosa congregation is capable of handling the task, which he feels is theirs, not his. Hugon rehearses again the fact that the bishop sold the old church and its lot for $1,000 in 1880, while keeping the money in trust for when the parish was ready to build a new building. Hugon quotes the bishop from a letter written back on December 17, 1885: "Of course, the $1,000 will be refunded whenever you are ready to begin building at Tallahassee." The congregation is ready to build now, but the bishop is offering nothing, not even the $1,000 held in trust, says Hugon. "If we can't trust our Bishop to fulfill his just duties, then who can we trust"? Here Hugon assaults the bishop's integrity and reliability, an accusation which must have struck to the core of Moore, since he perceived himself as a man a duty and responsibility. We have no record of his feelings about this assault on his person now made a public matter.[48]

Most certainly with the connivance of the pastor, two days later the Building Association wrote Moore, enclosing Hugon's letter to them dated March 11. As a result, their treasurer resigned, but a replacement was elected. The Association recently opened an account at the 1st National Bank of Tallahassee. They ask the bishop for the $1,000 he has held in trust since the sale of the old church in 1880 and for Hugon's back salary of $746.45 since 1890, which the pastor pledges to give this time for the construction of a parsonage. As soon as they receive this money from the bishop, "We will at once adopt plans and begin to build." We have no record of Moore's response to these parishioner demands. We can surmise that he was not pleased. The Building Association writes a second letter to Moore on April 1, asking him to come to Tallahassee and investigate matters for himself. The priest's living quarters in the old convent is "unfit to live in." They add that, not having received any reply from the bishop for two years, Father Hugon feels despondent and neglected. "If you will not help us, then [we will] lay our case before the Cardinal [Gibbons in Baltimore]. We ask you again for the $1,000 you hold in trust for us." They conclude: "It has been a long time since you visited Tallahassee — many need the Sacrament of Confirmation." The Building Association demands that the bishop reply to them by letter in two days, otherwise they will be forced to take their case to the Cardinal in Baltimore.[49]

The situation quickly moved from character assassination to the threat of appealing their case to a higher authority, namely the Cardinal. What did Moore do? We don't know precisely because we have no extant record of his response. We also have no further record from Hugon or the Building Association. We can surmise that the dispute was resolved. But most likely, Moore did not give the pas-tor the full $1,000 or the $746.45 in back salary, largely because he did not have on hand that kind of money and whatever he may have had on hand was going to finish up the work on the Cathedral.

This episode points out a clash of two models: the former French Missionary Model of Verot and Hugon and the new Modern Model introduced by Moore. The Missionary Model looked to the bishop to supply all the funds for most parishes and missions, including the priests' salaries. Moore's new Modern Model expected the parishes to be self-supporting, not dependent on the bishop for their upkeep (except in rare cases). Meanwhile, the diocese had its own projects that needed funding, such as rebuilding the Cathedral. Moore raised his own money for that elsewhere, unlike Florida bishops of the mid-twentieth century who would raise money for diocesan projects by taxing and assessing parishes. Ironically, Moore ended up doing to the pastor of Mater Dolorosa what was done to him earlier as pastor of St. Patrick's in Charleston. Recall that Bishop Lynch kept the money Father Moore had collected for his proposed parochial school (over $4,000); Moore ended keeping the money (or part of it) from the sale of the old church and lot in Tallahassee. In addition, as was the case with Moore's constant begging up North, Moore's episcopacy mirrored Lynch's. What this episode also reveals is how a pastor can use his parishioners as a tool to pressure the bishop toward a desired end. It is clear that Hugon was coaching the Building Association members. On the other hand, it is also clear that parishioners were able to stand up to their bishop by collective action. How successful pastor and parishioners in Tallahassee were in this case is not recorded, but what is a fact is that Moore did not vindictively remove Hugon from his post because of his tactics, his attacks on the bishop's character, or his cry for justice, but he remained on in Tallahassee until after Moore's death. Perhaps Moore realized that his own actions (or inactions) perpetrated the crisis.[50]

Which brings us to another important point, very few of Moore's relationships with his priests were contentious, rather they might be best characterized as fatherly and brotherly, even though his personality was reserved, and even taciturn (his priests nicknamed him "Silent John"). Recall how much the Tampa Jesuits appreciated Moore's solicitude for them, as well as his pastoral concern for Catholics in Tampa and Ybor City. The Golden Jubilee (fifty years since ordination) of Father de Carriere, SJ, was on October 4, 1894. On that occasion, Bishop Moore celebrated a 9 a.m. Mass at St. Louis Church with three of his diocesan priests, two Benedictines, and three Jesuits in attendance. Moore delivered what one Sister of the Holy Names characterized as a "touching sermon" on the historical vicissitudes of the Church in Florida. On that occasion he also paid high tribute to the Tampa Jesuits and recalled the circumstances of Father de Carriere's coming to Florida.[51]

Moore also supported many of his priests financially, but quietly. He sent the Father Felix Ghione $410 and Father Clavreul $90 in September of 1877, not long after he became bishop. Later, in 1884 Moore gave Father Langlade $159 in Mass intentions for the year; he also gave to the parish, St. Ambrose, Moccasin Branch, $300. In the Spring of 1891 Moore sent Father Hugon in Tallahassee $32 for Mass Intentions. He probably did much more, but these are not recorded.

Father Ghione was an Italian, recruited by Bishop Verot, and was pastor in Key West. In early 1879 he sent a letter while he was in Italy stating that he would retire if Moore would give him an annual pension of $200. Moore sent him $100 in response, but not the pension. By 1880, Ghione returned to Key West, having scotched his retirement plans. In late December 1897, Ghione decided to retire again, citing poor health. Once again he asked for $200 as his annual pension, which he said was a condition for his retirement. The bishop never agreed to the $200 a year pension; meanwhile, Moore assigned the Jesuits take over the parish in 1898. Retirement and a pension were not seen at the time as the norm by either priests or bishops.[52]

Moore's relationship with his priests, especially financially, was quite different than today. In the twenty-first century bishops expect parishes and pastors to support them and their diocesan bureaucracy through an annual tax or assessment or both. Although Moore moved Florida Catholicism from being largely missionary (financially dependent) to being modern (primarily self-sustaining), but some pastors continued to depend on his financial help, since they were too poor to help themselves. Chapter 9 describes how Moore did this.

Another category of diocesan priests that Moore had jurisdiction over, although loosely so, were those priests who visited Florida from other parts of the country, usually during the winter months, usually staying for several weeks, sometimes with friends or family. A few came for health reasons. Most often they would offer their services to the local pastor, sometimes in exchange for food and lodging at the rectory. With no central administration and no formal process permitting these priests to function, matters like this were handled on the local level by the pastor, who most often informed the bishop of the presence of an extern priest helper. Although their help was unpredictable regarding when they would arrive and for how long they would stay, they were a welcome supplement to the local parish. With extern help, the pastor was able to visit his attached missions and stations more easily, knowing that the Sacraments would be distributed by the visiting priest who was at the parish's home base. Parallel to the development of the railroads and resort hotels for the rich, this phenomenon of extern priests supplementing the pastoral care during the winter gradually increased during Moore's tenure.[53]

A final topic regarding the clergy of Florida is a unique one — the only native priestly vocation during Moore's tenure, namely Edward A. Pace. Pace was born on July 3, 1861, in Starke, Florida, the oldest of eight children. He spent his first four years in Nova Scotia with his mother and maternal grandmother, a wartime exile. With the War's end, he and his mother returned to Starke, where he attended elementary school, then high school in Jacksonville, until 1874, when he was sent as a seminarian to St.

7.7 *Father Edward Pace, c. 1886* Source: *ADSA*

Charles College, Ellicott Mills, Maryland, where he graduated with highest honors in 1880. Moore then assigned the promising student to North American College, Rome, where he was ordained in 1885 and received a Doctorate in Sacred Theology in 1886. Upon his return to Florida, Pace was assigned as rector of the Cathedral in late October 1886. Moore was relieved to have such a bright, able priest to assist him now, especially with diocesan administration, and particularly when Moore had to be gone from St. Augustine on parish visitation or on begging trips up North. In a diocese whose clergy lacked not only numbers but talent as well, Moore had great confidence in Pace and soon began treating him as his trustworthy administrative assistant. In April 1887, Moore delegated Pace to take over the responsibilities as Vicar General. "In the future whenever I am about, you have all my faculties and you can dispense as you think well to do," he wrote. Yet sadly for Moore, Pace was not destined to remain in his diocese for long. In early 1888, Bishop John Keane, the first Rector of the newly established Catholic University of America in Washington, DC, invited Pace to join the founding faculty of that new national Catholic university. After consultation with Moore, Pace accepted the new academic appointment in early 1888. This was a blow to Moore's plans, as he wrote "I am willing to let him go; I have come to believe that he will do better at teaching than he is likely to do on the missions [of Florida]." For Moore, the greater good of the Church and the best use of Pace's academic talents demanded that he release the young priest from his missionary diocese to teach at the Catholic University. Ironically, the only native vocation during Moore's tenure only spent two years in his home state. He went on to a long distinguished academic career, studying psychology at the Universities of Louvain and Paris, eventually getting a doctorate in Psychology in 1891 from the University of Leipzig. He served in various capacities at the Catholic University in Washington, until his death at age seventy-seven on April 26, 1938. To his disappointment, Moore lost his potential protégé to the greater needs of the Church in America. But, Moore admitted that the Florida frontier was no place for a bookish priest, but one who was more a missionary. Although Keane promised to replace Pace with another priest he would send, he never did.[54]

## CHAPTER EIGHT

# Women Religious

## The Sisters and the Academy

After the clergy, religious women were an essential group of cooperators with Moore's task of pastoral care. These special groups of women focused their efforts primarily on the education of youth throughout the diocese, a ministry that engaged them also with parents in the local community where they served. Although not the case in more urban dioceses where free parochial schools prevailed, such as in Philadelphia and Baltimore, Florida possessed no Catholic parochial education throughout most of the nineteenth century but instead had the academy. This institution, run and owned by particular women's religious order, charged tuition to both boarders and day students, although the boarders were a very small percentage of the entire student body. The Sisters lived in a convent within the walls of the academy and earned income from its tuition and extracurricular classes. Although the Benedictine monks had one school for boys and the Jesuits eventually another, most of Catholic education of the period was administered by women religious, primarily for girls, with some younger boys in separate classes. These academies also attracted non-Catholic students, since it was believed the education there was superior to the public schools, especially for girls, which in many cases it was. As a result, Sisters were often able to contact parents who would not otherwise be reached by the priests. They also ran free Catholic schools for Spanish, Cuban, Italian, and African-American children in Ybor City and Key West, and for African-Americans elsewhere, too. Not only was the Catholic school a place where the basics in education, Tridentine Catholicism, discipline and moral values were passed on, but the Sisters also engaged in a kind of "soft evangelization" in their work with various ethnic groups, as well as with their Protestant charges. For example, at the Sisters of the Holy Names Academy in Tampa, the Protestant enrollment was substantial: 58.6 percent in the 1888-89 school year; 53 percent in the 1896-97 school year; 48 percent in the 1900-01 school year. That enrollment of Protestants only begins to fall off after World War I, not only in Tampa, but in the other academies in Florida cities and towns with the improvement of public schools.[1]

## Benedictines

Father Gerard Pilz, OSB, the first Benedictine pastor of St. Anthony Parish, San Antonio, Fla., reached there on May 12, 1886. Soon after arriving, he realized the need for Sisters to take over two parish schools already in operation, started by the initiative of the laity. With the permission of Bishop Moore, Pilz invited the Benedictine Sisters of Allegheny, PA, (near St. Vincent's Archabbey) to run the parish schools at San Antonio and St. Joseph. Four Benedictine Sisters arrived in San Antonio on February 25, 1889, and their Abbess required them to immediately sever all connections with the community in Allegheny. The Sisters opened the independent Holy Name Priory on March 1 of that same year. But sadly, both Pilz and the newly-arrived Sisters soon were embroiled in controversy.[2]

On August 10, 1889, Father Pilz was observed driving a buggy to nearby Dade City, accompanied only by a Benedictine Sister postulant. A county commissioner accused Pilz of "sinning in a buggy by the roadside." Rumors spread like wild fire, fueled by such prominent citizens, as Judge Edmund Dunne, founder of the Catholic colony. Dunne may have found it convenient to cast aspersions on

Pilz's character since the priest had publicly challenged the judge's authority earlier. Then, the mere suggestion of sexual impropriety was enough to destroy a priest's reputation and remove him from office. Unfortunately, Pilz was not an innocent victim of hearsay. He admittedly engaged in inappropriate sexual advances with the postulant on a public road, witnessed by several citizens. He was about to be brought before a Grand Jury, when Bishop Moore intervened behind the scenes. The hitherto popular pastor was spirited away by his Abbot to teach at St. Mary's College in Belmont, N.C. He quietly departed San Antonio on November 9, 1889, leaving the Sisters' reputation under a cloud. Since the Benedictine monks had not as yet arrived to establish their new foundation, the embarrassing incident had time to blow over before they did.[3]

St. Anthony Catholic School began in the fall of 1883 with fourteen children taught in Mrs. Cecilia Morse's kitchen. The school moved into the church in April 1884, and a small frame building was constructed as a school house that fall. When the Sisters arrived, they took over the administration of both the San Antonio and St. Thomas Catholic schools on September 1, 1889. Just a month before, at the request of the pastor, St. Anthony Catholic School became San Antonio Public School #14, where the two Sisters who taught there were supported by the tax payers of Pasco County. In 1892 the county erected a two story frame building for use by the school and the town (as a meeting hall). In 1898 Sacred Heart Parish School in St. Thomas also became a public Catholic school, with the Sisters as administrators and teachers. Tax money was used for the Catholic schools' up-keep, with no qualms about the First Amendment raised, until 1918, when pressure from the anti-Catholic administration of Gov. Sidney Catts pressured Pasco County officials to terminate the arrangement.[4]

In San Antonio the Sisters established their own school, Holy Name Academy, "a select school for young ladies, on March 11, 1889, only eleven days after the foundation of their own independent Priory. Enrollments there peaked to forty in 1896. They continued teaching in both the Catholic/Public Schools and in their own Academy. In the 1890s an average of sixty-six students per year attended St. Anthony School, with a high of 103 in 1897-98, to a low of forty-six in 1890-91.[5]

In Quincy, twenty-one miles northwest of Tallahassee, an entrepreneur named Storm recruited workers from New York to establish a company town to cultivate tobacco and provide laborers to manufacture cigars there. Keeping an eye on the development there and wanting to get ahead of it, Bishop Moore sought assistance from Father Leo Haid, OSB, abbot of Mary Help Abbey, N.C., in December 1891 to supply a German-speaking priest for Quincy. Moore also had in mind that the Benedictine Sisters at San Antonio might establish a day school and academy there also. Moore pestered Haid again a month later. The abbot sent Father Patrick Dolan first, then in 1893 a faculty member from St. Leo's, Father Leo Panoch. The bishop had high expectations about the future of the Quincy mission (a church was built there in 1892), writing to Haid in early February 6, 1892, that Quincy would be "'the center of which [the tobacco cultivation and cigar manufacturing] will be in Quincy, which is destined to become the most important in Florida — to surpass even that of oranges. I think we may expect great developments there in the near future.'" As he previously did in Pasco County, Moore handed over the pastoral care of Quincy "'permanently to the Benedictine Fathers.'"[6]

The Benedictine Sisters at San Antonio assented to Moore's request, sending a delegation to Quincy in August 1892, headed by their Prioress, Mother Dolorosa Scanlan. Soon the five Sisters stationed there opened St. Mary's Academy, whose enrollment reached a high of 30 in 1896. Even through the nuns were initially well received, neither the bishop nor the Sisters had a crystal ball to foresee Quincy's future. On June 27, 1896, after four years of struggle, the Sisters abandoned Quincy and returned to San Antonio. Historian of early modern Florida Catholicism, Father Benedict Ross, OSB, explained that the departure was "owing to the local bigotry and for want of patronage, this Academy is now abandoned.'[7]

The Citrus Freeze of 1894-95, which seriously impacted Florida's citrus and other agricultural interests, had a deleterious effect on the OSB Sisters. Since the parents of the children they taught at their Academy in San Antonio were primarily farmers, they now lacked cash to pay for tuition, which was the main source of the Sisters' livelihood. The financial situation of the Sisters was still atrocious in the fall of 1897, due to the continuing negative economic impact of the Freeze of 1894-5. Moore wrote Mother Katharine Drexel, SBS, in Philadelphia thanking her for the hospitality she offered to two traveling OSB Sisters and explaining: "They are real objects of charity... [their convent and schools] are in the woods of Pasco County. They depend for their support on the farmers around, most of who were nearly ruined by the freeze of three years ago." He added that the Sisters now depend on the salaries of their numbers who teach in the two county public schools, since their Academy presently brings them little income.[8]

But the effects of natural disasters and financial distress were not the only problems the Sisters faced. In the of 1898 warfare was not limited to that between Spain and the U.S. By that summer, tension which was developing for sometime among the members of the Priory finally manifested itself with explosive force, threatening to break up their foundation in Pasco County. Earlier in 1895 their Prioress, Mother Dolorosa Scanlan, died at the age of forty-two. Sister Boniface Feldmann was elected to succeed her. Leadership switched from Irish to German, consequently ethnic pressures between the Irish/Irish American and German community members increased.

By 1898, the community, comprised sixteen members, was at the verge of imploding. Seeing a way out, Mother Feldmann wrote to Bishop Moore on August 4, 1898: "It seems impossible for me to save my soul where there is no peace and harmony, and the other Sisters who have been persecuted so terrible in the community feel the same as I do." Moore had the authority as bishop to adjudicate such disputes. Moore, who was begging in Buffalo, sent a letter to the Prioress immediately and told her to do nothing until he returns. Mother Feldmann named four German-speaking Sisters who wished to go with her to work in Alabama. Typical of his leadership style, Moore first consulted with Prior Charles Mohr, OSB, at St. Leo's. Father Charles states he is surprised by Mother Boniface's letters and complaints. He points out that when the new Priory is founded, the Mother house at Allegany continued to send money to help with the new foundation, but this was considered a loan to be paid back over time. Because of this, it would be difficult if the German Sisters go. But then Mohr tells Moore: "Let the Germans go!' He continues: "As you have paid for almost everything in San Antonio's Convent, you will have the right to say what help said convent may send to Alabama. I would let them go absolutely, that is — never to return."

Abbot Benedict Menges of St. Bernard's Abbey, Cullman, AL, needed some German-speaking Sisters to take over an elementary school there and wrote Bishop Moore for his permission for the OSB Sisters to come. The bishop responded in the affirmative: "'I will allow them to go in the hope that peace will be restored to the community of San Antonio. The spirit of nationalism has got into the community, and created discord and unhappiness, and I see no other way of exorcising [sic] that evil spirit but by the separation. It will surprise me if you ever have any reason to complain of the Sisters whom I send you.'" The five sisters departed for Alabama on September 12, 1898, one of whom was Mother Boniface Feldmann, but the San Antonio Nuns Priory remained intact.[9]

## Holy Names

Five Sisters of the Holy Names of Jesus and Mary of Canada arrived at Key West on October 24, 1868. They came at the invitation of the pastor of St. Mary Star of the Sea, Father John B. Allard, OMI, who was associated with the founding of the congregation in Quebec City in 1843 by Marie-Rose Doroucher (1811-1849). This religious community had as its purpose to serve the Church through Catholic education of poor youth, through the establishment of private girls' academies to support the work with the poor. Key West, and later Tampa, would prove fertile fields for their purposes. Bishop Augustin Verot sought the Sisters because he was concerned about education in Key West in the broad sense or, as he put it, with the "regeneration of the moral and religious life of the Island [sic.]." Upon leaving Montreal, one of the Sisters wrote: "Voluntary exiles, we go into a distant isle to make God known, to extend His Kingdom and do His Holy Will." One of the Sisters expressed shock at her first impressions of Key West, the largest city in Florida at the time: "The town, built in the northwest section, is noteworthy more for the number of its inhabitants than for the progressive development that characterizes the other growing cities of the Union. One can see no important public buildings, and the private residences, rarely more than one story in height, are all built of wood. The channel encircles the island in such a fashion that one gets a pastoral view of the whole, even before landing."[10]

The Sisters began their work by establishing a temporary academy in an abandoned Union barracks owned by Key West Catholic and former Secretary to the Confederate Navy, Stephen Mallory, who let the Sisters use the property for free and eventually deeded it out-right to Bishop Verot, who then handed over the deed to the Sisters. Their arrival was well-timed, since Key West was beginning a population spurt. Beginning in 1868, significant numbers of Cubans immigrated for both political and economic reasons ninety miles by sea to Key West, the result of Cuban's Ten Years' War (1868-78) with colonial Spain.[11]

By 1875, estimates were that 2,000 Cubans resided in Key West. All Cubans were Catholic, but most were not practicing their Faith, as judged by a lack of Mass attendance and reception of the Sacraments. In Cuba Catholicism was colonial, that is, virtually all priests were from Spain. The Spanish colonial government and religious orders financially propped up the Church there. Bishop Moore traveled to Havana in 1886, but penned Cardinal Gibbons that he was unfavorably impressed with the state of Catholic life there. He wrote that only about 2.5 percent of Catholics of the city practiced their faith, with many engaged in *Santeria*, a syncretism of Catholicism and religious practices from Africa. He also thought that the clergy were in a poor state of moral decay. Yet at the same time, Cubans were proud to be called Catholic, deeming it an insult if accused of being unfaithful.[12] Cubans in Key West brought their culture with them, including their ecclesiastical milieu.

Spaniard Vincente Martínez Ybor immigrated to Cuba, where he invested in the modernization of the cigar industry in Havana. When the Ten Years' War started in 1868, Ybor sided with the separatists. To escape arrest by the Spanish colonial authorities, he fled Cuba for Key West in 1869 and established a cigar factory there. By 1875 fifteen cigar factories operated in Key West, attracting even more Cuban emigration to the island from Cuba. However, lack of transportation and a series of devastating cigar-worker strikes at a time when ninety-one cigar factories operated on the island, forced Ybor to relocate again in the mid-1880s, this time to Tampa. Later in 1892, due to inflation and cigar labor strikes, 2,000 Key West Cubans moved to Ybor City. Key West's population in 1898 of about 18,000 was comprised of 44 percent Cuban, 22 percent African-American, and 34 percent Caucasian-American (who were from many different States of the Union). When the Jesuits took over Mary, Star of the Sea Parish in 1898, one wrote: "The practice of religion among the Cuban population, at least of the men, is not encouraging, but the women as a rule are better disposed." It should be noted that the same Jesuit commentator was not sanguine about the American Catholic population on the island either: "Even the American portion of the parish is largely made up of lukewarm Catholics. A great deal of work lies before us."[13]

The various backgrounds of Catholics in Key West presented the priests and Sisters there a serious pastoral challenge. The Sisters responded by offering Catholic education to the young people on the island. As previously mentioned, as soon as they arrived in 1868, they opened an academy in the abandoned Union barracks. In 1873, they opened a free school for Cuban girls, Our Lady of Mercy School. The Sisters had great expectations for the salubrious effect this school would have on both Cuban children and parents. For the Sisters, this school was an investment in the future. As a parish priest wrote the year after it opened: "The present generation is irrevocably lost to the faith and all our efforts towards saving the rising generation should receive a stronger impulse than ever — free schools for Cuban boys and girls should no doubt go far to achieve this end." But Our Lady of Mercy School was closed in 1878 because of declining enrollments and rising economic pressures. The Sisters welcomed any Cuban girls who may wish to enroll in their Academy, treating them with the "Same care and solicitude" as the American girls. This notion of "integrating" the Cubans with the Americans was a rather progressive view, given the contemporary racial and ethnic attitudes of segregation, but it was also economically pragmatic. How many Cuban girls entered the Academy is difficult to determine. Unfortunately, the economic well-being of the Sisters and their Academy trumped the pastoral needs of the Cuban children, as was noted by the local pastor.[14]

*8.1 Holy Names Academy, Key West. Source: ASNJM*

The economic pressures on the Sisters were the result of a $7,794.54 ($182,228.52 in 2017 dollars) outstanding debt on their newly constructed convent/academy, which was built in 1875 at a cost of $24,678.11 ($559,640.94 in 2017 dollars). It was a magnificent three story wood frame building with a mansard roof and a central rotunda. In 1887 the sisters opened St. Joseph's Parish School and St. Francis Xavier School for African-Americans (which remained opened until 1962). Both schools were tuition free. That year the Sisters taught forty pupils in the parish school, 125 in their black school, and a total of 253 in the Academy, eight of whom were boarders.[15]

In 1881 the Sisters had in mind to expand their ministry in Florida. They had already tried this earlier in 1872. Two Sisters arrived in Tallahassee in August of that year and opened a parish school, but hard economic times exacerbated by the failure of the cotton crop forced the Sisters to abandon Tallahassee in the Spring of 1874. As early as 1878, Father A. F. Bernier, a French Canadian and pastor of St. Louis from 1875 to 1879, asked the Sisters to open a school in Tampa. Bernier's successor, Patrick J. Lynch, went so far as to renovate a house in 1880 for the Sisters to reside. But the Mother General in Montreal replied that she could spare no Sisters for the enterprise. She reconsidered in 1881. On July 17 Sisters Augustine and Maurice left Key West for Tampa by boat with some food, a satchel of clothes, and $5.10 donated to them from the black students. Things started off bad and got worse. When the Sisters arrived in Tampa at 2 a.m. July 18, the pastor was not there to greet them. Uninformed as to when the Sisters might be arriving, Father Lynch was out of town visiting Catholics at various missions and stations. From the docks, a fellow passenger from the boat led the two Sisters to the home of J. John Jackson. Kate Jackson, his daughter, was a boarder at the Sisters' Academy in Key West from 1869 to 1873. The Jackson family was a great promoter of the Sisters coming to Tampa. The next day, Kate accompanied Sister Maurice to the Sisters' future home. The place was a broken down shack, a sight which brought Sister Maurice to tears. It seems that Father Lynch, unsure if the Sisters would ever come to Tampa, diverted the money collected to renovate the Sisters' future home to construct at the back of St. Louis Church sleeping quarters and an office for him, since heretofore he had neither. On July 20, both Sisters resigned to accept the shack as is and began cleaning the dilapidated place. An Irish-born U.S. soldier walked by and asked the religious women why they were working so feverishly. The Sisters said: "Because we are poor." The soldier gave the Sisters all he had on him, $2.50, and then he invited them to come to his military post to beg among the soldiers. On July 21 they did, collecting $34.50 for their efforts ($884.57 in 2017 dollars). Mrs. Jackson and some other women brought the Sisters fruit, vegetables, soup, and milk daily. Although three prominent male parishioners, Messrs. Ghira, Jackson, and Atkins, miffed at their pastor, refused to donate to a cause they had already subscribed to earlier (the Sisters' house), they did agree to loan the Sisters enough money for needed repairs. With a confidence that often inhabits religious women, the Sisters felt that Bishop Moore would eventually pay off the loan for them, which he did.

The pastor remained out of town for five weeks, an abnormally long time for a missionary journey. The Sisters were unaware that they had stepped into a hornet's nest, arriving at a time when St. Louis Parish was in complete turmoil, with parishioners at odds with Lynch, as we discussed in Chapter 7. Bishop Moore had to intervene. Lynch intended originally to abandon the parish for good, but was persuaded otherwise by his bishop. The Irish pastor finally returned to Tampa on August 28. The Sisters' presence may have played a conciliatory role in healing the divisions between the pastor and his people.

The Sisters' school opened Sept. 2, 1881, with thirty-five pupils, but no textbooks, in a former blacksmith/gunsmith shop adjacent to the Sisters' house on the corner of Zack and Franklin Streets, the same block that the church was on. Two other Religious came from Key West, making a community of four. By of the end of the school year, they had seventy pupils. Enrollments increased from there. It was a free parish school, but soon the Sisters began to take in student boarders to supplement their income and to aid families living too far for a daily commute.

The Sisters found Tampa to be an educational wasteland. In 1880 Hillsborough County had forty-nine schools, but not all were in operation. Each school had one room and one teacher, with less than thirty pupils per school. County schools were in session for only three months. Tampa had one private school, a high school.

The Sisters introduced educational innovations to Tampa. Their school year ran for ten months. Their curriculum was based on a broader range of courses than the public schools and was anchored with prescribed texts. In December 1881 the Sisters introduced an educational novelty: the "entertainment," where students sang, performed, and recited, demonstrating their well-rounded achievements to parents and friends, and additionally emphasizing the moral tone of Catholic education. The "entertainments" had another value: they raised money. This first one netted $88. These well-received "entertainments" became an end-of-the-year staple of school life for decades.

The Sisters offered their school and later their Academy for the entire Tampa community. In the early 1880s only two churches existed, the Methodist and the Catholic. The Catholic school run by the French-Canadian Sisters represented progress, order, moral values, and refinement beyond what public school and frontier existence provided, most especially for young women. Both Protestants and Catholics admired, supported, and attended the Sisters' educational establishments.

From the beginning, the ramshackle five room Sisters' house and the adjacent smithies shop-turned-school was inadequate. For a

*8.2 Holy Names Academy in Tampa. Source: ASNJM*

short time the Sisters rented a store-front on Franklin and Harrison Streets, then they purchased a lot on Twiggs and Central Avenue in May 1884. With the help of a $2,500 loan from Bishop Moore, they secured the lot and began construction of a three-story brick convent/academy, which opened in the 1889-90. It was slightly smaller than the Academy in Key West. Both buildings were used as hospitals during the Spanish-American War in 1898. Both communities of Sisters in Key West and Tampa ministered to the soldiers stationed there during that War, an unusual activity for the Sisters provoked by war-time conditions. The Sisters gave out thousands of meals to soldiers during the summer of 1898, while providing them with conversation, rosaries, medals, scapulars, and a connection with the churches and schools they knew from back home, many of which had the presence of religious women.

Bishop Moore was a great supporter of the Sisters in Tampa from the beginning, paying them his first visit on February 17, 1882. Every time he came to Tampa, which was at least three times a year after the Jesuits arrived, he visited the Sisters and their schools. His first Confirmation of the Sisters' pupils was in January of 1884. In March 1886, after returning from Rome, he gave the Sisters a Papal Blessing and some souvenirs. During that visit, he expressed his concerns over the Sisters' dilapidated living conditions, saying that it was "something not becoming for religious." He soon backed up his concern with $2,500 for their new Academy building. Then in December 1890, he helped the Sisters secure a loan of $5,000 from Msgr. Preston of the Archdiocese of New York to assist them with the debt for their new Academy building.

When the Jesuits came to Tampa, the Sisters got along well with them. They appreciated the Jesuits' experience as confessors and retreat masters. Despite these generally amicable relations, there was at least one instance of tension between the Sisters and the Jesuit clergy. It related to priorities of pastoral care versus the institutional needs of Sisters. Father de Carriere was chaplain and confessor to the Sisters of the Holy Names since the fall of 1889. He wrote of them in 1896 that they were good teachers, but they were not well adapted to teaching boys. "This deficiency," he wrote, "may prove regrettable in some cases for our parochial work." He perceived a possible conflict between the educational needs of the parish [free and for boys and girls] and the purposes of the Sisters' Academy [tuition and for girls]. An 1891 Agreement between the Sisters and the Jesuits stated that no child was to be refused from any of their schools if their parents could not pay, since the pastor would make up for any school deficit. Father de Carriere bemoaned that Tampa five years after the 1891 Agreement still had no "system of parochial schools." The majority of Catholic families sent their children to the public schools, since they could not afford the tuition for the Sisters' Academy. In short, de Carriere opposed the academy system because he felt it discriminated against the poor. Also, the academy system was under the control of the Sisters, whereas the parochial school was ultimately under the control of the pastor. Father de Carriere took an even harsher tone when he claimed that the Sisters of the Holy Names were trained in a very severe personal economy, coupled with what he characterized "a greedy instinct for getting occasionally all the pettier gains they can make for their community." He felt that the Sisters opposed parochial schools because they felt those free schools undermined their income-bearing academies. The Jesuit went even further in favoring the Sisters engagement in pastoral work, rather than just teaching in their insular academies, a remarkably prescient suggestion; he also knew that the Holy Name leadership would never permit this. Father de Carriere turned out to be a prophet since within two decades the academies would be

| Year | Sunday School S. Louis/S.H. | Academy H.M.** Board | Total | Day | Peter Claver | Academy Ybor | Ignatius P. Tampa | Academy W. Tampa | Anthony San An | Sacred Heart St. Joseph | Total Pasco | Total Tampa |
|---|---|---|---|---|---|---|---|---|---|---|---|---|
| 1889-90 | 40 | 2 | 112 | 110 | | | | | 54 | ? | 54+ | 112 |
| 1890-91 | 43 | 8 | 104 | 96 | | | | | 46 | ? | 46+ | 104 |
| 1891-92 | 70 | 18 | 175 | 157 | | 106 | | | 53 | ? | 53+ | 281 |
| 1892-93 | ? | 22 | 204 | 182 | | 176 | | | ? | ? | ? | 380 |
| 1893-94 | 100 | 12 | 286 | 274 | | 219 | | | 72 | ? | 72+ | 505 |
| 1894-95 | 116 | 20 | 284 | 264 | 80 | 225 | | | 55 | ? | 55+ | 589 |
| 1895-96 | 145 | 7 | 331 | 324 | 102 | ? | | | 58 | ? | 58+ | 331+ |
| 1896-97 | ? | 4 | 280 | 276 | 112 | 217 | 80 | 92 | 76 | ? | 76+ | 780 |
| 1897-98 | ? | 7 | 294 | 287 | 118 | 196 | 80 | 108 | 103 | ? | 103 | 796 |
| 1898-99 | ? | 19 | 286 | 264 | 106 | 229 | 81 | 103 | 90 | ? | 90+ | 805 |
| 1899-00 | ? | 11 | 269 | 258 | 156 | 186 | 66 | 111 | 85 | ? | 85+ | 788 |
| 1900-01 | 175 | 12 | 295 | 283 | 149 | 324 | 61 | 130 | 48 | ? | 48+ | 959 |

** Academy of Holy Names, Tampa: Boarders, Total, Day Students
? - Statistics Unavailable

*8.3 Tampa Bay Area Catholic Education, 1889-1901. Sources: ASNJM, ADSA, ASSJ*

in decline and seventy years
later religious women would serve in pastoral ministry, including the SNJM's.[16]

Despite Father de Carriere's critique, the Sisters of the Holy Names made a significant contribution to Catholic education in South Florida. Besides running their Academy in Key West, the Sisters of the Holy Names also staffed there St. Joseph Parochial School and St. Francis Xavier School for blacks. During the 1895-96 school year, of the 470 Key West students under their instruction, 252 were Catholics and 218 were non-Catholics (46.4 percent of the total).[17] In the Tampa area, besides their Academy in Tampa, they served in their Academy in West Tampa from 1896, St. Ignatius Parochial School in Port Tampa from 1896, St. Peter Claver School for blacks from 1894 to 1901. In the 1900-01 school year the Sisters of the Holy Names taught 635 students, or 66 percent of the total of 959 of Tampa's Catholic school students from that school year.[18]

The lifestyle of religious women reflected a mixture of monasticism with post-Tridentine activism. Religious women had two expressions: the choir Sisters and the lay Sisters, a distinction springing from medieval monastic life. The former were semicloistered and educated for teaching, while the latter were less educated cooks, housekeepers, buyers, and practical functionaries, dealing much more with everyday mundane affairs, as well as being exempt from communal prayer done in choir. In 1897 Holy Name Convent, housed in their Tampa Academy, had fourteen choir

| 8.4 Key West Catholic Education, 1868-1896 | | | | | |
|---|---|---|---|---|---|
| Year | Sunday School | St. Joseph's Boys School | Holy Names Academy | | St. Francis Xavier |
| 1868-69 | N/A | N/A | 7* | 7 | N/A |
| 1873-74 | N/A | N/A | 5 | 250 | N/A |
| 1875-76 | N/A | N/A | 4 | 382 | N/A |
| 1887-88 | N/A | 40 | 8 | 245 | 125 |
| 1890-91 | 100 | 120 | 16 | 260 | 67 |
| 1895-96 | N/A | 100 | 6 | 295 | 69 |

*Boarding students

*8.4 Key West Catholic Education, 1868-1896. Sources: ASNJM, School Reports; ADSA, Notitiae, St. Mary Star of the Sea, Key West*

Sisters and four lay Sisters. They were the most numerous and influential group of religious women on the West Coast.[19]

# Sisters of St. Joseph

Unlike the Sisters of the Holy Names, whose Motherhouse was in far away Montreal and who consequently relied on their own local leadership to determine the direction and priorities in Tampa and Key West, the Sisters of St. Joseph of St. Augustine had their Motherhouse in St. Augustine, but had two bosses: the local bishop, John Moore, and their General Superior in Le Puy, France. However, the SSJ's were much more responsive to the educational and pastoral needs of the people of the Diocese of St. Augustine because they were under the bishop's pastoral direction. Also unlike the SNJM's, who had academies in the Province of Quebec, in Oregon, in New York State at Rome and Schenectady, in California at San Francisco and Oakland, all before they came to Key West in 1868, the Sisters of St. Joseph from Le Puy were focused only in the Diocese of St. Augustine in Moore's time. But, whereas the OSB Sisters worked only in three Florida counties just North of Tampa and the SNJM Sisters worked only in Key West and the Tampa area, the SSJ's worked in various settings and capacities throughout the state.[20]

**8.5 Sisters of St. Joseph Schools, 1866-1891**

**1866:** St. Augustine Motherhouse academy and four free schools (two for whites and two for blacks) and two public schools (one white, one black)

**1868:** Jacksonville, St. Joseph's Academy and two free schools (one white, one black)

**1868:** Mandarin, St. Joseph's Academy and two free schools (one white, one black)

**1871:** Fernandina, St. Joseph's Academy and two free schools (one white, one black)

**1874-1884:** Mayport, St. Joseph's Convent

**1876:** Palatka, a free school for blacks

**1882:** Elkton, St. Joseph's Academy

**1886:** Jacksonville, St. Mary's Home for Children

**1887:** Pablo Beach, St. Joseph's Convent

**1888:** Orlando, St. Joseph Academy

**1891:** Ybor City, St. Joseph Academy

*8.5 SSJ Schools, 1866-1891. Source: Sister Thomas Joseph McGoldrick, Beyond the Call, 378-79*

The Sisters of St. Joseph were founded in Le Puy, France, in 1650 by Father Jean Pierre Médaille, SJ., who gathered six women as his spiritual directees and began forming them "'in a new way of life'" for service in the Church, shaped by the active service and spirituality of Ignatius of Loyola. Their purpose was to serve "'in perfect love of God and neighbor.'" There was to be no canonical cloister and no restrictions on doing any specific work. They would be free to respond to the local needs. Each foundation was to be parish-centered and under the direction of the local bishop. In 1646 Médaille referred to the group as the Daughters of St. Joseph. In 1650 the Bishop of Le Puy gave the six Sisters canonical status as a diocesan Congregation. Their first mission was to run an orphanage in Le Puy, where they established their first convent. After the French Revolution and the Papal Concordat of 1801, the Sisters of St. Joseph were one of the first teaching Congregations to be revived. By 1827, they operated fifty-eight schools throughout the Diocese of Le Puy. Although charging tuition, their schools were affordable and ubiquitous. Most of the recruits for the Congregation were peasants from the areas surrounding Le Puy. Most of them lacked a dowry or pension upon entry, but that did not deter their entrance. The Sisters day began with prayer, Mass, meditation, followed by teaching or caring for the sick and the poor.[21]

Bishop Augustin Verot, the first Bishop of St. Augustine in 1870, was from Le Puy. Immediately after the American Civil War, Verot had in mind to improve the lot of the newly freed slaves by offering their children the benefits of an education, heretofore denied them as slaves. To this end, he sailed to France in June 1865 to obtain teaching Sisters for the blacks living in the territory of his jurisdiction. He asked for women religious from the St. Joseph Sisters in Le Puy. Sixty volunteered, but he could only afford to sponsor eight. To their Mother Superior, Verot made clear his purpose: "'I want you to understand fully and clearly that it is for the Negroes and for them almost exclusively that I have arranged for the daughters of your Order to come into my diocese. I have five or six hundred thousand Negroes without any education or religion... for whom I wish to do something.'" The eight pioneering Sisters left Le Harve in August 1866 with Verot. On the ship he gave them a crash course in English, then more of his personal English language instruction after they arrived. A month later, on September 2, they disembarked at Picolata, the mail station for St. Augustine on the St. Johns River, after stops in New York and Savannah. Only five months later, in January of 1867, the Sisters opened a school for black children in a small building (the former Academy of the Mercy Sisters) on the northwest corner of St. George Street and what is now Cathedral Place, near the Cathedral. The Sisters taught the children in the daytime and in the evening had literacy classes for the adults. Simultaneously, the Sisters established their convent in the former house of Father Michael O'Reilly on Hospital Street (now Aviles Street) not far from their school. O'Reilly bequeathed his house to the Church in 1803. More Sisters arrived from Le Puy in 1867 and 1868. By May 1868, the Sisters had sixty black pupils in St. Augustine, meanwhile they opened two other such schools in Savannah and Jacksonville. As early as December 29, 1866, five postulants came from Savannah, all were either born either in America or Ireland. The group was now not just exclusively French. In 1869 in Jacksonville and in 1871 in Fernandina they founded other schools for blacks. Verot financed the whole enterprise from money from the Society of the Propagation of the Faith and from his begging tours up North. Meanwhile, the Sisters provided for their necessities by selling the French lace they made, by conducting fairs, and by giving lessons in French, music, painting, drawing, and lacemaking. Throughout the nineteenth century the Sisters struggled financially. They founded tuition academies for whites. Even though the tuition from those academies provided the majority of their income, their own extracurricular work was an essential supplement to their expenses. At St. Joseph Academy in 1881, the Sisters' extra work provided 19.7 percent of their total income; in 1882 in was 30.9 percent. Without their considerable extra efforts, neither their institutions nor they would have been able to stay afloat. Verot himself built the Motherhouse/Academy in St. Augustine for the Sisters in 1874, despite the objections from some of his priests about the cost of that expenditure.[22]

As was the case with other religious communities of women, they found they needed to establish tuition-producing academies in order to support themselves and the other work in which they were engaged. By the time Moore arrived in 1877, the Sisters of St. Joseph had five schools for blacks which were accompanied by five academies, each in St. Augustine (1866), Jacksonville (1868), Mandarin (1868), Fernandina (1871), and Palatka (1876). By Moore's death in 1901, the Sisters established seven new foundations: 1882 - Moccasin Branch (St. Ambrose, Elkton); 1886 - Jacksonville, St. Mary's Home (orphanage); 1887 - Pablo Beach (Jacksonville Beach); 1889 - Orlando (St. Joseph Academy); 1891 - Ybor City (St. Joseph Academy); 1896 - Ybor City (St. Benedict the Moore - school for blacks); 1898 - St. Augustine (St. Benedict the Moore - school for blacks). As was true with the SNJM's in Tampa, Bishop Moore made annual visitations to the Sisters of St. Joseph houses and institutions, examining and signing their account books, inspecting other records, and speaking with the Sisters. He also gave the Sisters financial help, both in terms of donations and loans. For example, from 1885 to 1896, Moore loaned them $15,421.29 ($460,920 in 2017 dollars). By 1896, they paid back $7,509.00, but they still had a balance of $7,912.29.[23]

Under Moore's administration, the SSJ's ran most Catholic schools, served the most varied constituency, were stationed in the most varied and difficult settings, and taught the most pupils than any other women religious in Florida. Unlike the SNJM's who were becoming increasingly academy/institutionally oriented, the SSJ's, true to their founding charism, were more pastorally accommodating. They served in more black Catholic schools, in more different locales, and more parish Catholic schools than any other group of women religious in Florida. By 1901, the Sisters of St. Joseph operated an orphanage, eight academies, eleven free schools (six of which were for blacks), and two public schools. They educated over 1,300 children in these institutions, and their community numbered just over eighty.[24]

As was the case with the SNJM's during the Spanish-American in 1898, the SSJ's broke from their usual routine in order to respond to the needs of all those living in the military encampments around Florida the summer of 1898. Although they paid especial attention to Catholics, the Sisters served all to the edification of all. The SNJM's served soldiers in Key West and Tampa. The SSJ's served soldiers stationed not only in Tampa, but in Pablo Beach and Fernandina. They cared for and nursed the fever-stricken and wounded soldiers. They even opened up their summer cottage at Pablo Beach as a temporary hospital where two Sisters were assigned as nurses and two prepared soups and delicacies for the patients. In Fernandina, three Sisters transformed their Academy's auditorium into a make-shift hospital. When this auditorium became too crowded, the Sisters made their two parlors into wards to alleviate the overflow. Even though St. Joseph's Academy in Ybor was the poorest of all their establishments, the Sisters still made extra-efforts there during the summer and fall of 1898. Since the Ybor City Convent was some distance from where the soldiers were encamped, three Sisters visited the sick in the afternoons, bringing with them also soup and custards.[25]

We have seen that depending on the circumstances and his judgment of the situation, Moore could be firm with his clergy if he felt the situation warranted it. In 1895 he sent his first Circular to his priests on the Papal condemnation of the three fraternal organizations: the Odd Fellows, the Sons of Temperance, and the Knights of Pythias. Moore sent a printed copy in English of the Papal condemnation to all pastors, admonishing his priests to read the Papal document from the pulpit to the people, adding: "Exhort your people to yield prompt and full obedience to the decision and command of the Holy See. Now that Rome has spoken, there is no longer room for doubt and the line of duty is clearly marked for all Catholics. I trust and pray that their obedience will be cheerful and sincere."[26]

For Moore obedience to the will of the Holy See was para-mount for everyone: bishops, priests, religious, and people. Usually reserved, considered, and circumspect in his decision-making, his sense that the leadership of the Sisters of St. Joseph had flaunted the will of the Holy See and his express admonitions drove him to uncharacteristic action toward the end of his life.

In 1836 the first SSJ's to leave France (from Lyon) for America arrived at the nine year-old Diocese of St. Louis. Up to 1901, three other foundations came directly from France: New Orleans - 1855 (from Bourg), St. Augustine - 1866 (from Le Puy), Lee, Massachu-setts, - 1885 (Chambéry). The early works of these communities involved teaching in grade schools, teaching in their academies, catechizing women, caring for the sick and orphans, visiting the homes of the poor. Although a few other Sisters came from France after these initial foundations, from the beginning the future of these communities in the U.S. depended on encouraging recruits from America, not from France.[27]

The process of the Americanization of the SSJ's began almost immediately after their arrival. The first American joined the Sisters in Carondelet, Missouri, in 1837. The process of Americanization was enhanced when the Sisters engaged with civic structures through their operation of orphanages, schools for the deaf, and in some cases being teachers in what were public taxed-based schools. In Missouri in 1847 the Constitutions of the Order had to be translated into English because of the number of the American candidates they attracted did not read French. The decade of 1847 to 1857 saw tremendous expansion of the Order to Philadelphia, St. Paul, Toronto, Hamilton, Wheeling, Buffalo, Brooklyn, and Albany. Who was in charge of all of these foundations? The Constitutions stated that the local female Superior and the male ecclesiastical superior (the local bishop or his delegate) were. The local bishop had the right to confirm elections, impose corrections, and even appoint or remove a Superior. Only in 1858 did the revised Lyons Constitutions allow for a Superior General at Lyon. But even this notion was adapted to the American scene. When new houses were founded from Carondelet, by 1860 the Mother Superior of that house acted as the virtual Superior General, having extensive powers over other of their foundations. Also by 1860, there was no longer a formal dependence on France by the Sisters of St. Joseph in the U.S. and by that time also the Congregation had the numerical dominance of Americans in their membership. By then, the greatest numbers of candidates were Americans, followed by Irish, and a small number of Germans and other nationalities. The Carondelet Sisters elected an American Superior earlier in 1857. But their French roots were not completely eradicated; for example, thirty-nine Sisters came from France to Carondelet between 1854 and 1887. But the upshot was, by 1870 the SSJ's became independent diocesan congregations in Philadelphia, Toronto, Hamilton, Wheeling, Buffalo and Brooklyn, while Albany and St. Paul remained under Carondelet. The Carondelet Sisters' service as nurses in the Civil War and in the War of 1898 further pushed their assimilation, not only into American culture, but also into the American Church.[28]

This was the process that was taking place in the country among the Sisters of St. Joseph. It was about to take place in a less gradual and more calamitous form among the Sisters of St. Joseph of St. Augustine through the instrumentation of Bishop Moore.

The Americanization of the SSJ's of St. Augustine did not go as smoothly or as naturally, as was the case in other parts of the country. For one thing, until 1877, the Sisters had a French diocesan bishop in Bishop Verot, thus reinforcing their French character. Also, throughout the nineteenth century their religious superiors in St. Augustine, who may have had to act largely independent from Le Puy, were French: Mother Sidonie Rascle (1866-69), Mother Stanislas Bertrand (1869-78), and Mother Lazarus L'hostel (1878-1899). The latter came from LePuy in 1867, making her part of the second group who came out of France. She was the Provincial Superior in St. Augustine for twenty-one years, that is since they became of Province in 1878. The French connection also remained strong with a steady supply of recruits coming from Le Puy: 1867 - four; 1872 - three; 1874 - three; 1879 - three; 1880 - three; 1883 - one; 1884 - four; 1886 - four; 1894 - four; 1897 - one. Even though from 1886 to 1900 more SSJ candidates came from other nationalities (ten Irish, seventeen from Canada, eighteen Americans, four Floridians), the French minority (25 percent of the total of 142 Sisters up to 1900,) were in all the leadership positions and, although physically distant from Le Puy, were spiritually and emotionally connected to their roots. They would not have an American-born Superior until 1946.[29]

In 1899 Bishop Moore did two things that shaped the future of the Sisters of St. Joseph of St. Augustine: he removed their Superior from her office and he severed their relations with Le Puy. On November 14, 1899, he wrote to the Superior General in Le Puy:

> Years ago [1891] I promulgated in all these communities of the Sisters of St. Joseph in this Diocese the Pope's Decree *Quemadmodum* [December 1890] which treats the manifestation of conscience and other practices of religious life and I ordered said decree to be read to the whole community each year on the feast of St. Teresa [Oct. 15 - the day the Sisters renewed their vows]. I drew your superior's attention to the excommunication which the Pope attached to the non-observance of this Decree, and I made the observation: "If we do not obey the Pope, [then] who will we obey?"
>
> The decree has not been read annually as the Decree itself prescribes, and as I ordered should be done on the Feast of St. Teresa. Hence the Pope's decree has been flagrantly violated, and your superior has incurred the Pope's excommunication.

A community whose superior has incurred excommunication, and probably received the Sacraments in that state, cannot expect to have God's blessing upon it.

> Wherefore, in order to make some reparation to the sanctity of the Pope's decree which has been violated and to deter other superiors in future from the neglect of its observance, I hereby depose Mother Mary Lazar from her office of superior in this community, and I declare her forever ineligible to said office of superior in any community of Sisters in this Diocese. For the unexpired term and until this

next election I hereby appoint Sister Mary Eulalia
Ryan superior of this community.[30]

Moore did not excommunicate Mother Lazarus, but he felt that
she did receive Papal excommunication by not reading the document
annually as required, and also perhaps not following the intent of the
document, though Moore never directly says this. Moore deposed
Mother Lazarus because "the Pope's decree has been violated." Was
it violated just because it was not read annually to the Sisters or
because its content was not being followed under her leadership?

Only nine days later, on November 23, 1899, Moore wrote the
Superior General again, this time severing all connections between
Le Puy and the Sisters of St. Augustine. That Superior General
responded to Moore on December 14, 1899, by accepting the
bishop's decision for separation from Le Puy:

> The blow which strikes us is assuredly very
> unforeseen; nevertheless we are accepting it with an
> entire submission to the designs of Divine Providence.
>
> The consequence of the action you have judged
> appropriate to take is that our French Religious may
> return to France, if they wish.
>
> Another consequence seems to us equally required
> of your justice, Your Excellency, that expenses of
> returning to their homeland should be the obligation
> of the Florida mission. That is, moreover, the opinion
> of our ecclesiastic Superior [the Bishop of Le Puy]
> here.[31]

At the end of January 1900 Moore fired back a response.

> I wish to inform you that I do not acknowledge
> any obligation to furnish the Sisters who want to
> return to France either the costs of the journey or
> of apparel, and much less [to furnish] dowries or
> provisions for those who have served the diocese for
> many years.
>
> I am not dismissing them; they are all free to
> remain. Many of them had expressed the intention
> of remaining, but I am told lately that almost all have
> changed their mind as a result of encouragement
> which you wrote to them, and they want now to go.

I believe I see a necessity to have only Sisters who are entirely diocesan, Sisters who obey the Bishop of the Diocese...

Nevertheless, I would not desire the Sisters to go away; on the contrary I would want them to stay even though at present the efficaciousness is questionable because of the persuasions to return to France [from you].

I repeat, I want Sisters who obey me like their bishop; and who are not in any manner subject to orders of a Superior in another distant country.[32]

In the above letter Moore also points out how all the SSJ Superiors of their local convents throughout the State are French, that is all the leadership is French, and he questions where their loyalties are — to Le Puy or to the bishop and the people of the diocese?

Moore's decision in early 1900 could not have come as a complete surprise to Mother Lazarus. While in Europe in 1885, he visited the Motherhouse in LePuy with the express intention of getting the SSJ's of St. Augustine made as a separate Province. Both she and he must have discussed this matter before he left for Europe. Mother Lazarus at that time must have acquiesced or perhaps even promoted the idea. Moore wrote Mother Lazarus that the authorities in Le Puy refused to create the new Province, and the St. Augustine SSJ's remained a dependency of Le Puy.

But the bishop's action did have unintended consequences. He had no desire of "dismissing" the French Sisters, including Mother Lazarus, as he pointed out the Mother Superior in Le Puy in early 1900. "They are free to remain," he wrote, but those who did must accept his authority. But, almost 50 percent of the French Sisters did not and left Florida for France.

Meanwhile, as he had done earlier with Father O'Boyle, Moore disciplines Mother Lazarus. He sends her to St. Joseph's Academy in Ybor City, the poorest of all the SSJ establishments and the most challenging, not as the Superior of the house, but as an ordinary teaching Sister. This action created discord among the members of the entire Community, but especially in the Ybor City Convent. As one Sister there wrote in the convent's diary, with Victorian understatement: "There is an unavoidable constraint in our intercourse." As result of the tensions within the community because of Moore's actions, some of the French Sisters in the congregation sought repatriation back to France. The French Sisters still recognized Mother Lazarus as their true Mother Superior and leader. Ultimately, Moore ordered Mother Lazarus to return to France for the good of the unity of the Congregation. Mother Lazarus departed Ybor City on April 27, 1900, and the U.S. on May 3, 1900, with four other French Sisters. Two others left July 19, 1900, while four more returned to France shortly, thereafter, making a total of eleven departures. Ironically, just as one door was closing for those Sisters, another opened. Seven of them returned to the U.S. in July 1902 to a new foundation of Le Puy's in Fall River, Massachusetts. Of the nine founding Sisters who went there, seven of them had been in Florida. It is also ironic that Mother Lazarus who claimed such a love for Le Puy, left there again in 1902 for Fall River. Perhaps she loved it best from afar.

Twelve of the French Sisters decided to stay in the Diocese of St. Augustine. Surprisingly, then a slight majority of the French Sisters remained in Florida, suggesting that even the Sisters from France were divided over these events. The leadership vacuum was filled largely by the Irish-born Sisters. Moore appointed Irish-born Mother Mary Eulalie Ryan to fill out Mother Lazarus' term, which was to expire in 1901, when the Community then elected Mother Mary Sidonie McCarthy from New Brunswick, Canada, as their new leader. Meanwhile, in June 1900 Moore gave permission and the funds for two Irish-born SSJ's to travel to Ireland to recruit Irish candidates for the Congregation. As he did for his clergy, so it was now for his Congregation of Sisters, Moore chose Ireland as the preferred field for harvesting candidates for religious life. From 1866 to 1900, a total of 140 SSJ's were in Florida. The national origin of the Sisters during the period were as follows: France - 25 percent; Ireland - 13 percent; Florida - 13 percent; out of state Americans - 37 percent (making Americans in the community at 50 percent); Canada - 12 percent. If there were any "winners" in Moore's decision of 1899, it was the Irish Sisters, who took over most of the leadership positions. From 1891 to 1904 the Community acquired twelve Sisters and five novices from Ireland. In 1908 alone of the twenty-one women in formation, nineteen were Irish-born. The first American-born, as well as the first Floridian, General Superior elected by the Congregation was in 1946, Mother Anna Joseph Dignan, a native of Jacksonville, FL.[33]

The documentary evidence about this split and its effects comes from the French Sisters, most especially from those who left Florida. In September 1908, Mother Lazarus, who was then in Fall River, gave her explanation of the events of 1899-1900 in a letter written at the request of her Superior General in Le Puy. She stated that "three or four years before this matter happened" Bishop Moore and ordered that in every [local] community the Superior" was to read the Decree of the Holy Father [*Quemadmodum*] on the Feast Day of Teresa of Avila. The Sisters gathered locally and at the Motherhouse to profess Sisters and to renew vows. Mother Lazarus said that in St. Augustine, because of the schedule set for that day, there was no time to gather the Sisters to have the document read to them, so she asked for and received permission from Moore to read it during the Sisters annual retreat, which was in January. "One year I forgot it, but every year at the retreat the decree was read and explained by the Father who gave the retreat." On the morning of November 14, 1899, Mother Lazarus received a note from Bishop Moore saying that she was to gather all the Sisters at 3 o'clock so that he might speak with them. "Contrary to his custom, the bishop gave no reason; I knew no cause for the order." Moore read from a paper which was substantially from the contents of the letter he sent to the Superior General in Le Puy that same day. That letter has previously been quoted here in full. Sister Lazarus added that Moore deposed her in the presence of all the Community and said that she is now in the state of a Papal excommunication. Moore did not excommunicate her himself personally, but felt she was already excommunicated by Papal mandate for not following the Decree. She asked him if she could receive the Sacraments. He said no, but she could remedy the Papal excommunication, adding: 'You will go to Confession and you will do what the Confessor (a Tampa Jesuit) will tell you. I will give him the authority." He provided her with an easy remedy for her Excommunication and therefore an easy access to the Sacraments. She followed the path that Moore laid out for her and was restored to the Sacramental life of the Church.

Ten days later the bishop announced to her, in the presence of the new Superior and her Assistant, that the Sisters of St. Joseph of St. Augustine are no longer a dependent of Le Puy. "That blow was more terrible to me than the first," wrote Sister Lazarus. At the same time, Moore made it clear to Sister Lazarus that she could stay in Florida, if she so wished. She requested to go to Mandarin; Moore sent her instead to Ybor City, the establishment farthest away from St. Augustine, with "orders not to stop in our houses which were on the way." Sister Lazarus said she was happy in Ybor City, unburdened from the responsibilities of leadership and teaching the younger children. She also wrote that she was torn between her Le Puy Superior General wanting her to return to France and her St. Augustine Superior, Mother Eulalie, wanting her to stay. She thought she would leave it up to obedience, by getting Mother Eulalie to ask the bishop what he might prefer. Sister Lazarus recorded the bishop's response was: "Tell her that it would be better to leave and return to France." This reported response by the bishop to Sister Eulalie about Sister Lazarus, some-thing that he never put in writing to her or told her directly, had a becalming effect on her and she decided to reply by obedience. She left Florida on May 3, 1900. She concluded by writing in 1908 that "What I regret is the separation; still one must see here the will of God."[34]

Sister Lazarus did admit to forgetting to have the Papal document read one year, but she never mentions anything about the contents and purpose of the Papal Decree, that is the issue of forcing Sisters to reveal their conscience to their Superiors (what in effect were matters for the Sacrament of Penance). She seems so focused on defending herself and the letter of the law (Moore's request to have it read annually), but not its spirit. She omits any mention as to why Moore may have so insisted on the annual reading of the document and why he reacted to her the way he did. In fact she says that Moore "had been a good and devoted Father to us; in my difficulties I used to go to him without fear; he was my support." Epistolary evidence seems to verify this. In spring and summer of 1885 he wrote to her in a friendly and supportive manner from Baltimore, from Rome, from Buffalo. In the summer of 1889 he wrote her from Buffalo, approving the opening of an Academy in Orlando in the fall and encouraging the Sisters to attend the Teacher's Institute, part of the Public School System. He wrote her an encouraging letter from Chicago in June 1890. If they had such a good relationship up to late 1899, and from all indications they did, then what suddenly changed? Her silence on these matters is deafening.

We do have an epistolary record of the turmoil these events created, not only for Mother Lazarus and some of the other French Sisters. On the other hand, we practically know nothing about the feelings of the non-French Sisters, who were in the far majority. We have no witness from any of the priests of the diocese, including the Jesuits who were confessors and retreat masters for the SSJ's. Even more importantly, we do not have any extant explanation from Moore for why he did what he did. We can only speculate.[35]

We do know that these actions were extremely unusual ones for Moore. He generally did not operate in this directly authoritative manner. Also, by his own admission, Moore would consult with Mother Lazarus or inform her ahead of time if he had something to tell the Community. In his decision-making, Moore inevitably consulted with others, getting the facts, before rendering a decision, as was the case when he dealt with problems that arose with his priests. Who did he consult with before rendering his decision about Mother Lazarus and the Sisters of St. Joseph? What were the facts that he gathered?

We don't know precisely whom he consulted, but we do know that it was not a characteristic of him to act imperiously, impetuously, or independently. Certainly, he must have consulted with Father Kenny, the Vicar General and pastor of Immaculate Conception Parish, Jacksonville. He had worked with Kenny as Vicar General since 1889, entrusting him with the wealthiest parish in the diocese. Moore trusted Kenny to run things in the diocese when he was out of town, which was often because of his numerous pastoral visits within the diocese and his many begging trips outside the diocese. He had Kenny with him when he made that fateful announcement to the Sisters about Mother Lazarus. What Moore said and did that day could not have been a surprise to Kenny.

For Moore the issues that resulted in his actions were what he perceived as: the flaunting of a Papal Decree, the flaunting of his direct orders on the annual reading of the document, and something else that was unspoken, namely, the disregard for the spirit of the document, not just its letter. The issue could not simply be that the Papal document was not read annually, but its purpose may not have been observed. The content of the decree forbade religious communities forcing their membership to reveal matters of conscience, confes-sional matters, specifically to their Superiors. We know that some religious Communities of women, even in the U.S., did expect their members to reveal their faults to the local Superior, in the manner of the monastic "Chapter of Faults." We also know that some Commu-nities (for example, the Sisters of the Blessed Sacrament) sought to correct this practice as a result of Pope Leo's 1890 Decree *Quemadmodum* ("On Certain Abuses to be Eradicated which have Crept into Religious Institutes").[36]

So the issue for Moore was not just a legalistic one, not just disobedience of Papal or Episcopal authority of the requirement of the annual reading of the document, but the suggestion that the French leadership might have coerced their membership to reveal matters that were on the purview of the Sacrament of Confession. If Moore lacked such suspicions, he would have never pressed for the reading of the document so forcefully. He never did such for any other Papal document. Moreover, he made no such requirement for the other two religious communities of women in the diocese, nor the two orders of men. Had he gotten wind of the fact that the French Superiors were forcing to reveal their member's inner consciences to them and the reading of this recent Papal document was a necessary corrective not only for the Church Universal, but the Church particular?

How would he have known that the document was not being read as he requested and that its contents may have been abused by certain practices among the French leadership? Somebody had to have told him and that somebody could certainly have been one or more of the Sisters themselves. They and Moore would have never written about such a delicate matter. They would have only communicated it verbally. Another potential source of information for Moore on this matter may have been the Tampa Jesuits. They were in frequent communication with the Sisters at the Ybor City Academy and were regular retreat masters for the Sisters' annual retreat in St. Augustine. They would have been aware of any irregularities in the life of the SSJ's. Whoever were his sources, Moore kept quiet, not only about their identity, but also about the true reasons for his taking strong uncharacteristic actions. Something very serious moved Moore to act in this way. He perceived that the spirit of *Quemadmodum* was not being kept and that the highest authority in the Congregation, the Mother Superior, did not promulgate the annual reading of that document as he had ordered nor did she implement the spirit of the document.

A fundamental flaw with the Sisters of St. Joseph's polity as it existed in Florida is that they had divided loyalties. They were to obey their Superior General in Le Puy and their local bishop. "No one can serve two masters. That person will either hate the one and love the other, or be devoted to one and despise the other" (Math. 6:24). Mother Lazarus was known to be very devoted to LePuy, as were many of the French Sisters, attached to its French customs, one of which could have been the revelation of a person's conscience in obedience to one's Superior. By 1900, the French Sisters were at most only 25 percent of the membership, but held 100 percent of the positions of authority. While most of the Sisters of St. Joseph in the U.S. were Americanizing in customs and leadership by 1900, the St. Augustine Sisters were not. They continued to recruit Sisters from Le Puy through the 1880s and 1890s as best they could, but from 1886 to 1900 they only received five Sisters from France. In order to bolster their French-speakers, they decided to recruit in French-speaking Canada. From 1886 to 1900, they obtained seventeen Canadians, while, encouraged by Moore, they enrolled ten from Ireland. After the separation and even after Moore's death, Ireland would be the chief hunting ground, not only for priestly recruits for the Florida Mission, but also for religious women. While between 1866 and 1900 only nineteen of the SSJ's were from Ireland, but from 1901 to 1920 fifty-one Sisters of their total number of eighty-five came from Ireland. The Congregation became to be predominated by the Irish-born through the 1950s.[37]

Bishop Moore would have been familiar with the Americanization process among the SSJ's in the U.S. due to his extensive travels among the major cities in the U.S. for the purpose of raising money for his poor diocese. But another attractive feature of the Americanization process in the Northern branches of the SSJ's, especially for local American ordinaries, was that through it divided loyalties were eliminated. By cutting off ties with France, the local bishop became the only ultimate authority for what was now a diocesan community of religious women. As Moore explained to the Mother General in Le Puy in January 1900: "'I believe I see a necessity to have only Sisters who are entirely diocesan, Sisters who obey the Bishop of the diocese, and who are not in any manner subject to orders from a Superior in another distant country.'"[38]

So his first decision was to remove Mother Lazarus from her leadership, his second determination, taking place a little more than a month later, was to sever connections between the SSJ's in his diocese and Le Puy. He could not have taken these decisions lightly, but felt that they were best for the future of the SSJ's and the Church of Florida. He was not a vindictive, selfish, or petty man, but dutiful, self-sacrificing, and pastoral.

Sister Thomas Joseph McGoldrick, SSJ, former SSJ archivist, former Superior of the SSJ's, and author, recognizes how uncharacteristic this action by Moore was, but attributes his decisions to his unsettled state of mind that was the result of the recent stroke he suffered in August 1899. This post-stroke condition made him not quite himself, since relations between him and Mother Lazarus had been up to that time "professional, healthy, and friendly." His relationship with all the religious in the diocese, both male and female, was good and positive. He annually visited each school of the three Sisters' congregations in his diocese, he often gave them money or loans, he made an appearance at the SSJ's annual retreat and commencement exercises. His relationship with the religious women in his diocese might be characterized as fatherly, in the best sense of the word. One example of his paternal care was that in June 1890 Sister Mary Ann, SSJ, who ran the orphanage in Jacksonville (she was dubbed by all the citizens of that city, Catholic or Protestant, "The Angel of Jacksonville," so respected was she and her work), had some medical problems and needed to go to a hospital. Moore wrote to Mother Lazarus that he thinks that Irish-born former Mercy Sister Sister Mary Ann should go to St. Joseph's Infirmary in Philadelphia (run by the Philadelphia SSJ's) "and submit to an operation, since the doctors judge it necessary, but I do not compel her; I leave it to her own choice to decide for herself as she likes."[39]

Although he did have a stroke that summer, we have no evidence of any debility, mental or physical, on Moore's part in late 1899 or early 1900. He wrote letters, traveled, conducted business as normal during that time. As we shall see later, only in the summer of 1900 had Moore's health discernibly deteriorated, yet as late as November 1900 he celebrated two Confirmations, one in St. Leo and one in San Antonio, although his handwriting in the Confirmation Register is slightly different than before, a little more shaky, less sure and fluid. At that same time, as we shall see later, he was still busy finishing up renovations on the Cathedral in 1900 and even into 1901. There is no conclusive evidence that his mind was beclouded and that he was a man not fully in possession of himself in late 1899 and early 1900.[40]

But, in the end what we have is a lack of evidence from Moore himself about his real motivations for the removal of Mother Lazarus and the subsequent separation from Le Puy. His inclination was to do business verbally, as he did with Henry Flagler. He kept no journal or diary. He very rarely retained copies of correspondence he sent. For example, he kept no copies of his two letters to Le Puy in late 1899 and early 1900, as important as they were. Another matter might also apply to this case: he had trusted Mother Lazarus, considered her a friend in the past and he did not want to besmirch her reputation by putting in writing the details of his decisions against her. The diocesan priests' nickname for Moore was "Silent John." In this case in particular, the priests got it right. Moore is silent about the exact reasons for these significant decisions made in late 1899 and early 1900. We may never be able to penetrate through that veil of silence.

CHAPTER NINE

# *The Laity*

## Frontier Catholicism

In 1880, just a couple of years after Moore became bishop, the population of Florida was thirty-fourth out of the thirty-seven States in the Union. Exactly 90 percent of the population lived in rural areas, that is on the frontier. The population density of the State was 4.9 persons per square mile, well below the U.S. average of 16.9. The standard definition for a frontier is six persons per square mile, so Florida qualified as being called a frontier. By the end of Moore's episcopacy, the State still had 79.7 percent of its population living in rural areas (as compared to 15.2 percent in 1990). Florida's largest urban centers from 1880 to 1900 were Key West, Jacksonville and Tampa. Key West was the largest city in 1880 with a population of 9,890; Jacksonville was the largest city in 1900 with a population of 28,429.[1]

Frontier life in Florida was far from romantic, as the American myth of the cowboy might suggest. Florida had its cowboys, but most on the frontier lived on farms, where life was hard. There was back-breaking work, no creature comforts, subsistence living, little social life. Before the days of refrigeration, people lived off pickled beef, dried beef and fish, pork sausage, white and blood puddings, salted meat, domestic animals and game, garden vegetables, and dairy products. The animals had to be fed, crops needed water and tending, other chores had to be done daily. The unrelenting constant work could be numbing and socially isolating. No wonder young people would flee to life in the city if they had a chance. One young lady from Moccasin Branch, a small rural community west of St. Augustine, poetically described frontier life in Florida in this way:

> We are having gloomy weather.
> It is enough to depress anyone's spirits,
> Particularly in this low, west region.
> I never saw the like of swamps and branches.
> Nearly every house is encompassed by
> An impassable branch.

The positive side to frontier life is that it incubated innovative and practical people. People who lived there were an enterprising and restless lot, lured by the offer of cheap land, of starting out fresh, of chasing dreams of a better life, of independence, of forgetting or reinventing their past. Then and now, Florida has always attracted this kind of person. Frontier society was less aristocratic, less class conscious, less socially static, more fluid and flexible than urban life. Transiency was a fact of life; for every pioneer who came and stayed, three or four came and left. Yet at the same time the fluidity of the frontier created a people who were conservative, who clung to past loyalties, especially religion, which provided a moral structure and stability to frontier family life.[2]

For a Catholic living on the frontier, the "domestic church" was central, since living on the fringe of parish life, they saw a priest infrequently and periodically, when he visited the missions or stations. They probably would have never seen their bishop, except if they went to the closest parish for Confirmation. So without the easy accessibility to a priest, Mass, and the Sacraments, which were available to those living in a city or town, the frontier family and home were the center of Catholic life, the focus of devotional piety, practice and catechesis. In the "domestic church" the mother played an indispensable role. Distant from the parish and a Catholic school, mothers taught their children to pray, drilled their children in the Catechism, read them Bible stories and lives of the saints, led in family prayers and devotions, placed Crucifixes and statues in the home, taught moral values, decorated the home and prepared special meals at Christmas, Easter, and other religious holidays. Although these things went on in every Catholic home to a greater or lesser extent, on the frontier the "domestic church" took on special significance. Also, leading Catholic men and women on the frontier maintained the mission church building and offered their homes to the visiting priest as a station.[3]

## Urban Catholicism

Curiously, the "domestic church" took on a special meaning in the city also, most especially among the Latins of Key West and Ybor City. For them, Catholic culture and ethnic culture were intertwined. Religious and ethnic culture was passed on in the family and homes of Spaniards, Cubans, and Italians, who displayed visual and tactile reminders of Catholicism with domestic shrines to the Virgin Mary and saints, crucifixes on the walls, special meals on religious holidays. Here, once again, mothers, grandmothers, and aunts played a crucial role in perpetuating the power of the "domestic church." Among ethnic Catholics the "domestic church," with its family devotions and traditions, with its popular piety, was sometimes more important than the institutional church with its parishes and schools. Latin families perpetuated what might be called a Medieval Catholicism, versus the Tridentine Catholicism promoted by priests, parishes, and Catholic schools. Latins had a very broad view of what it meant to be a Catholic, not as constrained in their viewpoint as the proscriptions of Tridentine Catholicism. On the other hand, the Church always taught doctrinally and Canonically that anyone baptized a Catholic was a Catholic, regardless of their level of participation in the Church liturgically or Sacramentally. For example, virtually all the residents of Ybor City considered themselves Catholic and almost everyone was baptized a Catholic. Everyone had a *padrino* and a *madrina*, a godfather and godmother. These persons not only were honored by the family who chose them, but they had ongoing responsibilities to their godchild throughout their lives. They were mentors and guides. But Latins did not always practice their faith as Trent proscribed. Ybor City was a very religious and Catholic place, as its residents would concede, but it was not so much a Tridentine place.

*9.1 Sisters of St. Joseph outside their convent in Ybor City*
*Source: ASSJ*

Trent sought to replace Medieval Catholicism with authorized doctrinal and moral teaching, as well as the regular practice of the Faith through Mass attendance and participation in the Sacraments. Latin mutual aid societies, their corporate communal society, their strong family life, their preoccupation with justice and fairness, their devotion to the saints as personal patrons, their celebration of religious feasts, were all expressions of Medieval Catholicism. When Ybor City's Latins claimed to be *muy Catolico*, to be solidly a Catholic, they neither deceived themselves nor their listeners. The Latins were also influenced by anti-Church and secular socialist ideas that sprang from the Italian Nationalist Movement, the ideals of the Cuban Revolution, and Spanish post-Enlightenment ideas. Meanwhile, the Jesuits and the religious women who taught in the Catholic schools sought to work with the next generation to introduce them to Tridentine practice through their educational institutions.[4]

Bishop Moore kept apprised of developments in the Tampa area by his frequent personal visitations, as well as by letter. Moore himself would have been familiar with the texture of Latin Catholicism since he had studied in France and Italy, as well as traveling to Cuba. Father William Tyrell, SJ, pastor of St. Louis, Tampa, wrote Moore in January of 1893 giving his assessment of things in Ybor City. Tyrell says he has tried to convince the Cubans to allow a priest into their homes to visit the sick, especially children, but with little success. Apparently, Cuban men were suspicious of priests visiting their homes when they were away at work. Tyrell also mentioned that the dead are buried without benefit of a priest because the local undertakers don't suggest that people contact a priest and the undertakers themselves don't either, thus depriving the dead of a proper burial, the family of a proper religious ceremony in their grief, and the Church of extra income through stole fees. Tyrell states that he goes every day to Ybor City, where he feels the people there need to know that a priest is not an officer of the government "with a *per capita* tariff on his ministrations," as was often the case in their home countries. Tyrell adds that "the Sisters (the SSJ's) are doing well in Ybor." The people, especially the men, "have the greatest respect for the Sisters." But, he claims that the Sisters work too hard in the school all day to have the energy to visit the families in the evenings, "which otherwise would yield great profit," especially since the priests are not welcome in the homes.[5]

The SSJ's opened St. Joseph Academy in Ybor City in the Fall of 1891 in the nave of Our Lady of Mercy Church, with four Sisters - two French, one Irish-American, and one Floridian. They lived in the back of the church the first four years. Not only were those they ministered to challenging, but also were their living conditions. No wonder they were unable to visit the families of their students! The cultural differences and religious differences between the Sisters and their students were palpable. As one Sister wrote of her initial impressions of her students:

> The wildest, strangest little things... Teaching, under existing circumstances, was difficult. The children were bright but not accustomed to restraint. They would speak aloud in school, leave their places without permission, and, as it was necessary to have someone interpret all that was said by teachers or pupils, there was unending confusion.

The posting was difficult economically too. In the mid-1890s tensions ran high between Cubans and Spaniards over the War of Cuban Independence. Yet the Sisters persevered, making slow progress among their charges. By the fall of 1896 seven Sisters were assigned to their academy, which was now a modest two-story wooden building. Convinced by Sicilian Father Achille Vasta, SJ, to open a school for Italian children in Ybor City, the SSJ's did so in the fall of 1897 in a spare room in the church. It only lasted until December. Meanwhile, the Sisters of the Holy Names also began working with the Latins of West Tampa, also a cigar manufacturing area. Buying land in 1895 in West Tampa, the Sisters opened a three-story brick school there in September 1896 (the Academy of the Holy Names), through the generous benefaction of Col. Hugh MacFarlane, developer of West Tampa. Bishop Moore approved of the expansion of ministry among the Latins of the Tampa area, especially through Catholic education, and that work would bear fruit in the years to come.[6]

## Tridentine Piety and Spirituality

Except for the Latins in Ybor City, West Tampa and Key West, and the African-American Catholic parishes and schools, the parishes of the diocese were not ethnic enclaves and nor ethnic parishes (personal or national parishes). The frontier was the great equalizer where no one nationally dominated. Not everyone was American-born, but English and the America-style parish prevailed, albeit influenced by the Irish Catholicism of the growing number of Irish pastors who carried with them across the ocean their style of Tridentine Catholicism.

The Catholic school and parish were the center of Catholic Tridentine piety and spirituality. Catholic preaching was almost always done in a liturgical setting, at Mass or at Sunday Vespers, by a priest or bishop. Sermons followed the legislation outlined by the Council of Trent (1545-63). The pastor had the obligation to preach at the principal Mass on Sundays and on Holy Days of Obligation, adapting his message to his listeners. He was to be brief, plain in speech, and speak in the vernacular. But, the content of the Tridentine sermon was not the Scriptures of the liturgy of the day, but the Catechism of the Council of Trent (the Roman Catechism), which was in Latin and which presented the teachings of the Church under four major headings: The Apostle's Creed, the

Sacraments, the Commandments and Church Precepts, and Prayer. Tridentine preaching was thematic, doctrinal, moral, catechetical, and systematic. Its purpose was to educate the listener to a deeper understanding and practice of the Faith.

Catholics did not come to church to listen to a sermon so much as encounter the Mystery of God through the celebration of Mass (which was in Latin), through Benediction (a ritual which focuses on the adoration of Jesus in the form of a Consecrated Host in a special vessel, called a monstrance), through the celebration of Vespers (a rite performed on Sunday afternoon as Evening Prayer), and through the celebration and the reception of the Sacraments. A city or town's typical Sunday liturgical schedule was; 7 a.m. Low Mass (not sung and with no music); 10 a.m. High Mass (sung by priest and with music); 2 p.m. Catechism for children was taught by the priest in the church; 3 p.m. Vespers and Benediction. Because of the heat of the summer and fall, morning Masses were moved to an earlier hour.

People would come to the church also for special occasions, such as a Baptism, First Communion, Confirmation (only administered by the bishop), Matrimony, or a funeral. They would also come for communal prayers said in the vernacular, such as the Stations of the Cross, novenas (nine days of prayers for special intentions), Forty Hours Devotion of the Blessed Sacrament, and the parish mission (conducted occasionally by a visiting priest invited by the pastor for the purpose of renewing and reviving faith and practice). These parish missions involved a different style of affective, vivid, and emotional preaching, which in Florida the Jesuits often conducted. People also came to church for private prayer also: lighting a candle for a deceased loved one, praying silently before the Blessed Sacrament, private recitation of the rosary or the Stations of the Cross. For Catholics the church building, whether full or empty, was a sacred place and space where one could encounter the presence of God.

In the hinterlands where there were only missions and stations and where a priest only visited occasionally, prayer was centered in the home of the "domestic church." Prayer books, devotional guides, meditation books, books on the saints, the Bible, the Catechism in the vernacular, rosaries, statues, Crucifixes, and special family meals shaped the piety and spirituality of those who lived on the frontier. For example, in 1877 Father Bernier, pastor of St. Louis in Tampa, wrote Bishop Moore asking that the bishop send him some children's catechisms and some rosaries since "I am entirely out of them and have many calls for them." The bishop was expected to supply his priests on the missions with devotional aids.[7]

In the urban environment there were also school and parish organizations which promoted lay piety and spirituality. Women and girls were predominating in these pious societies. Small St. Anthony of Padua Parish in Benedictine territory in 1886 (comprised of 318 parishioners, 46.2 percent of whom were children) had a Rosary Society (forty-five members), a Young Ladies Sodality of the Blessed Virgin Mary (twenty-one members), and the Altar Society (forty-five members). The latter society was an ubiquitous one in every parish and even every mission, usually the first organization formed. The Altar Society was comprised of women who cleaned the church, the altar linens, and sanctuary vessels and vestments. They also oversaw flower and other decorations, especially for special liturgical events such as Christmas and Easter.

When the Jesuits arrived in Tampa in 1889, they immediately set out to establish more parish organizations, beginning with the Apostleship of Prayer. In 1895 Father Tyrell, SJ, pastor of St. Louis Parish, established the Young Men's Catholic Club, a social and educational organization. By April 1895 Tyrell erected a two-story wooden clubhouse on the corner of Twiggs and Marion Streets for $5,500, from contributions by Tampa's Protestants and Catholics alike. The organization was folded into the Boy's Jesuit High School when it was founded by Terrell in September of 1899. By 1900, St. Louis Parish had the following parish organizations: Young Men's Club (twenty-eight members); the Children of Mary (forty members); the St. John Berchman's Altar Society (fifteen altar boys); Holy Angels Sodality (twenty girls); the Ladies Altar Society (eighty-four women), the Memorial Society (twenty members); the St. Cecilia Society (twenty-four women choir members); the Apostleship of Prayer (over 500 members, which said certain prescribed prayers daily, but never had meetings). Only in 1902 was a Men's Club founded to encourage men to participate more in parish life. In March 1902 eighty men received Holy Communion as a body at the 7 a.m. Mass, after which they had breakfast together (called a Communion Breakfast). Soon on April 11, 1902, the Tampa Council #667 of the Knights of Columbus was established with forty members. The K of C was a men's national organization founded in Hartford, Connecticut in 1882 to fight anti-Catholicism, promote American patriotism, share in mutual aid, and encourage male participation in Catholic life.

The kinds and numbers of pious organizations founded at St. Louis Parish existed in all of the diocese's parishes at the time, although participation was more numerous in the larger urban parishes. Their purpose was to engage people in parish life and communal life and to deepen Tridentine piety. As can be seen, they were largely for women and children. Often the same person overlapped their membership into more than one organization.[8]

Music was valued and an essential part of a High Mass, wherein both priest and choir sang. In the late 1880s and early 1890s St. Louis Parish had an excellent mixed choir of men and women, a women's choir, and a children's choir, all led by the parish organist and choir master, Prof. W. Warwick Parker. After his parish visitation in 1891, Bishop Moore sent the pastor a list of matters he wished him to attend, two of which related to church music. One was that a Catholic cannot be an organist at a Protestant church; the second was that religious women were not to play the organ or sing in the choir, except with the school children. It would seem that both of these things were happening at St. Louis and the pastor needed to remedy these matters. Ever dutiful and exact, Moore was concerned that church law was being implemented in his diocese.[9]

Of course there were times when the laity were not always engaged in pious societies and praying — sometimes they were protesting to their pastor and to their bishop. Although not formally part of the parish decision-making process (very few missions and one parish, the Cathedral, had lay trustees (a group of laymen who owned church property as a corporation), yet they sometimes interjected themselves into decision-making process of the local pastor or the supreme decision-maker — the bishop.[10]

## Conflict Resolution

We saw earlier in Chapter 7 how Bishop Moore was drawn into pastor-parishioner disputes with Father Lynch in Tampa, with Father O'Boyle in San Antonio, with Father Creed in Orlando. He responded to these problems with a consistent approach. After receiving the concerns of the people, he then investigated the allegations by presenting the pastor with them and allowing

9.2 San Antonio, Fla. Source: ADSA, Notitiae, San Antonio Parish, January 1, 1886

him to respond, finally then Moore acted, as was his responsibility, based on his reasonable judgment of the situation.

But not all the problems Moore adjudicated were between the pastor and his people. In the Catholic Colony of San Antonio, Pasco County, in 1884 the problem was intramural, between the colonists and its founder/owner, Judge Edmond Dunne. Some of the colonists were disaffected with Dunne and claimed that when he was recently away from the colony for four months he left no one in charge to sell land or attend to other affairs of the settlement. He advertised land at $2.50 to $5 an acre, but in fact sold no land under $25 per acre. He even refused to sell any land to John Flannigan. "He has kept much of the land only for himself or forced colonists to buy railroad land for $1.25 per acre. The church that Dunne was in the process of building is only partially complete, since it had neither roof nor floor." The complaints were signed by six men (four of whom were Irish), identifying themselves as members of the St. Anthony Society. Their petition was given to Dunne, who passed it on to the bishop on January 14, asking him to adjudicate the dispute, stating that he had "no time to attend to this matter [himself] now...," and adding "I know that I have a good case in your court."[11]

On January 24, 1884, Dunne sent a twenty-four page hand-written memorandum to the bishop explaining "the troubles" at the San Antonio Colony. Dunne wrote that he founded the colony July 1881 from 50,000 acres he obtained from Hamilton Disston (it was payment for legal services Dunne had rendered Disston, although Dunne does not mention this in his memo). In April 1882 George Mullen, who hailed from Baltimore where he crafted marble altars for churches there, arrived in the Colony, then he left. On February 23, 1883, Mullen returned with L. W. Reilly (both of whom were signers of the "Report of Disaffected Colonists" of early 1884 and Reilly was editor of the *Baltimore Mirror*). Both men now wanted to purchase land near the lake and church. Dunne responded that Mullen had a chance to purchase the year before but did not, consequently the land they want is now unavailable. Dunne did let them purchase ten acres each at $5 an acre of town plots. Dunne feels that part of the present 1884 dispute is based on these two men's grievances against Dunne for not selling them the land they wanted. Dunne goes on and on in excruciating detail defending himself. Bishop Moore had no desire to cut through the Gordian Knot of these complicated personal and financial entanglements, nevertheless Dunne pulled him in. Moore personally visited the San Antonio Colony in February in an attempt to adjudicate the matter. While there, he received title for the church and the land near it.

Moore's answer was to send priests to disaffected San Antonio. Father Dunne and Father D. Hishen from Chicago came temporarily until Easter (they were winter visitors). Moore promised to send a priest to the Colony permanently, which had about 150 persons at the time. True to his word, Moore sent Father F. X. Augustus Stemper, "a gentle, refined old gentleman." Stemper was formerly the pastor of St. Joseph's Church, Steven's Point, Wisconsin. Expressing an interest to Bishop Moore in coming to Florida, the bishop had just the place for him. Upon arriving in San Antonio, Stemper wanted to build a Catholic school and have the Blessed Sacrament reserved in the church (now finished and seating c. 150). Dunne would have none of it. The developer was very much in charge of affairs in the

Colony. As a result of tension between Stemper and Dunne, the former Wisconsinite asked Moore to relieve him. Some parishioners signed a petition to the bishop to keep Stemper and pledged to support the construction of a Catholic school. Moore approved the construction of a school house and visited San Antonio again in April 1884, announcing that a schoolhouse would be built. Dunne, acting as the master of the plantation, was not happy, expressing his displeasure in a letter to the bishop. Its tone was "impudent," wrote colonist Alex Dallas. Moore read Dunne's letter in the presence of Alex Dallas, a colonist, and Father Charles Peterman, pastor of St. Louis, Tampa, whom Moore called in as a witness. Meanwhile, Father Stemper left for Tampa, no longer able to endure Dunne and the situation in San Antonio. But the bishop would not run away nor would he be bullied or dictated to by Dunne. The bishop asked Alex Dallas to build the schoolhouse, which he agreed to do. Meanwhile, Moore sent Father John O'Boyle, pastor of St. Michael's, Fernandina, to San Antonio as pastor of St. Anthony's to calm the waters. O'Boyle was not received well by the leading colonists, who felt he was in Dunne's pocket. Instead of calming the waters, O'Boyle put gasoline on the fire. Chapter 7 describes the problems that O'Boyle engendered, although his story must be put in the larger context of the ongoing problems at San Antonio. Moore had to return to San Antonio in March of 1886 and then again the following month to deal with the tensions between pastor and people. As a result of his on-site inspection, he removed O'Boyle, sending him to the Central Florida Missions. Moore thought he had finally solved the disturbances in San Antonio with the coming of the Benedictines and the assignment of Gerard Pilz, OSB, as pastor in May of 1886. As was recounted in Chapter 7, Pilz started off well, but then created a scandal and had to leave in November of 1889. Father Roman Kirchner, OSB, was assigned to replace Pitz and finally San Antonio was at peace.[12]

This long-lasting episode shows Moore's method of problem-solving, his desire to provide pastoral care for Catholics, and his persistence. These problems in that small community lasted five years, and through it all Moore did not give up trying to find a solution, including numerous personal visitations into the eye of the storm.

Eventually, his tenacious efforts and patient pastoral solicitude bore fruit.

# The People Petition for Pastors

More often than not, people petitioned the bishop, not so much to settle disputes, but to send them a pastor, so they could move from being a mission visited occasionally by a priest, to becoming a parish with a resident priest. One example of this kind of petitioning came from the people of Ocala, which had been a mission chapel since 1883, St. Philip Neri. But instead of petitioning Moore for a pastor, in October 1893 they went over his head to the Apostolic Delegate in Washington, DC, an Italian. This leapfrogging over Moore might have been due to the fact that of the 237 signatories, 171 were Italian-born. There was another curious thing about the petition. Its 237 signatures were not signed primarily by parishioners. When Moore assigned a resident pastor to Ocala in 1894, Father B. O'Reilly, he counted merely eighty Catholics in the parish, only 50 percent of whom made their Easter Duty. If they had sent the petition to Moore, the excessive number of people on the petition would have aroused suspicion. By going to the Apostolic Delegate, they could both disguise their inflated numbers, as well as put pressure on Moore.[13]

# Benefactors

A very important group of lay people were the various benefactors who supported the growth of the diocese, especially with special projects designated by the bishop, pastors, or religious women. One of the most important of these was not even a Catholic, but none other than railroad magnate, Henry Flagler. Curiously, there is no correspondence either in the Moore Papers in the Diocesan Archives of St. Augustine or in the Flagler Archives to or from Moore. As we have seen, Moore did a lot of business verbally in person. This would have been particularly the case with Flagler, who himself did not wish to have his benefaction to the Catholic Church made public or a matter of record. He even went so far as to not write checks to Moore from Florida banks. After the St. Augustine fire of 1887, he even established an account with a northern bank which

Moore could draw from as needed. As Moore wrote to Father Pace in the Cathedral Rectory: "He [Flagler] does not want it known in St. Augustine, even at the bank, what he gives [donations to the bishop], and therefore does not like to send his checks there. We must keep it a secret." Both Moore and Pace did, as well as Flagler.[14]

During his very successful and lucrative career in Standard Oil, Henry Flagler specialized in bargaining with various railroads to secure favorable shipping rates for Standard Oil's products. He was good at it, one might even say ruthless. He appreciated the value of railroads and also got to know something of their operations. He first traveled to St. Augustine in December 1883 with his wife Alice and John and Laura Rockefeller. After leaving Standard Oil, he resettled in St. Augustine in 1885, when he began transforming that sleepy town into the winter Newport. St. Augustine had only one large hotel at the time, the wooden four-story St. Augustine Hotel built in 1869 on the northeast side of the plaza. Flagler went about building more luxurious, ornate hotels in St. Augustine for wealthy winter visitors who could now arrive by train from their homes in the North.

The three hotels in St. Augustine were made from concrete and not wood, having a Spanish Renaissance style of architecture — the Ponce de Leon, the Alcazar, and the Moorish-styled Cordova. Not satisfied with transforming St. Augustine, he extended his railroad, along with his string of posh hotels for the Gilded Age's well-heeled, down Florida's East Coast — Ormond Beach, Palm Beach, Miami, Nassau (reached by steamship from Miami), and eventually all the way to Key West. By 1887, Flagler took up residence in the Ponce de Leon Hotel, still under construction and a block from the bishop's residence. The Ponce de Leon opened to the public in January of 1888.[15]

Flagler became a benefactor of Moore as a result of a tragedy. On April 12, 1887, the bishop's Cathedral was ruined by a fire which started in the St. Augustine Hotel, then spread to destroy a single city block just north of the central plaza of St. Augustine. The Cathedral's roof caught fire, collapsed into the interior, gutting the building, leaving only its charred coquina walls. In addition to all of the other financial burdens of his poor diocese, Moore was saddled with the task of rebuilding the Cathedral. Flagler hired New York architect James Renwick, Jr., who designed St. Patrick's Cathedral and who was staying at the Ponce de Leon Hotel during the fire, to rebuild the Cathedral and to design a new campanile for it. Flagler himself paid for the campanile. In the summer of 1887, he also contributed $5,000 deposited in a northern bank for Moore to draw from in the reconstruction effort. From then on the millionaire became an important ally and benefactor of Moore, not only in St. Augustine, but throughout the state, while always remaining quietly behind the scene. Flagler biographer Thomas Graham estimates that Flagler donated at least $75,000 just for the rebuilding of the Cathedral alone.[16]

In 1889 Flagler gave $1,000 to Moore so that the bishop could purchase a $5,000 lot in Ybor City for a proposed church there. After the railroad got to West Palm Beach in 1894, Flagler contributed, along with some of his wealthy guests staying at the Royal Poinciana Hotel, to the building of the wooden St. Ann's Church, dedicated in March 1896, built on land he donated. He then had it moved to a better location in 1900. The Tampa Jesuits served there during the season, because Flagler erected a three-story rectory there also. When his railroad reached Miami in 1896, Flagler gave land for a Catholic church (Holy Name), rectory, and school. In the 1890s Flagler loaned to Moore a building in St. Augustine which was used as a Catholic school for black children. On the board of directors for the Plant holdings, Flagler even proposed in 1901 to have the Jesuits take over the Tampa Bay Hotel to use as their high school.[17]

Some have suggested that Flagler's benefactions were usually self-serving and with strings attached. In some cases, this was true. When Flagler was giving money to Moore to rebuild his Cathedral, the businessman was angling for a piece of property which the diocese owned between the Cathedral and the Ponce de Leon Hotel. Moore conveyed the property to Flagler, one businessman to another. In return Flagler agreed to help Moore with his Cathedral reconstruction. Flagler's benefactions in West Palm Beach and Miami might be seen as a good business and public relations decision, because of his Catholic railroad workers, hotel workers, and for his hotel guests. Yet some of what he did, and we do not all that he may have done for Moore since much was done secretly, did not seem to be self-serving. Much was based on a personal respect and trust that both men had for one another. Benefaction over time is always based on trust and personal relationships, and not simply grounded in self-interest.[18]

The attraction of Flagler to the bishop was due to more than just the tragedy of the Cathedral fire, but also based on the fact that both men were leaders, both men appreciated the value of religion in society, and both men were quite familiar with the tragic in their lives. We have discussed earlier aspects of Moore's life which connected him with human suffering. Flagler, like Moore, had a "close to the vest" nature. As a leader, he projected the "Mask of Command." Even the most traumatic events in his life produced no outpouring of grief, such as the loss of his first wife and daughter. Such was also the case from Moore. Flagler's diary entries were typically terse. Moore never kept a diary. Flagler only revealed something of his inner self in his letters and parts of his diary. Such was also the case with Moore. His letters sometimes reveal his warmth and passion, but most of them are terse and business-like. One commentator in 1910 called Flagler excessively modest, with an elusive personality who has no intimates, adding: "You realize that you are before a man who has suffered and has never wept... He is without redeeming vices, without amiable inconsistencies, without obsessions. He simply does not 'classify.' You cannot accurately adjectivize [sic] him. He does not defy analysis; he baffles it." Much the same could be said of Moore. His priests called him "Silent John," suggesting an elusive personality. Moore did have friends, but most were in New York. His relatives were in Charleston, whom he kept in contact, but whose letters to him are not extant. At age seventy-four, Flagler said this of himself: "My diet is always been simple and the only excess I believe I have indulged in has been that of hard work... I possess as much vitality and can do as much work as the average man of forty-five." Flagler must have seen in Moore the qualities of modesty, personal simplicity, energy, and hard work which he himself possessed.[19] Hence his desire to be supportive of what he may have seen as an ecclesiastical version of himself.

Moore writes to Cardinal Gibbons in March 1893 calling Flagler "my friend." It seems that there was a plan to have a bishop's meeting in St. Augustine. "Mr. Flagler has offered to provide for the entertainment of the bishops." But the meeting never took place there, to Moore's disappointment. Moore mentions to Gibbons of his promised visit to St. Augustine with the new Apostolic Delegate "next winter." No doubt Flagler would have hosted them also, but the proposed trip never took place. The railroad tycoon was willing to demonstrate his friendship with Moore in a public setting by entertaining bishops in his hotels. This public display was something of a change in Flagler's earlier secret benefactions, signifying their deepening friendship.[20]

Another benefactor, but from afar, was James W. Willcox, Jr., of Philadelphia. His family was a long-time supporter of the Catholic Church, going back to Colonial times. It was Willcox who paid for the construction of the church and rectory in Orlando (St. James). The Maitland area in Central Florida was heavily settled by Philadelphians. Willcox paid for the construction of a mission chapel there in 1881, and for the building of a mission chapel at New Smyrna. Later, with Moore's Cathedral rebuilding and his begging trips to Philadelphia, Willcox made some contributions to that project in 1887. Earlier in 1883, he invited Moore to visit him in July and August when his family will be spending their summer in Newport. There is no evidence that Moore did so.[21]

But the majority of benefactors that Moore had were not big captains of industry, but ordinary people who donated land, lumber, and labor to build mission chapels or parish churches or schools. In 1893 a parishioner at St. Louis, Tampa, donated a carpet for the parish's sanctuary. That same year a Tampa parishioner donated a cow to the Sisters of the Holy Names.[22]

As often as not a benefactor was a woman. Mrs. Margaret K. Plant, wife of the West Coast railroad and hotel man, was a Catholic and a generous benefactor to St. Louis Parish and Holy Names Academy. Mrs. Mercedes Ybor donated several statues and improvements to Our Lady of Mercy Church, Ybor City, in 1897 at the death of her husband. Kate Jackson, former student of the Holy Names Academy in Key West and daughter of a prominent Catholic family in Tampa (the Jacksons orchestrated the Holy Name Sisters coming to Tampa), was a single woman of considerable means and talent. She gave repeatedly to St. Louis Parish/Sacred Heart Parish and the Academy of the Holy Names. Mother Katharine Drexel, founder of the Sisters of the Blessed Sacrament in Philadelphia, sponsored institutions for African-Americans and Native Americans throughout the U.S. In 1898 Mother Katharine gave $5,000 to Bishop Moore for the construction of a new school building for blacks in St. Augustine. Moore thought he could build the structure for about $8,000; it ended up costing $7,500. The building had classrooms on the first floor and a meeting hall on the second floor. Now, the black Catholic men's group, the Knights of St. John, would be able to use that hall for their functions. There were about 100 black Catholic families in St. Augustine at the time. Although Moore tried to get Sisters of the Blessed Sacrament to teach in it, Mother Katharine could spare none. The new two-story brick school for blacks was located in Lincolnville, where most African-Americans lived in St. Augustine. It was called St. Cecilia School, named for the previous black Catholic school located near the Cathedral at the old St. Mary's Academy, whose use was given gratis by Mr. Flagler, who owned the building since c. 1888. In 1914 St. Cecilia School was renamed St. Benedict the Moor, to complement the name of the new parish church built on that site.[23]

Of all the various groups of laity, it was the benefactors that Moore knew personally the best, since building a relationship with them translated into benefits for the Church.

## Numbers of Catholics

Just how many Catholics were in the Diocese of St. Augustine in Moore's time? Most numbers are guesstimates, especially given that a Catholic is defined as anyone who is baptized such. Whether a person practices the Faith after Baptism or not, does not disqualify a person from calling oneself a Catholic or being called one. Being a Catholic is a very inclusive status. The best source of estimating the numbers of Catholics in the period is Moore himself. He made two *Ad limina* reports to Rome, one in 1886, the other in 1892. In the 1886 Report, he estimates the Catholic population to be 10,200 out of a total of 226,798 as of 1880, that is, that Catholics comprised 4.5 percent of the total diocesan population. His 1892 Report cites the total population as of 1890 to be 328,211 (of whom 43.4 percent were black), while the Catholic population stood at 22,800 (a figure which also includes blacks and Cubans). Catholics were at 6.9

percent of the total population. Though a small minority, Florida Catholicism was growing in terms of numbers and in relation to the total population during Moore's tenure. He strove mightily to sustain pastoral care amidst a period of population growth and urbanization during Florida's First Boom.[24]

CHAPTER TEN

# *Priorities*

L eadership is about choosing priorities. You can't do everything and everything is not of equal importance. The discernment of priorities and the implementation of them is crucial for effective leadership. For Moore, some of his priorities were shaped by his own choosing and his skills of implementation. On the other hand, some were imposed upon him by circumstances beyond his control. Unlike his contemporary titans of business in Florida, Moore's priorities were not about profit share, ruthless competition, controlling markets and governments in a manner favorable to your business, but rather about the delivery of pastoral care to the needs of his people, a skill that took a careful management of personnel and finances. Unlike the "Robber Barons" such a Flagler, Plant, Ybor, and Disston, Moore produced no goods and services which generated a profit to fuel his ecclesiastical business. Yet, it takes money to support clergy and religious women, build missions, parishes, and schools, as well as supplying ecclesiastical services and goods. Unlike his contemporary business leaders who had not only profits, but sophisticated corporate structures and specialized personnel to advertise their products and to finance the building of railroads, the construction of resort hotels, and the promotion of property sales, Moore ran a charitable organization which lacked any bureaucratic structures and specialized personnel. Financing came from freewill donations of parishioners or benefactors and from his own personal engagement in begging, for lack of a better term. Moore did a lot of begging, mostly outside of Florida.

## Pastoral Care

Moore's top priority was always providing pastoral care for the people in his diocese. He expresses his anxieties about providing pastoral care in a letter to Archbishop Gibbons in mid-1883:

> I could not express to your Grace the anxiety I feel on account of the wanting of priests in this diocese. Catholics are coming to all the little towns that are now springing up so rapidly all over the southern part of this State, and I find everywhere I go the very best dispositions in our regard on the part of non-Catholics. Oh, if I only had priests to minster to them all![1]

This is why, for example, he invited the Jesuits and Benedictines into the diocese, since he lacked the personnel to provide the necessary ministrations for the growing number of Catholics on Florida's West Coast and Southeast Coast. One means he implemented to keep track of the pastoral needs within the diocese was the *Notitiae*.

The use of the annual *Notitiae* began in the Archdiocese of Baltimore during the episcopacy of Francis Peter Kenrick, archbishop from 1851-1863. These forms were standardized by Archbishop James Roosevelt Bayley (1872-1877) in 1872. Moore simply took the Baltimore standardized forms and applied them in his own diocese, beginning in January 1878 (for the year 1877). At that time he had eight parishes and nine priests, all of them diocesan. Two forms were sent to each of the eight pastors: one to be filled out and sent to the bishop, the other copy to be archived in the parish. Some pastors did not embrace the new requirement with enthusiasm, since only four of the total of eight parishes initially responded. Some of the French pastors, recruited by Bishop Verot, were particularly resistant to the idea of annual report, especially regarding parish finances. Father Joseph L. Hugon, pastor at Mater Dolorosa in Tallahassee, was particularly irked about the requirement, even through the 1890s. Father Henry Clavreul, at St. Joseph's, Mandarin, also was recalcitrant, giving a very minimal report every year, although he was generally more cooperative and less belligerent than Hugon.[2]

The annual *Notitiae* was a one-page two-sided printed form folded into two. The pastor filled out the various categories and could elaborate adding additional sheets of paper. The categories to be responded to were as follows: parish statistics (numbers of parishioners — men, women, children; Sacramental numbers — baptisms, marriages, burials, Easter Duty, etc.; numbers of kids in catechism class and in the parish school; the numbers of stations and missions, along with their populations); the second page was a detailed Financial Statement of Receipts and Expenses. This latter reportage seemed to gall the Gallic priests the most. These annual reports taken individually and corporately gave Bishop Moore a good picture of each parish and the diocese as a whole. The *Notitiae* of 1878 showed that St. Mary, Star of the Sea, Key West, was the diocese's largest parish with 560 parishioners. It also had the largest income. But most parishes in that year were much smaller, between 100 to 300 parishioners, and most of their finances put them barely in the black, with a few in the red, not allowing some pastors even to take a salary of $200 a year. For example, St. Louis in Tampa in 1878 claimed ninety-nine parishioners total, fifty-four of whom made Easter Duty (receiving Confession and Holy Communion during the Lenten or Easter Season). The annual income was $356.51, but that amount was exceeded by expenditures which amounted to $375.02. Although not reporting in 1878, Father Dufau did make a report for 1880 for Immaculate Conception Parish, Jacksonville. That account claimed a total of 1,280 parishioners, 400 of whom made Easter Duty. The parish received $4,045.48 in income, making a gain for the year of $12.86, with $2,119.27 in debt on the church and rectory. This made the Jacksonville parish the biggest and most lucrative in the diocese at the time. Although Key West had a larger Catholic population, counting the Cubans, many Catholics there were not as engaged in parish life or as generous to the parish as were the parishioners in Jacksonville.[3]

By the end of Moore's episcopacy in 1901, the diocese had seventeen parishes, twenty missions, and 110 stations. In 1901, the largest and wealthiest parish was Immaculate Conception in Jacksonville. Most parishes had a couple of hundred congregants.

There were thirty-one priests — seventeen religious and fourteen diocesan (nine of whom were Irish-born). Moore concentrated on recruiting Irish-born seminarians, preferring them to be trained in Rome. By 1901 his Irish strategy was beginning to pay dividends. James Nunan received his doctorate in Rome in June 1898, while James Veale did so in 1900. Moore sought learned and well-trained priests, as he was, who had a broad vision of the Church that came from Roman training. So successful was his Irish recruitment, a process continued by his successors, that by 1921, in a mutually and amicably agreed-upon arrangement, the Diocese of St. Augustine had enough of its own priests to relieve the Jesuits from their pastoral responsibilities for most of South Florida. At that time, over 80 percent of the diocesan priests were Irish-born. It was an Irish-born man, recruited by Moore, sent to Rome to study, ordained for the diocese in 1904, who became Bishop of the Djiocese of St. Augustine in 1914. It was he who negotiated the transition in South Florida from the Jesuits to the diocesan priests in 1921, Michael J. Curley. That same year, he was transferred to the Archdiocese of Baltimore.[4]

In addition to collecting data yearly from each parish, Moore received annual "Statistical and Financial Reports," that is *Notitiae,* from the various schools in the diocese, a fact alluded to in Chapter 8. But Moore did not simply sit at his desk reading reports, he personally visited every parish and most of the schools annually. He routinely celebrated Confirmation in the parishes from 1878 and also in the Sisters' Academies from 1885. Parishes that were farther away, such as St. Louis, Tampa, and St. Mary, Star of the Sea, Key West, he confirmed every two years from 1880. The Cathedral and St. Mary, Star of the Sea, consistently had the highest number of Confirmands. As did Bishop Verot and as did most bishops is the South, Moore carefully noted the Confirmation of African-Americans separate from Caucasians. As the number of parishes increased in the late 1880s, Moore's Confirmation schedule expanded. For example, with the development of the Benedictine parishes and the Jesuit parishes on the West Coast, Moore started making annual visits for Confirmation there from 1893.[5]

As we saw in Chapter 7, he also visited parishes that demanded his personal attention because of problems. Moore did not supervise pastoral care from behind a desk in some Chancery Office Building, but was constantly on the road, making pastoral visits and also traveling up North. On the other hand, he did not supervise by micromanaging. He used the principle of subsidiarity, although he would not call it that, since the concept was articulated after his death by Pope Pius XI in his 1931 encyclical *Quadragesimo Anno*. This socio/political principle maintains that it is a "harmful disturbance of right order to turn over to a greater society of higher rank functions and services which can be performed by lesser bodies on a lower plane."[6] In other words, the parish and school, the pastor and school Sisters, were the first and primary locus of decision-making regarding the pastoral good of the people in their respective institutions. Moore relied on and trusted his pastors and school Sisters to provide appropriate pastoral care which was administered locally. This is why his interventions in a parish or in the case of the Sisters of St. Joseph in 1899 were so rare and exceptional. Moore's local visitations were meant to be of moral support for those in the local pastoral field and to put flesh on the bones of the annual reports he received. Sometimes his visitations also provided financial support from the bishop as well.

This principle of subsidiarity also played out on how new parishes were formed, not by some "master plan" coming from a central office, but organically and locally based from stations becoming missions, then missions being made parishes when they had sufficiently matured numerically and financially. Missions and stations were created from the mother parish through the cooperation and collaboration of priests with their people. The bishop simply ratified this process with the appointment of a resident pastor for the newly named parish which was previously a mission.[7]

Despite all of his various preoccupations, Moore felt that delivering pastoral care was his key priority. For example, he estimated there were 6,500 Spaniards and Cubans in Key West and 3,000 of them in Tampa in 1889. As he wrote Pace, rector of the Cathedral, about the unique pastoral needs of Hispanics in his diocese in May 1889: "I must make an effort to provide for their [the Hispanics] spiritual wants and I cannot do otherwise than with the help of a religious order. I could not get Spanish secular priests for that work, or if I got one or two now, how could I keep up the occupation?"

He ended up recruiting the New Orleans Jesuits for the task and supported them in their extensive ministry in South Florida.[8]

# Begging

Bishop Moore made up his mind in early 1883 that he needed to travel on begging trips. As he wrote to Archbishop `:

> I am struggling down here with poverty, fewness of laborers in the vineyard, and wants of [the] missions growing yearly beyond what anybody expected in a short time ago, and trying to do my best. I dislike the idea of going out to beg in some of the rich dioceses of the country, but I have no Father White down here and I may be compelled to undertake the labor myself sometime or another.[9]

Moore spent a lot of time outside of the diocese, especially after 1887. He was perpetually traveling to beg for money because he was perpetually in need of cash for his missionary parishes and institutions, many of whom were not self-supporting or were just barely meeting expenses from their collections. His benefactors in Florida were not sufficient financial fuel available to maintain and expand pastoral care. He and the diocese were unceasingly out of money and in debt, but through his constant strenuous efforts and skills, the diocese remained solvent and pastoral care was able to increase during his tenure. Ironically, the very thing that he criticized Bishop Lynch for when he was a young priest of the Diocese of Charleston, that is, Lynch's being constantly absent from the diocese, Moore himself was forced to do when he became Bishop of St. Augustine. Both men were constrained to travel outside their dioceses in order to keep their dioceses afloat.

Moore traveled by boat or train to dioceses and parishes in the Northern states. Meanwhile, the Southern economy lagged in the post-War Period, due to the fact of its failed-state (the Confederacy), its relative lack of economic engines (such as industry and railroads), and due to the fact that most of the War and its ravages took place on Southern soil. The post-War Period in America, often called the Gilded Age, was one of growing economic vitality, especially in the North, which is why the railroads and hotels built by Plant and Flagler were so popular among those who were benefitting from the economic boom, opening up Florida to high-end tourism and to markets for their agricultural products. As a result, Florida experienced its first economic boom in the late nineteenth century, as is evidenced by the growth in the Tampa area, along the Southeast coast, and in Jacksonville, all coinciding with Moore's tenure. But that prosperity did not sufficiently trickle down to most Florida Catholics so that they might be able to sufficiently support their parishes and missions; hence, Moore traveled North and appealed to his fellow Catholics there on behalf of his missionary diocese, his struggling parishes, his people.

Train connections, good from Jacksonville north, improved during the First Florida Boom. Better railroad connections enabled Moore to visit the parishes within his diocese, as well as to travel up North. Riding the rails was a modern marvel, shrinking distance and time, with relative comfort and ease.

Moore visited New York in September and October of 1880, but it was a personal trip, not a begging tour. He had two priest friends from his Roman days in Gotham City, Father Richard Burtsell (ordained in 1862) and his classmate Father Edward McGlynn. Also while in New York, Moore wrote Archbishop Gibbons of Baltimore asking for assistance to pay for seminarian Edward Pace's education in Rome. Later, Moore would return time and again to New York, not only to visit his friends, but to make appeals for his diocese.[10]

In July 1884, Moore journeyed to Boston, then to New York, where amidst fundraising, he met with historian John Gilmary Shea about the status of Church property in Spanish Florida. In February 1885, Moore is in Baltimore, and then sails for Rome in April as part of a team of bishops tasked with getting the enactments of III Plenary Baltimore approved by Rome. He used his presence there to deliver his first *Ad Limina* Report (a ten-year report about a diocese given to the Holy See by the bishop in person). Moore returned to New York in early 1887, visiting Father McGlynn on Jan. 3. The next day he dined with Archbishop Corrigan. On Jan. 10 he left New York for Florida.

In mid-May 1887, Moore is back in New York, staying there until the end of July, when he pushes on to Philadelphia through November. Why such an unusually long absence from his diocese?

One reason was that his Roman classmate, Father Edward McGlynn, was in very serious trouble with his archbishop, Michael J. Corrigan, because of the pastor's political activities. The extent of Moore's engagement in what might be called the McGlynn Affair will be discussed in full in Chapter 13.[11]

But Moore did not just go up North for an extended period in the summer of 1887 only because of his loyal friendship with McGlynn, or because his diocese needed money for its various pastoral care activities, but primarily because his Cathedral burnt down and he needed money to rebuild. Previously in Charleston, he experienced that city's Cathedral conflagration in 1861, but now as the Bishop of St. Augustine, he had the primary responsibility to find a way to restore his Cathedral.

Early in the early morning hours of April 12, 1887, a fire started in the boiler room of the four-story wooden St. Augustine Hotel, which was on the same city block as the Cathedral. Rapidly, the entire hotel was aflame and sparks shot into the air like white-hot rivets, setting ablaze adjacent buildings. Soldiers from St. Francis Barracks and workers from Flagler's various construction projects acted as volunteer firemen, trying to limit the spread of the flames to St. George and Treasury Streets, thus protecting Flagler's new Ponce de Leon Hotel. The Cathedral's roof caught fire from the flying embers and soon collapsed into the interior, destroying the building. Only the thick coquina stone walls of the church stood, as the Philadelphia Archdiocesan newspaper, *The Catholic Standard*, reported: "Nothing but the walls remain." The Cathedral was insured for $10,000, a mere drop in the bucket to actually reconstruct the church. Fortunately, the breeze was calm and by nightfall the fire was contained to only one downtown block, on which the Cathedral stood. But still, estimates of the property damage amounted to $250,000 ($6,922,239.40 in 2017 dollars). Flagler's hotel, still under construction, was spared. The millionaire sent his laborers to clean up debris littering the burnt-over block, agreeing to help with the rebuilding effort, including the Cathedral reconstruction. This tragic episode marks the beginning of a decade-long collaboration between the two men. Thomas Graham, a Flagler biographer, estimates that the railroad magnate quietly donated at least $75,000 over time to Moore to rebuild his Cathedral. In addition, it was Flagler who

*10.1 Cathedral of St. Augustine, 1886, prior to the fire. Source: Maurice F. Egan, The Hierarchy of the Roman Catholic Church of the U.S., Vol. I (1888), 34.*

commissioned and paid for the new campanile, designed by James Renwick, who was the architect of St. Stephen's in New York (McGlynn's parish) and of St. Patrick's Cathedral, New York. Because of the secrecy which Flagler demanded in his benefactions to Moore, the exact amount Flagler donated to Moore for the Cathedral and other projects remains unknown.[12]

So now, not only did Moore have to provide for the pastoral needs of his people by begging for funds, but also the necessity of rebuilding his Cathedral was thrust upon him. He wasted no time collecting money for that project. By mid-May 1887, he was in New York, using it as a base for collecting throughout the Northeast during his whirlwind tour of 1887.

Even before he left, donations began coming in: the first from his New York friend, Father Richard Burtsell; then from the proceeds of minstrel entertainments given by a Savannah-based troop in parishes in Jacksonville, St. Augustine, and Palatka; from Father Denis O'Connell, rector of the North American College, Rome; from various individuals in New York City; from the Drexel Company and family in Philadelphia. But most of the Cathedral restoration money came by his own personal begging efforts. By the end of 1887, Moore reported collecting a total of $15,037.10 for Cathedral repairs. He sequestered those funds into especially designated accounts. By way of comparison, the total receipts for the Cathedral for 1887 were $4,448.39, of which $794 was applied specifically to Cathedral rebuilding, which was exactly the difference between the Cathedral's expenditures and income. Moore had to endure the strenuous begging trips up North because he knew that the resources of the Cathedral, of all his parishes in the diocese, and even his Florida benefactors, were insufficient for the rebuilding task at hand.[13]

While attending Burtsell's 25th Anniversary on August 10, 1887, he raised money in a few wealthy New York parishes; meanwhile he shuttled back and forth to Philadelphia, speaking at several larger urban parishes there in July and August. He collected $333 ($9,220.42 in 2017 dollars) at the Philadelphia Cathedral, plus he received a check for $375 ($10,383.36 in 2017 dollars) from one individual. He also begged at the following Philadelphia parishes: Annunciation, St. Augustine, St. John the Evangelist, St. Michael's, St. Patrick's, St. Philip Neri. He returned to New York, then left there on August 27 for Philadelphia again, until September 28, when he embarked for St. Augustine.[14]

While in New York, not only was Moore raising money in 1887, but he was also meeting there with Flagler and architects regarding the Cathedral's rebuilding. Earlier, with Flagler's consent, Moore discussed with Joseph McDonald, a Catholic and Flagler's construction chief, about obtaining some of the concrete being used to build the Ponce de Leon Hotel and the Alcanzar Hotel for the Cathedral's reconstruction. During the first of the three times Moore met with Flagler in New York in 1887, the bishop discretely did not bring up the matter of the concrete, since he already had both Flagler's and McDonald's promise to supply the concrete. Moore also met with Renwick, who had submitted architectural plans to him in early June. Moore was very hands-on with the project, wrestling over details like the pews, the windows, and the organ. As an example of his attention to detail, in September he wrote Pace at the Cathedral rectory that he never considered heating the whole church, although heating the sacristy might be a good idea, especially in helping to preserve the vestments from dampness. Earlier in 1883, Moore had gotten permission from the Acting Secretary of War, William T. Sherman, to quarry coquina rock from the Federal government's land on Anastasia Island. He instructed Pace that if there was any coquina left after using it for cathedral reconstruction, it should be saved and used for a "colored church" that he was planning to erect, as well as for Our Lady of Leche Chapel.[15]

Moore returned to the Northeast in mid-January 1888, collecting first in Washington, DC, begging at St. Matthew's Cathedral, where he collected $330, plus obtaining another $300 from wealthy parishioners. He wrote Pace at that time, saying: "My health is good, but I feel the cold very much." No Floridian wants to be in the Northeast in the winter! The next Sunday made an appeal at St. Patrick's, then the weekend after at St. Peters, then at St. Aloysius, then at two other parishes. After he finished covering the Washington parishes, he moved on to Baltimore, then going back again to New York.

He traveled to St. Augustine mid-February (probably to thaw out), hoping to catch Flagler when he was expected to arrive between February 13 to the 15th — "I may find him there when I come," Moore wrote Pace. That same month, Moore composed a letter to O'Connell, Rector of North American College, Rome, apologizing: "This year I will be tardy in making my remittances [payments for the seminarians at North American College] as the work of restoring my Cathedral absorbs all my funds... I have already paid out over $41,000 on it [in restoration costs] and will need fully $30,000 more." He added: "I have to beg and borrow the best I can." He returned North in mid-March, at which time he visited Richmond, Norfolk, then back to Washington again to collect at St. Augustine Parish. His whole task was a worrisome burden, arduous and exasperatingly slow work. As he wrote Pace in mid-March from Norfolk: "The indebtedness, of which you sent me in a statement, is startling to me, when I see how slowly I am able to collect. Some Good Samaritan will, I hope, come to our relief." On March 18 he was at St. Augustine's, Washington, when he received a check from a Jersey City pastor who gave a donation of $200 in lieu of a promised parish collection. Later in 1897, Moore reckoned he garnered $14,707 in 1887 and 1888 for Cathedral restoration, $4,282.87 coming from Philadelphia alone, and the biggest contribution he received from a single diocese. But recall that usually the diocese itself did not contribute to his cause; rather, it was Moore's speaking at the Masses in individual parishes which generated the funds he needed. He worked hard for what he got. On March 19, 1888, he went to New York City to catch a steamer to Savannah, and then return to St. Augustine by rail.

In the summer of 1889, he was on to Chicago begging, then to parishes in the Diocese of Buffalo, returning to St. Augustine in November. In the summer of 1890, he was back in Chicago. By the fall, he moved about the Northeast, once again using New York as his base. He did not travel out of Florida in 1891, but in the summer of 1892, he proceeded to St. Louis, collecting and confirming, since the archbishop there was ill. Moore spent the summer of 1893 raising funds in Chicago, "but I have got very little money — barely enough to save me at the bank. But the end of the crisis must come." The "crisis" Moore is referring to is the Panic of 1893. He barely collected enough money in Chicago to cover his checking account expenses and loan payments. From the fall of 1896 into January 1897, Moore based himself again in New York, collecting in parishes throughout the Northeast. In the summer of 1898, he was in Buffalo once again. In the fall of 1899, he journeyed to Pennsylvania, where on September 6, 1899, he suffered a heart attack, having a stroke which partially paralyzed him for a time. After that, he no longer traveled out of the State; he soldiered on in his diocese, until he became more debilitated in 1901.[16]

All of this traveling by boat and train up and down the East Coast in a compressed time frame in 1887 and 1888, as well as throughout his episcopacy from that point on, had to have been physically and mentally exhausting, while all the time feeling pressured to make payments for ongoing Cathedral repairs and bank loans. These begging tours demanded lots of organization and energy: transportation to and from the various locations; scheduling speaking venues; getting permissions from bishops and pastors to make appeals; speaking at all parish Masses; living out of a suitcase from rectory to rectory; depositing the money collected and keeping track of all of it; meanwhile attending to pastoral matters that arose in Florida, beyond Cathedral construction. Moore was fifty-three, going on fifty-four, years of age during 1887-88. All of these complicated burdens, which he had to do himself, must have aged him prematurely.

So while traveling, speaking, and managing his collections, he is also keeping eyes on all the details of Cathedral reconstruction, often from afar by letter. Moore writes to Pace from Baltimore in July 1888, complaining that collections there "are very small... I shall have to hang around here all summer." Meanwhile, he tells Pace that Cathedral costs are amounting to more than anticipated. "Renwick is horrified," he comments. Up to this point, Moore was able to pay as he goes from his collections, but now he can't. He has to borrow. His "Good Samaritan Friend," as he calls him, is Flagler who "allows me to call upon him for a loan whenever I want it, nor does he limit the sum I ask for." It was Flagler's secret loans that enabled Moore to continue work on the Cathedral in mid-1888.[17]

Throughout his correspondence, Moore constantly asks Pace, who is at St. Augustine, how work in the Cathedral is progressing — is the roof on yet? He trusts Pace to implement his wishes regarding Cathedral reconstruction. Renwick gets into a dispute with William Cotter, architect and builder from Sanford, Fla., about the costs. Cotter in late August 1888 writes Renwick defending his expenditures to date: a total of $70,000 ($1,938,227.03 in 2017 dollars). He breaks down the various disbursements, including the campanile at $13,000 ($359,956.45 in 2017 dollars) and the pulpit at $497. Construction outlays embraced both the church and the rectory, the latter being also seriously damaged by the fire. After reviewing Cotter's statement of accounts, Renwick wrote to the builder and the bishop apologizing for his criticism, saying that he was unaware of the number of items included were not on the original plans (sewers, gutters, sidewalks, furniture changes). He was unaware that the amount of change orders and cost overruns amounted to $20,000. However, in November, Renwick remains rankled about the construction expenditures, as he writes Moore: "It's too bad the work is done by the day and not by contract."[18]

Nonetheless, the work proceeded, but ended for a time in December 1888, when Moore had to come to aid Kenny, pastor of Immaculate Conception, Jacksonville, who was infirm due to yellow fever. All the while Moore was engrossed with his Cathedral rebuilding, he dealt with the priest shortage initiated by yellow fever in Tampa and eventually negotiated with Jesuits for the pastoral care of all of South Florida. Meanwhile, Moore writes Gibbons in Baltimore in early December telling him that "My Good Samaritan Friend" [Flagler] had given Moore $30,000 and loaned $15,000

*10.2 Rebuilt Cathedral of St. Augustine.*
*Source: TLPC postcard, no date*

without interest, adding "Still I need more." He gently reminds Gibbons of the $1,000 he promised him at the end of 1888. He reports that Cathedral reconstruction costs are at about $80,000 ($2,215,116.61 in 2017 dollars), "and there still remains much to be done." Yet, the Cathedral was back in operation in October 1888. By mid-May 1889, Moore believes construction will cost $20,000 more, since he still needs the Bishop's Throne, three marble altars, and stained glass windows. He intends to look into the stained glass on his next trip to Europe. He will suspend work on the Cathedral for now, since he needs to pay back some of the loans he has taken out and the Sisters of St. Joseph require a new convent and orphanage in Jacksonville. He adds: "But where is the money going to come from?" He says that "I trust in good measure to Sister Mary Ann's capacity for begging." Sister Mary Ann, SSJ, was a beloved figure in Jacksonville among all of its citizens. Known as the "Angel of Jacksonville," she ran the orphanage there. She was Irish-born and had formidable persuasive skills, of which obviously Moore was well aware. Moore planned a trip to Chicago to beg for the two new Jacksonville institutions, which he thought will cost about $37,500 for land and construction. Another reason for the cessation of the work on the Cathedral was that Moore prioritized his attentions to the pastoral needs of the Tampa area and beyond with his negotiations with the Jesuits.[19]

Moore did go to Chicago in the summer of 1890, where he collected $6,000. As usual, he worked hard at it. "I had to preach from three to six times every Sunday... the heat was great, [but] I had to try to make hay while the sun shone." Sadly, all of his work to build the convent and orphanage in Jacksonville literally went up in a puff of smoke with the great fire there in May 1901, when both of the relatively newly constructed buildings were destroyed.[20]

For the rest of his episcopate, Moore continued to complete the details of Cathedral restoration, which also necessitated continued periodic begging trips to the North. In the Fall of 1893, he signed a contract for $2,200 for a marble and masonry altar to the Blessed Virgin Mary, paying for it by the end of 1897. In the October of 1897, he purchased a St. Joseph's Altar which cost $2,200, plus $224 for the architect's commission. Although he suffered a stroke while on a begging tour in Wilkes-Barre, Pa, in early September 1899, Moore was still focused on executing the main marble altar and reredos in mid-1900.

To aide with that project, the ladies of the Cathedral Parish put on a fair at the end of February 1900 (when wealthy winter visitors were still in town), which netted $1,482.40 ($44,306.83 in 2017 dollars), but such local fundraising was inadequate for the task at hand. After Easter, he traveled to New York to raise more money, despite his declining health. On October 13, 1900, he approved the altar, reredos, and statues of Pius IX and of Francis Borgia, along with a bas relief of the Sacred Heart of Jesus and two angels, all done in Italian marble at a cost of $6,900 ($206,231.19 in 2017 dollars). Renwick wrote Moore on October 15: "We are sorry to hear that you are progressing so slowly in your health..." In spite of not being fully himself, he remained ever the man of detail, duty, and exactitude, asking for changes on the carving of the Pius IX statue in early December. Moore made the first payment of $1,500 on December 6; he paid the last installment on March 28, 1901. The main marble altar, reredos, and statues were delivered as Moore had requested right after Easter 1901 (in April).

However, in early May he received some very bad news which would entail more rebuilding, not in St. Augustine, but in Jacksonville. The Great Fire of 1901 happened there on May 3, destroying 146 square blocks and over 2,000 buildings, including Immaculate Conception Church and Rectory, the Sisters Academy and the Orphanage. That rebuilding would be left to his successor. His health continued to decline.

He died in St. Augustine on July 30, 1901.[21] An ever dutiful man of business and a leader in pastoral care to the end, he completed his responsibilities of Cathedral rebuilding almost right up to the hour of his death. It was as if he willed himself to live until his duty was completed.

## Soliciting by Pen

But Moore begged money for the diocese in other ways besides his personal appeals in northern parishes. One way was by raising money by writing letters to the Society of the Propagation of the Faith (the SPOF) in Lyons and Paris, France. Moore's predecessor, Frenchman Bishop Augustine Verot, received money from them annually. In 1876, Verot requested 14,000 francs from the SPOF. Moore continued his predecessor's tradition, receiving donations from the SPOF from 1877 to 1889.[22]

The SPOF was conceived by Pauline Jaricot of Lyons when she was a mere 19 years of age in 1818. She sold her idea to the French Directors of Foreign Missions. On May 3, 1822, the "Society for the Propagation of the Faith" was established and approved by Pope Pius VII the following year. Its purpose was to pray and support with alms foreign Catholic missionary efforts in non-Catholic countries. As soon as a particular mission was able to exist on its own, the SPOF withdrew funding. With revised rules drawn up in 1834, the SPOF had two councils, one in Paris and one in Lyons, each with eight members and a cashier. Both councils had to agree on disbursements, which were pro-rated on the annual donations received. The SPOF had no investments. All funds donated in a given year were to be disbursed that same year. Donations came not just from France, but from throughout Europe, and eventually from the U.S. The first National Director of the SPOF in the U.S. was appointed 1897. From 1822 to 1861, the U.S. received a total of $7,020,974 from the SPOF.[23]

Moore was required to make a report to the SPOF annually regarding the state of the diocese, how much support he requested, and how he intended to disburse the money. For example, in November of 1877, he wrote a three page letter in French asking for a total of 90,800 francs, 4.8 times more than previous year's request which was submitted by the Diocesan Administrator, Father Peter Dufau, who had been Vicar General under Verot. With his usual financial precision, Moore declared the diocese's income to be 10,600 francs (mostly revenue from parishes and missions, dividends, and property rentals). His projected expenditures were as follows: personnel (clergy salaries) — 15,000 francs; operations of six Catholic schools — 6,500 francs; interest on debt — 200 francs; seminarians (five at St. Mary's and St. Charles's Colleges, Baltimore) — 5,000 francs; for a total of 26,700 francs needed. He also listed as another expenditure construction debt, totaling 64,100 francs, for the churches in Moccasin Branch and Green Cove Springs and the SSJ convents in Palatka, Fernandina, and St. Augustine. Moore ended up getting 20,000 francs from Paris and 30,000 francs from Lyons, plus an additional bonus of 385.50 francs from Lyons. Moore also received extra donations from three individuals connected with the SPOF, amounting to 1,925 francs. So, all told, Moore's powers of persuasion earned him 52,310.50 francs from the SPOF during his first year of making a request. Although it was not the precise amount he asked for (that requested amount was slightly "padded"), it would be the largest annual amount he would ever receive from the SPOF for the rest of his episcopacy. Moore continued his style of asking for more than he received. For example, in 1884, he petitioned for no specific amount since his diocesan income exceeded his expenditures by 1,530 francs, but he is quick to point out that he had construction debts of 116,000 francs; he received 9,200 francs from the SPOF that year.[24]

In January 1888, he made an appeal to the SPOF as a result of the "grand calamity" of the burning of his Cathedral in April 1887. He solicited 113,500 francs, his largest request ever. He does not get it; in fact, he gets nothing from the SPOF from that point on. No explanation is given either by the SPOF or by Moore. Perhaps the SPOF was disinterested in sponsoring construction projects, especially massive ones such as Moore was undertaking in rebuilding his Cathedral. Moore tries requesting the SPOF one more time in 1895, on behalf of the Benedictine parish, St. Anthony, which had an outstanding debt of $1,800. Due to the citrus freeze of 1895, the orange crop was ruined, resulting in farming congregation's inability to pay the debt. Moore's begging letter to the SPOF on behalf of St. Anthony Parish went unanswered.[25]

However, this did not end Moore's epistolary begging. In early 1893, he received $1,000 from the Commission for Catholic Missions among the Colored People and Indians (from a national collection taken up on every American parish for Blacks and Native Americans, the nation's first, established in 1887). The Diocese of St. Augustine received what was the average amount given to dioceses. The Diocese of St. Augustine only collected $72 for that collection in 1893, the lowest of any diocese in the country. Also in the years 1888, 1891, 1893-94, 1896-99 the Benedictine Parishes of Pasco County received around $200 a year from the Ludwig Missionary Association in Germany. Moore must have been aware of this fact, even though he himself was not directly involved with that request for money, the monks of St. Leo's were.[26]

Moore had annual diocesan collections for both the SPOF and the Negro and Indian Missions, the former beginning in 1886, the latter beginning in 1888. Of course, he received much more from those organizations than he was able to give to both those organizations.[27]

## Borrowing

Unlike his contemporary corporate leaders, such as Flagler and Plant, Moore had no corporate bureaucracy or a team of financial experts to manage the diocesan financial accounts. He had to do it all himself, from raising money to managing it.

Another way he augmented his finances was by borrowing. The First National Bank of St. Augustine was his favorite place to borrow money. From 1888 through 1895, he borrowed fourteen times from that institution, notes from $500 to $5,000 each, due from three months to one year. The earliest notes were at 6 percent interest, then at a flat fee of $100, while later notes were interest and fee free. Although Moore always paid back the money, he did not always pay it back on time. A number of the notes due dates were extended three to eight times! That bank was certainly friendly to Moore and forbearing, but then in the end they always got their money back, eventually. Moore borrowed similar sums at least once from the Germania Bank of Savannah, Ga.; once from the State

Savings Bank of Tallahassee; and twice from the Southern Savings and Trust Company in Jacksonville. But with those banks, he had to pay between 6 and 8 percent interest.[28]

Moore also borrowed from individuals. Cardinal Gibbons of Baltimore loaned him money at least once. He extended his repayment on the Gibbons loan, for which he was particularly apologetic for taking three years to repay. He also borrowed from wealthy laity in Florida and New York: Matthew Hays, M.R. Cooper (three times), Dr. E.T. Sabal (twice), and of course Henry Flagler. Each of these loans was at 6 percent interest. Moore paid each in a timely fashion (except for one, Cooper's 1889 loan), but the July 1899 note for $1,000 from Dr. Sabal was the only note he ever neglected to pay, probably due to his ill health and then death. There is only one note from Flagler, recorded July 31, 1895, at 6 percent interest, yet we know from other sources that the railroad tycoon loaned and even donated to the bishop's causes; he just did not want to leave a paper trail.[29]

## Other Means of Raising Money

From 1878 until 1883, Moore did invest some of the diocese's money in stocks. In 1878-79 he asked his friend, Father D.J. Quigley of Charleston, to invest for him in some municipal bonds and in St. Lawrence Cemetery stocks. From 1879 to 1883, he had a stockbroker in Baltimore buy and sell U.S. Bonds, municipal bonds, and B&O Railroad shares (perhaps at the recommendation of Cardinal Gibbons). Moore kept in touch with his Baltimore stockbroker every three months. But in 1883, the bishop sold out all his diocesan stocks and bonds. Good thing, because the Panic of 1893 would have wiped him out![30]

Besides being a fundraiser, a banker, a dabbler in stocks, Moore was a realtor, preoccupied by necessity with the buying and selling of church property, as well as paying taxes on unused diocesan parcels. From 1878 to 1892, Moore accumulated eight deeds for property he bought on behalf of the Church. In 1892, he reckoned that the Church owned at least seventeen parcels of untaxable land, which he estimated to be worth $428,530. He also kept close track of and paid all tax bills for diocesan property. In St. Augustine he was fortunate because in 1897 the City Council voted to exempt all Catholic Church property there from taxation; however, such was not the case elsewhere.[31]

Beginning in 1885, Moore even tussled with the governments of Spain (in Cuba) and the U.S. over the Spanish King's grant of 1796 of ten lots in Havana, the rents from which were to be used for the upkeep of the parish and Franciscan Convent in St. Augustine. Moore even went to Havana in February 1886 to investigate pertinent documents for his case. He claimed to "have been partially successful." He sent historian John Gilmary Shea in New York his findings. With the American occupation of Cuba in 1898, Moore stepped up his Cuban claim, demanding $200,000 from the U.S. government, the second largest amount from among an aggregate total of $726,452 in claims. Moore died before any of this could be resolved. His successor tried to pursue the matter, but to no avail.[32]

Always a man of detail, Moore was dutiful and meticulous in his financial record-keeping, which shows how important monetary affairs were to him and to the exercise of his office. Every promissory note was kept and dated "paid," every deed, every tax bill, every lawyer's correspondence was filed, with his scribbles on them. Every cancelled check from 1891 to March 1901 was also preserved, banded with either rubber bands, or paper bands, or stuck together with pins. He himself kept track of all of his financial dealings on behalf of the diocese right up to his final illness and demise.[33]

## Specialized Pastoral Care

Moore was not just interested in rebuilding his Cathedral, or in raising money, or rationalizing parish reportage. His priority was giving his people good pastoral care, which of course necessitated a financial aspect. For him, reaching out to the outcast, who may not have been Catholic, was an important aspect of his pastoral solicitude, a subject which will be discussed in our next chapter.

CHAPTER ELEVEN

# *Concern for Those on the Margins*

Moore had a personal identification with people on the margins of society, since he himself was in that position several times in his life. As a young boy, he was forced to leave his homeland for a new country and a new life. At the College of Combrée in France and then at the Urban College of the Propagation of the Faith, Rome, Moore experienced being a foreigner and an outsider, compelled to learn new languages and adjust to new cultures. When the North American College opened in 1859, Moore did not transfer there as his classmate Edward McGlynn did, because he was Irish-born and not as yet an American citizen. Upon his return home, he experienced the terror of the bombardment of Charleston and the depressing defeat of the Confederacy, which had long-lasting effects, economically, socially, and psychically, on Southerners long after Reconstruction was over. When he came to Florida as bishop in 1877, he was an outsider, unfamiliar with the Church there and its clergy, religious, and laity. He had some sympathy with those on the margins of society because he had been there himself many times in his life.

## Native Americans

From 1870 to 1878, Cheyenne, Kiowas, Comanches, and Arapahos were prisoners of the U.S. Government, victims of the Indian Wars, and some were sent to Fort Marion (*Castillo San Marcos*) in St. Augustine for brief periods of incarceration. Beginning in 1886 and into 1887, over 300 Apaches from Arizona and New Mexico lived in Army tents pitched on grounds adjacent to the *Castillo San Marcos* in St. Augustine for several months. Among those in custody of the U.S. Army were women and children. While on his way to New York in early January 1886, Moore arranged for a contract with the Catholic Indian Bureau, which was the agency the U.S. government permitted to do pastoral work among Native Americans. Under this contract, the Sisters of St. Joseph, with Moore's encouragement, set about establishing a school for fifty-six children at the *Castillo*, as well as educating the adults; all told 300 persons were under instruction by the Sisters. But this effort was short-lived, since soon the government moved the Apaches to a reservation out West.[1]

In February 1872, Bishop Verot sent his Vicar General, fellow Frenchman Peter Dufau, to Miami to deliver a letter written by the bishop dated January 28, 1872, addressed to the Chief of the Seminole Indians. In it Verot offered to send priest, as well as Sisters, to teach the Seminole children how to read, write, and how to "please the great Spirit." While in Miami, Dufau stayed with the only Catholic family there, the Wagners. At that time, Miami was populated by about fourteen families along with a few single men. Scattered from Cutler, eighteen miles south of the Miami River, to ten miles north of it, they made a living making starch, sponging, or wrecking (salvaging from wrecked ships). Very few of them traded with the Seminoles, who lived west in the depths of the Everglades. As a result, Dufau was unable to deliver the bishop's letter because he could find no one who would take him into the South Florida interior to meet the Seminole chief and because Dufau understood that the Seminoles themselves were indisposed to receive messages or initiatives from non-Seminoles. Later in 1886, Moore expressed a desire to be of some service to the Seminoles, but demurred because he needed one or two missionary priests for the task, but he presently had none to spare.[2]

In early 1891 a judge in Orlando inquired of Moore if Father John O'Boyle, the missionary priest assigned to the Central Florida missions, would be interested in being the Seminole Agent for the Indian Bureau. Apparently there were 110 nominally Catholic Native Americans living at Cow Creek, near Titusville. O'Boyle seems disinclined to the suggestion, as the writes Moore in his *Notitiae* for "The Missions of Volusia and Brevard Counties," dated January 1, 1891: "There are 110 nominally Catholic Indians in this mission. They are well disposed and seem to be willing to follow my advice, but a lack of means prevents me from visiting them as often as I would wish." Could these have been the descendants of the Catholic Indians from Florida's original tribes, evangelized by the Franciscans in colonial times, the remnants of whom amalgamated with the Seminoles? O'Boyle blames Moore for the lack of resources to minister to these people. "This mission [to Volusia and Brevard Counties] has not received a cent for the past two years. The money realized from the sale of the church lots here, last April, was taken elsewhere and Titusville, as a result, has no church." Most probably Moore, prioritizing the rebuilding the Cathedral, took whatever financial resources he could gather for that task, to the detriment of some others, like O'Boyle's. Nothing further is mentioned in the existing archival documentation about O'Boyle's engagement with the Catholic Seminoles of Cow Creek.[3]

Bishop Moore made one final attempt to initiate pastoral care for the Seminoles in the Everglades. In early 1894, he writes to Mother Katharine Drexel, SBS, who devoted her family fortune to minister to those on the margins of American society, African-Americans and Native-Americans, and who founded a religious community of women, the Sisters of the Blessed Sacrament, to serve those forgotten, segregated, and impoverished peoples. He penned: "I believe that the time is now favorable for an effort to Christianize them [the Seminoles]." He notes that in the previous year the Episcopal Bishop of South Florida "was introduced to the Indian chief by the U.S. [Indian] Agent, but the chief told him [the Agent] not to bring that man [the Episcopal Bishop] there again." Shortly after this episode, "Father Conrad Widman, SJ [the Tampa Jesuit missionary to the East Coast], with two Catholic laymen, went to the camp of the chief and was most kindly received by them." The chief and other leaders said that upon their next visit they would take the Jesuit to see their families and "they would all come to hear his instruction." Moore adds that: "I had been frequently told that the Seminoles in the Everglades had preserved a kindly remembrance of the Spaniards and some traditions of the Catholic Church, but up to the present time I had no priest whom I could send to them." He now believes that the time is ripe for such evangelization and Father Widman is the man for the task, since he is "learned, pious, zealous, and experienced." Moore added with pastoral solicitude that after Widman's next visit "I will be able to say what the prospects are of bringing these poor Indians to embrace the Catholic Religion and to save their souls." It seems unlikely that Widman ever made a second visit to the Seminoles. In April 1894, he was in the Ocala area and called on the Seminoles of Cow Creek. But despite Moore's plans for Seminole evangelization, Widman was transferred from Tampa by his Jesuit superiors in August 1894. With no other candidate to send and with a lack of funding to support the mission (Mother Katharine never committed herself to any monetary support of the enterprise), Moore was forced to abandon his pastoral plans for the Seminoles.[4]

## Latins

"Latins" is a generic word used to refer to the Cubans, Spaniards, and Italians who lived in Ybor City and worked in the Cigar industry there. But, the origins of the Latins of Tampa was Key West. With the War of 1868-78 in Cuba, the cigar industry in Havana moved to Key West, as did eventually about 4,000 Cubans who worked in the ninety-one cigar factories that sprung up on the island. There were a few Spaniards also, mostly cigar factory owners, such as Vicente Ybor.[5]

The Cubans in Key West and later the Latins in Ybor City presented pastoral challenges for Bishop Moore, and for the priests and Sisters who served them. Moore had a very negative impression of the state of Catholicism in Cuba because of a visit he made there in 1886, staying at the Archbishop's residence in

Havana and investigating possible claims on the former Franciscan Convent in St. Augustine [converted to a military barracks since 1763, with the British take-over of Florida]. "There is a scarcity of native priests," Moore wrote Archbishop Gibbons in Baltimore about Cuba, claiming that the Faith of Cubans "degenerates into superstition... the state of religion here is practically sickening." Moore also commented on the clergy being in a poor state of moral decay and on the frustrations of the Spanish Archbishop of Havana trying to discipline such a group of priests. The Cubans brought this unpleasant experience of the Church from their home island with them to Key West and Tampa, thought Moore. Later in 1895, Moore became so exasperated with the Cubans in Key West and Ybor City that he decided to no longer include them as part of the total number of Catholics of the diocese. He explains: "In estimating the Catholic population of the diocese I have heretofore counted the Cubans, because they call themselves Catholics, but as very few of them go near the church and many of them even allow their children to die without Baptism... I now leave them out of the count." Despite his experience of Italian Catholicism while in Rome as a student, he seems incapable of grasping Cuban Catholicism, using his knowledge of Irish Catholicism and Tridentine Catholicism as the litmus for his negative judgment of Cuban Catholicism.[6]

Moore was not the only one who was skeptical of Cuban Catholicism and aware of the pastoral challenges Cubans presented. From 1877 to 1901, there were four pastors of St. Mary, Star of the Sea Parish: Paul La Rocque (Canadian), Felix Ghione (Genoise), D. Bottolocio (Genoise), and Alexander Friend, SJ (Swiss). They all found ministering to the Cubans in Key West difficult.

Father LaRocque excluded the Cubans in Key West in his report of parishioner statistics in 1878, although he does mention that there are about 4,000 of them and they presented him real pastoral challenges. He states that Cuban Protestant ministers are preaching among them, drawing them even further from Catholicism. While the Sisters of the Holy Names had opened Our Lady of Mercy School for Cuban girls in 1873, they charged tuition. It was closed in 1878, due to a lack of enrollment. LaRocque felt a need to establish a free Catholic school for all Cuban children, as well as establishing a separate church for them. These institutions "might save many women and the younger generation in the Faith," he noted. In 1879 a separate Cuban chapel was established (Our Lady of Charity) by Father Ghione, but was closed by 1898. Apparently, LaRocque had little hope for the Cuban men. He adds: "Secret societies are the greatest curse on this island." These male dominated enclaves where political ideas were discussed and debated, as well places of socialization. LaRoque "strongly recommends" that the Catholics of the island, especially the Cubans be entrusted to "a poverty loving [his emphasis] religious community of men whose corporate presence would exceed what talents any single man may possess," namely himself. "The present incumbent would gladly retire tomorrow [his emphasis] to make way for such a religious community." Twenty years later, in 1898, Moore did send a religious community, the Jesuits.[7]

The Northern Italian, Felix Ghione, sent a letter to Moore along with his *Notitiae* for 1888. He estimates 6,500 Cubans were in Key West. "Cuban infidels and apostates [Cuban Protestant clergy] have opened schools near our own and their opposition to anything Catholic is simply diabolical." Ghione charges a nominal tuition of 50 cents a month at the Catholic Cuban school. In response the Protestant Cuban school reduced its tuition from $2 a month to 15 cents a month. Ghione comments: "This is simply one example of what we have to contend with here in Key West!" He continues: "The Catholic school must be open *gratis* to the Cubans, but even then it probably won't be patronized." Ghione feels that Cubans' Catholicism is tepid. Of the parish's 513 burials in 1888, only 185 were Cubans; of the total marriages of 315, only 112 were with Cubans. "How light is the hold of the Catholic Church on Cubans." He says that only 5 percent of their burials are in the Church and only 5 percent call a priest at the point of death for the Last Rites. Barely 10 percent of their marriages are in the Church. But there is one bright spot, 75 percent of the total of infant baptisms are of Cubans. "This is the only oasis [his emphasis] on this island." He states that the Cubans in Key West need their own church, "like the French Canadians, the Germans, and the Italians" in other parts of the country. Later, Ghione sends Moore in 1890 a "Census of Catholics in Key West." The "floating population" of Cubans amounts to 2,500 whites and 300 "colored." The "settled population" of Cubans amounts to 3,800 whites and 400 "colored." He states the total Cuban population is about 7,000. American parishioners amount to 265 whites and 154 "colored."[8]

In 1894, Father D. Bottolocio, also from Northern Italy and Assistant Pastor under Ghione, included separate statistics for the Cubans, since they now had their separate parish, Our Lady of Mercy. The Americans of the St. Mary, Star of the Sea Parish in 1894 amounted to a total of 142 whites — twelve men, thirty women, 100 children; of the total of seventy-six Baptisms that year, four were "colored." The total annual Offertory was $70.66, while stole fees (for Baptisms, burials, funerals) exceeded the annual collection, totaling $105.50. Comparing total receipts to expenditures, the parish was in the black by $128.26, although it had a $50 debt still to be paid. Bottolocio added this to the *Notitiae* about the Cubans of Key West: "Although the Cubans appear to be good, they are very superficial in their outlook toward God and the Church. I cannot understand them at all!"[9]

In 1898 the Tampa Jesuits took over St. Mary, Star of the Sea, with Father Alexander Friend, SJ, a Swiss, as pastor. By then, at least 2,000 Key West Cubans had moved to Ybor City. Key West's population of about 17,000 was 44 percent Cuban, 22 percent black, and 34 percent American Caucasian, from almost every state in the nation. Father Friend gave his impressions of the state of Cuban Catholicism as he encountered it in 1898. "The practice of religion among the Cuban population, at least of the men, is not encouraging, but the women as a rule are better disposed." But, he also was disquieted by the state of Faith of the American Catholics on the island: "Even the American portion of the parish is largely made up of lukewarm Catholics. A great deal of work lies before us."[10]

Despite pastoral efforts, pastors' perceptions of the state of Key West Cuban Catholicism remained virtually unchanged for twenty years. The situation of Latins, including Cubans, in the Tampa area was on a larger scale and more complex than in Key West, yet at the same time it was more hopeful for those engaged in pastoral ministry there.

Unlike Key West, which only had Cubans, with a few Spaniard owners, as its Latin contingent, Ybor City had Cubans (the majority group), Spaniards, and Italians, all of whom worked in the cigar industry and lived in company housing. Gary Mormino calls them "an ethnic *paella*" (a Spanish saffron-rice casserole flavored with meats, seafood, vegetables and herbs) unique in the South. Each group brought their own historical experiences of the Church and the state from their homelands and their own culture. But they also had a lot in common, beyond simply working in the cigar industry. They shared a strong sense of the value of family life, where the domestic church was a stronger influence than the parish church. Their spirituality and view of the Church was shaped more by the Medieval Church than by the prescripts of the Council of Trent. Their political views were shaped by the rise of nationalism, which in Italy especially meant being anti-clerical and anti-Church. In Ybor City, Cuban, Italian, and Spanish social clubs and mutual aid societies were more popular gathering places on the weekends, especially for men, than the parish church. Not only were the Latins set apart by living in the separate community of Ybor City, but they were also set apart from the American community by language, customs, political views, and cuisine, as well as a different experience and view of the Church. For example, Americans were used to giving to their parish in the weekly collections and for special fund drives. Because of the First Amendment, the Church could expect no financial help from the state. If Catholics in America wanted a church or school, they had to build it and support it themselves. Latins experienced a Church usually supported by the state or in the case of the Cubans, supported by the colonial power, so much so that virtually all clergy were Spaniards. Latins also experienced a church in their homeland that was often weak and corrupt. None of their previous ecclesial experiences inclined them to give regularly for the support of the Church or its institutions. When they needed the Church, say for an infant Baptism or for a special supplication, especially by a favorite saint, they came to the parish church, otherwise they stayed away. The domestic church provided them with objects of devotion and moral teaching within family life.[11]

The Jesuits of Tampa were much better equipped to deal with the pastoral challenges of the Latins than were the diocesan priests in Key West because of their numbers, their grasp of different cultures and languages, and their cooperative relationship with the religious women there. Most Jesuits stationed in Tampa before 1900 were foreign-born, at least 80 percent. The largest ethnic group was French, followed by the Irish, Germans, and Swiss, respectively. In 1897, the Tampa Jesuits comprised seven different nationalities and spoke five different languages. They were well prepared to deal with the Spanish and Italian languages of the Latins of Tampa. In addition, their Order was founded during the turmoil of the Catholic and Protestant Reformations and molded by Tridentine spirituality and prescriptions. Their community was action-oriented, so much so that they were forbidden to say the Divine Office (the official daily prayer of the Church) in common. No one Jesuit was "a star," but rather they saw themselves as interchangeable, subject to the will of their superior. As Father Philippe de Carriere, SJ, wrote in 1896: "He [any Jesuit] ought to be ready and willing at all times [to allow] any other laborer [who] would and should come to facilitate him [in] the work of salvation [and] in the share of souls he has received for Christ and not for himself only." This interchangeability and resignation to obedience is personified by Tampa pastor, Father William Tyrell, SJ, whom we discussed previously in Chapter 7.[12]

The Jesuits established a mission in Ybor City in 1891, called Our Lady of Mercy (named for a nineteenth century devotion to Mary by Cubans). In 1900 it became a parish. In West Tampa, another enclave for Latins, a mission church was built in 1896 and on its second floor the Sisters of the Holy Names founded an academy. In 1903, a larger church was built and it too became a parish, St. Joseph's, with a resident Jesuit pastor. Mass attendance by the Latins of Ybor City was poor, less than 3 percent of the total Latin population. Despite all their qualifications, talents, and efforts, the Jesuits of Tampa needed the help of women religious to reach the Latin community. For although it was difficult for the priests to engage their Latin parishioners, women religious had access to family life through home visits and to the next generation through their schools. The Catholic school was the bridge for Latin children between the society of their parents and American life, between Medieval Catholicism and Tridentine Catholicism, between the domestic church and the parish church. Both Bishop Moore and the Jesuits were extremely supportive of the Sisters' work among the Latins of Tampa.[13]

Without doubt, the indifference of Tampa's Latins to parish life was a challenge to all who ministered to them. The priests and Sisters who labored among the Latins in the Tampa area were often discouraged by a lack of measurable results for their efforts. Frenchman Father de Carriere, SJ, disparaged the lack of religious practice (Tridentine style) on the part of Latins, as he wrote in 1896: "Alas, the Catholic Faith and Religious feelings and practices are dying more and more, are already almost dead, among those pretended Catholics from Spanish origin living in Florida." It seems that Father de Carriere subscribed to a "myth of decline," that somehow in the past Cubans, Spanish, and Italians in Tampa had at one time been good Tridentine Catholics, but now in Florida their former practice of the Faith was in decline. His misapprehension was surprising, given his Gallic past. A French Canadian Sister of the Holy Names observed in her community's diary in 1895: "Their [the Latins] ignorance of our religion is extreme. They do not know God, nor [sic] Faith, consequently, have no piety."

But no Tampa Latin would have concurred with that assessment; in fact, they would have been insulted by it, since most felt they were *muy Catolico*, especially in their devotion to the Blessed Virgin Mary and the saints, whom they considered their friends and patrons. Another French-Canadian Sister diarist wrote in 1896: "The greater number of Catholic Cubans, who had little faith had not heard Mass on Sunday for a long time. A large number of them work on Sunday. What [a] difference between those people and our people of [French] Canada! It grieves pious hearts to see God so little known and so little loved!" What we have here is a clash of culture and a clash between Medieval Catholicism and Tridentine Catholicism. Sister Hubert, SNJM, who taught in the West Tampa Academy, wrote in 1896 that teaching the Cuban children "was justly considered one of the most irksome and thankless tasks ever undertaken by the Holy Names Sisters." Yet despite her frustrations and discouragement, she remained a teacher there from 1896 to 1913 and again from 1914 to 1926, for a total of twenty-nine years of service among Tampa's Latins.

Despite the disheartenment of many of the priests and Sisters who worked with Tampa Latins, they kept at it. They persisted and persevered in service to them well into the twentieth century.

This persistence of service and presence, especially among the next generation of young Latin people, gave time as their long-term ally. Never once from 1889 to 1900 did one priest or Sister write anything about withdrawing from their efforts, no matter how difficult or exasperating at times. Meanwhile, the Latins kept coming to the parish to have their children baptized Catholics, a sign of their continuing personal identification with the Church. Also godparents extended the nuclear family with another set of care-givers and mentors for young people. It was an honor and an obligation to be a *padrino* or *madrina*. Baptism not only adhered the child to Christ and His Church, but also kneaded the godparents into the bread of the child's family and community, forging bonds of allegiance and loyalty among and between families. Sacramental records indicate that the celebration of Baptism at the parish brought to the Church mothers and father, grandparents, uncles and aunts, godparents, other relatives and friends. The sacred and social came together; the domestic church met the parish church; Medieval Catholicism encountered the Tridentine Church. Tampa's pastors, when reporting on Sacramental statistics of Latins, which were well below Tridentine sacramental standards, took encouragement that virtually all of the Latin infants were baptized. It was a promising sign that the clergy felt could be built on in the future.[14]

Teaching Latin children in Catholic schools was the most significant investment made for the future of Catholicism among the Latins of Tampa. Although a few attended the Academy of the Holy Names in Tampa, most Latins who attended Catholic school went to the Academy of St. Joseph, opened by the Sisters of St. Joseph in 1891 with Bishop Moore's encouragement. In Ybor City, the Latin mission church was established the same year as the academy, no coincidence, since the Catholic school was considered vital to parish life. Unlike most other Academies, it took in no boarders. That first year they had 106 students. By 1893-94, they had 219 students; by 1900-01 they taught 324 students, a population greater than that of the Academy of the Holy Names in that same year. Meanwhile, cigar factories began opening in West Tampa in 1890; the municipality was incorporated in 1895. In September 1896, the Sisters of the Holy Names opened a three-story brick school, the

Academy of the Holy Names, constructed by Hugh MacFarlane, the developer of West Tampa.[15]

Catholic Schools taught the basics of elementary education, as well as the Tridentine model of Catholicism, discipline, moral values and guidance, and Catholic Church teaching. The schools were also centers of evangelization, not so much by the priests and Sisters, but by the children themselves. They often drew their parents closer to parish life. As a result, those children who may have not been baptized, were and some families who were not practicing the Faith, did so. At the schools, Latin children participated in various Sodalities, which were designed to deepen Tridentine piety. Another extracurricular activity was music, which was particularly appealing to Latin children. As one Sister of St. Joseph wrote in 1891, the children's choir "proved a good way of bringing them [and their parent's] to Mass." At the Feast of the Holy Rosary in 1896 at St. Joseph's Academy in Ybor City over 125 children sang for Sunday evening Benediction, accompanied on the flute by Father Albert Biever, SJ. As a way for the graduates of St. Joseph's Academy to continue to attend Mass, the Sisters of St. Joseph organized a graduates' choir in 1899.

Schools also served another function: they were the presence of the Church amidst the Latin community since the Sisters and pastors lived where they taught and ministered. The Sisters sought the children out at their parents' homes after school through home visitation at times of sickness, family hardship, or truancy. Priests could not do home visitation because of Latin males' suspicion about priestly intentions toward their women folk. But they had no such fears about the Sisters, who were highly respected. Therefore, the Sisters had access to the Latin family in ways priests did not.

The Catholic school was also a medium of adjustment and accommodation for immigrant children and their families, for at the school, unlike home, the children learned English and American ways, since the language of instruction was English. Catholic schools prepared Tampa's Latin children to negotiate with the broader culture, a skill essential for moving out of the cigar industry and Ybor City.[16]

## African-Americans

Of all those on the margins of late nineteenth century America, Moore was most personally engaged with the African-American community. Moore became bishop in 1877, the very year that Federal troops pulled out of occupying the South and when race relations began to deteriorate due to ever increasing Jim Crow laws.

The Archdiocese of Baltimore set the tone for Catholic bishops in the South with the Tenth Provincial Council of Baltimore in May of 1869. All suffragan bishops of the Archdiocese of Baltimore, which included the Bishop of St. Augustine, agreed to follow the example of Baltimore and provide special missions for blacks, separate parishes and schools for them, and special collections for them. Archbishop Spalding encouraged the Oblate Sisters of Providence, a black community of religious women, to extend their schools beyond the archdiocese. Spalding also introduced the Mill Hill Fathers (founded in England in 1866 to evangelize in Africa and Asia). In 1874, four Mill Hill Fathers arrived at St. Francis Xavier Church, a former Jesuit parish, to work with African-Americans at the request of the Archbishop of Baltimore. Later, they took over St. Augustine's in 1881, St. Monica's in 1883, and St. Peter's in 1886. The Franciscan Sisters of Mill Hill arrived from England in 1882 to teach in the schools for blacks and run a home for the aged and an industrial school. In 1892, the American branch became independent from England and was named the Josephites, headquartered in Baltimore, to work exclusively with African-Americans throughout the U.S.[17]

But actually, Florida was engaged early on with the African-American community. During Spanish Colonial times, Fort Mose was established by Spanish officials in 1738, as a defense two miles north of St. Augustine with a free black militia who were to militarily protect the northern approaches to St. Augustine. The soldiers there and their families were Catholics and comprised the first free black settlement in North America.[18]

Even before becoming the diocese's first bishop in 1870, Bishop Verot, although short of finances and personnel after the War, nonetheless sought to serve the newly freed blacks by helping them to learn to read and by giving their children an elementary education, as during enslavement they were neither permitted literacy nor given a formal education. The first black Catholic school, St. Cecilia's, was opened in St. Augustine in 1867 in the former Sisters of Mercy Academy on St. George Street by the Sisters of St. Joseph, who were personally recruited by Verot from Le Puy, France, specifically for the purpose on educating the children of former slaves. By 1869, St. Augustine Parish had five black Catholic societies for men and women, girls and boys. The Sisters directed these lay pious organizations, which met weekly for catechism, prayers, hymn singing and preparation for Confession before monthly Holy Communion. The establishment of a black Catholic community during Spanish Colonial times provided the foundation for the Sisters' relative success among blacks in St. Augustine. Such was not the case in Jacksonville. The Sisters began their work there in 1872 among blacks, but with less satisfying results. Of the 5,000 African-Americans in the city, only thirty were Catholic. The problem, as one Sister confided in a letter to Le Puy, was that most blacks were already affiliated with one of eight black Protestant Churches in the city, whose black pastors "hold firm" to their congregants. The Jacksonville A.M.E. Church was founded in 1867; by 1875 they claimed 13,000 members. Nonetheless, the Sisters of St. Joseph persevered in their dedication to Florida's African-Americans, with four schools opened by them and another two operated by the Sisters of the Holy Names in Tampa and Key West by 1900. These schools were not designed so much to make converts, as to provide educational opportunities, especially given the poor state of public schools for blacks at the time.

Florida's black population was substantial. In 1890 the diocese's white population was 185,925, while blacks were 142,286 or 43.4 percent of the total population of the Diocese of St. Augustine. They were less concentrated on the West Coast and in South Florida, with the exception of Tampa. They were 32.2 percent of Monroe County (Key West and only the Keys), but 55.6 percent in Duval County (Jacksonville and vicinity). By 1900, they numbered 193,775 in the diocese, but only about 1 percent of them were Catholic.[19]

The establishment of St. Peter Claver School in Tampa provoked a racial backlash which engaged Moore personally. Father Tyrell, SJ, pastor of St. Louis, encouraged by Moore, purchased a former Methodist church and parsonage in 1893, recruiting two Holy Names Sisters directly from Montreal to come to teach Tampa's black children. The school opened in the church's parsonage on February 2, 1894. Early in the morning of February 14, the former Methodist church was set ablaze by arsonists, with the following notice tacked onto a nearby tree:

> This inscription is posted in this place to say that the late fire on these grounds was not caused by any ill feeling to the Catholic Church. But because citizens do not propose to submit to a Negro school in the midst of the white and retired resident portion of the city. And warn that in case another institution of the same character is operated in this vicinity, it too will meet the same or a worse fate, and to persist in the same line will certainly cause destruction of the con-vent and your other churches. REMEMBER, THIS IS POSITIVE.

A group of Tampa business/professional male vigilantes, who controlled labor disputes in the cigar industry with the blessing of the factory owners and those who controlled town politics, let Catholics know that they were upsetting Tampa's racial arrangements of segregation and Jim Crowism by opening a black school in a white neighborhood. The parsonage where the Sisters held classes was only slightly damaged, but the church, which was going to be used as an African-American Catholic mission, was destroyed, although no one was injured. Father Tyrell, fully aware of who was behind the conflagration, was quoted in the *Tampa Daily Times* as saying that the lamentable event was "an act of lawlessness which injures the business interests of Tampa." In effect, Tampa's business, social, and political elites could be lawless and violent to protect what they perceived to be their self-interests and the status quo). Out of defiance, Tyrell instructed that the school stay open for several days as a gesture of strength amidst persecution, and then closed it out of fear of further violence.

Moore heard about the incident and immediately hurried to Tampa to investigate the matter himself. His personal inclination was not to buckle under pressure and threats from bigots. His courageous Celtic heritage and his sense of justice for the underdog moved him to dig in and fight, but after consulting with Tyrell, whom he greatly respected and trusted, he decided to go against his own personal inclinations, rather submitting to the course of action recommended by Tyrell. Instead of remaining on the former Methodist church property and possibly fueling more racial violence, Moore, following Tyrell's advice, purchased another piece of property on Scott and Governor Streets, well within the territory of the segregated black community. Moore admitted that "I feel humiliated at the thought of doing this, but the rector of the mission, Father Tyrell, who is on the spot and therefore best able to judge, deems it the best course to take and I consent, very reluctantly indeed." As was his custom, he consulted with others and sometimes changed his viewpoint as a result. Here also the principle of subsidiarity was in play. A two-storied frame house was opened as a black Catholic school there on October 2, 1894. By the end of the school year, the two Holy Name Sisters taught eighty-five students in St. Peter Claver School. Later in 1909, a chapel was housed in the school. A separate concrete mission church was eventually built adjacent to the school in 1915, also called St. Peter Claver. It became a parish in 1926.[20]

With the help of religious women, Moore continued and expanded Bishop Verot's outreach to the black community in Florida through Catholic education, one that grew in the first half of the twentieth century.

Bishop Moore also expanded parochial presence amidst the black community, most especially with the building of his new Cathedral. Before the fire of 1887, blacks had to climb up one flight of stairs to the lower gallery on the back wall of the church, which was under the second and upper gallery designated for the all-white choir, an arrangement going back to Spanish Colonial times. With the destruction of the Cathedral, this seating arrangement was rethought rather than just rebuilt. Moore decided to add two transepts onto the interior of the Cathedral, the eastern one designated for the exclusive use of blacks. Now black Catholics could worship at the same level as everybody else and not have to trek up a flight of steep stairs in order to attend Mass.[21]

When Moore first came to the diocese in 1877, he made an assessment of the state of ministry among the black community in the diocese. At the Cathedral parish, he noted five black Catholic societies for men, women, girls and boys, all directed by the Sisters of St. Joseph. He also counted two chapels specifically for

African-Americans, St. Monica and St. Benedict the Moore, were served from the Cathedral parish, so "numerous" were black Catholics in St. Augustine, he added. The Sisters of St. Joseph operated four black Catholic schools, in Fernandina, Mandarin, Jacksonville, and St. Augustine. Such efforts were not as successful in other places due to a lack a clergy and other resources.[22]

It is worth observing that Moore expanded these efforts of Catholic outreach to Florida's blacks in the 1890s, at the very time that Jim Crow was growing stronger in the South. What he needed initially was money, and he found a willing benefactor in Mother Katharine Drexel, SBS. With her family's background in business, she, like Flagler, gave of her fortune under very specific conditions and also without fanfare. She had a whole file of the exact amounts she donated and the agreements she made with those who received her benefactions. For example, stipulations for a grant included that the buildings to be erected would be for the exclusive use of African-Americans or Native Americans.[23]

Moore moved ahead expanding ministry to blacks in Tampa without any promise of funding. He sent his first begging letter to Mother Katharine in early January 1894. He explained to her that he had bought a former Methodist church in Tampa for $2,750, which he considered a bargain. He paid $800 down, and took out three notes for $650 each at 8 percent interest. He will need extra money to properly outfit the church (it had no pews) and has altered the parsonage for a school at the cost of $500. The Jesuits will be in charge of Tampa's new black mission. He adds that the school is being encouraged by some black pastors since the public school for blacks "burned down some months ago and it has not been rebuilt." Moore writes Mother Katharine again in March 1894 thanking her for her promise of help, especially in light of the recent troubles associated with the burning of the former Methodist church and the threat of more destruction of church property (he enclosed a Tampa newspaper article). He delves into more details about the church burning episode: "I feel little inclined to yield to a threat, especially by one so cowardly, made by an anonymous ruffian, but Father Tyrell thinks it best to do so." Moore did not want to back down in the face of prejudice or even appear to back down. He adds that "the Sisters are in mortal dread lest their new convent building [the Academy] be burnt down." They had a debt on it of $19,000. Moore tells Mother Katharine that he deferred to his man on the local scene [Tyrell] to judge best the situation and appreciates the Sisters' fears. He says insurance on the burnt church was for $1,100, which he hopes to get, but is unsure because he has heard that pressure was put on the insurance company not to pay up. He will sell the present property and buy a lot in the black community for a school and church. He assures Mother Katharine that the sixteen children in the school will have their education "interrupted as little as possible." He ends one of the longest letters he ever wrote, expressing his confidence that she will help. She did. On April 13, 1894, she gave Moore $2,000 "to aid in the building and fitting of a church" in Tampa and promised to send another $1,000 in the near future. True to her promise, she sent a second check to Moore for that amount in June 1895. In April 1894, Moore thanks her for her check, which he is forwarding to Father Tyrell. After he goes to Tampa May 20th for Confirmations, he will inform her how the money was used. Again the principle of subsidiarity is at work by his allowing Tyrell the discretion to use the money as best he sees fit, but will get a report from the Jesuit, to pass on to the lady in Philadelphia. He also mentions Father Widman, SJ, efforts to reach the Seminoles, a project which, if it develops, he suggests might also be funded by her.[24]

Moore writes Mother Katharine again in May 1895 begging for $1,000 for "the Negro school of Tampa." Since September 1894, the new school has operated. They presently educate thirty-six kids, thirty of whom are Protestant, but are taught Catholic prayers and the Catechism, "with the full consent of their parents." The school needs to be enlarged, "making them [the accommodations] more healthy and pleasant." He includes a photo of the school and the kids. In June Mother Katharine sent a check for $1,000.[25]

Mother Katharine continued to be an essential component in the expansion of ministry to blacks in Tampa. The bishop was always careful to inform his Philadelphia benefactor precisely how her money was being used and what results were coming from her investment, as one person of business to another, and as one person of the Church to another, which is probably why she continued to support his efforts. Moore thanks her again in October 1897 for her ongoing support of "the colored school of Tampa." He reported that last year the school had twelve converts. "We expect even greater results this year." At that time 100 kids matriculated in the school, which, Moore comments, contains "the most respectable colored children in Tampa." As if almost in passing, he mentions Father Tyrell is planning to open another black Catholic school in Ybor

11.1 *Mother Katharine Drexel, c. 1895. Source: ASBS*

City. Moore thanks her again for the $2,000 she sent in June 1899 for the new school in Ybor City. In April 1900 he informs her of the delay in opening the Ybor City school since Father Tyrell was recently transferred and the lot for the school had a defective title. He found another lot for just over $1,000 and plans to erect a two-story brick building with four classrooms on the first floor and a hall (which also can be used as a chapel) on the second floor. The bids for the construction of the new school are $5,800 and $5,785. He needs $5,000 to begin building. In June Mother Katharine sent $3,000, then another $3,000 in August. Moore tells her that the school should open in January 1901. He also informs her that the Tampa 'Colored School" is prospering with 114 students at the close of the 1899-1900 school year.[26]

Mother Katharine also funded other enterprises in Florida. In June 1899 Moore begs her for money for a black school in Old Town, two miles from Fernandina, where a black Catholic mission church was built earlier, but the pastor of St. Michael's, Fernandina, Father Maurice Foley, wants a "colored school" to complement it. Mother Katharine promised $2,000. She ended up sending him $5,000, for a school building and a priest's house. In early 1901 the Philadelphia benefactor gave $100 for one teacher's salary, with the proviso that attendance be increased the next year to at least twenty students.[27]

But the greatest collaboration between Mother Katharine Drexel and Bishop John Moore was the building of a new black Catholic school in St. Augustine.

The Sisters of St. Joseph arrived in St. Augustine on Sept. 2, 1866. The French Sisters initially lived at the Mercy Sisters Convent on St. George Street. The Sisters of Mercy came to St. Augustine at Bishop Verot's request in 1859, but withdrew in 1869 because their academy could not sustain itself due to the War and the post-War poverty of the people of St. Augustine. Besides, St. Augustine was not big enough for two different women's religious communities and the institutions which they would operate. The Mercy Sisters returned to their Motherhouse in Hartford, Connecticut, except for two Irish-born Sisters, who became SSJ's, Monica Nicholson and Mary Ann Hoare. The latter became the more noteworthy of the two, as she later headed the SSJ orphanage in Jacksonville and became beloved as "The Angel of Jacksonville."

Earlier in December 1866, the SSJ's moved from the Mercy Convent to the O'Reilly House, adjacent to which they had already begun their first black Catholic school in November 1866. But the Sisters needed money to live on and it was not being supplied by their work among the poor blacks. The SSJ's purchased St. Mary's Academy in 1869 and opened a free school for white girls there that October. In 1874, Bishop Verot completed a Convent/Academy building, despite the objections from some clergy over the expense of the construction. With an academy, the SSJ's would have the means to supply for their needs. In 1883 the school for blacks moved to the old St. Mary's Academy, west of the Cathedral, and became known as St. Cecilia's School. As mentioned in Chapter 9, Moore deeded over the block west of the Cathedral on which the former St. Mary's Academy stood to Flagler in 1887, but the millionaire allowed the Sisters to continue to operate St. Cecilia's School in the old building of Mercy Sisters, rent free.[28]

But that building became very dilapidated and a new black Catholic school building was needed. Moore made his appeal to Mother Katharine beginning in October of 1897, presenting her the problem and his desire to solve it. "My greatest solicitude is for the new school for colored children in St. Augustine." He tells her that there 110 black Catholic families in St. Augustine who are "very

*11.2 Students and teachers at St. Benedict the Moor School in St. Augustine*
*Source: ASSJ*

good Catholics, but very poor." Last year the black Catholic school had 105 pupils, but this year only forty-five returned. The rest have gone to public school since the Catholic school has no attraction for them. The building is in poor condition, consequently "A remedy for this state of things is urgently needed."

Moore's plans to rectify the situation were years in the making. Back in 1880 Father Thomas Farrell died, a mentor of Father Richard Burtsell (Moore's friend from New York) and former student at the Urban College in Rome. Farrell's will left a provision for the founding of a black Catholic church in New York. Burtsell was Ferrell's executor of the will and as a result in 1883 St. Benedict the Moor Parish was founded in lower Manhattan. Surely Moore knew about this and it may have planted a seed in Moore's imagination. At that very time Moore was in New York, well aware of the execution of Farrell's will and the establishment of the black parish as a result. In July 1887 Moore was contriving upon converting the old Methodist Church at St. Augustine into a church for blacks. He was waiting for a decision from Flagler, since he owned the building. It turned out that Moore was unable to secure that building for his purposes. He wrote Pace in St. Augustine in September 1887 to save any coquina left at the quarry on St. Anastasia Island to use in the construction of a "colored church." But that plan was never implemented. In early 1890 Moore met Mother Katharine for the first time. She was visiting St. Augustine with another religious woman when Bishop James O'Connor of Omaha was there recuperating from an illness. She soon left with the other Sister escorting the bishop to a hospital in Pittsburgh. He died in Omaha on May 27, 1890.

Undaunted by his previous frustrated objectives, he bought one city block 310 x 253 feet within the black community of Lincolnville for $7,312 in 1890. Since then, he admits being offered "a fortune" for the property, but he has refused sell it. He did not buy it on speculation, but for a purpose. His vision for it was specific and carefully thought out. His intention was to build a black Catholic Church, school, and rectory on the property. The school would be two stories: three classrooms on the first floor and a hall on the second, a place "entertainments" could take place and where the Knights of St. John could meet. He reckons the school would cost $8,000. He requests that Mother Katharine donate $5,000 for the project; he will raise the other $3,000. Talking about the new church, he writes her saying that although he provided a wing of the Cathedral (the east transept) that is exclusively for them, he wants them to have a new church that they can call their own. But he will not to force them to attend the new church, adding "the old people would scarcely be willing to leave the Old Cathedral. I will leave [it] to them. They are perfectly free to do as they please. The wing of the Cathedral will always be theirs." He assures Mother Katharine: "I want to treat my colored people the best I can." He also tells her that the school, rectory, and church will be recessed twenty feet from the street, so as to provide space to walk around the block in procession, an act of devotion which he says the black Catholics "take great delight in."[29]

In March 1898 Mother Katharine agreed to give $5,000 for the school. A proviso came with her donation, namely, "that the school be kept in perpetuity for the Colored and in case it were ever abandoned or the property sold, the $5,000 she gave should revert to some other Colored work in the Diocese of St. Augustine." Moore was delighted with Mother Katharine's help. He writes her that same month that the school will be completed in two weeks. Besides her donation, he got $1,200 from the annual national collection for the "Colored and Indians," which he applied to the cost of construction. "The colored people are jubilant over their new school," he writes. "The Knights of St. John "call it their House of Refuge." Moore renamed the school St. Benedict the Moor (formerly called St. Cecilia's), the same name given to Father Ferrell's bequeath of a black parish in Manhattan and the same name at the new black parish.

The Chairman of the Board of Public Instruction elected to send some kids attending the black public school to St. Benedict's, because of overcrowding, which Moore says "will extend the influence of our school." As a result of the Chairman's action, the new school now brought another benefit. Since it was now part of the public school system, the SSJ Sisters who taught there would be paid from public funds. Moore admits that heretofore he was unable to compensate the Sisters when they taught at St. Cecilia's, since he "had not the money." When Moore mentioned to the black Catholics that the school was made possible by Mother Katharine's benefaction, they applauded her "most heartedly." In June 1899 she gave another $2,000 for the school, as well as $2,000 to the black school in Tampa. But her generosity was not limited to Tampa and St. Augustine. Moore mentions her donation of $500 for the black school in Old Town (Fernandina) and the "colored school" in Mandarin, which was nearly completed. He writes her about the new black school in St. Augustine: "The white children of the public school nearby are, I was told, jealous that the colored children shall have a better school house than theirs. The colored people are flattered and encouraged."[30]

Given the atmosphere of Jim Crow and "separate but unequal" model of education for African-Americans, Moore's personal efforts on behalf of black Catholic education were remarkable, especially given the financial constraints of the diocese. It is undeniable that his actions would have been impossible, but for the benefaction of Mother Katharine. It was a remarkable partnership for the good of those on the margins. The reason Mother Katharine was so generous to Moore was that his requests were very specific in nature and targeted to her interests, as well as to his perceived needs of those on the margins. He was also meticulous in giving her updates about the progress of her benefactions. He proved accountable and transparent. In addition, sometimes he promised to raise part of the money needed himself, an approach Mother Katharine appreciated.

Sometimes Moore persuaded Mother Katharine to invest not just in institutions, but in individuals. Moore wrote her in late March 1898 about a seventeen year old black man he met on a recent visit to Key West. The man (whose name was Wiggins) presently works as a cigar maker, but wants to be a medical doctor, but the problem is that being a black-Cuban, he has little command of the English language. The pastor at St. Mary, Star of the Sea, assured Moore that the young man is a good practicing Catholic. He has attended night school to learn English at the Methodist Church. The Methodists offered him money for his further education, so he converted to Methodism. A lady associated with the night school called upon Moore when he was at Key West, attesting to the man's talent and moral conduct. Moore wrote to Father Slattery (Superior of the Josephites) in Baltimore, who responded that Wiggins should attend the University of Michigan at Ann Arbor, since blacks are accepted into their medical school. Moore adds that it would be very beneficial to have a black medical doctor in Key West. In April Moore sends Mother Katharine a letter he received from Wiggins which states that $150 per year would cover his educational expenses. Moore asks her for that much, adding that he would make up "any balance that might be required." He tells her that "I am anxious to help this young man on account of his many good qualities." Mother Katharine does agree to help and is willing to send the same amount annually, if he continues his course of study. Because of a sickness in the family, Wiggins does not get to Ann Arbor until the summer of 1899, at which time Mother Katharine sent to Bishop Moore the money she promised for Wiggins, and does so the next year also. The record is unclear as to whether Wiggins ever does become a physician, but if he didn't, it was not due to a lack of financial support.[31]

Mother Katharine was not the only source of help in Moore's expansion of services to African-Americans in the 1890s. The Annual National Collection for Ministry to Blacks and Indians gave Moore money for that ministry in his diocese from 1887. The Diocese of St. Augustine took up the annual collection, giving in less than $100 a year, while it received an average of $1,000 annually from the fund during the 1890s.[32]

But in April 1898, Moore complained to Cardinal in Baltimore about not getting what he considered his diocese's fair share from the fund. Moore stated that he spent over $8,000 for a new black Catholic school in St. Augustine. He had asked the fund for $3,000 to help defray the cost. Since he did not receive what he asked for, he offered to come to Baltimore to plead his case before the Board of the annual collection. He added that the chair of the Board, Father Dyer, had some years ago expressed surprise that Southern bishops had not protested the fact that "'large sums were given to rich dioceses where Negroes are few comparatively.'" Moore added: "We Southerners who have no means should be aided more abundantly." He writes Gibbons in September requesting once again that he come to Baltimore to beg the Collection's Board for more money. Another reason he wants to go to Baltimore is to see a wealthy benefactor, Miss Abell, whom he met on the train from Buffalo the summer before. He wants to ask her for a loan or better, a donation. It is unclear if he ever got to Baltimore, but in November Father Dyers sent him a check for $1,500, a slight increase from the usual. Moore repeats to Dyer what he told Gibbons: "We Southern bishops were hardly getting our legitimate share of this fund, as we have so many Negroes within our jurisdiction and absolutely no resources." Moore's protestations had some effect. In 1899 the Board sent him $2,250 (the third largest appropriation to any diocese that year, exceeded only by New Orleans and Baltimore, who received $3,000 and $2,900 respectively) and then $2,000 in 1900.[33]

Still, no one equaled Mother Katharine in her consistent and expanding support of Moore's outreach to those on the margins of late nineteenth century American Society. Moreover, her benefice did not end nor diminish with the death of Moore. She continued to help the Diocese of St. Augustine in its care for African-Americans into the first half of the twentieth century.[34]

*A Shepherd of the Church of the United States,*
*1877–1901*

John Moore

CHAPTER TWELVE

# *Collegiality*

I t is unlikely that Bishop Moore would have used the word
"collegiality." It only came into common usage after Vatican
Council II, as that Council's Decree on the Bishops' Pastoral
Office in the Church states:

> Sharing in the solicitude for all the churches,
> bishops exercise this episcopal office of theirs, received
> through episcopal consecration, in communion with
> and under the authority of the Supreme Pontiff. All
> are united in a college or body acting in the name
> of the entire Catholic episcopate, it will at the same
> time demonstrate that all the bishops in hierarchical
> communion share in the responsibility for the
> universal Church.

But Vatican II did not invent the concept; rather it stretches
back to the earliest centuries of the Church, as evidenced by early
episcopal synods. A bishop's responsibility is never limited only to
the particular diocese entrusted to him. Moore was aware of this
universal responsibility, not only theologically, but personally. His
life experience as an exile from his homeland, as a student in France
and Rome, as a priest in Charleston during the War, as a friend
to priests in New York, all impressed upon him the universality of

his responsibilities as a bishop. In particular, his Roman experience not only gave him life-long friendships, but a vision of the Church that was bigger than just Charleston, or St. Augustine, or even the United States.

## The American Bishops and Vatican I

Although individual bishops felt some concern for broader issues in the Church, not all agreed on the same response to those issues. At the heart of these divisions was the relationship of the Church to American society. The founders of this country were heavily influenced by the Enlightenment. The First Amendment to the U.S. Constitution does something that no other country had ever enacted — the separation of Church and state. Our first bishop, John Carroll, took a positive view of the relationship of Roman Catholicism and the U.S. government. During Carroll's episcopacy (1789-1815), Catholics were a small minority of the population, about 3 percent. The First Amendment protected a religious minority like Catholicism from the dictates of the majority. Moreover, Carroll observed first-hand the machinations by governments against the Church, as he taught in Europe when the Jesuits were suppressed. As a result, he preferred governments to be hands-off regarding the life of the Church.

On the other hand, his view of ecclesiastical polity was synodal not monarchical; he saw the Church not as an absolute monarchy, but as a communion of Churches centered in Rome. Infallibility for him resided in the body of bishops united with their head, the Bishop of Rome. Up to 1870, most U.S. bishops would have shared the same view of Church polity as Carroll. The II Plenary Council of Baltimore in 1866 articulated a synodal and collegial view of the Church's authority. Most U.S. bishops at the time located infallibility in the college of bishops united with the Roman Pontiff. The pastoral demands of a missionary country like the U.S. and the challenge of unprecedented immigration beginning in the 1840s forced American bishops to be more practical than theoretical in their theological and pastoral approach.[2]

Of the just over 700 bishops who attended Vatican Council I (1869-1870), 52 percent were Italians and French, while forty-nine bishops attending were Americans. Even though a third of the prelates came from outside Europe, the Council was largely a European affair by reason of its issues, its overwhelming European membership, and by virtue of its leadership, who steered the Council's direction. Most Americans were largely uninformed about Ultramontism or Papal Infallibility, key issues which surfaced. When the formal vote on Papal Infallibility took place on July 18, 1870, Bishop Edward Fitzgerald of Little Rock was one of only two bishops that voted against it. Fifty-five bishops absented themselves from the formal vote because they did not want to vote against the measure publicly and in the Pope's presence. Of the fifty-five absentees, three were Americans: Archbishop Peter Kenrick of St. Louis, Bishop Michael Domenec of Pittsburgh, and Bishop Augustin Verot of St. Augustine. Even Bishop Bernard McQuaid of Rochester, who acceded to the Papal Infallibility decree of Vatican I, clung to a synodal, collegial view of ecclesiology, as he stated: "... to the last I opposed it [Papal Infallibility decree]; because somehow or the other it was in my heart that Bishops ought to be consulted."[3]

The declaration of Papal Infallibility at Vatican I signified a shift in the established Roman approach to devotion, discipline, theology, jurisdiction, and jurisprudence throughout the Church Universal, a process that had already begun at the Council of Trent, but the implementation of Trent was slow in many places in the world, stymied by local rulers or cultural conditions. With Vatican I, the Pope and his centralized bureaucracy of Curia officials commandeered the leadership and direction of the Church, thereby diminishing any synodal, localized approaches.

The reception of Vatican I by U.S. Catholics was tempered by recent upheavals in American society — the challenges of nativism, immigration, the trauma of the Civil War, the forces of centralization, and massive industrialization. Throughout America and in American Catholicism the desire for security, stability, unity, and identity amidst all of the social turmoil prevailed.

The crisis of the Papacy over the loss of its temporal power and the rise of Italian nationalism fostered in American Catholic journals of the day a sympathy for and personal devotion to the Pope Pius IX. During the II Plenary Council of Baltimore in 1866, the bishops authorized an annual collection for the Pope in every U.S. parish.

*12.1 Fathers of the III Plenary Council of Baltimore, 1884. Source: Frederick J. Zwierlein, The Life and Letters of Bishop McQuaid, Vol. II (1926), 304*

This personal identification for the sufferings of the Pope helped facilitate the concept of Roman centralization and standardization fostered by Vatican I. For example, the appointment of bishops was increasingly appropriated by Rome, especially in missionary countries, such as the U.S., which was under the direct supervision of the Roman Congregation of the Propagation of the Faith. Roman titles like "Monsignor" and "Cardinal" were now appearing more readily in America. By 1884, twelve priests in the U.S. were given the title "Monsignor," including Thomas Preston, the Vicar General of the Archdiocese of New York and James A. Corcoran, a priest of Charleston, SC, who was on the faculty of St. Charles Borromeo Seminary, Philadelphia. Roman Pontifical colleges and universities were the nurseries of Ultramontane theology and sources of future ecclesiastical advancements. More national Roman colleges were being founded, including the North American College for the U.S. in 1859. Roman liturgical trends and a massive devotional revolution affected a uniformity of discipline, liturgy, and piety. These new devotions, such as Eucharistic-centered Forty Hours and First Friday, a multitude of Marian expressions, and devotions to the Sacred Heart of Jesus and the Holy Family, were most often promoted by religious orders of men and women, especially through periodic revitalization efforts known as the parish mission. Unlike the liturgy, which was in Latin, these various devotions were recited in the vernacular. They provided Catholics in America with both local and universal solidarity, especially giving newly arrived immigrants a connection with the Faith expressions of their homeland, also offering some sense of stability and cohesiveness amidst the social chaos and dislocation created by migration and resettlement.[4]

## III Plenary Council of Baltimore
## and Its Acceptance by Rome

One consequent of Vatican I and the new prominence of the centralized Papacy in the last decades of the 1800s was the III Plenary Council of Baltimore. The Church in missionary America was governed locally through the nine Councils or Synods of Baltimore from 1829 through 1866. Vatican I signaled an end to such regional synodal collegiality. Unlike the previous Baltimore Councils, the bishops in the U.S. were summoned in 1883 to meet at the request of the Vatican with the intention of bringing the American Church firmly in line with Roman practices. Plans for the Council and its agenda were drawn up in October 1883 by Rome's Congregation of the Propagation of the Faith, namely its head, Cardinal Johann Baptist Franzelin, a leading theologian of Vatican I. That agenda, which was only slightly modified by American Archbishops, who were called to Rome for a consultation in November 1883, did not include some of the pressing national issues of the American Church that surely would have been

12.2 *Cardinal James Gibbons, 1884.*
Source: Maurice F. Egan, <u>The Hierarchy</u> <u>of the Roman Catholic Church of the U.S.</u>, Vol. I, (1888), front piece.

on the agenda if the American bishops had initiated it. Franzelin signaled out the Seminary of St. Charles Borromeo in Philadelphia as the most Roman in its instruction, over other American seminaries in Baltimore, Troy, N.Y., Boston, Cincinnati, and Milwaukee. Roman officials were intent on bringing American Canon Law more in line with Roman Canon Law. For example, Rome insisted that American bishops provide for irremovable rectors (pastors) with tenure, an idea that many American bishops disapproved, but one now to be sanctioned upon the advice of Archbishop Gibbons. Although Rome called for the establishment of irremovable Cathedral Canons, the Americans modified the proposal by establishing instead diocesan consultors, whom the bishop must confer with before buying or selling property, or disbanding or erecting a parish, but the bishop is not compelled to follow their advice. Also the consultors were now to draw up a list (a *terna*) of possible candidates for vacant episcopal sees. Those *ternae* would be examined by the bishops of the metropolitan province in which the vacancy occurred. One of the few items initiated by the bishops themselves was the establishment of a national theological school, the Catholic University of America in Washington, D.C. But neither Rome nor the American bishops addressed the pressing problems surfacing in the Church in America at the time, not the least of which was the ethnic tensions and power struggle between the Irish and the Germans. The Roman orchestrators of the Baltimore Council did make one concession to the Americans; Archbishop Gibbons of Baltimore was constituted as the Papal Delegate for the upcoming Council, after American bishops protested the appointment of an Italian, Archbishop Luigi Sepiacci, a consultor to the Congregation of the Propagation of the Faith.[5]

On November 8, 1884, fourteen American archbishops and coadjutor archbishops, fifty-seven bishops, seven abbots, and thirty-one superiors of men's religious orders met in Baltimore from November 8 to December 7, 1884, the largest such meeting of U.S. bishops to date. Bishop Moore attended, along with his chosen theological advisor, Father Richard Burtsell, his friend from New York and the most prominent Canon lawyer in the country. Earlier on April 3, Archbishop Gibbons sent Moore, and all his suffragan bishops, Chapter 1 of the *schema, De clericorum* (On Clerics), to study and prepare to comment on. In addition to the previously mentioned subjects of seminary education, irremovable rectors, and diocesan consultors, the American bishops modified some other of Propaganda's proposals. Regarding secret societies, any statements about such were to be reviewed by the archbishops. If they could not reach an agreement regarding action, the matter would be referred to Rome. Concerning parochial schools, the Council declared that every parish should erect a school within two years of the Council's termination "unless in the judgment of the bishop the building or maintenance of a school is impossible." One piece of new legislation not part of the Roman generated agenda was the establishment of the Catholic University of America in Washington, DC, a project long promoted by Bishop John Lancaster Spalding of Peoria. This institution was envisioned

*12. 3 Bishop John Moore, lithograph c. 1884. Source: Maurice F. Egan, The Hierarchy of the Roman Catholic Church in the U.S., Vol I, (1888), p. 33*

as a seminary, a graduate school of theology for diocesan clergy.[6]

With the III Plenary Council of Baltimore concluded and its 319 decrees elucidated, they now had to be delivered to Rome for final approval. Gibbons tasked three men to convey the documents to Rome: Father Denis O'Connell (Gibbons' secretary) and Bishops John Moore and Joseph Dwenger, CPP.S., of Fort Wayne. The three arrived in Rome in March 1885. Shortly, they were joined by a fourth Gibbons appointee, Bishop Richard Gilmour, Bishop of Cleveland since 1872. From a Roman perspective, there were several controversial points in the Baltimore decrees: the advice or consent of diocesan consultors in financial matters, the erection of parochial schools, and the role of religious. Bishop Moore told Pope Leo XIII on July 3: the "Bishops of America feared too big a dose of cannon [sic] law might be given them all at once...'" Ultimately, the legislation on the role of diocesan consultors was to stand for ten years, but in grave matters, the local bishop was to consult Propaganda. In all other cases, bishops were to take the advice of his consultors, but were not obliged to follow it. Baltimore's decree

*12.4 BishopRichard Gilmour, left, and Bishop Joseph Dwenger, c 1885. Source: Frederick J. Zwierlein, <u>The Life and Letters of Bishop McQuaid</u>, Vol. II (1926), 352*

on the erection of parochial schools was modified to allow the bishop to grant only an extension of time before the parish school was to be built. Lastly, the decree on religious owning property was suspended until another Plenary Council was called (which in fact never happened). The III Plenary Baltimore decrees were basically an American formulation of Roman documents and perspectives. They indicated more Rome's concern about the American Church, than the real issues that were actually pressing on the American Catholic community. These issues were not addressed in the decrees of III Plenary Baltimore, but would nonetheless surface in the U.S. almost immediately after the decrees were approved by Rome.[7]

Moore, although previously aware of certain national and international issues through his friendships with some priests of New York, was exposed to not only those issues, but to episcopal personalities as a result of his attendance at III Plenary Baltimore. Two men who attended in Council and whom he would have heard about from his New York friends were Bernard McQuaid of Rochester and Michael J. Corrigan of New York.

McQuaid had early on tried to influence events of the Council in 1883 when he wrote directly to Cardinal Franzelin suggesting a meeting in Rome of a few Archbishops and bishops (presumably himself included) to discuss the improvement of the Church in America. Gibbons seems unaware of these machinations. In May Franzelin invited only U.S. Archbishops to Rome in November 1883 to discuss proposals for the upcoming Council.[8]

McQuaid penned Gilmour in December 1884 that he disliked Moore and O'Connell being the ambassadors of the Baltimore decrees to Rome. Corrigan agreed. In particular, he felt Moore too reticent to stand up to the anticipated opposition from Rome, while Dwenger he perceived as more German than American. McQuaid feared that since Moore and O'Connell are Roman products, they would collude with Roman authorities to prune, add, or even wipe out what the U.S. bishops decided in Baltimore. Always confident in his own opinions, McQuaid preferred that Corrigan and Gilmour go instead of Moore and Dwenger. "If we cannot have a strong representation in members of our body, it would be better to have no one there." In January 1885, McQuaid heard a rumor that Gilmour alone will be dispatched with the decrees. McQuaid expresses to Gilmour that he strongly favors him as the sole envoy, since he is clear in thought, can find a way through "a muddle of bewildered minds," and will not throw in the towel when the opposition might get rough. Gilmour himself writes to Gibbons in February and then again in March expressing his opinion that the Baltimore decrees should not be touched or changed by Rome. He volunteers himself to travel to Rome to get the decrees approved. He adds that Dwenger, a religious order man, will not defend the bishops against the religious and will cower before Roman authorities. He suggests that he and McQuaid should be sent to Rome instead of those announced to go.[9]

Gibbons responded to Gilmour that he did not want to retract the appointments he had made. He also feels that it is inappropriate to have too many bishops go to Rome, giving the impression of unduly pressuring the officials there. He will not credential both Gilmour and McQuaid. Gilmour informs McQuaid of Gibbons' decision, which he adds shows the archbishop's lack of courage. He also appends: "I don't trust Dwenger." The reason for this distrust is that Dwenger is both German and a religious. There were tensions within the American Church and especially among American bishops with both groups. McQuaid responds that "it is better that neither of us go to Rome at present." He declares he no longer wants to go, especially without official sanction. He is convinced that the Romans will radically change the decrees which will be a disaster, and this will be all due to the "weakness and timidity" of Archbishop Gibbons, who wants the red hat so much that he will do nothing which might endanger it. McQuaid opines that Franzelin is the one to dread because "he is a German and a Jesuit; his prejudice against us is very strong."[10]

In May 1885 Gibbons pens to Gilmour stating that, after consultation with five American bishops, he feels that "your presence in Rome is very desirable," especially since Gilmour was so active in formulating many of the Baltimore decrees. Gilmour accepts the appointment and leaves for Rome on May 21, arriving on June 5. O'Connell had already left the city for the summer villa of the North American College. The final approval of the decrees had seemingly already been completed by the time Gilmour arrived in Rome. Despite his and McQuaid's misgivings about Moore, O'Connell, and Dwenger, Gilmour admits to McQuaid that the status "of the *Acta* is good, up to now."[11]

Gilmour was right with his addenda "up to now." In August Propaganda suddenly changed its mind. Now it said that bishops needed the consent, not just the advice, of diocesan consultors. This was an unacceptable alteration of the decrees for the American bishops. Gibbons told Corrigan that such an emendation would have dire consequences. Corrigan advised Gilmour to appeal directly to the Pope, since the Vatican Secretary of State, Simeoni, favored consent over advice also. Because of the impending crisis, O'Connell now returned to the team in Rome from the summer villa of the North American College. Gilmour scribbled in his diary: "All now depends on the Pope." Dwenger was reluctant to go over Propaganda's head by appealing to the Pope, but Moore and Gilmour persuaded him to join them in a united front. Gilmour cabled Gibbons on September 11 that the Pope confirmed the Baltimore decrees. Bishops would seek the advice, not the consent, of the diocesan consultors. But there was a string attached. U.S. bishops had to write Propaganda for permission to borrow large sums and write a report on their financial operations every three years.[12]

Gilmour felt that he and Moore worked well together, but Dwenger was the odd man out, since he declared his determination to act independently of the two other members of the team. He needed to be coerced to cooperate. Both Gilmour and Moore were obliged to write jointly in October to Gibbons, complaining of Dwenger's attitude. Not only did he speak Latin poorly, but he "lacks prudence, tact, and humility." They claimed he showed a marked desire to please Franzelin and Propaganda in everything, currying favor at every opportunity. They declared that he only went with them to the Pope "half-heartedly." Gilmour added that throughout the process he was scandalized by those who governed the Church, all the more convinced that the Church is ultimately guided by the Holy Spirit, not by the foibles of human agents. There is no evidence that Moore was so scandalized, which does not mean that he was unaware the limits of the human heart and Roman governance, but that he was more circumspect about it all.[13]

Unlike Gilmour, Moore did not keep a journal of his time in Rome in 1885. Being a very private, reserved person, he never kept a journal or diary his whole life. But we do have some reflections of his experience in letters he wrote about it, especially to Archbishop Gibbons. Moore composes a letter to the Archbishop upon his arrival in Rome on March 16, 1885. The next day, March 17th (St. Patrick's Day) he dined at the Irish College, but he stayed in what he called the "excellent accommodations" at the North American College. There resided Edward Pace, the Floridian seminarian, with whom Moore had an opportunity to know better as a result of his stay in the Eternal City. On April 1 Moore wrote Mother Lazarus, SSJ, telling her that he has little to do right now. He said Mass at the tomb of Peter, then at St. Paul's, offering the Masses for the "priests, Sisters, and people of the diocese." That same day, he wrote to Gibbons saying that the he dined with Bishop Dwenger and Cardinal Howard. He likes Howard, but makes no reference to Dwenger. He says that Cardinal Franzelin is unhappy with the American bishops since he believes that they "oppress" their priests. Franzelin mentioned that he has received letters of complaint from U.S. priests. Moore cites that these are likely one-sided accounts, "probably exceptional cases, and likely an exaggerated form." Franzelin points to cases where priests were treated unjustly by their bishops. Despite these misgivings, Franzelin feels that Church discipline in America is in need of attention, but that the bishops' work on the Baltimore decrees is timely, and will most probably call for very little correction. Moore adds that as yet the American team has not yet seen the Holy Father.[14]

Moore mentions to Mother Lazarus that April 9 was his 25th Anniversary of priestly ordination. Instead of celebrating his anniversary in his home diocese, duty called him to Rome. For that occasion, he sang Pontifical High Mass and preached to the North American College students. That evening at dinner, the students honored him with music and recited prose and poetry. Mindful that the occasion afforded him an opportunity to "advertise" his diocese, he made an impromptu speech on "the beauties of Florida, its past history and future prospects." He announces to her that this past Sunday the American team had their first audience with the Pope, who sent his special blessing to the Sisters of St. Joseph of St. Augustine, commenting that: "Our work is now beginning in earnest.[15]

Gibbons had instructed Moore back in February that he would not have to remain in Rome until the decrees were approved since the details could be left the O'Connell to mop up. But things did not turn out that way. Moore writes Gibbons in mid-June under "great distress." O'Connell, appointed Rector of the North American College (to the displeasure of Franzelin and other members of Propaganda) on June 8 was dangerously ill with an inflammation of the bowels (intestines), so much so that a priest was sent for to administer the Last Sacraments. A week later Moore writes that O'Connell's health is somewhat improved. He got out of his sick bed on June 19.[16]

Moore had an audience with Leo XIII and told him of the American bishops' fear of being forced to accept "too big a dose of cannon [sic] law" all at once. The Pope agreed with Moore and reported to him that all the Cardinals and Propaganda officials, with the exception of Franzelin, favored the acceptance of the American decrees. In the same letter that Moore wrote to Gibbons on July 6, with this very good news from the Pope himself, he included also what he told the Pope forthrightly regarding Franzelin:

> [Franzelin] has a hard head, he is full of speculative theology, abstract principals, and scholastic distinctions, whereas our matters not being questions of dogma but of discipline and practice require, in order to judge them correctly, a knowledge of the habits and customs of the people and of the dispositions of the priests, of the laws of the several States and of the Constitution of the United States, of the decisions pronounced in the courts all over the country in cases similar to those which may be expected to arise between priests and their bishops, and from the government of temporalities of the church. With this knowledge the Bishops possess, they can best foresee what laws are likely to work well, and what laws if imposed on them would probably have the effect of thwarting the progress of religion. Holy Father, what is the use of imposing laws on the church of America, which in the judgment of the Bishops will probably remain dead letters, printed in a book, but which cannot be put in execution?

With the Pope and with Gibbons, Moore is uncharacteristically direct and frank. He also betrays his preference, and that of his fellow bishops, of a synodal not centralized Church polity, where the local Church, that is in the U.S., is respected for its unique cultural and political context which the central Church bureaucracy should respect by not imposing some kind of universal uniformity, which was the tendency after Vatican I. With everything looking now more favorable, he felt that the team turned the corner on getting the decrees passed, so much so that he hopes to return home in September. Gilmour and Dwenger could remain in Rome until around Christmas if needed. But, Moore's buoyant optimism was soon to fade quickly.[17]

On July 15 Moore wrote to Gibbons in the longest letter he ever wrote to anybody, so stressful was the moment for him. He was all packed and ready to leave Rome, when Gilmour came to him "in the most solemn manner," begging him to remain. Dwengler was becoming more and more problematic and O'Connell was still recuperating at North American College. Gilmour needed Moore's presence and support. After such an entreaty, Moore agreed to stay. Moore comments on Dwenger, "whose vanity and selfishness are simply sickening." He tells Gibbons that the Bishop of Fort Wayne is working more to become the archBishop of St. Louis and for German interests in America, than he is working to get the decrees passed. Moore added that Dwenger's attempts to get St. Louis "should be prevented." He and Gilmour tried to show members of Propaganda how some are trying "to Germanize [sic] the Church in the United States," and how they are using the POF to control episcopal appointments in the U.S. For Moore and Gilmour the "German Question" was already a major problem and those promoting German interests in the U.S. had already vaulted over the U.S. hierarchy to capture the ears of Propaganda. Meanwhile, Moore reports that he and Gilmour work well together and have drafted strong arguments in favor of the decrees. Moore himself translated them into Italian. He hopes to have the decrees ready the first of August and to hear back about them by mid-August. The problem for Propaganda is that they feel they will have less power, not more, over the U.S. Church. "It is astonishing to me with what tenacity they [Propaganda] hold onto every shred of power and authority. They now feel that some of it has slipped from them [in the decrees]."[18]

Moore's optimism was deflated in August. Propaganda responded with requiring a major change, influenced by Franzelin. They demanded that the diocesan consultors have a truly deliberative, not just a consultative role. This reversal took Moore by surprise, as well as Gilmour. Moore, Gilmo z, Dwenger (who had to be cajoled) went to Franzelin with strong arguments against this change, but "he is determined not to be convinced." Cardinal Czacki from Propaganda advised the three go at once to appeal to the Pope and present their case before a final decision is made. The three got a Papal Audience within days, on August 22. Moore wrote their supplication in Italian and read it to Leo XIII, leaving it with him, along with another document by Moore and Gilmour, also translated by Moore. After the meeting with the Pope, both Moore and Gilmour felt confident that the consultive (*concilium* not *concensus*) role of the diocesan consultors would be restored, as was in the original decree. Moore's reading of Leo XII response was correct.[19]

The Cardinals at Propaganda met again on August 24, modifying the decree on diocesan consultors in this way: 1) the bishop can act alone in the alienation of church property or contracting debts up to $3,000 ($83,066.87 in 2017 dollars); 2) from $3,000 to $5,000 the bishop must take council only with his consultors; 3) anything over $5,000 ($138,444.79 in 2017 dollars), the bishop must consult the Holy See. Moore related that the team felt that this might be a big problem for the U.S. bishops. "They will feel their liberty of action injuriously restricted." Moreover, the strictures of #3 would create huge delays. Propaganda responded that only under conditions #1-3 will the decree be restored as it was produced in Baltimore previously. Moore asked Gibbons to respond by telegram to this present problem as to how the team should respond. We have no extant record of Gibbons response, but he must have agreed to the stipulations.[20]

Moore writes Gibbons on September 9 communicating that Propaganda met four times the week before and terminated their examination of the decrees. The word *concilium* (consultation) was restored completely for ten years. Only in cases of severe gravity would the Holy See have to be consulted. A Papal message given to the Propaganda consultors broke the log jam. Moore said there were only "very slight changes" to the original decrees. Final Papal approval would take place next day (Sept. 10). "Our work is done," wrote Moore in relief, adding "This is considered by all an immense triumph." But the victory was not without considerable difficulties, not the least of which was with one of their own members. Moore added that he and Gilmour "have had a great deal to suffer from the vanity and selfishness of Bishop Dwenger." Both Moore and Gilmour (who left Rome on October 10) jointly felt it necessary to write Gibbons on October 3 about their assessment of Dwenger, lest he be considered for higher office. They agreed that he constantly acted independently of other members of the team. Only when threatened by Gibbons of his possible removal from Rome did he decide to begrudgingly cooperate with the team, and with that only half-heartedly. His exhortations lacked clarity and precision, going on interminably. "We suspect that his private interviews with the Cardinal of Propaganda (Franzelin) may have undermined the Committee's work." Moreover, "He continually boasted of his great talent and lacked Prudence [sic] and tact. He sought to curry favor for himself and sought to please Propaganda." Through Dwenger, Rome was hearing the German side of the "German Question," as interpreted through Franzelin. Moore sent a final letter to Gibbons from Rome thanking him for his Dec. 11 letter, thanking him for the opportunity of serving the American Church, and thanking him for approving of his work in Rome. The Bishop of St. Augustine left Rome just in time to be home for Christmas.[21]

Moore played an important, if not indispensable role, in the success of the American team to get the decrees of Baltimore approved by Rome. His contribution has often been overlooked. He was Gibbons' personal choice, and arguably his best choice for the team. He knew the ways of Rome, having been a seminary student there. He also could write and speak several languages — English, Latin, Italian, French, and Spanish. Despite his initial discomfort with Moore, Gilmour writes McQuaid in November 1885 that the Bishop of St. Augustine made a significant contribution to the proceedings.

> Msgr. Moore proved a firm and steady quality, [although] lacking in the power of initiative, but [was] excellent in sustaining, when measures were proposed. He and I worked well, and alone we would have done well, but Fort Wayne would not work in harness. Either he or *nihil* [nothing] was his motto.[22]

Moore possessed a temperate, composed, calm, reserved, diplomatic demeanor. He was able to stick to the point amidst distractions and difficulties. Above all, he was also competent, rational, and intelligent, with a grasp of the Church in America and of its hierarchy. He was an all around good choice to promote the Baltimore documents to the Holy See. It is hard to argue with success, despite being initially opposed by McQuaid and Corrigan, despite internal divisions among the team members, and despite the resistance on the part of Propaganda, especially Franzelin. Gibbons chose well in choosing Moore, his suffragan.

O'Connell, on the sideline of the process of getting the Baltimore decrees approved after his appointment as rector of NAC in early June 1885, did play a key role in the publication of the approved decrees of III Plenary Baltimore, spending from November 1885 through February 1886 in Baltimore, with Father Sebastian Messmer, supervising the publication of the decrees, after which he returned to Rome in March 1886. The III Plenary Baltimore's decrees governed the Church in America from that point on, being modified in 1917 by the Code of Canon Law. They were at best American formulations of previous Roman enactments. They did not address some burning questions that divided the American Church, including "the German Question," or other nationality questions, or ecclesiastical discipline, or divisions in the American hierarchy (for example, between Gibbons and Corrigan, or Archbishop Ireland and Corrigan), or secret societies, or unionism, but it did introduce an original idea: the establishment of the Catholic University of America in Washington, DC.[23]

Ever mindful of his pastoral and personal responsibilities, Moore used his free time in Rome to take care of some other business while in Europe. In March 1885, he traveled to Le Puy, on his way to Rome, where he arrived on March 16. He investigated whether a Sisters of St. Joseph province would be created for St. Augustine, thus releasing the Florida SSJ Sisters from any dependence upon Le Puy. He had to leave before he got his inquiry answered, which was ultimately "no." Five novices in Le Puy offered to come to Florida. Four were eventually sent in 1886.[24]

Although he was not due to give his *Ad limna* report until 1887 (bishops, then as now, are to give a written report on the state of their diocese to Rome, preferably delivered in person, every ten years), Moore decided to give his while in Rome in 1885. On July 5, just before he was planning to leave on July 9, he had a special audience with the Pope to present his *Ad limina*. In it he reports having 12,000 Catholics in a diocese with a total population of 270,000 (4 percent were Catholics). The diocese also has 4,000 Cubans and 800 Negroes. With a total of ten parishes in St. Augustine, St. Ambrose (13 miles West of St. Augustine), Jacksonville, Mandarin, Fernandina, Tallahassee, Palatka, San Antonio, Tampa, and Key West, the largest and most lucrative one is Immaculate Conception in Jacksonville, which is the only parish with two priests assigned. Only four of the ten are self-supporting—St. Augustine, Jacksonville,

Palatka, and Key West, all the rest are supported by the Society of the Propagation of the Faith, which gives about $3,000 ($83,066.87 in 2017 dollars) a year to the diocese. Each parish had missions and stations attached. Only one parish, in Tallahassee, presently has no resident priest. Eleven priests are in the diocese: three Frenchmen, two Italians, one German, three Irish, one American, one born in England of Irish parents. During his eight years as bishop, he has lost six priests: three died, two were recalled by their bishop, one went out to the Western U.S. As for seminarians, he has two theologians, one studying in Rome (Edward Pace), the other in Quebec City, while he has five studying philosophy, three in Baltimore and two in Limerick, Ireland. He adds that one of his great difficulties he has is finding "good priests willing to work for God and not for money."

Moore made a second *Ad limina* trip to Rome in August of 1895. He estimated the Catholic population at about 14,000, out of total population of 260,958, or about 5 percent of the total. Now he had fourteen parishes, all with missions and stations attached, and twenty-eight priests: eight Americans, eight Irish, six French, two Italians, two French, one Bohemian, one German. The diocese contained four Jesuits and five Benedictines. At that point, Moore sent all his theological students to NAC or to Carlow in Ireland.[25] Since mid-April 1885, Moore's sister was in Paris with her cousins.

He left Rome for France, sometime at the end of July and early August to see her, returning to Rome on August 13. He also visited the College of Combrée, where he had matriculated as a seminarian. There he met some former classmates and professors. "Many came from throughout the diocese to greet me," he writes Mother Lazarus. He then traveled to Nantes to visit the grave sites of his uncle, his aunt, and two of his cousins. Next he went on to Paris to visit his sister, who was still there and recovering from an illness. He sent her to Ireland for a visit; she would return to the U.S. before him. Moore intended to visit Le Puy one more time to try to get more Sisters for Florida. From there he goes on to Ireland to recruit some postulants of the SSJ's, to recruit some seminarians for Florida, and to recruit a priest for Florida. He did one more task while in Ireland, an act of filial piety, which was to erect a headstone for his father's grave in Clonmellen Parish Cemetery, County Westmeath.[26]

# Fraternity

Moore demonstrated his collegiality not only by actively participating in III Plenary Baltimore and his membership on the American team promoting the acceptance of its decrees in Rome, but also by his efforts to show solidarity with his brother bishops. In particular, he continued to show interest in events in his home Diocese of Charleston.

Thomas Muleahy wrote to Moore in 1878 asking for money. Moore, who had not forgotten Muleahy's kindness to him during the War, sent him a postal order for $15 ($387.07 in 2017 dollars). He also wrote to Bishop Lynch for rent money for Muleahy so that he could, as he put it to Moore, get "out of this difficulty and prevent me from being out on the street." Even though Reconstruction meant hard times for many in the South for people like Muleahy, he, like many, were not looking for a hand-out, but the opportunity of helping himself, as he confided to Moore that "with the help of God, I hope that some job will come my way."[27]

Moore kept in touch with his former bishop, Patrick N. Lynch of Charleston, by other means. On his way to an episcopal consecration in Richmond of Francis Janssens in 1881, he stopped by Charleston to visit Lynch. In January 1882 Moore traveled to Baltimore for the Consecration of Henry Pinckney Northrop as Vicar Apostolic of North Carolina. Northrop was a priest of Charleston, ordained in 1865, and the pastor of St. Patrick's, Moore's former parish. Gibbons was the primary consecrator, with William Gross of Savannah the first assistant consecrator and Moore as the second assistant consecrator. On March 2, 1882, Moore attended the funeral of Patrick N. Lynch in Charleston, along with Gibbons (the celebrant), Corrigan, and a handful of other bishops. Lynch had specifically written in his will that he did not want a funeral sermon, "I distinctly forbid it." To do an end run around his wishes, while at the same time trying to respect them, Moore was designated to say a few words from the sanctuary (not from the pulpit) after the *Agnus Dei* (the Lamb of God after the recitation of the Our Father, but before the reception of Holy Communion). Moore read a section from Lynch's will, including the part about no funeral sermon, then made a few brief comments as a tribute to his former bishop:

His memory will be ever fresh in our souls and our hearts as long as we live — that we will cherish for him the dearest recollections - we who have grown up around him, his children, will always look back with fond remembrances of him... Do we not recall the lessons learned from him? Did you ever see any act of his except an act of kindness?... Do I not speak your sentiments, when I say that his memory will be cherished with filial affection? Will you not recall his indomitable spirit, especially in paying off the debts of the diocese over seventeen long years [1865-1882]? He endured mental and physical labor to do this. The one ruling object of his life — to transmit to the diocese a name unstained, to uphold the honor of his religion. He asked forgiveness of no debt... I am satisfied that his memory will be cherished truly and tenderly by all who knew him and that you will transmit your love and attention for him to your children... we will always look back with fond remembrance of him.

Moore's wartime and post-war antipathy for Lynch as his absentee bishop had long dissipated, perhaps because of his own episcopal challenges which had parallels with Lynch's. Now he understood Lynch in a way that he was unable to do before. In his heart-felt and tender words, it seems that he may have been speaking as much about himself as Lynch.[28]

Moore traveled to Baltimore for a consultative meeting called by Gibbons to decide on Lynch's successor. Also attending that meeting of March 22, 1882, were the following bishops: John Keane of Richmond, John Kain of Wheeling, Thomas Becker of Wilmington, Henry P. Northrop of North Carolina, and William Gross of Savannah. Later, Moore returned to Charleston in September 1882 to attend the funeral of Claudian Northrop, age 37, the brother of Bishop Henry Northrop. In March 1883 Moore was back in Charleston for the installation of Bishop Henry P. Northrop as Bishop of Charleston. Moore delivered the sermon on *Matt.* 28:19 "go into the whole world and baptize." A few months later that same year Moore returned to Charleston for the rededication of St. Joseph's Church on December 17. The edifice was blessed by Bishop Moore, while Bishop Northrop was the celebrant and Bishop Gross preached. In a ceremony that must have delighted Moore, he attended the dedication of a new church building at St. Patrick's, Charleston, on May 15, 1887. The new church cost $60,000 and seated 700. Msgr. Daniel Quigley was pastor, as well as being the Vicar General of the Diocese. Northrop was the celebrant and Becker, now of Savannah, preached. On May 26, 1896, Moore consecrated the newly renovated altars at St. Mary Church, Charleston, largely because Bishop Northrop was ill. In March 1901 the newly renovated St. Mary's was consecrated by Northrop, but Moore did not attend because of his own declining health.[29]

But Charleston was not the only place where Moore visited out of friendship, to fulfill ecclesiastical duties in response to request for episcopal consultations or installations, or simply to show support to his fellow bishops.

In July 1877 he sent a congratulatory letter to Archbishop Gibbons who had just been transferred to the Archdiocese of Baltimore, American's Primatial See. "You will leave Richmond and dear North Carolina for which you have labored so faithfully and with so much success, yet Baltimore is your home [Gibbons was born there in 1834, through his parents returned to Ireland in 1837, then in 1853 moved back to the U.S., settling in New Orleans]." Moore was confident that Gibbons would have "the hearty good will of the people, which will help lighten the burden of your administration." In October of that same year, Gibbons as Moore's Metropolitan consulted Moore regarding who should be his successor in Richmond, since Moore was unable to attend the meeting of the bishops of the Province of Baltimore where the matter was discussed. Moore says he agrees with the *terna* and the order of candidates proposed by the bishops at the Provincial meeting, namely: 1) Msgr. S. Chatard of Newark; 2) Rev. John J. Keane of Baltimore; and 3) Rev. Henry Northrop of Charleston. Moore adds that if he was present at the meeting, he would have made some observations on each of the candidates. It was Keene who was finally chosen as the next Bishop of Richmond. In May of 1880, the Vicar General of Richmond, Francis Janssens, was consecrated bishop by Archbishop Gibbons in St. Peter's Cathedral, Richmond, because he was chosen to be the Bishop of Natchez.

Bishops Keane and Becker were the co-consecrators. Bishop Moore attended the ceremony, along with Archbishop Elder, and Bishops Kain, Gross, and Lynch. That same month, Moore was asked to give his opinion about Harry Northrop, a priest of Charleston, who was on the *terna* for the Diocese of Louisville. Bishop Lynch of Charleston stated that he would like to see Northrop succeed him in Charleston. In April 1882, Moore wrote Archbishop Gibbons and Cardinal Simioni in Rome about the *terna* for Charleston. He felt that F. Wegrich would not be a good fit because "he is a Prussian." He thought that Northrop would be a better choice, although "if Father Quigley was allowed one year as Administrator, the whole diocesan debt would be cleared out," so much confidence did Moore have in his financial acumen. It was Northrop, who was a priest of Charleston and recently Vicar Apostolic of North Carolina, who was installed in Charleston in March 1883. Since Gibbons was supposed to attend but couldn't, Moore escorted Northrop to his episcopal chair at the Cathedral, as the principal consecrator, along with Bishop William Gross of Savannah and Bishop John Tuigg of Pittsburgh. Moore also preached at the occasion.[30]

Moore continued his involvement in consultations, in episcopal ordinations, and in installations, most especially in the Southeastern U.S. throughout the 1880s and 1890s. In mid-1883 Moore penned Gibbons (enclosing a letter sent him in June by Philadelphia layman James M. Willcox and Maitland, Fla., benefactor). Willcox claims that the Church of Philadelphia is in a "great crisis" because of the failure to appoint a successor to the late archbishop. "The diocese is so important, so conspicuous, so powerful... and the elements are not harmonious." Philadelphia needs an archbishop "of ability, experience, and force, one long tried and proved both as a man of God and a Bishop [emphasis by Willcox]." In 1884, Moore opines to Propaganda in Rome about the vacancy in Philadelphia. He disputes the claim that the diocesan finances there are in good shape. Rather, he observed that they were a disaster, plus the morale of the diocesan clergy was poor. Archbishop Wood's "kindly disposition gave rise to a relaxed disposition among the clergy." He added that none of the Philadelphia suffragans were up to the task; hence he felt that Bishop Kain of Wheeling would be the best candidate since he was "eloquent, courageous, and acceptable to the clergy."

Cardinal McCloskey of New York favored Patrick J. Ryan, the coadjutor Archbishop of St. Louis, while Gibbons thought O'Farrell of Trenton or Spalding of Peoria would be best for Philadelphia. Neither Moore's nor Gibbon's candidates won Philadelphia, but Ryan. When Gibbons was made a Cardinal, he received a Cardinal's *biretta* in June 1886. Moore attended that ceremony in Baltimore. Later in July 1888 Abbot Leo Haid, OSB, of Belmont Abbey, was consecrated Bishop of the Vicar Apostolic of North Carolina. Moore attended the ceremony and the bishops of the Province gathered along with Gibbons to discuss the appointment of the new Bishop of Richmond, since John Keane resigned as Bishop of Richmond so as to devote all of his energies as the first rector of the Catho-lic University of America. Augustine Van de Vyver, a Belgian and Vicar General of the Diocese of Richmond, was consecrated Bishop of Richmond in October of 1889.[31]

Gilmour's and Moore's paths crossed one final time in an instance of Moore's collegiality and hospitality. In the fall of 1889 Gilmour took seriously ill. As his health continued to deteriorate, in the spring of 1891 doctors advised him that a warmer climate might enhance his recovery. He left Cleveland on March 11, 1891. After staying briefly in Cincinnati, then Atlanta, he reached St. Augustine on March 19, with a small entourage of Cleveland priests to attend him. Upon arriving in St. Augustine, with Moore's aid, he was the guest of Capt. Leopold R. Vogel, whose mansion overlooked the sea. Bedridden for a week because of the ardors of the journey, by April 7, thinking he was dying, he made out his will and received the Sacrament of Extreme Unction. Bishop William McCloskey of Louisville paid him a visit before his death in St. Augustine on April 13, 1891.[32]

Moore's closest friend among the hierarchy was Thomas Becker, especially after the latter moved to the See of Savannah in 1886. Their friendship first began when they both traveled by ship to Rome in 1855. They were students together at the Urban College, until Becker's ordination in June 1859. Moore had Becker, Bishop of Wilmington from 1868 to 1886, as co-consecrator at his ordination as Bishop of St. Augustine in Charleston in 1877. They reconnected at the periodic meetings of the bishops of the Province of Baltimore, as well as at the consecration of Janssens as the Bishop of Natchez in

May 1881. It was Becker who was chosen to preach at the dedication of the new church of St. Patrick's in Charleston in May 1887. At Christmas, Moore would send Becker in Wilmington a basket of fresh oranges, always a welcome treat in the dead of a Northern winter. Becker in turn shared that gift with the Sisters of Visitation Convent.

When Becker was installed as the sixth Bishop of Savannah in May 1886, Moore was present at the ceremony, along with Bishop Northrop of Charleston. When Cardinal Gibbons received his red biretta in Baltimore on June 30, 1886, Moore and Becker journeyed together from Savannah to Baltimore for the event. The two friends also traveled on vacation together in the summer of 1886 and in April of 1889 Becker vacationed with Moore in St. Augustine. Undoubtedly, Moore also visited with Becker in Savannah on his way to his various begging trips to Northern cities. Sadly, Moore was unable to attend the funeral of his friend in Savannah in August 1899 due to his own ill health. Interestingly, Becker's Cathedral burned in 1898 and he was unable to restore it before he died on July 29, 1899; Moore's Cathedral burned in 1887, but he did complete its restoration just before his death on July 30, 1901.[33]

## National Collegial Issues

During their time in Rome together in 1885, as we have seen, Gilmour and Moore were at odds with Dwenger over the "German Question," that is what the best pastoral approach was in coping with Germans and German-Americans in the U.S. Correspondence to Franzelein from Germans in America was discovered by Gilmour and Moore during their time in Rome in 1885. This tension between Germans and German-Americans in America and some members of the American hierarchy, along with the Germans dragging Rome into the fray, was only one of several national and international issues which preoccupied some members of the American hierarchy, with Cardinal Gibbons of Baltimore, made Cardinal in 1886, trying to arbitrate matters among the hierarchy. Corrigan and McQuaid were often pitted against Archbishop Ireland, Bishop Keane, and Msgr. O' Connell, Gibbon's agent in Rome. All of these issues culminated in the Americanism Crisis of the 1890s and ultimately with the condemnation of "Americanism" by Papal Decree in 1899.

With the rebuilding of his Cathedral from the 1887 fire, the necessity of his frequent traveling to raise money for its reconstruction, and with his keeping up with the growth and development of his diocese, he hardly had the luxury of time to be engaged in national episcopal debates and in-fighting, especially since most of those issues did not impact directly on the pastoral care of his priests, women religious, and laity in Florida. Often the late nineteenth century ecclesiastic infighting was about personalities, politics, power, and various views of the polity of the Church in America regarding ethnic groups and the relationship of the U.S. Church with Rome. Moore's temperament and mind were reserved rather than flamboyant; his aspirations were humble rather than ambitious. He was inclined to work quietly behind the scenes, rather than in the glare of the limelight, seeking conciliation rather than controversy. His vision of himself was more localized than national, more pastoral than ideological. Yet never shrinking from what he felt was his duty, no matter how difficult or personally sacrificial, but he did not perceive it his duty to engage in some of the national controversies of his day. However, Moore kept up on national ecclesiastical affairs throughout the 1890s, especially by reading the minutes of the annual national meeting of Archbishops, and through his conversations with bishops and priests during his numerous fund-raising travels throughout the country.[34]

There were however a few notable exceptions to Moore's disinclination to personally engage in national issues: the establishment of a Papal diplomat in Washington, the banning of secret societies, the Catholic Total Abstinence Union, and the Edward McGlynn controversy.

Moore's initial position was to be opposed to the establishment of a Papal Nuncio in Washington. Rome was pushing for it, but Gibbons and some bishops were averse to it. Moore wrote Gibbons in August 1886 protesting the establishment of a Delegation in the U.S.: "We are better off as we are, free from government interference in ecclesiastical matters." Moore even thought that such an establishment might be unconstitutional and cause a serious uproar in the country against the Church. Firstly, it went against the earlier notion of synodal governance, rather than centralized control in the style of Vatican Council I. Secondly, there was the ongoing tension with Germans in America with the majority of the American Hierarchy. The Germans had used communication with Roman officials to express their grievances and demanding justice, especially in the form of more German bishops in the U.S. In this way they found a way to get a hearing for their concerns, circumventing the American hierarchy altogether. Some thought that the establishment of a Papal Nuncio on American soil would only aggravate the various issues surrounding the "German Question."[35]

Gibbons had expressed to Rome this opposition to the establishment of an Apostolic Delegation to the U.S. as early as 1878. At that time, he conveyed his opposition to the concept on political grounds. A Roman presence in the U.S. would give the wrong impression of Catholicism to the government and people of the U.S. Instead, Gibbons favored having an American agent residing in Rome, just as was the case with England. When Moore was in Rome in 1885, he picked up information that Roman authorities thought the American bishops were trying to tie Rome's hands with the idea of the agent in Rome. Instead they proposed having one or two American bishops in the U.S. receive appeals from throughout the country and treat matters there for Rome. Moore, speaking for Gibbons, said he felt that plan was agreeable, as long as there was also an American prelate in Rome who could represent the American Hierarchy there. Gibbons thought he found a compromise when his associate, Denis O'Connell, was appointed rector of the North American College in Rome on June 15, 1885. Now O'Connell could be the agent for the U.S. hierarchy and also be Gibbons' man in Rome. Meanwhile, Rome had not given up on the idea of having an Apostolic Delegation in Washington, and it seems Bishop Dwenger, the nemesis of the American team trying to get III Plenary Baltimore decrees approved in 1885 and an agent of German interests in America, was working behind the scenes, encouraging the establishment of the Roman delegation in the U.S. Moore convinced Gibbons of Dwenger's machinations, which the Metropolitan strongly disapproved. In October 1886 Moore suggested to Gibbons to bring the issue of the Apostolic Delegate to the upcoming meeting of the American bishops, since

Gibbons' opinions on the matter were apparently being ignored by Rome. Moore informs Gibbons that Dwenger was in Washington "a few weeks ago," probably working behind the scenes for the establishment of the Apostolic Delegation. In December 1886 Moore tells Gibbons that he does not know what legislation the Germans want, but "If they succeed in obtaining the sanction from Rome for their efforts to Germanize [sic] the Catholic Church in this country, I venture to predict that serious evils will follow. The Irish are likely to take up the alarm," which will lead to "religious discord and strife... The Church and religion will suffer... We cannot fail to become the laughing stock to the American people... I entirely agree with Bishop Gilmour." After a trip to New York City, Moore informs Gibbons in mid-January 1887 that Dwenger might be angling to be appointed the Apostolic Delegate himself. "What a calamity!" exclaims Moore. While in Rome, Moore testifies that Dwenger said that if offered the position, he would not refuse it. Moore advises Gibbons to vigorously oppose Dwenger's appointment during his upcoming visit to Rome. Moore also suggests that English-speaking bishops be encouraged to write letters to Rome on the subject of the appointment before "we are at the mercy of the Germans."[36]

Circumstances changed in 1892 with preparations for the World's Columbian Exposition to be May 1, 1893, in Chicago. Managers of the Fair sought maps and charts which were contemporaneous with Columbus's first voyage. Only the Vatican Library had them. On behalf of the Exposition's planning committee, John W. Foster, Secretary of State, wrote a letter to Cardinal Mariano Rampolla, the Papal Secretary of State, asking for the loan of the fifteenth century maps. Foster said not only the Exposition's promoters, but the American people would greatly appreciate this gesture by the Holy See. He also suggested that if the Pope so wished the documents could be conveyed to the U.S. through a personal representative of the Pope and that the President himself assures that "such representative shall receive all possible courtesy upon his arrival and during his sojourn in [t]his country.'" Archbishop Francesco Satolli was chosen as the Papal representative to accompany the maps.[37]

Bishop John Ireland of St. Paul and Gibbons were very concerned about keeping in the company of Satolli at all times during his U.S. stay, for fear that he be unduly influenced by opposing ecclesiastical forces. Both Msgr. O'Connell and Father Edward A. Pace, the Floridian now at the Catholic University of America, accompanied Satolli from Europe to the U.S. After Satolli went to Chicago with the maps, he came to Washington, residing at the Catholic University of America. Gibbons and his allies were anxious to spirit him back to Rome as soon as possible, but Rome and Satolli has other ideas, taking advantage of the warm welcome by the U.S. Government. On January 3, 1893, Gibbons sent a letter to Pope Leo XIII in the name of the American Archbishops outlining their reasons for not wanting an Apostolic Delegate in the country. In brief, the Church in the U.S. was not yet ready to receive a Delegate because of continuing anti-Catholicism and because a Delegate would appear to be sent for the express purpose of controlling the American bishops, a perception that would injure the esteem that the Catholics have of their bishops. In addition, there were already a number of negative press accounts of Satolli's visit. Archbishop Ireland blamed Archbishop Corrigan of New York for fomenting some of the bad press. Be that as it may, on January 14, 1893, Gibbons received a cablegram from O'Connell in Rome stating: "American delegation established. Satolli first Delegate." It seems as if Satolli was the guest who came to dinner, and then refused to leave the house. The establishment of an Apostolic Delegation in Washington was now a *fait accompli*. Gibbons and other American bishops who opposed such an establishment now had to accommodate themselves to this new reality and its new oversight. Moore's position changed on the matter, as did Gibbons' along with most of the American Hierarchy. They assented to the will of the Holy Father. As the old Latin dictum said: "When Rome has spoken, the matter is settled." As Gibbons wrote O'Connell from Chicago in September 1893; "I hope that Satolli will be kept here. The bishops might become reconciled to him. It was decided here [in Chicago] by the Archbishops to build him a residence."[38]

After Moore's work on getting the Roman approval for the decrees of III Plenary Baltimore, Cardinal Gibbons did not consult Moore on national controversies as before and Moore did not put forth his opinions to Gibbons unsolicited. An exception, however, was Gibbons seeking Moore's opinion on the banning of secret societies. Moore wrote Gibbons while on a less than successful begging trip to St. Louis in 1892. The Bishop of St. Augustine urged caution: "We must not be hasty to condemn secret societies, but the refusal of the Knights of Pythias to give their _____ [the handwritten word is indecipherable] to Archbishop Janssens [of New Orleans]. We need to get all the information about them and this matter, then refer it to Rome." In August 1894, Rome condemned Catholics being members of the Knights of Pythias, the Odd Fellows, and the Sons of Temperance, but allowed Catholics continued membership only if four specific conditions were met. The decree directed that American bishops be notified of the action of the Holy Office and that their people be warned against membership in these societies. Ever dutiful, Moore sent out a circular letter in early January 1895 to all his pastors explaining the Papal condemnation of the three secret societies and asking them to inform their parishioners that Catholics are not to be members of those societies by reading the circular from the pulpit. One priest asked Moore if he could delay making the announcement about the Papal condemnation. John F. O'Boyle was the priest who tended the surrounding missions and stations of Central Florida. At the time, he was building a mission church in Titusville to be used as his base of operations. Because he was in the midst of raising money and constructing St. Teresa of Avila Church in Titusville, he felt it inopportune to make an announcement about the condemnation of secret societies to his parishioners: "To make it public just now would place me in a very embarrassing position. Can I not hold off until the church building gets closed in?" Apparently a number of his flock were members in one or the other of those condemned societies. We have no record of Moore's reply, but we can presume that he assented to O'Boyle's pastoral concerns.[39]

The one national issue which Moore was personally engaged was the Catholic Total Abstinence Union. Father Theobald Mathew was born in Thomastown, Tipperary, on October 10, 1790. He was ordained in Cork in 1814. By 1838, he formed in Cork the first members of what he called the Total Abstinence Society, initially thirty-five in number. Five months later, 150,000 members took the pledge in Cork. The pledge was this: "I promise, with the Divine Assistance, to abstain from intoxicating drinks, to prevent by advice and example the sin of intemperance in others, and to discontinue the custom of drinking in society." In a decade Father Mathew spoke throughout Ireland and then in England and Scotland, where he persuaded over 5 million Irish men, women, and children to take the pledge. He came to the U.S. at the age of sixty in July of 1849, speaking first in New York, then Boston, Philadelphia, and Washington (where he addressed the U.S. Senate, even getting some Senators to take the pledge). By Christmas, he was in Richmond, then on to Charleston, then on to Savannah, Augusta, Macon, and Atlanta. By March 1850, he visited Mobile, then New Orleans, Vicksburg, and Little Rock. By October, he traveled to St. Louis, then back to New Orleans. In March 1851, he set off for Nashville, where he suffered a stroke and decided to return to Ireland. He departed for Ireland from New York City in November 1851, a physically broken and financially impoverished man. During his American tour he pledged 500,000 people. He died in Ireland on December 8, 1856. Many of the men who took the pledge under Father Mathew were founders of the Catholic Total Abstinence Union of America (CTAU), established in 1872. Bishops John Ireland and John Keene took the pledge from Father Mathew as boys, as did Bishop Gilmour as a young man in Pottsville, PA, even before he became a Catholic.[40]

Moore too was a member of the CTAU. While in Philadelphia on his first fund-raising tour for the rebuilding of his Cathedral, he attended the Seventeenth Annual Convention of the CTAU and gave the toast to the Holy Father at the gathering. On October 10, 1899, in Scranton, PA, the CTAU celebrated the Fiftieth Anniversary of Father Mathew's coming to the U.S. with a big rally and parade. Moore suffered his first stroke earlier in August 1899 in Wilkes-Barre, Pa., therefore was unable to attend, but if that had not happened he may have attended, especially if he was still fund-raising in the area. He did keep a news clipping about the August 1899 event. Although a life-long teetotaler, Moore never established a branch of the CTAU in his own diocese, nor did he promote the cause in Florida.[41]

The final national issue in which Moore was engaged was the dispute between Archbishop Michael Corrigan and his priest, the Rev. Dr. Edward McGlynn, which will be discussed in the next chapter.

CHAPTER THIRTEEN

# *The Edward McGlynn Affair*

B ecause of John Moore's physical distance from the Northeast and Midwest, because of his pastoral burdens in Florida, because of his personal engagement in rebuilding his destroyed Cathedral, and because his temperament was naturally calm and sedate, he was disinclined to involve himself in a public fray. Although he sometimes commented on ecclesiastical matters in person or by letter, he never sought the limelight. Therefore, his entanglement in the McGlynn Affair was extremely untypical. His desire was to help a friend who was in real trouble. For him, it was personal.

## The New York Connection

Moore matriculated in Rome with some New York priests and had a connection with others who had previously studied in Rome. Among his contemporaries in Rome were three New York priests: Richard Burtsell, Michael Corrigan, and Edward McGlynn.

As a result of their shared experience, these men formed life-long associations.

Jeremiah W. Cummings (1814-66) was the first American graduate from the Urban College of the Propaganda in Rome. In 1848, he was the founding pastor of St. Stephen's in Manhattan. He was a counselor of Orestes Brownson, contributor to *Brownson's Review*, and an acerbic critic of seminary formation in the U.S. Cummings, along with Father Henry Brann of the Diocese of Newark, another graduate of the Urban College, founded the priests' organization, the *Accademia* (or the Theological Society), in the Spring of 1865. Approved by the archbishop, this group met monthly and was comprised primarily, though not exclusively, of Urban College graduates. Its purpose was to continue the theological education of its members and to foster priestly fraternity. They read and discussed original papers presented by their members. When Edward McGlynn returned to New York with his doctorate from Rome in November of 1860, he joined the organization. The theological opinions of the membership varied, but some of the ideas discussed were decidedly progressive: abolitionism, Radical Republicanism, Finianism, opposition to the temporal power of the Pope, optional celibacy (which Burtsell and McGlynn opposed), the authenticity of Mosaic authorship of the Pentateuch, the Church's extreme legalism, the use of the vernacular in the liturgy, the opposition to the establishment of national parishes, the gradual assimilation of immigrants. They believed that the Church in the U.S. should take the lead in social reforms, introduce more democratic processes, and promote public schools over a parochial school system. But on September 14, 1865, the group disbanded, in order to reformulate their society. Father Richard Burtsell, a member, said that the *Accademia* "was not acceptable to many of the clergy" because it was seen "to be a clique of Romans and abolitionists" and because its principal founder, Dr. Henry Brann, was not a priest of New York. Consequently, the

13.1 *Msgr. Richard Burtsell*
Source: Sylvester L. Malone,
*Dr. Edward McGlynn*
*(1918), no page number*

group disbanded, with only Brann and another priest objecting. McGlynn persuaded Father Thomas Farrell to approach Archbishop McCloskey about approving a new society for priests. As it turned out, no formal approval of the new group came from McCloskey, but from the initiative of Father Thomas Farrell, who began hosting weekly meetings of about a half-dozen priests interested in ongoing theological education. Burtsell confided to his diary in early 1867: "We need a revision of the fundamental principles of our theology and I am commencing '*ab ovo*' ["from the very beginning," literally "from the egg"] my theological studies, which were narrowed down by Roman prejudices."[1]

Where did the theological ideas of these New York priests come from? Although almost all of the association had in common their studies in Rome, the genesis of the group's more radical approach to theology did not revert to the theological content that they learned there. If anything, they were reacting to what they previously had received. Both Burtsell and McGlynn were conservative seminarians with very orthodox ideas. Some commentators suggest that it was the trauma of the Civil War that was the catalyst that radically committed them to American democracy and to a unique expression of Catholicism in the U.S. As Michael Gannon puts it:

The Civil War (1861-1865) was probably a watershed in the maturation of the American Church, for with the onset of sectional warfare, bishops and priests for the first time entered national politics on an issue not directly affecting Catholicism as such... Only after the guns began to roar, when it appeared that they could no longer stand apart from the civil agony and still claim the full loyalty of their subjects, did the clergy commit their pulpits to the fire of politics and war. As everyone else, bishops and priests lined up along geographical lines. It was a strange moment for the Church that had "left to worldlings [sic] the cares and anxieties of political partisanship." But by the time peace settled over the charred ruins and the flag of the Confederacy was furled forever, it was clear that the American Church, like the nation, had changed. In October

1866, the bishops of the North and South assembled at Baltimore for a Second Plenary Council, as though nothing had happened, but something had happened, and because of it the Catholic clergy were of necessity more closely bound up with the nation, with her problems, social and economic, with her commonweal in general, with her destiny.[2]

But most of the New York's clerical theological radicals had more than the Civil War as a common experience. They also had their studies in Rome. Even though the content of those studies was traditional and orthodox, the way they thought about theology was different from that of those who studied in the U.S. In Rome they experienced the long history of the Church by living in an environment where structures from Roman times through the Middle Ages and modernity were clearly visible. Roman students saw Church history as a tactile reality all around them, and one of the aspects of that history was that the Church changed over time, as did the development of theology. They also observed that the Church had taken the shape of the times and culture which surrounded it. Their experience of the Church and of doing theology in Rome gave them a different perspective on the present and future of the Church in America.

One of the issues of concern to members of the *Accademia* and those that followed them in New York and other similar groups of priests, such as in Cleveland, was the erosion of priestly canonical rights and independence because of the often heavy-handed exercise of episcopal authority in America. Since the U.S. was considered a missionary country until 1908, it was not under the normal provisions of Canon Law. Most American bishops viewed this situation as giving them a *carte blanc* regarding the appointment or removal of priests from their assignments. As Orestes Brownson wrote in 1862: "Each bishop [in the U.S.] is well-nigh absolute in his own diocese, and the freedom of the second order of the clergy has no security but in the will and conscience of the bishop."[3]

Some priests began to act in defense of their canonical rights. Father Eugene O'Callahan was part of a group of priests similar to the *Accademia* that began meeting in Cleveland in 1862. O'Callahan wrote a series of articles under the name "Jus" in James McMaster's

New York *Freeman's Journal* in 1869. He called for an ecclesiastical juridical process to replace the existing arbitrary method in which American bishops transferred or dismissed priests at will or whim. The situation was only aggravated by the missionary status of the country — parishes were not canonically erected as parishes and pastors in the U.S. were technically only rectors. Over 1,000 priests responded to the *Freeman's Journal* supporting the perspective of "Jus." Meanwhile, in Newark, Father Sebastian Smith published his *Notes on the Second Plenary Council* in 1874 in which he took the American bishops to task for not observing the provisions of Canon Law or even their own conciliar decrees. But the most notorious of the clerical dissidents were in New York. Some bishops, such as Corrigan of New York and McQuaid of Rochester, were convinced that all clerical progressive groups were part of a national conspiracy to dethrone episcopal authority. In fact, these groups were local in composition, and no evidence exists of any nationwide conspiracy.[4]

## The Cast of Characters

At the forefront of the movement for priests' rights in America were the New York priests Richard Burtsell and Edward McGlynn. Both were good friends with John Moore.

Richard Lalor Burtsell was born in New York City on April 13, 1840, from an old and prosperous New York Catholic family. At age 11 he was sent to the Sulpician Seminary in Montreal to study the classics and in 1853 at age thirteen to the Urban College in Rome, where he received his doctorate in theology in 1862 and where he was ordained that same year. He returned to New York the fall of 1862 and was assigned to assist the pastor of St. Anne's, Thomas Preston. In December 1867, he became the founding pastor of Epiphany Parish. But because of his open support of McGlynn, Archbishop Corrigan transferred him to St. Mary's, Roundout, near Kingston in December 1889. But he did not arrive there until November 1890, due to his unsuccessful appeal to Rome regarding his transfer. During his productive years, he wrote scholarly articles for academic journals and for newspapers. In 1898, Archbishop Corrigan named him a irremovable rector (pastor) and Archbishop John Farley designated him a monsignor in 1904, a gesture of vindication and reconciliation. He died in Kingston, NY, in 1912.[5]

Burtsell was one of the few American priests at the time who had a special expertise in Canon Law and for many years developed a national reputation as a successful counselor and defender of priests who had problems with their bishops, a reputation that hardly endeared him to the American bishops or to his own archbishop. Nearly all of the cases that Burtsell undertook were appealed to Rome successfully. He wrote a series of articles in the *New York Tablet* in 1887 titled: "The Canonical Status of Priests in the U.S.," even though McGlynn was listed as the author. The articles covered the same themes he outlined earlier in his anonymous pamphlet of 1883 called "The Rights of the Clergy Vindicated or A Plea for Canon Law in the United States." Burtsell promoted due process for American priests.[6]

With so many priest cases remitted to Rome, officials there decided to investigate. In 1878 the Irish Bishop of Ardagh, George Conroy, was sent to Canada as a temporary Apostolic Delegate. He was also directed to visit the U.S. After an extensive tour, he wrote a lengthy report to Propaganda about the Church in America. In it he said that U.S. bishops attached a good deal of importance to the skill of managing finances, both in choosing candidates for the episcopacy and in assigning pastorates. He also noted "'the ever increasing discord between bishops and priests.'" He added that there were two major areas of complaints from priests: 1) the manner which episcopal candidates were chosen (priests wanted to be included in the process); 2) bishops took little or no account of Canon Law when they exercised their authority. In response to the Conroy's Report, in 1879, Propaganda sent out new instructions to the U.S. Bishops. Each American bishop was to form an investigative commission of from three to five priests, elected at a diocesan synod, to examine criminal and disciplinary cases of priests. The bishop was to listen to the commission's advice on the particular case before acting against the priest in question. American bishops were not pleased with this new legislation since they had not been consulted by Propaganda beforehand. Among those discontented was Corrigan, then Bishop of Newark, and McQuaid of Rochester. In response to an American episcopal push-back, Propaganda reformulated their instructions, saying that the bishops should not move priests without a serious and reasonable motive. Moreover, these newly mandated diocesan commissions were only consultative; the final decision on any matter was left to the bishop's discretion. McQuaid extolled this outcome as "'so grand a victory for the American Church,'" which he seemed to always identify with his perspectives and opinions.[7]

*13.2 Archbishop Michael Corrigan, c 1884*
*Source: Maurice F. Egan, The Hierarchy of*
*the Roman Catholic Church in the U.S.,*
*(1888), front piece.*

In October 1883 Johann Cardinal Franzelin of Propaganda in Rome wrote up a report on the state of the American Church. It was a document written in preparation for the Roman instigated meeting of American bishops the next year in Baltimore. Franzelin noted that although a new procedure was established for choosing American bishops, it was not working well. Secrecy was not observed and the details of the procedure were not always followed, which resulted in American bishops promoting their own favorites. Moreover, too few Roman trained priests were made bishops in the U.S. (Franzelin counted only six or seven as he wrote). Although U.S. priests felt that they should have more say in who was chosen as bishop, the U.S. bishops did not share their perspective. The Report went on to say that U.S. seminaries do not have enough Roman trained priests on their faculties and consequently they promote anti-Roman ideas, except for the seminaries in Baltimore, Emmitsburg, Milwaukee, and New York. But the most Roman of all American seminaries was St. Charles Borromeo in Philadelphia. Although American bishops send some of their better students to Louvain, Innsbruck, Quebec, and Montreal, not enough are assigned to North American College, Rome. Regarding clerical discipline, Franzelin noted that many European priests reside in the U.S. without clear permission from their bishops back home or without incardination into the American dioceses in which they work. Although priests in the U.S. are technically rectors of missions, not canonical pastors of parishes, bishops act like tyrants suspending priests, often leaving them destitute with no financial help from their bishop. There is an atmosphere of distrust between bishops and priests. Franzelin feels that now is the time to introduce normal Canon Law to the U.S., to no longer see it as mission territory, to inaugurate Canonical Chapters in dioceses (as was introduced into Scotland in 1883), to institute irremovable rectors in qualifying parishes, and to broaden the consultation process in the selection of bishops. As we know, III Plenary Baltimore did not institute Cathedral Chapters of Canons, but rather consultors, 50 percent of whom were chosen by the diocesan bishop and 50 percent chosen by the priests, but they were only advisory. In addition, one tenth of the missions (parishes) were to be designated as irremovable pastors. Despite these suggestions, the missionary status of the U.S. remained a fact until 1908. Many U.S. bishops, including Gibbons of Baltimore, were unwilling to accept many of Franzelin's ideas since they were unwilling to relinquish their power over their priests.[8]

*13.3 Father Bernard McQuaid Source: Frederick J. Zwierlein, The Life and Letters of Bishop McQuaid, Vol. III (1927), front piece.*

The next three persons were great believers in episcopal rights and authority. Consequently, they were easily threatened when any priest or priests might appear to be challenging that authority.

Michael Corrigan was the Archbishop of New York from 1885 to 1902. Corrigan was born in Newark, NJ, on August 13, 1839. One of nine children, his father, Thomas, a cabinet maker, was from County Meath and arrived in the U.S. in 1828. Thomas married in 1831 and became a small businessman — a grocer and tavern proprietor. Michael attended St. Mary's College, Wilmington, DE, Mount St. Mary's College, Emmitsburg, MD, and beginning in

1859, the North American College in Rome. Burtsell was a year ahead of Corrigan, Moore was three years ahead, as was McGlynn. Antipathy between McGlynn and Corrigan most probably started back in Rome when McGlynn was prefect at the North American College. McGlynn was bright and athletic; Corrigan was clever, pious, studious, and slightly effeminate. Burtsell confided in his diary in 1865 that Corrigan "'whom I formerly esteemed... I find to have been despised by the American students as too girlish and narrow-minded.'"

Upon his ordination in September 1863, Corrigan remained in Rome another year to complete his Doctorate of Divinity in June 1864, then he returned to his diocese in September 1864, when he was appointed to the faculty of Seton Hall Seminary, where Bernard McQuaid had been rector since the institution was founded in 1856. McQuaid was Corrigan's pastor when he was a boy. When McQuaid was appointed the first Bishop of Rochester, Corrigan became the president of the college and director of the seminary from 1868 to 1877. He was also Vicar General of the Diocese of Newark from 1868 to 1872 and Administrator of the diocese from 1869 to 1870, and again from 1872 to 1873. He was named the Bishop of Newark in 1873. McQuaid preached at his episcopal consecration. One of his first acts he did as the Bishop of Newark was to consolidate all church property under his name, eliminating parish trustees. He implemented annual reports for each parish in 1873, and generally centralized power under his command. McQuaid was a mentor and model for Corrigan as bishop. McQuaid fought vigorously to maintain his monarchical power, especially over his priests. Corrigan agreed with McQuaid's approach. As early as 1872, Corrigan wrote in his diary: "'Bishops rule dioceses, not priests.'" As bishop, Corrigan believed he had the prerogative to remove priests from their assignments whenever he felt it necessary, no questions asked. Rarely challenged by his priests, he was particularly harsh on priests with alcohol problems, or those whom he even merely suspected of such.

In 1880, he became the coadjutor of the Archdiocese of New York, which was the largest diocese in the country at the time, with 600,000 Catholics, 200 churches, and 379 priests. He succeeded to the metropolitan see of New York in October 1885, remaining there until his death on May 5, 1902.[9]

Emmet Curran, in an 1978 biography of Corrigan, assessed him in this way: Corrigan had practically no pastoral experience before becoming the Bishop of Newark. Moreover, little in his past prepared him to take over the See of New York. He lacked the common touch or even contact with ordinary people. He had no illusions about his limited intellectual powers, but that did not cause him to be especially cautious in making extremely consequential judgments about ideas or persons. He, like McQuaid, had what could be judged as an almost pathological fear of what he considered ubiquitous conspiracies. As a response to these perceived plots, he would equivocate, dissemble, and even utilize spies against those whom he thought were undermining him and the Church (like McQuaid, he did not distinguish between himself and the institution). This all led to a misuse and abuse of power, as well as a corruption of authority, which ironically he was trying to preserve.[10]

Bernard McQuaid might be characterized as a cheerleader and supporter of the Archbishop of New York, Michael Corrigan. Born of Irish parents in New York City in 1825 and baptized in Old St. Patrick's Cathedral, McQuaid's family moved to Jersey City, where his father was a glass worker. McQuaid's youth was filled with tragedy and rootlessness, things that scarred his personality. His mother died in 1827 and his father in 1832. His stepmother abused the children, a bitter memory that stayed with Bernard throughout his life. In 1839, he began his studies for the priesthood, first at Chambly College, near Quebec City, Canada, where he was bullied by his burlier, healthier immigrants from Ireland. Making fun of his emaciated frame, his health only declined amidst an environment of constant harassment. In 1843, he is transferred to St. Joseph's Seminary at Fordham. While at both seminaries, he spent his summer vacations at an orphanage. He was ordained by Bishop John Hughes of New York on January 16, 1848. During the early days of his priesthood, McQuaid was, by his own recollections, "a frail and delicate man, apparently destined for a short career." During his first twenty years as a priest, he recalled being poor — never at any one time having more than $25 in cash. He had no savings, no investments, and no property, besides his clothes and books. On

January 21, he was assigned as an assistant in a parish in Madison, New Jersey, which included three counties and parts of two others. By that April, he was named pastor there. He made the rounds of his extensive parish, mostly to stations. In 1853, James Roosevelt Bayley was appointed the first Bishop of Newark, thus putting McQuaid in the new diocese. Bayley knew him when he was President of the seminary in Fordham, where McQuaid matriculated as a seminarian. In October 1853, Bayley charged McQuaid as rector of St. Patrick's Cathedral, in Newark, where he remained for fifteen years. Besides being the Cathedral Rector, he was Bayley's right hand man. He helped build and rebuild Seton Hall College, introduced the Sisters of Charity into the diocese, and in 1866 was named Vicar General and also President of Seton Hall. On March 3, 1868, he was appointed the first Bishop of Rochester, dying there on July 18, 1909.[11]

*13.4 Msgr. Thomas Preston circa 1892. Source: Albert Shaw, ed. (1892) The Review of Reviews, 518*

As soon as Corrigan became the Archbishop of New York, McQuaid became his staunch ally, but their friendship went back to their days together in Seton Hall. Both men had similar ideas, similar views about episcopal authority, and similar paranoid personalities. They shared one other thing in common: both despised Edward McGlynn. McQuaid's personal animosity toward McGlynn extends back to when he visited New York in April 1875, on the occasion of Archbishop John McCloskey of New York receiving the red *birettum*, signifying his being made a Cardinal a month before, America's first. McQuaid met McGlynn at the event and invited him to visit Rochester. McGlynn never took up the invitation and the Bishop of Rochester took offense and never let it go. Around the same time, McQuaid had a problem with one of his priests whom McGlynn supported and whose case McGlynn made known to Rome. This was another black mark against McGlynn as far as the Bishop of Rochester was concerned. McQuaid also took umbrage with McGlynn's promotion of public schools over Catholic schools, of Irish Home Rule, of the Irish Land League, and later of Henry George's Single Tax Theory. By February 1887, McQuaid writes venomously to Bishop Gilmour: "What a bad egg the fellow [McGlynn] has been all these years! Our worst enemy, but a concealed one! I made no mistake when years ago I forbade his preaching in my diocese."[12]

Another ally of Corrigan's lived in Rome, journalist Ella B. Edes. She was born in Charlestown, MA, in 1832, the only surviving child of merchant Capt. Robert Edes, who perished at sea in 1836. After her father's death, she converted to Catholicism in 1852, living with her mother in Elizabethtown, NJ, until the latter's passing in 1856. As the sole heiress of a considerable fortune, in 1860 she decided to move to Rome with her life-long companion, Eliza McBride. Ella found employment as secretary to Cardinal Alessandro Barnabò, Prefect of the Congregation for the Propagation of the Faith. Over time she became a lobbyist without portfolio for bishops like Corrigan. She grew into a dangerous partisan agent, accessing decisions and judgments even before they were officially promulgated, cabling her friends in America with insider information. She also leaked confidential information of secret meetings at Propaganda to both Corrigan and McQuaid. She kept dossiers on leading clerics and bishops. She also planted false stories and erroneous details, stole and forged documents, even bribed Propaganda personnel, as is often the case with spy masters and political operatives. For her, the end justified the means. She was famous for hosting dinners for Roman officials which facilitated her cultivation of friendships and connections, further enhancing her ability to ask for and give favors. Her enemies referred to her as "*La Signora*," whom they perceived as the source of most of their frustrations in Rome. As a journalist, she wrote letters to English language secular and religious journals and newspapers. Her work was characterized by a concise mocking style, which combined both venom and vitriol. She was a formidable adversary but was unfailingly loyal to her friends, such as Corrigan and McQuaid. During her latter days in Rome, she began to destroy all of her papers and encouraged those who were her correspondents to destroy her letters. She left Rome in 1900 due to poor health

*13.5 Dr. Edward McGlynn, bust portrait on political campaign poster, 1887. Library of Congress*

and died in Priscina in northern Italy in 1916.[13]

The next actor in this drama was more Corrigan's personal servant, but he also had his own personal convictions which complemented both Corrigan's and McQuaid's. Msgr. Thomas Preston, born on 1824, became an Episcopal priest in 1847, but was received into the Roman Catholic Church in 1849 and ordained a Roman Catholic priest in 1850. First named pastor of St. Mary's Church in Yonkers that same year, then in 1863 became pastor of St. Ann's in Manhattan, where he remained until his death in 1891. He was Chancellor of the archdiocese from 1853 to 1891 and Vicar General from 1873 until his death. Richard Burtsell was assistant pastor at St. Ann's under Preston. Burtsell opined that Preston had a limited knowledge of theology, was rigid, and was an extreme Ultramontane regarding the Papacy. He was particularly fearful and hostile toward the New York priests who met with Thomas Farrell, which included Burtsell and McGlynn. The danger of this group, and those like them, Preston thought was that they sought "'to establish an American school of theology with liberal ideas, by minimalizing [sic] the authority of the Holy See and adapting Catholicism to democratic forms and institutions.'" Preston remained a staunch ally of Corrigan and McQuaid in the upcoming McGlynn controversy.[14]

Edward McGlynn was the primary actor in the drama that would follow. Born September 27, 1837, of Irish parents, his father was a successful contractor, who died in 1847 when Edward was quite young. His father, Peter, left his widow and eleven children financially secure. After studying first in New York's public schools, he was sent at the age of thirteen by Archbishop John Hughes in 1850 to Rome, where he matriculated for nine years at the Urban College of Propaganda, with his last year of 1859-60 spent at the newly opened North American College. This is where he encountered Corrigan and where their rivalry began. The young, frail, studious and introvert Corrigan was subject to the older, athletic, brilliant and extrovert McGlynn who was the student Prefect. As an outstanding student, McGlynn won the gold medal for excellence at the end of his studies, being proficient in both Italian and Latin. Ordained in Rome on March 12, 1860, he received his Doctor of Divinity that same year. Propaganda proposed that he be the vice-rector at NAC under the newly appointed rector, New York priest, William McCloskey. But McCloskey refused to accept McGlynn on the grounds that he did not know him and that it would not be good to have two priests from the same diocese in leadership positions at NAC. Upon his return to New York in December of 1860, he was assigned in rapid succession to the parishes of St. Joseph, St. Brigid, and St. James, and then made pastor of St. Ann's in December 1861, where he was but one year, when he was assigned to St. Joseph's Military Hospital in Central Park in December 1862. This move was engineered to make room for Thomas Preston to become the pastor of St. Ann's, with Richard Burtsell as his assistant. The transfer was also as a disciplinary action by Archbishop Hughes, since McGlynn had traveled to Rome without permission (he went there to recover from a hemorrhage caused by overwork). By the end of the Civil War, Jeremiah Cummings, the founding pastor of St. Stephen's (created in 1848) and the first Roman alumnus from New York, was dying and asked that McGlynn be his assistant and successor. Cummings had played a substantial role in the development of McGlynn's vocation. With the death of Cummings, McGlynn was appointed at age 29 as pastor of St. Stephens on January 1866.[15]

St. Stephen's, the largest parish in the archdiocese with 28,000 parishioners, presented many pastoral challenges to McGlynn, whose pastoral accomplishments were many. He enlarged the Gothic-style church to seat 2,500, opened a home for destitute children, organized a Sunday school with 1,600 students and with a faculty of 120 (he did not favor Catholic parochial schools since he felt they did a better job of making young people Americans and that education was the job of the state not the Church, except in regards to religion), was especially attentive to the liturgy and music. But he was well-known beyond the confines of the parish, as a social activist, a popular orator, and a man deeply interested in the plight of the poor. Also after his return from Rome, he became a member of the *Accademia*. When Archbishop John McCloskey traveled to Rome for Vatican I, Preston called a meeting of the pastors of the city about the well-publicized views of McGlynn regarding public education. Fifty-four pastors signed a public protest against McGlynn and his views. Only three pastors refused to sign. They were all members of the *Accademia*. Preston forwarded to McCloskey in Rome the result of the pastors' vote, as well as an article in the *New York Sun*, April 30, 1870, in which McGlynn was quoted, among other things, as advocating an Amendment to the U.S. Constitution forbidding the Federal Government from supporting Catholic schools or Catholic charitable institutions. Not only did McGlynn have a bad feeling regarding Preston when the latter became pastor of St. Anne's, but now over Preston's orchestration of getting pastors against him.[16]

McGlynn was one of the first priests of New York to see the importance of the rapidly developing social problems created by industrialization. For him, charity was not a substitution for justice, hence structural changes in society and politics were necessary. By 1879, McGlynn was absorbed by Irish nationalism and the cause of Irish social and economic reform. Crop failures in 1879 in Ireland aggravated chronic unrest. One out of five Irish were tenant farmers and agricultural laborers; it was said that one-fourth of the Irish were paupers. That same year, Michael Davitt founded the Irish Land League, whose goal was to induce or compel the British Government to buy out the mostly absentee landlords and sell the land to the tenants. Davitt also pledged to work with Parnell, the leader of the Irish Home Rule Movement. On the other hand, the English were convinced that the Irish were unfit for self-rule, an opinion widely shared in America also. In 1880, the American Land League was formed to help Davitt's cause. America soon supplied 90 percent of the funds for Davitt's movement. McGlynn threw himself into

Irish political crusade and was a much sought-after speaker by New York proponents of Home Rule and the Land League. However, it was also in 1880 that two events changed the direction of his life: the appointment of Michael Corrigan as Coadjutor of New York and McGlynn's sudden conversion to the economic ideas of Henry George.[17]

## The Drama

Almost from the moment he arrived in New York in October 1880, Corrigan had a bead on McGlynn, spurred on by Preston and McQuaid. McGlynn, on the other hand, may have underestimated Corrigan, thinking him weak. Interestingly, Burtsell made no entrance in his diary in October 1880 about Corrigan's coming to New York, so insignificant did he perceive the event. It should be added that McGlynn's troubles were not simply due to the machinations of his enemies, since he could be his own worst enemy — impatient, single-minded, impetuous, too sure of himself and his opinions.

At the time of Corrigan's arrival in New York, McGlynn was already absorbed in Irish nationalism and Irish social/economic reform. That same year of 1880, Henry George published Progress and Poverty, which was influenced by his experiences in Ireland as a correspondent for New York's *Irish World* from 1879-80. George, born in Philadelphia in 1839, promoted the Single Tax Theory, a concept he did not invent, but which he popularized. The Theory allowed for private ownership of land, but disallowed profiting from that ownership. The State was obliged to seize the entire profit from land as a tax. In doing so, the State would take in so much money, that it could abolish all other taxes, hence the name the Single Tax Theory. All this tax money would fuel not only the State's operational expenses, but also vastly expanded social programs. Although he thought his Theory was applicable everywhere, George believed it to be particularly applicable to Ireland. McGlynn enthusiastically embraced George's ideas, but differed with him on the private ownership of land. McGlynn sensed that private ownership of land should be abolished. McGlynn met George for the first time in the fall of 1882, and remained friends throughout their lives.[18]

Rome was at the time trying to reestablish diplomatic relations with England and was getting pressure from leading English Catholics to rein in the Land League's efforts. Cardinal Giovanni Simeoni, Prefect of Propaganda, wrote Coadjutor Archbishop Corrigan in August 1882 that statements attributed to McGlynn were contrary to the teachings of the Church. Simeoni penned McCloskey again saying that by Papal Decree McCloskey could suspend McGlynn, unless he thought McGlynn's attitude had improved. McCloskey chose not to do this, as long as McGlynn abandoned his political activities. Cardinal McCloskey, who liked McGlynn, reluctantly rebuked him for his socialistic addresses and McGlynn in turn agreed to abstain for all future political gatherings. But he did not keep his promise and drifted back into his public pronouncements on political issues. Since preparations for the gathering of and the Roman acceptance of the III Plenary Council of Baltimore absorbed the American episcopacy from 1884 to 1886, McGlynn's activities were not well noted. Meanwhile, McCloskey died on October 10, 1885, when Corrigan took the full reins of the Archdiocese of New York.[19]

In New York City widespread unemployment and a prolonged transit strike agitated the public. It was in this context that the New York mayoral race took place in 1886. Henry George ran for Mayor as a candidate of the United Labor Party. Abram Hewitt and Theodore Roosevelt were also in the race. George was supported by Robert Ingersoll, an agnostic, Father Edward McGlynn, and Samuel Gompers, who founded the American Federation of Labor in 1886, as well as by Socialists and the Central Labor Union. McGlynn was a Republican and his endorsement was thought to influence Irish Catholics, who normally would have supported Tammany Hall candidates. By September 1886, McGlynn was at the peak of his fame and influence, locally and nationally. He possessed an exceptional gift as a speaker, combined with unusual magnetism along with a commanding presence. But he also was impatient with details, extravagant in speech, unskilled in parochial administration, and inattentive to correspondence. Not only did he endorse George, but he actively campaigned for him. Archbishop Corrigan had a public challenge in McGlynn that he could not ignore. On September 29, 1886, Corrigan wrote McGlynn forbidding him to attend a rally for George on October 1 or take part in any future political meetings, without the prior consent of Propaganda in Rome. McGlynn responded to Corrigan that he was already committed to the October 1st rally, but promised that he would take no further part in George's campaign. Due to his flamboyant language at the rally, McGlynn was privately suspended by Corrigan for two weeks, beginning the next day. McGlynn kept his word about making no further campaign speeches, though he did appear on the podium with George at some rallies. Hewitt, the Democratic candidate, won the election, but George beat out Roosevelt for second place.[20]

One may have thought that with the end of this election, McGlynn's tensions with Corrigan would have subsided, but things only got worse. On November 26 Corrigan resuspended McGlynn until December 31 for an alleged interview with a *Tribune* reporter in which he was quoted as encouraging people to read Progress and Poverty. At the same moment, Corrigan wrote Cardinal Simeoni in Rome that McGlynn persisted in preaching doctrines that were both against Catholic teaching and unacceptable to the vast majority of Americans. Moreover, Corrigan accused McGlynn of denigrating the Pope and expounding the heresy that priestly ministry derives not from the bishop, but from the people. Many of these theological points were attributed to McGlynn by the secular press. Corrigan cabled Rome at the beginning of December demanding some definitive action against his classmate. On December 4, Simeoni cabled Corrigan to have McGlynn come immediately to Rome. In January 1887 the Pope himself issued the same order and appropriated the McGlynn case to him personally. Very quickly the issue moved from one of local politics and a local dispute between a priest and his bishop, to a Papal investigation on doctrinal grounds.

McGlynn responded to Corrigan on December 20 that he was unable to go to Rome for three reasons: his poor health, his meager financial resources, and his family obligations. He defiantly added that he would continue to teach that private ownership of land is "against natural justice" and that he would, if given a chance, confiscate all private property without any compensation. He denied the right of anyone "Bishop, Propaganda, or Pope" to punish him for opinions on political economy which have never been condemned by the Church. McGlynn laid down the gauntlet. On January 14,

1887, Corrigan removed him from his pastorate at St. Stephen's. In May 1887, with Corrigan's encouragement, Pope Leo XIII ordered McGlynn to come to Rome within forty days under the pain of excommunication, which would be automatically imposed on July 1, 1887. McGlynn pleaded conscience over obedience, did not go to Rome, and was thereby excommunicated on July 1st. Corrigan wrote McGlynn on July 3 verifying the excommunication. McGlynn responded at an Academy of Music speech on July 10, which was reported in some newspapers in New York and Rochester. McGlynn denounced, not the Church of Christ, but the ecclesiastical machine [Corrigan's and Tammany Hall's] "with nothing but the cupidity and lust for money and power." He also vehemently denied and dismissed the canard, spread by McQuaid, that he had a secret wife. "I was wedded to St. Stephen's as truly as to a pure and innocent wife. I desired no other bride, and I desire none other today." On February 4, 1888, the popular McGlynn wrote to his parishioners at St. Stephen's urging them to be faithful to the teachings and ministrations of the Church and asking them to refrain from protesting against his suspension from ministry. "I need to assure you that my faith and sense of reverence have not suffered and will never suffer any change."[21]

Throughout the first half of 1887, McGlynn continued public speaking and conducting interviews for the press. On March 26th he and his friends founded the Anti-Poverty Society, for which he was President and Henry George was Vice-President. Beginning in May, they met weekly at the Academy of Music, usually before a crowded house, where McGlynn orated for two hours without notes. He also spoke in Boston, Buffalo, Chicago, Cincinnati, and even Rochester.

Meanwhile, in April 1887, fifty-five German priests signed a declaration of support for Archbishop Corrigan. In May a similar declaration was signed by 357 of the 450 non-German priests of the archdiocese. Only two of the signatures were Roman-trained.

On the other hand, on June 18th, a massive rally took place to support him and to protest or prevent his impending excommunication. About 75,000 attended. That evening he used a theme that would be recurrent in his talks in the years to come. He denounced "the ecclesiastical machine" which for thousands of years "perpetuated blunders and mistakes" and even crimes. The Doctor compared his own case to that of Galileo and Copernicus. These public statements did not help his cause and only reinforced in the mind of Corrigan and others that McGlynn was a dangerous radical, perhaps even a heretic. The battle lines were definitely drawn. All the bishops that McGlynn and his friends appealed to, including Archbishop John Ireland, gave him the same advice: Go to Rome, go quickly, and don't try to impose terms on the Pope. After the excommunication was imposed, McGlynn lost many supporters. This very public episode created divisions within New York political society and ecclesiastical society, among presbyterate and among the laity.[22]

Corrigan soon came to the realization that Burtsell was the man behind the scenes in the McGlynn affair and a fomenter of clerical opposition to this authority. He decided to move against the pastor of Epiphany Parish, Manhattan. This action received the full encouragement of McQuaid in Rochester because of a run-in he previously had with Burtsell. In 1869 American-born Father Louis Lambert was appointed rector of St. Mary's Church, Waterloo, NY. In 1877, Lambert founded a newspaper, *The Catholic Times*, published in Waterloo. By 1880, Lambert and his paper adopted the platform of Irish Home Rule and of the Irish Land League. McQuaid wrote to Lambert objecting to the newspaper's recent attack on the Bishop of Ogdensburg (Edgar Wadhams) and on the rector of the Cathedral in Rochester. By June 1880, McQuaid decided that Lambert was undermining his authority and rising up a faction of obstructionists. In April 1881, the bishop restricted Lambert's faculties to his parish only. In April 1884, Lambert appealed to Rome, but lost. In June 1887, Lambert persuaded Burtsell to take his case to Rome once again. In September, McQuaid suspends Lambert and removes him from St. Mary's, but instead Lambert remains in Waterloo. Then, McQuaid proceeds to excommunicate two Waterloo laymen for supporting Lambert and his ideas. In January 1890, Rome decides in favor of Lambert, but declares he cannot go back to Waterloo. For this and other reasons, McQuaid bore no love for either Burtsell or for McGlynn.[23]

Although he wanted to suspend him but felt that action would create too many problems, Corrigan chastised Burtsell by removing him from Epiphany Parish on December 6, 1889, transferring him to St. Mary's Parish, Roundout, a rural mission in Kingston County, and miles from the city. Burtsell appealed to Propaganda, but lost his appeal in July 1890. After helping so many priests out when bullied by their bishops, Burtsell could not help himself. With the appeal resolved, in November of that year he took up his pastoral responsibilities at St. Mary's, where he would stay until his death in 1912, having received the consolation prize of Monsignor from Archbishop Farley in 1904.[24]

To further isolate McGlynn, Corrigan pursued the condemnation by Rome of George's <u>Progress and Poverty</u>. In October 1887, the archbishop formally petitioned the Pope to put the work on the <u>Index of Forbidden Books</u>. Cardinal Gibbons vehemently opposed such an action and recruited his agent in Rome, Denis O'Connell, Rector of NAC, to appeal against any such condemnation, but rather let the work die a natural death over time. Gibbons also wrote Cardinal Manning of England to forestall the condemnation, saying that except for about six bishops, the U.S. Hierarchy deplores the proposed condemnation on the grounds that the censure would only awaken Protestant sympathy for George and would label him a martyr to Catholic intolerance. With typical Roman compromise and deliberation of action, a year and a half later Rome condemned George's book, but refused any public promulgation of the condemnation. Preston and Corrigan were frustrated and hoped some bishops would leak the decree, but none did. Undaunted, Corrigan pressed Rome for a declaration on the right of private property in May 1890, as a way to put down McGlynn and George. The Papal Encyclical *Rerum Novarum* (May 1891) did promote the right of private property, but it is unclear as to what effect, if any, Corrigan's petition had on the Pope. Corrigan's friends felt that the Papal Encyclical was a great vindication of the archbishop's long struggle with McGlynn and George.[25]

The impasse between McGlynn and his archbishop seemed to be heading nowhere. McGlynn maintained his speaking engagements; Corrigan continued to try to eat away at his classmate's power base. Then something unexpected intervened, the process of creating an Apostolic Delegate to the U.S.

Pope Leo XIII appointed Francisco Satolli as an Apostolic delegate to the U.S. in August 1892, the ostensible purpose was to represent the Pope at the World's Columbian Exposition in Chicago in 1893. The hidden agenda was to establish a permanent Apostolic Delegation in Washington and also to bring about a reconciliation of McGlynn with the Holy See, and ultimately with Corrigan. Satolli confidentially told John Farley, now Corrigan's Vicar General, that many in Rome felt that Corrigan acted too hastily, and perhaps even too harshly, in the handling the McGlynn case. Cardinal Mariano Rampolla, the Papal Secretary of State, who was taking a more active role in American affairs, was dismayed over Corrigan's actions against McGlynn and thought that they may have been unduly influenced by the political machinations of Tammany Hall. With Eda Edes' power diminished and the mood in the Vatican changed, Corrigan was finding more doors in Rome closed to him. Meanwhile, the official U.S. envoy in Rome, Denis O'Connell, along with Archbishop Ireland, backed the establishment of the Papal delegation in Washington.

The time was ripe for McGlynn's reconciliation. He had been out of the headlines for some time. His Anti-Poverty Society, now five years old, was losing membership. His Sunday addresses at the Academy of Music were noted for their number of empty seats. By mid-December 1892, McGlynn was asked to submit a statement of his economic principles, which were examined by four professors from the Catholic University of America (one of whom was the Floridian Edward A. Pace). They found nothing contrary to Catholic doctrine in McGlynn's statement. On December 23, 1892, Satolli restored McGlynn in good standing with the Church, without so much as any consultation or communication with Corrigan. As it happened, McGlynn did not have to go to Rome to make an account of his activities, rather Rome came to him.

Needless to say, Corrigan and McQuaid were not pleased. Corrigan refused to accept McGlynn back into the archdiocesan clergy until he made public reparation for the scandal that he had given. But in January 1893, the newspapers carried the headline of accusations against Corrigan, as the instigator of letters and articles against Cardinal Satolli and Archbishop Ireland that appeared in newspapers throughout the country earlier in November 1892. Yet

Corrigan remained stubborn, refusing to give McGlynn a parish or even allow him to say public Mass.

In the spring of 1893, McGlynn left New York secretly for Rome, but Corrigan caught wind of it, sending his Italian-born secretary, Father Gherardo Ferrante, to represent the archbishop. Corrigan sought to take advantage of the divisions between the Secretary of State and Propaganda. As of February 1892, Propaganda's Prefect was Cardinal Mieceslaus Ledochowski, who was not consulted about the establishment of the Apostolic Delegation to the U.S. and was smarting from the slight; he supported Corrigan. Although things seemed to have been resolved for McGlynn, they were certainly not with his local ordinary. The Pope suggested that Satolli give Corrigan some public sign of esteem. On August 15, 1893, the Delegate made his public peace with the Archbishop of New York at a Pontifical Mass at St. Patrick's Cathedral. December of 1894, found McGlynn in Brooklyn still waiting for Corrigan to welcome him back and give him a pastorate. Finally, the Apostolic Delegate persuaded Corrigan to name McGlynn pastor. Corrigan and McGlynn met, with the result of the archbishop appointing him as pastor of St. Mary's, Newburgh, NY, a small town up the Hudson River, far removed from New York City, effective January 1, 1895. While there, McGlynn continued to promote his views on the Single Tax Theory, parochial schools, the plight of American labor, and the need for the Church in America to be more fully American. In late October 1897, McGlynn gave the funeral oration for Henry George. As late as 1899, still obstinate, Corrigan composed a letter to the Apostolic Delegate in Washington asking what he should do about McGlynn and his teaching. The Delegate advised him to do nothing. McGlynn died at age 63 in Newburgh on January 7, 1900, and ironically Leo XIII condemned Americanism less than a year before. McGlynn's funeral was held at St. Stephen's on East 28th Street on January 9. Over 45,000 people paid their respects. Moore was unable to attend. Corrigan's battles with McGlynn were over. Meanwhile, the condemnation of Americanism seemed to validate Corrigan and McQuaid. Their Ultramontane views had triumphed. But more importantly for them, they had defeated their episcopal rivals such as Keane and Ireland. Their struggles with McGlynn were vindicated in their minds.[26]

## Moore and the McGlynn Affair

Up to this point, we narrated the outline of the McGlynn Affair, but excluded one *persona dramatis*, Bishop John Moore. He is often left out of accounts of the episode or barely mentioned. His role might easily be overlooked, since this was the only significant national ecclesiastical issue in which he ever engaged. But, his contribution to the resolution of the matter was no small one. In his usual style, he worked quietly behind the scenes. For him, his personal engagement was not about wrestling over theological issues, or the exercise of power, or ecclesiastical political infighting, but about justice and friendship.

As was mentioned earlier in Chapter 4, Moore took his first trip to New York to visit his Roman schoolmates in the fall of 1866. While there, he spoke freely with his friends and discussed ecclesiastical matters with those with whom he shared a personal and intellectual experience in Rome. He stayed with his classmate Edward McGlynn, who took up a collection for the parish school that he was attempting to establish in Charleston. Moore was particularly grateful for McGlynn's kind hospitality, as he wrote Bishop Lynch: "Nothing can equal Dr. McGlynn's kindness to me."[27]

Moore returned to New York in September and October of 1880, this time as bishop; yet he came not to beg, but rather to make a personal visit. Once again, he stayed at St. Stephen's with McGlynn. Always attending to some business when traveling, Moore writes from New York to Gibbons in Baltimore about Edward Pace being sent to NAC in Rome, but all the burses (scholarships) for Baltimore are filled. Moore asks Gibbons if he can be of help with Pace's education, but if not, Moore will find a way somehow to pay for it himself. In early September 1882, he stops by New York again for a brief stay. During the III Plenary Council of Baltimore in November 1884, Moore chooses Burtsell as his theologian, so they work together while in Baltimore. Burtsell also served on the Commission of the Rights of Pastors and co-authored *The Baltimore Catechism*. But Burtsell was not tethered to Baltimore. Unwilling to relinquish his love for the urban culture of Gotham City, he shuttled back and forth from Baltimore to New York by train to attend lectures, plays, and dinners.[28]

It is rare indeed when someone from Florida leaves the State in early January for New York City. But when Moore heard of McGlynn's troubles, he decided to travel to New York in early 1887 to investigate matters for himself, under the guise of an invitation from Burtsell to a liturgical event at Epiphany Parish. He arrived at Burtsell's Parish of the Epiphany the evening of January 3. After contacting Archbishop Corrigan, Moore and Burtsell were invited to the archbishop's residence for dinner, along with Msgr. Preston and the Archdiocesan Consultors. It was Preston who brought up the McGlynn case and how it was creating scandal. The archbishop deliberately changed the subject to Henry George's theories. Burtsell admitted the right of private property, while pointing out that George proposed that the fruit of a man's labor should not be taxed, but only the land itself. Preston stated that George's theories were unjust and opposed to the Faith. The Bishop of St. Augustine is not recorded as saying anything that evening. Moore attended the consecration service of the relics at Epiphany Church on Jan. 9, along with Archbishop Corrigan, Bishop James O' Connor of Omaha (he was a Philadelphia priest and urban College graduate), and Msgr. Preston who preached. After the ceremony, Corrigan mentioned that the McGlynn case appeared in the current edition of *The New York Times*, but the paper seemed unaware of McGlynn's resolve not to go to Rome. Burtsell pointed out that *The Times* was unaware of McGlynn's plans because McGlynn purposely did not tell the reporters of his intentions. Corrigan quickly interjected that it was not he that initiated the idea that McGlynn appear in Rome to defend himself; rather, it was Bishop Jacobini in Rome that suggested it. Burtsell told the archbishop that he would like to talk to him more about the case, but only when fewer people were around. Not taking his cues from Burtsell, later at the dinner the archbishop reengaged in the conversation about McGlynn. He said that friends of McGlynn's had reported him to Rome back in the summer of 1882. Propaganda informed Corrigan of this in August 1882, when he was coadjutor. He passed the information on to Cardinal McCloskey, who took the matter to himself, telling Corrigan that he wished him not to have anything to do with the question. Burtsell stated that he was also aware that Bishop Gilmour had raised complaints against McGlynn because of Land League activities in Cleveland. At the end of the meal, the archbishop agreed to meet with Burtsell about McGlynn the following day. Meanwhile, Moore left for Florida on Jan. 10 with $50 Burtsell gave him for traveling expenses and $25 for Mass stipends. Burtsell had his meeting the next day with the archbishop. Corrigan insisted again that it was not he who insisted on McGlynn proceeding to Rome to explain himself. He had just received a letter from Propaganda asking that McGlynn go to Rome. Burtsell countered that Msgr. Preston is vehemently opposed to McGlynn and has no right to insist on his recantation and that he, unlike the archbishop, had read George's Progress and Poverty and discussed it with theologians. Corrigan replied that he would have to remove McGlynn from St. Stephen's and did not wish him to say public Mass until he went to Rome. At the same time, he stated that did not consider McGlynn suspended. Both before and after this meeting, Burtsell tried to contact McGlynn, but was unable.[29]

It would seem that Moore, while in New York, was also unable to contact McGlynn. But typically, while there Moore observed the situation and immediately upon his return to St. Augustine sprang into action with his pen. On Jan. 15 he wrote to Gibbons. "The McGlynn Case is bad; blunders have been made on both sides." McGlynn disobeyed the archbishop and for that he is to blame "and no one attempts to defend him" for that. But his suspension is not based on his disobedience "but on the supposed heterodoxy of George's Theory, which he was ordered to retract, and which he refused to do, maintaining that it [George's theories] does not conflict with Catholic doctrine." Information on this case reached the public not through McGlynn, but through "the Archbishop [sic] himself, his household, and his Chancery." In an attempt to use the press for his own purposes, Corrigan himself telegraphed *The Tribune* that McGlynn was ordered to Rome. Moore feels that this was "a grave error" on Corrigan's part. Moore explains that McGlynn never said that he would not go to Rome, just that he does not wish to go at this time, since his present state of health is poor and he is under severe mental strain. Moore adds that Msgr. Preston is the prime mover in the actions of Corrigan against McGlynn. "The whole affair is doing great harm; many workingmen are ready to throw the Church overboard... some of them even now refuse to go to Mass."[30]

Corrigan became aware that Gibbons was now in play for the first time in the McGlynn Affair and sought to make his position known to the Baltimore Cardinal. Corrigan invited Gibbons to be his guest before Gibbon's departure for Rome to receive the red hat. Gibbons demurred, saying that he had received a previous invitation to stay with Major Keiley of Brooklyn, but Gibbons did promise to see the archbishop some time on the Thursday before he sailed for Rome. Burtsell met with Gibbons while he was at Keiley's on Jan. 28, the same day that Corrigan was to meet the Cardinal. In an encounter that lasted about an hour, Burtsell outlined the history of the problem in New York. Gibbons admitted that he did not know McGlynn personally, but had heard of his excellent character. He acknowledged that he found George's land theories complicated and debatable. Although Burtsell had told the Consultors that McGlynn should be allowed to explain his actions before them, Msgr. Preston would hear none of it and Corrigan sided with Preston. Gibbons urged Burtsell to encourage McGlynn to go to Rome where "he would be sure to set himself a right." He thanked Burtsell for all the information and said he would use it while in Rome to persuade the authorities to receive McGlynn, not as one on trial, but as one who has come to explain his principles. We do not have a record of Corrigan's meeting with Gibbons. What we might conclude is that, given Gibbon's temperament, he would be disinclined to enter into the dispute in New York.[31]

That same day, Jan. 28, in a desperate attempt to stave off a disaster, Moore cabled Propaganda asking that any excommunication of McGlynn be suspended for a time, promising to send a letter explaining his reasons for his request. However, he did not send any such letter until June. There were intervening circumstances, not the least of which was the burning of his Cathedral on April 12, 1887.[32]

As a final gesture of solidarity with McGlynn, Moore penned a letter to Burtsell, which was received on February 3, 1887. In it was a check for McGlynn for $1,000 to pay off a note Moore borrowed from him two years past. He asks Burtsell to give McGlynn the check "with a message of sympathy." Realizing that McGlynn was under financial constraints, Moore assists his friend with some financial support, not as charity, which may have insulted McGlynn, but as just paying back a loan from two years past.[33]

On May 21, 1887, Moore returned to New York to use it as a base for his fund-raising efforts to restore his destroyed Cathedral, but he also spent a considerable amount of time working on the McGlynn case. While in New York, he stayed with Burtsell at Epiphany Church. Two days later they both visited McGlynn, whom Burtsell observed "looked tired and flabby." On May 25, Moore met with Corrigan who asked him to do some Confirmations for him. On May 30 after dinner, McGlynn came to Epiphany where he had an extended discussion with Burtsell and Moore. On June 7, Burtsell read to Moore a collection of articles and letters about the McGlynn case. That same day, Moore departed for Baltimore with Gibbons to participate in the ceremony at the Cathedral celebrating the Cardinal's return from Rome with his red hat. Moore used the opportunity to talk to Gibbons about the McGlynn case. Although Moore communicates well in his letters, he always preferred the face to face conversation rather than a letter, especially when dealing with delicate matters.[34]

At the end of June and early July, Moore proceeded into an epistolary frenzy on behalf of McGlynn, just before his excommunication would take effect. On June 27, he sent a cable to Simeoni, the Prefect of Propaganda, saying: "If it is possible, suspend for the time being the secret excommunication in the McGlynn case." On June 28, he writes to Simeoni saying that he feels a "duty of conscience" to seek a "remedy to the evil which has developed in New York in this dispute between McGlynn and Corrigan." "I don't think I could be accused of intruding myself in somebody else's affairs" since the problem is not just New York's, but affects the whole Church in the U.S. McGlynn feels strongly that Corrigan has dealt with him too rigorously and even unjustly. To Moore, it seems that McGlynn is right, although he can't approve of McGlynn's disobedience to his archbishop. Moore suggests certain remedies. One, instead of Corrigan throwing McGlynn, who is sick and without money, into the street, he could transfer him anywhere and he thinks McGlynn would go. However, this has not been done. Second, Corrigan accuses McGlynn of absconding with $37,000 in St. Stephen's funds. This accusation could be adjudicated in New York, and if that process did not satisfy all parties, they could appeal to Rome. But this has not been done. The newspapers, with their exaggerated reports, are only exacerbating the problem. McGlynn's excommunication will only extend and intensify the scandal, making his return to the Church even more difficult. Moore urges Propaganda to order Burtsell to come to Rome with McGlynn, so as to plead his case. Also, McGlynn's faculties should be restored, at least on the condition that he go to Rome. Moore concludes that his only motivation in his intervention in the matter is to save "such a virtuous and talented priest" as McGlynn. For Moore, there was nothing at all in this for him, but simply he is doing what he feels is the right thing for his friend. Then on June 29, Moore forwards to Gibbons a letter from Burtsell, the cablegram he sent to Simeoni, and a letter he wrote to Simeoni. Moore asks if Gibbons might send a dispatch to Rome: "Approving the steps I have ventured to take in this matter lest no attention be paid to my writings but of course, that is a point I must leave to your own discretion." Gibbons never intervened as Moore had asked.[35]

Gibbons wrote Moore in July 1887 saying that he had received Moore's correspondence of June 29. Gibbons find McGlynn's excuses for not going to Rome "unacceptable." Gibbons asserted that he did not endorse Moore's cablegram while in Rome. "I do not think that such an endorsement was necessary, as you are well known and respected in Rome and your suggestions were expressed in respectful and filial language and no one could question the purity and disinterestedness of your motives." Simply put, Gibbons refuses to get involved. Gibbons made of copy of his letter to Moore, something he rarely did. He wanted to have on record his disengagement from the McGlynn Affair.[36]

On July 9, Burtsell received Corrigan's letter excommunicating McGlynn. Then on July 14, Moore and Burtsell "had a long talk about the Doctor's case." Moore shares with Burtsell Gibbons' July letter, something which discouraged both men. The Cardinal has found the documents on the McGlynn case sent by Burtsell in March "not very satisfactory." Moore leaves for a month of fund-raising in Philadelphia the next day. It is clear from Burtsell's diary that Moore is personally fully engaged in the summer of 1887 in the McGlynn affair, in concert with Burtsell.[37]

On August 10, 1887, Burtsell celebrated his 25th Anniversary as a priest. Moore was there, along with Fathers McGlynn (whom Burtsell specifically requested), McSweeney, McLaughlin, Nillan, and Burtsell's assistant pastor. "Jokes were the order of the talk" wrote Burtsell. After dinner, McGlynn gave a good portion of one of his poverty speeches. At 5 p.m. Burtsell left for a picnic given for the poor of the parish at Harlem Park. He returned to the rectory at 8:30 p.m., where he found Moore and Nillan. "We had a bottle of champagne before going to bed." On August 12 Burtsell persuaded Moore to join him on Long Island for a family gathering. There McGlynn talked privately with Burtsell and Moore. Soon thereafter, a New York priest denounced Burtsell to the archbishop for having McGlynn at the 25th Anniversary. On August 17, Burtsell showed Moore a newspaper account of Burtsell's meeting with McGlynn. That same day, Moore pens Gibbons. Moore refers to Cardinal Simeoni's reply to Moore's cablegram and his letter to the Cardinal. "They reached too late to stay the action the Holy See had determined to take. I do not see what further effort can be made to help McGlynn." On Sept. 3, Burtsell submitted to McGlynn "all of the correspondence between Bishop Moore and myself about removing censures from the Doctor on condition that he would go to Rome." That same day, Burtsell writes Moore outlining the state of the McGlynn case to date. In a final attempt to engage Gibbons in the McGlynn case, Moore passes Burtsell's letter on to Gibbons two days later, suggesting that at the upcoming meeting of the U.S. bishops there should "be at least some informal talk about the McGlynn Case." Gibbons did not respond to Moore's suggestion or his letter.[38]

Moore leaves New York for another round of fundraising in Philadelphia, but returns to Epiphany on September 19. The news about Gibbons' attitude toward the McGlynn case was not encouraging. Moore had met the Cardinal on June 10 when he said: "Archbishop Corrigan does not want Dr. McGlynn to go to Rome." Moore responded: "What does he want? Does he want the ruin of the poor man?" The Cardinal just walked away, as if what Moore said was true. Moore added that although Gibbons had initially said he would help McGlynn, now the Cardinal has decided to take no further action. Gibbons "has as much as accused Bishop Moore of a breach of confidence" in sharing Gibbons' correspondence to Moore with Burtsell and McGlynn. Gibbons tried to persuade Moore to have nothing more to do with the McGlynn matter, and even not return to New York. Roman authorities, said Gibbons, would not be pleased to receive any further communication from Moore on the matter. Moore suspects that Bishop O'Connell at NAC wrote Gibbons to this effect. Moore's strenuous attempts to engage Gibbons and Roman authorities in the case led to a dead end. Moore, disheartened, felt he had a better relationship with Gibbons than apparently he had. Moore is very unhappy with what he calls "the selfishness of the Cardinal." In an uncharacteristic tone of negativity, the exasperated Moore mentions that the priests in Philadelphia find the Cardinal's response to the McGlynn case unsatisfactory. In fact, they applaud Moore "for what he has done." Moore adds snidely that the Baltimore priests have a nickname for the Cardinal: "Slippery Jim." On Sept. 20, McGlynn dined with Burtsell and Moore, at which time Moore repeated the account he gave from the night before. Burtsell read a letter to be sent to Cardinal Giovanni Simeoni, Prefect of Propaganda, composed by Burtsell but in McGlynn's name, with emendations by Moore and McGlynn, asking for a reopening of the case. McGlynn said that he will go to Rome if the censures are removed and if he can be told of the charges against him ahead of time. He also expressed his personal thanks for all that Moore has done for him. Two days later Moore reports to Burtsell that priests in Philadelphia are circulating the report that McGlynn has had improper relations with a woman, even with several women. This rumor was generated by Corrigan, who said he even had proof of its veracity. Now, the McGlynn issue devolved into dirty tricks.[39]

Moore left New York for Philadelphia on September 23, where he continued fundraising until September 28, when he returned to the Diocese of St. Augustine. For now, his work on behalf of McGlynn would be suspended, but not completely abandoned.[40]

Unsurprisingly, McQuaid of Rochester was irritated and discontented with Moore's involvement in the McGlynn Affair. He writes his ally, Corrigan, in August of 1887 of his displeasure with McGlynn dining with Moore and others at Burtsell's 25th Anniversary. Even as late as October, McQuaid was still smoldering about what he called "the dinner scandal." "The presence of the bishop [Moore] added to the offence," which McQuaid characterized as "loudly scandalous and therefore wickedly sinful." In December McQuaid writes Bishop Gilmour in Cleveland railing against McGlynn and referring to his public assault on the man, adding "There is no love lost between Burtsell and myself." McQuaid admits that his public attack on McGlynn was more intended for Moore and Burtsell, than for McGlynn. In December McQuaid writes Corrigan going even farther by harshly suggesting that all who helped McGlynn, including Burtsell and Moore, should be excommunicated. Fortunately for Moore, he never had to ask McQuaid to fundraise in Rochester for the restoration of his Cathedral.[41]

As was mentioned in Chapter 10, after only three months in Florida, Moore was back on the fundraising circuit in mid-January 1888, at Washington, Richmond, Norfolk, and Baltimore. By mid-March, he returns to New York. While there, he shows Burtsell the letter that Propaganda sent Moore about McGlynn, which Moore characterized as hasty in its action. Both men met with McGlynn. Before leaving New York for Florida, Moore instructs Burtsell to have McGlynn's response to Propaganda to him for review by April 8th.[42]

By the fall of 1890, Moore decided on a new tact regarding the McGlynn Case. Instead of trying to work with Cardinal Gibbons and Propaganda, approaches that ended in a *cul-de-sac*, Moore came upon the idea of working through the Vatican Secretary of State, Cardinal Rompalla. The latter wrote Moore at the end of September 1890 that the complaints about Archbishop Corrigan's exercise of his pastoral ministry reached Rome. Meanwhile, McGlynn agreed to go to Rome under the conditions laid down by Moore in his letter to Cardinal Simeoni of Sept. 23, 1887. Moore writes Rompala in late October, then again in mid-November 1890, about the latest developments with McGlynn.[43]

The McGlynn case takes on new life in 1892, as a result of the strenuous efforts of Moore, who confides to O'Connell in March 1892 that he is going to bring up the McGlynn case to Roman authorities one more time. "If I fail this time," he writes O'Connell in Rome, "I suppose it must be my last effort." Yet Moore has hopes that McGlynn's offer will not be rejected since there is a new Prefect of Propaganda (Ledochowski) who "is not committed to past action of Propaganda and the case can be presented to the Pope in a new light." So Moore takes on a two-pronged approach: one through the new Prefect of Propaganda; the second through the Pope and the Secretary of Vatican State. Moore writes Archbishop John Ireland, who is in Rome, on March 1892, begging him to stay there until Moore's letters to Cardinal Ledochowski, Prefect of Propaganda, and to the Pope arrive. Also included is a letter from McGlynn, instigated by Moore, in which he states his desire to be "restored to my priestly ministry," and in which he also agrees to go to Rome if all censures are removed from him. Moore asks Ireland to urge the Roman authorities to accept the conditions: McGlynn must be relieved of all censures, including the Papal excommunication and Corrigan's suspension. Now the Pope and Propaganda must "treat him as a man and not impose humiliations on him... if they do not seek to degrade him, I am convinced that they will have in him a devoted and faithful son of the Church." Apparently O'Connell was not too confident in Moore's efforts; nevertheless, Moore confides in him on May 19: "If I should fail this time, I suppose I might as well abandon the effort. At any rate, I can say that I have done what I could, and if I had not made the attempt, I might have felt regret." Moore is driven by his sense of duty, justice and friendship with McGlynn. By the time Ireland left Rome in June 1892, he learned that the McGlynn case would be reopened "with splendid chances for the poor man." But Ireland also commented on the effect this news would have on the Archbishop of New York: "This will break Corrigan's head and heart."[44]

Meanwhile, something unexpected was afoot. The Pope desired to establish an Apostolic Delegation in Washington. Francesco Satolli arrived in Washington in October of 1892, setting up temporary headquarters at Catholic University of America. On Nov. 18, 1892, he asked Cardinal Mariano Rampolla, the Secretary of State, for faculties to absolve and restore McGlynn with two stipulations: 1) McGlynn must retract any statements at variance with Catholic doctrine; 2) once all censures are lifted, McGlynn must go to Rome and meet the Holy Father. Rampolla gave these faculties to Satolli. A week before Christmas, Satolli got four CUA faculty members (one of whom was Pace) to review McGlynn's statements of economic theory which he had submitted to Satolli. The faculty committee said there were no doctrinal errors either in George's or McGlynn's writings, especially in light of *Rerum Novarum* (1891). The Apostolic Delegate absolved McGlynn of any censures and restored him. With Burtsell at his side, he offered three Christmas Masses in 1892, the first Mass he said in five years. That evening he was at the Cooper Union at an Anti-Poverty Society Meeting. After years of effort, all of Moore's efforts had borne fruit.[45]

In January 1893, Bishop John Keane, rector of the Catholic University of America, gave a banquet in Washington in honor of the now officially appointed Apostolic Delegate, Satolli. McGlynn was a prominently featured guest and Bishop Moore was also present. This event did little to endear Corrigan to Keane or Satolli or McGlynn or Moore. McGlynn and Moore left for Savannah by ocean liner on Feb. 8, but not before McGlynn announced publicly that he would soon travel to Rome to meet the Pope. The two then traveled to Jacksonville by train, staying for about a week in that city, where McGlynn preached a Lenten series. They then traveled by train to St. Augustine, which McGlynn used as his base during his series of Lenten Sermons throughout the Diocese of St. Augustine. Moore's invitation to McGlynn got him out of New York, gave him something to do, and allowed him to spend some time with his classmate. Flagler even lent McGlynn his private railroad car for a preaching trip to Rockledge. He was also the guest of Flagler at a stag dinner at Kirkside with Bishop Moore and the pastor of the Presbyterian Church in St. Augustine, Rev. Smythe. McGlynn spent five weeks in Florida. He drew large crowds in St. Augustine and in Tampa. Moore described one of McGlynn's sermons at the Cathedral as lasting two and a half hours in which he explained eloquently the dogma of the Church, at the same time without giving offence to anyone. When McGlynn's Florida stay ended in March, Moore traveled with him as far as Charleston, SC, from where McGlynn journeyed on to New York. Moore wrote Gibbons at the end of March praising McGlynn's "immense service to religion in Florida." Moore recounted that his classmate preached a lecture five times a week for the five weeks he was there. "Whenever he preached in the Cathedral, the Protestant churches were nearly empty and his sermons produced [a] great impression." Mr. Henry

B. Plant, the Florida West Coast Railroad man, said that McGlynn had persuaded him of the justice and fair dealing that is part of the Catholic Church's teaching. Ironically, Corrigan visited Florida, just as McGlynn was leaving. The archbishop arrived in Florida at the end of February and left by March 16, 1893. While there, he toured St. Augustine and met with Bishop Moore (we have no record of that conversation), then he visited Jacksonville, departing the State by March 16, 1893. Since Corrigan did not frequent the State, it seems odd that he picked the same time that McGlynn was there for a Florida trip. Was he there to snoop on McGlynn? He did not encounter his nemesis while in Florida, but did remark that the weather was great during his stay.[46]

Still supportive of his friend, Moore wrote in early May 1893 to Satolli in Washington and Rampolla in Rome that McGlynn would be coming to Rome soon. Moore assured Satolli that McGlynn has toned down his rhetoric in public speeches and would be happy to devote himself entirely to pastoral ministry after his Roman visit, especially since the Anti-Poverty Society is now defunct. McGlynn turned down the offer by Henry Flagler of a loan of $200 to finance the Roman trip and also asked Moore not to accompany him to Rome (Moore had offered to go) lest it appear he needed an advocate. Burtsell advised him to work through Rampola to arrange an audience with the Pope. Moore, now in New York in early May, teamed up with Burtsell to push McGlynn to go to Rome now. McGlynn finally set sail for Rome at the end of May. He had his audience with the Holy Father, which lasted twenty-five minutes. The Pope asked him if he accepted the right of private property. McGlynn said "yes." The Pope then asked McGlynn: "Do you feel like going with Bishop Moore to Florida?" McGlynn said: "It is very remote. There is little to do there and it is far from my home and associations." The Pope then asked if he could accommodate matters with Corrigan. "It would be difficult," responded McGlynn. And so it would. The meeting concluded with the Pope giving him an Apostolic Blessing. McGlynn left Rome immediately on June 14, exactly five days upon arriving there. Ella Edes immediately cabled Corrigan in cipher about the Papal meeting with McGlynn.[47]

Like the glum elder son in the Parable of the Prodigal Son (*Luke* 15:1-32), Corrigan did not rejoice at the restoration of McGlynn. In fact, he was truculent and petulant. He still refused him a parochial assignment or a salary. Moore claimed that Corrigan had instructed one of his priests to refuse permission to say Mass at his parish if McGlynn asked. "I ask myself," muses Moore to Gibbons, "is Dr. McGlynn returned or is he not?" Exasperated with Corrigan's antics, Moore asks rhetorically: "Is it optional for a bishop to defy the action of the Pope's delegates?" Moore felt strongly that somebody owes McGlynn an apology after his five years as "a victim of gross injustice." In November Moore pens O'Connell in Rome that McGlynn is living in Brooklyn and hearing Mass only. Permission for him to say Mass "was given so grudgingly and with so many restrictions that the Doctor thought he would not avail himself of it." Moore comments about McGlynn's present predicament: "The poor man is restored, but he is no better off than before - he [is] like a leper, whom nobody dares to touch. This is a terrible condition for a man like McGlynn to be in; it may drive him to desperation... But I hope not. I have hopes to get him down here for the winter, where he will be removed from the temptation of talking foolishly. He did a great service for me last winter and he can do even greater this season ... The Protestant churches are mainly deserted when he preaches." But Moore was unable to persuade McGlynn to return to Florida again. Finally, Moore mentions that he hears that Corrigan is trying to reopen McGlynn's case in Rome and a petition has been sent by Tammany Hall politicians to Rome. He also asks O'Connell to help Burtsell all he can, for "his cause is a righteous one." Burtsell went to Rome on October 14 and stayed until May 12, 1894, appealing his own case against Corrigan, but with little effect.[48]

After two years of obstruction, of the hounding McGlynn through his surrogates, Corrigan finally assigned McGlynn as pastor. It was the Apostolic Delegate, Satolli, who pressured Corrigan to finally give McGlynn a pastoral assignment. McGlynn had written to Corrigan asking for an official assignment on Dec. 20. Corrigan agreed to meet with McGlynn on December 21, 1894. It was their first meeting in two years. Since St. Ann's, Manhattan, (Msgr. Preston's old parish) was without a pastor; McGlynn suggested that it be his assignment, probably tongue in cheek. Corrigan said that was out of the question, instead he suggested St. Mary's, Newburgh.

McGlynn accepted it, then knelt down and asked the archbishop for his blessing. Corrigan in turn asked pardon for anything he had said or done inadvertently against him. McGlynn added that we all needed pardon from God. The next day, Corrigan cabled McGlynn, assigning him to St. Mary's Parish, Newburgh, NY, far removed from the city, 100 miles north up the Hudson River, effective Jan. 1, 1895.[49]

Encouraged no doubt by Burtsell and driven by his own sense of injustice, and his less than cordial reinstatement by Corrigan, in the summer of 1895, McGlynn asked his archbishop two things: 1) compensation for a loss of past salary (eight years of it); 2) a better parish assignment closer to the city, namely returning to St. Stephen's, his old parish. In June 1895, he requested Father John Farley, Vicar General of the archdiocese, to endorse a loan for $1,500, the first step toward just compensation for his back pay, threatening to bring the matter to Secretary of State, Rampolla, if he failed to receive just compensation. Ever stubborn and self-righteous, Corrigan refused to endorse the $1,500 note, and also refused McGlynn's demand for $1,000 in back salary, denying that McGlynn was entitled to any compensation and that the loss in salary was all McGlynn's own making. For Corrigan, McGlynn's return to St. Stephen's was totally out of the question.

Moore went to bat for McGlynn again during his second *Ad limina* in the summer of 1895. During his audience with the Pope on August 27, Moore stated that he received assurances from the Holy Father that McGlynn would be restored to St. Stephens. With no such restoration forthcoming, Moore wrote Rampolla on June 26, 1897, reminding him of Leo XIII promise to McGlynn and that Corrigan had been instructed to treat McGlynn with charity and kindness. Moore also mentioned the eight years that McGlynn received no salary or stipends, an amount that would easily come to $2,000 per year. Justice, wrote Moore, demanded that this back pay be given to him. Rampolla forwarded the matter to Archbishop Sebastiano Martinelli, the new Apostolic Delegate in Washington. He contacted Corrigan, who got Father Henry Brann to respond to Moore's criticisms. Brann denied that McGlynn was due any back pay and that if McGlynn was brought back to St. Stephen's, Corrigan would be humiliated. Besides, the present pastor would have to be removed to make room for McGlynn, something that would unsettle the New York clergy. Martinelli wrote to both Rampolla and Ledochowski in Rome, repeating much of Brann's response and agreeing with it. Martinelli was not as kindly disposed to McGlynn as was Satolli. Rampolla replied to Moore saying that McGlynn has been treated with charity by Corrigan since his restoration; after all he was given a nice parish with a school. This letter had the tone of finality, clearly giving Moore no ground for further recourse. This was Moore's final action for his friend, ending his epistolary defense and promotion of McGlynn that began back in 1887. It was Moore who wrote time and again to Roman authorities about the McGlynn case, and it would be hard to imagine McGlynn receiving any justice or recovering his human and priestly dignity without the forceful and persistent pen of Bishop John Moore.[50]

The principals in the McGlynn Affair passed from this world in rapid succession. Henry George died on October 29, 1897; McGlynn died at St. Mary's on January 7, 1900 (Burtsell gave the eulogy at the funeral Mass); Corrigan died May 2, 1902; Burtsell died at St. Mary's, Roundout, on Feb. 4, 1912; Ella Edes died in Piscena, Italy, on February 27, 1916. Bishop John Moore passed away in St. Augustine on July 30, 1901.

CHAPTER FOURTEEN

# *The Final Journey and an Assessment*

## Final Illness and Funeral

Bishop Moore made out his first will on September 1, 1881, and his second and last will on November 5, 1891. The second one was not substantially different from the first. In it he bequeaths all real and personal property to Cardinal James Gibbons of Baltimore and appoints Father William J. Kenny, the Vicar General and Rector of Immaculate Conception Parish, Jacksonville, as his executor.

As early as the summer of 1898, Moore's health was failing. There was no specificity regarding the malaise, but some observed a decline. While on a begging tour throughout the Diocese of Scranton to rebuild his Cathedral, he preached at all the Masses on Sunday September 3 at St. Mary's Church in Wilkes-Barre, Pa. He spoke of the Cathedral fire, of the Diocese of St. Augustine being too poor to rebuild, especially because of the economic woes due to the lemon and orange tree frosts of five years ago and last year. Moore had a stroke on September 6, 1899, and recuperated at St.

Mary's Church, Wilkes-Barre. Two priests were summoned from St. Augustine by a cable from Moore, one of who was Father Kenny, his Vicar General. The local Catholic newspaper account said that he had a stroke, but it was not considered serious and that his recovery was expected in a timely fashion. The same newspaper reported that he was sixty-nine years old, although he was actually sixty-four years of age. After nine days at the parish, Moore traveled to St. Agnes Sanitarium, Baltimore, continuing to improve and staying there for five weeks. Moore writes in December 1899 that since he returned to St. Augustine he was able to say Mass daily, for which he is grateful. "The doctor gives hopes for my complete recovery," he writes. *The Pittsburgh Observer* reported falsely that Moore had a second stroke while on another begging tour at St. Mary's Parish, Allegheny, PA, in early June 1900. Moore was sensitive about the "fake news" and wrote the editor of *The Pittsburgh Observer* that the whole story was a fabrication. He had no such episode at St. Mary's, Allegheny. He did admit to having a stroke the summer before at Wilkes-Barre in the Scranton Diocese. This denial by Moore also appeared in the June 9th edition of the *Catholic Standard* and *Times* (Archdiocese of Philadelphia). Architect James Renwick wrote Moore at the end of June about estimates for the Main Altar and expressing regret about his continuing illness. Apparently Renwick heard about the *Pittsburgh Observer* story, but not about its falsity. Although Moore did not have a second stroke in June 1900, his health had not snapped back as some had predicted and as he had hoped. While still carrying on the business of the diocese, especially the Cathedral reconstruction project, he admitted that he did not have the energy that he would like. He wrote Mother Katharine Drexel on June 2 thanking her for her help with the Ybor City Catholic School for black children. "I am collecting here (near Allegheny, Pa.), but I am physically very weak and unable for this work." His handwriting appears shaky. Mother Katharine notes on the letter that she gave $3,000 for the Ybor City School. He writes her again in September 1900 from St. Augustine that: "I am very feeble, but my health is otherwise good." He asks for her prayers. His handwriting in this letter to her is degraded.

Despite his debility, Moore soldiers on attending to the details of the Cathedral restoration. Renwick presses him in February

1901 for a payment owed to the architects of $3,345 for the new altar. Moore already wrote to Renwick, in a letter dated the same date as Renwick's, apologizing that his illness has caused a delay in payment. Their letters crossed in the mail. But ever dutiful and conscientious, despite his declining health and low energy levels, Moore paid the last installment for Cathedral construction on March 28, 1901. The altar, reredos, and sanctuary statues were installed right after

*14.1 Bishop John Moore, c late 1890s. Source: ASSJ, 130.1, "Memoriam to Moore," Pascua Florida, III, Oct. 15, 1901, 3*

Easter (in April), which is quite remarkable given that Moore was bedridden from January 1901. He died at 10 a.m. on July 30, 1901, with his sister, Mrs. Katherine Levy of Charleston, at his side. She had taken care of him during his last two months. He was also attended by some of the Sisters of St. Joseph, Father J. Nunan, Cathedral Rector, and Father Patrick Maher, associate rector of the Cathedral.[1]

Moore's funeral took place on August 8, 1901, at the Cathedral, giving time between the death and the funeral for people who lived at a distance to arrive. The obsequies began on the evening of August 7, when the bishop's body was transferred from the Cathedral Rectory to the Cathedral itself. Vespers commenced at 4 p.m. Many lay societies, all the Sisters, as well as many priests and dignitaries were in the procession. "The catafalque on the body of the Bishop reposed was borne by six priests... The dead bishop was robed in the vestments of his office, and the body was on an angle, so that the full figure could be seen from all parts of the church." During that evening, hundreds of people, both Catholics and non-Catholics, processed by the catafalque for a final farewell to the man. Various parish societies, both black and white, women's and men's, kept vigil throughout the night. The morning of August 8 at 8:20 a.m., the Office of Requiem with nine readings was sung by various priests of the diocese, as well as Bishop Patrick J. Donahue of Wheeling, West Virginia. Next came the Pontifical High Mass. Bishop Henry P. Northrop of Charleston was the celebrant; Father William J. Kenny was the assistant priest; Father William Tyrell, SJ, now president of Spring Hill College in Alabama, served as the deacon; Father Patrick J. Lynch of St. Patrick's, Gainesville, the subdeacon; Father J. Nunan, the Cathedral Rector, the other sub-deacon; and Father Michael Maher of the Cathedral as the Master of Ceremonies. Father Daniel X. O'Sullivan, SJ, of St. Louis and Tampa, delivered the sermon. Besides a large number of the priests of the diocese, also in attendance was Bishop Benjamin J. Keiley of Savannah, Abbot Charles Mohr, OSB, of St. Leo's, and Msgr. Daniel J. Quigley of Charleston. At 11 o'clock with the service ended, the funeral procession began taking Moore's mortal remains to San Lorenzo Cemetery, where the bishop's coffin was placed in a vault. Father Richard Burtsell and Cardinal James Gibbons were unable to attend. Bishop Thomas Becker of Savannah and Father Edward McGlynn, both contemporaries of Moore's at the Urban College, were already deceased.[2]

## Character

Moore's human and spiritual formation began in the "domestic church," in the home of his family in Ireland, which was marked with a sense of loss. His ancestors once held property, but that was taken away during Oliver Cromwell's invasion of Ireland in the mid-seventeenth century. This initiated a more pervasive English occupation, leaving only some lands in Catholic proprietorship in Connacht, the poorest province in Ireland. John grew up in a small rented cottage on land that once belonged to the Moore's. His father's death and the courageous faith of his mother shaped him. The Irish famine and his family's flight from Ireland to Charleston only deepened his experience of separation and sorrow as an exile at an early age. All of which forged his character as a "silent man."

He continued his intellectual and spiritual formation at St. John the Baptist Seminary (Charleston), at the College of Combrée (France), and at the Urban College (Rome). His seminary formation forged his priestly character and shaped his habits of prayer, discipline, and considered action. These seminary experiences also broadened him intellectually, not simply from his classes, but from associations with his classmates and learning from the rich culture of France and Italy. He became not just a citizen from Westmeath or Charleston, but a citizen of the world and a man of the Church universal. As a result of this international experience, he developed linguistic skills in both classical and modern languages, something highly prized in the nineteenth century, especially given the aridity of theological studies in Rome at the time. Away from friends and family for nine years from the age of seventeen to twenty-six, Moore undoubtedly felt loneliness and loss, but at the same time developed inner strength, both psychologically and spiritually. He learned to appreciate friendships with those with whom he shared formation, but he chose his friends wisely. Moore befriended the best and the brightest, not just the most cunning, ambitious, or powerful. In particular, the totality of his experience in Rome gave him a broad vision of the Church, a self confidence in his intellectual abilities, and a sense of thinking with the Church. He acquired lifelong habits of learning, which permitted him to think through problems and integrate the many facets of his life.

In wartime Charleston he faced practical, personal, and pastoral challenges for which his seminary experiences could not possibly have prepared him. Yet, his seminary formation did provide him with the interior resources to enable him to adapt to an innovative pastoral responses to war-torn Charleston. The stress he experienced under fire drew out the best in him and provided him a foundation of competence and confidence which allowed him to face the complexities of his pastorate in Charleston during Reconstruction and later the many challenges during his episcopacy in Florida, including the conflagration of his Cathedral. St. Finbar Cathedral, Charleston, burned down on December 1861; his Cathedral in St. Augustine was razed by fire in April 1887. His life-long formative experience of the love of learning and the desire for God made it possible for him to think through problems and challenges in creative and imaginative ways. His spiritual and human formation empowered him to trust in the presence of God in his life.

These formative experiences of John Moore produced a man of character and integrity, a Christian leader. As he combated Arian bishops almost 1,600 years ago, Gregory of Nazianzus understood that the problems he faced in Arianism were not just doctrinal, but also a lack of character in his opponents, "A man's character," he wrote, "is the most persuasive thing of all."[3]

For the Christian Catholic, the Gospel is normative regarding a person's character, especially a leader. "The greatest among you must be your servant. Whoever exalts himself will be humbled, but whoever humbles himself will be exalted."(*Matt.* 23: 11-12). During his formative years, Moore conformed himself as a servant of his Master and Teacher, Jesus the Christ, and allowed the Gospel and the Paschal Mystery to shape his character in the midst of his family, as well as his educational and pastoral experiences. Later, "Silent John" would draw from those experiences as "a self-sacrificing bishop of an obscure diocese" and respond to the Church in his day with quietude, tenaciousness, and creativity. Moore would have agreed with Gregory of Nazianzus, who wrote in 381:

> A priest should have one function and one function only, the sanctification of souls by his life and teaching. He should raise them towards the heights by heavenly impulses. He should be serene, high-minded, reflecting like a mirror the godly and unspotted images that he has inside. For his flock he should send up holy offerings, until the day when he too shall perfect them into an offering.[4]

One inherits character from one's ancestors and family, from one's formation and life experiences, and from one's personal efforts at the cultivation of the garden of one's soul. Moore combined learning, intelligence, priestly piety with a strong sense of duty and responsibility. He was a man of remarkable character, selflessness, and generosity. A priest in the diocese who knew Moore well called him "a self-sacrificing bishop of an obscure diocese... Simple, studious, diffident, yet approachable, he proved a successful administrator."

Some of his contemporaries nicknamed him "Silent John," a nickname which captured his quiet considered demeanor. The 1877 *terna* for the then vacant see of St. Augustine succinctly described Moore as "firm and steady, devoted to learning, conspicuous in piety."[5]

## Leadership and Legacy

Newspaper reports at his death assessed his legacy quantitatively. When he arrived at the diocese in 1877, he had only nine priests; when he died there were thirty-two. When he arrived there were less than 500 children in Catholic schools; when he died there were 2,245. He established nine new schools, nine new parishes, and seventeen mission churches. He rebuilt the Cathedral after the fire, constructed a black Catholic school in St. Augustine, enlarged and built many churches and convents. Under him the Church in Florida made rapid progress. He was an "able financier and a man of business." His manner was approachable and simple, unostentatious, not desirous of attracting attention.[6]

But Moore's legacy was much more than the newspapers could quantitatively measure.

In our contemporary society there is a great deal of discussion about leadership. Widespread anti-authoritarianism in America began with the enactment of Prohibition. The 18th Amendment was adopted by the majority of States on January 16, 1919, and then the Volstead Act was passed by Congress on October 27, 1919, over a Presidential veto. Prohibition became the law of the land on January 16, 1920, unleashing the disparagement of authority for fourteen years, accompanied by lawlessness and corruption, both private and official. Later in post-1960s America, institutions and authority figures, especially males, were again under attack, spreading a cloud of doubt and distrust from the Office of the President of the U.S. on down. Now with the most recent scandals in the Church, the office, veracity, and authority of the episcopacy is questioned by some. So some reflection upon Moore's leadership style is relevant.

Contemporary historians have tried to capture the essence of leadership through examining political and military leaders.[7] But perhaps the most useful work on the topic was written in 1987 by British historian John Keegan, in his book titled <u>The Mask of Command</u>. In it he analyzes the military leadership of Alexander the Great, Wellington, U. S. Grant, and Hitler. In his study, Keegan identifies five characteristics of leadership.

1. Leadership is exercised in dialogue, real or implicit, that is, it develops a rhetorical and real consensus between the leader and the led, and between ideal principles and socio/cultural realities of a particular time and place.

2. Leadership is persuasive. It can "carry both society and army farther than they believed they wished to travel."

3. Leadership is power and as such is prone to corruption by the politics of court. "Power corrupts, but its real corruption is among those who wait upon it, seeking place, jostling with rivals, nursing jealousies, forming expedient cabals, flaunting preferment, crowing at the humiliation of a demoted favourite [sic]. The life of the camp corrupts less than that of the court: battle tests the real worth of a man as politics never can."

4. Leadership is a matter of character, but the revelation of that character must be both carefully hidden and carefully revealed, so as to create a certain mystique, what Keegan calls "The Mask of Command," the public face and the hidden inner character.

> Heroic leadership — any leadership — is... a matter of externals almost as much as internalities [sic]. The exceptional are both shown to and hidden from the mass of humankind... The leader of men in warfare can show himself to his followers only through a mask, a mask that he must make for himself, but a mask made in such form as will make him to men of his time and place as the leader they want and need.

5. Leadership is both distant and penetrable, not necessarily by personal access but by "the diaphragm of intimates and associates which surrounded the commander. Their selection and quality was crucial to the relationship that the general established with those to whom his orders were transmitted." The commander must demonstrate a skill in selecting effective and good men as his intimates.[8]

If we compare Moore's leadership style with that of Keegan's analysis of military leadership, we find some interesting parallels and some differences.

Leadership is exercised in dialogue. Moore's annual administration of Confirmation, parish visitation, and school visitation thrust him into dialogue with his people, especially his priests and religious women. When there was a problem that he needed to solve, he began by investigating it either in person or more often by correspondence, before making a decision. His faithful, persistent and long-standing support of his friend, Father Edward McGlynn, was fueled by both personal conversations and letter-writing. Also as bishop, he was accessible at his parish and school visitations and when he was at the Cathedral rectory. His advice was sought out by priests and prelates, and also by "a poor colored man or a little child." He knew his people because he talked with them.[9]

In the exercise of his pastoral ministry in Florida he almost always gave reasons for his actions, but he exercised his authority in the manner of his day, that is, orders were given and expected to be obeyed. This authoritarian style was not only exercised by bishops, but also by women religious superiors, by heads of big businesses, such as Flagler and Plant, and also by parents in relating to their chil-dren. Where persuasion was particularly used by Moore was in his ongoing defense of McGlynn. In his letters, especially to Roman authorities and to Cardinal Gibbons, he is always in a persuasive mode, marshaling arguments for a particular course of action.

Leadership is power and power can corrupt, more in court than in camp. Moore had no court to corrupt him. He had no diocesan bureaucracy or Chancery or Pastoral Center. He had no team of diocesan administrators that stood between himself and his priests, religious, and people. Of course the Church in Florida was simpler in his day. The Sisters ran and taught in the schools; the priests ran the parishes. The principle of subsidiarity reigned. One hard-working man could pretty much run everything, including the finances and rebuilding of the Cathedral of St. Augustine. Under Moore's leadership, the Church in Florida moved from a frontier style to a more urban style, as a response to Florida's First Boom in the latter part of the nineteenth century. In addition, Moore had no "court" because he was traveling so much, living out a suitcase most of the time, either visiting people and institutions throughout the State or insistently raising money to rebuild his Cathedral. The poverty of resources and personnel that Moore faced in Florida, as well as his frustrations in trying to rehabilitate McGlynn, gave him a sense of humility, rather than the pride and arrogance that comes with the isolated power of court.

Unlike Keegan' leader, surrounded by handpicked associates who buffer him from those he commands, Moore had no such cadre. He possessed neither bureaucracy nor court. Except for the Irish seminarians and the Irish Sisters of St. Joseph he later recruited, he did not handpick any of the people who served the schools and parishes of his diocese. He worked with what and who he had, while at the same time making provisions for future leaders with his Irish recruitment.

Leadership is a matter of character, which we had already discussed in regards to Moore. But Keegan goes on to point out that character in leadership is to be hidden, The Mask of Command, as he calls it. Completely foreign to him is what many corporate and political leaders have today — "spin doctors," a media liaison officer, the cultivation of a public persona. However, he did not wear his person or his character on his sleeve. He was a quiet man. His priests called him "Silent John." To those who did not know him, he may have appeared tough, taciturn, distant, or stern, but those who did know him "understood him to be learned, silent, thoughtful, as simple as a child, kind as a father, indulgent as a mother... But he was not too high or too great to soothe a child's pain or counsel or cajole a querulous old woman." We see Moore's hidden personality is his loyalty to his friend McGlynn. Although all of his letters are handwritten and are usually short, concise, and business like, a few were quite personal and even emotional, qualities he never displayed in public. One commentator wrote of his tenderness: "To him, Silent John as they called him, came prelates and priests of the Church for counsel and advice; to him as easily, also came the poor colored man, when sorrow or trouble darkened his life, or a little child whose treasured toy was broken. He opened his loving heart and tender sympathy to all... To us who knew him, he was as simple as a child, kind as a father, indulgent as a mother." Yet that same commentator noted: "his was a life of suffering and loneliness."[10]    Perhaps for

Moore the suffering fashioned "The Mask of Command," as well as the tenderness hidden underneath.

This leads us to another aspect of Moore's leadership style, but one not discussed in Keegan's book. The bishop was a Christian leader who took his inspiration from Gospels and from his relationship with Jesus Christ, the Jesus of Scripture and Tradition, the Jesus who mystically unites us with Himself at Baptism as His beloved disciples and remains with us as our friend and companion on our journey from this life to the next, the Suffering Servant and sacrificial leader. It was Moore's relationship with Jesus that made him a Christian leader, which ultimately shaped his character, which he brought with him in his struggles, in his loneliness, in his exercise of his leadership as a bishop, and in his sense of duty and responsibility. James Renwick, the architect of the Cathedral's campanile and the rebuilt church, whose letters are usually very businesslike, filled with details about construction and payments due, uncharacteristically writes in November 1888 about the quality of Christian leadership he admires in Moore:

> I thank God that you have recovered from the fever [yellow fever] and have been enabled to do so much good among your people. How small every other thing seems in this world when it is compared with the self-sacrifice of a Pastor [sic] who gives up everything for the welfare and well-being of his people. If it were proper to covet anything, I could envy you for the good work you are doing and I am very thankful that you have been spared to do it.[11]

# *Endnotes*

## Introduction

[1]Interview with Bishop John Moore in *The Catholic School &
Home Magazine*, c. 1892, John Moore File 130.1, ASSJ.

[2]John Keegan, The Mask of Command (New York: Viking
Penguin, 1987), 11.

[3]Michael J. McNally, Catholicism in South Florida, 1868-1968
(Gainesville, FL: University Presses of Florida, 1984), 11-16, 47;
McNally, Catholic Parish Life on Florida's West Coast, 1860-1968
(St. Petersburg, FL: Catholic Media Ministries, 1996), 81-94,
100-01; McNally, "Moore, John." in American National Biography
ed. by John Garraty and Mark C. Carnes (New York: Oxford,
1999), vol. 15, 762-63; McNally, "Reconstruction and Parish Life
in Charleston, South Carolina, 1895-1877: A Pastor's Perspective,"
*American Catholic Studies* 117 (Spring 2006): 45-67.

[4]For example: John Tracy Ellis, The Life of James Cardinal
Gibbons, Archbishop of Baltimore, 1834-1921, Vol. I
(Westminster, MD: Christian Classics, 1987), 145, 156, 160,
252, 260-61, 344-45, 350, 568, 573, 609; Patrick Henry Ahern,
The Life of John J. Keane: Educator and Archbishop, 1839-1918
(Milwaukee, WI: Bruce, 1955); Gerald P. Fogarty, The Vatican and
the American Hierarchy from 1870 to 1965 (Wilmington, DL:
Michael Glazier, 1985), 34, 37, 97-99, 105-07, 111, 116; Marvin R.
O'Connell, John Ireland and the American Catholic Church (St.
Paul, MN: Minnesota Historical Society, 1988), 361.

[5]OCD-1879, 382-84; OCD-1900, 480-82.

[6]Richard J. Purcell, "Moore, John" in Dictionary of American
Biography ed. by Dumas Malone (New York: Charles Scribner's,
1934), vol. 13, 132; *Acta,* Sacred Congregation of the Propagation
of the Faith, Jan. 2, 1877, vol. 245, fols. 1rv, 2rv, 3r, APF at AUND;
[Unknown author], "Memoriam to Moore," *Pascua Florida*, III
(1898-1903), October 15, 1901: 3-5, ASSJ.

## *Chapter 1*

[1] Sean Duffy, ed., The Macmillan Atlas of Irish History (New
York: Macmillan USA, 1997), 31, 37; Ida Grehan, The Dictionary

of Irish Family Names (Boulder, CO: Roberts Rinehart, 1997), 260; Liam Kelly, The Diocese of Kilmore, c. 1100-1800 (Dublin: Columba Press, 2017), 393.

[2]Patrick Duffy, "Westmeath, County" in The Encyclopedia of Ireland, edited by Brian Lalor (New Haven, CT: Yale University, 2003), 1130-31; P.W. Joyce, Atlas and Cyclopedia of Ireland, Part I (New York: Murphy and McCarthy, 1902) [no pagination]; Liam Kennedy, Paul S. Ell, E.M. Crawford, L.A. Clarkson, Mapping the Great Irish Famine: A Survey of the Famine Decades (Dublin, Ireland: Four Courts, 1999), 103; David W. Miller, "Irish Catholicism and the Great Famine," *Journal of Social History* 9 (Sept. 1975): 85-87.

[3]"1895 Ad limina for the Diocese of St. Augustine," New Series 119/621-37, APF at AUND; "Moore, John" in Herringshaw's Encyclopedia of American Biography of the Nineteenth Century (Chicago: American Publishing, 1898), 670; Richard J. Purcell, "Moore, John" in Dictionary of American Biography, vol. 13 (New York: Charles Scribner's Sons, 1934), 131. Printed sources disagree as to the date and place of Moore's birth. I have used Moore's own writings in his "1895 *Ad limina*" to verify his birthday and birthplace. His birthdate and place is also verified in Olive C. Curran, compiler and editor, History of the Diocese of Meath, 1860-1993 (Mullingar, Westmeath, Ireland: Diocese of Meath, 1995), 321.

[4]Christine Kinealy, This Great Calamity: The Irish Famine, 1845-52 (Boulder, CO: Roberts Rinehart, 1995), 31, 34; Kerby A. Miller, Emigrants and Exiles: Ireland and the Irish Exodus to North America (New York: Oxford, 1985), 284, 292; Clive Irving, "Passages," *Conde-Nast Traveller* (March 2004): 103-04; Michael Coffey, ed., text by Terry Golway, The Irish in America (New York: Hyperion, 1997), 3; J. Matthew Gallman, Receiving Erin's Children: Philadelphia, Liverpool, and the Irish Famine Migration, 1845-1855 (Chapel Hill, NC: University of North Carolina, 2000), 2; Kennedy, Mapping the Famine, 27, 29, 71. See Also: Colm Toibin and Diarmaid Ferriter, The Irish Famine: A Documentary (London: Profile Books, 1999); Ciaran O'Murchadha, The Great Famine: Ireland's Agony, 1845-52 (London: Continuum, 2011).

[5]Kennedy, Mapping the Famine, 105-06, 108, 114, 116, 121; *Florida Times-Union & Citizen*, July 31, 1901; Mullingar Library, Mullingar, Ireland, Michael O'Conlain, ed., Partial List of Some Memorials in Westmeath Church Yards, vol. 5, Clonmellon Parish,

"William Moore," 212 (Courtesy of Gretta Connel, Mullingar Library, Senior Library Asst., and Father Peter Dolan).

[6]Gallman, Erin's Children, 4, 28-29; Miller, Emigrants, 294; Coffey and Golway, The Irish, 24-26; Oscar Hanlin, Boston's Immigrants, 1790-1880, rev. ed. (New York: Atheneum, 1977), 49; Edward Laxton, The Famine Ships: The Irish Exodus to America, 1846-51 (New York, Henry Holt, 1997), 7-9, 28-29; U.S. Census-1850, M-432, Roll 850, 126, 149, NARA-P. Moore himself stated he arrived in Charleston in October 1848. After searching passenger lists of ships arriving in New York from July 1847 to March 1849, it is clear that Mrs. Mary Moore and her children from Westmeath did not come to the Port of New York, then ship to Charleston. Although passenger lists for Charleston in 1848 are non-extant, it is almost certain that the Moores came directly from Liverpool to Charleston. "Interview with Bishop John Moore," *The Catholic School & Home Magazine*, c. 1892, John Moore File, 130.1, ASSJ; Ira A. Glazer, ed., The Famine Immigrants, vol. II & III (Baltimore, MD: Genealogical Publications, 1983). Why the Moores went to Charleston is unknown, but one might speculate that Mrs. Moore had relatives in Charleston with whom she could find some kind of support.

[7]Duffy, ed., Atlas of Irish History, 64-67; Michael J. O'Brien, "The Irish in Charleston, South Carolina" *Journal of the American-Irish Historical Society* 25 (1926): 134-44; David A. Wilson, United Irishmen, United States: Immigrant Radicals in the Early Republic (Ithaca, NY: Cornell University, 1998), 158.

[8]O'Brien, "Irish in Charleston," 144; Richard C. Madden, Catholics in South Carolina: A Record (Lanham, MD: University Press of America, 1985),17-33; Peter Guilday, The Life and Times of John Carroll, vol. I, (New York: Encyclopedia, 1922), 737; Peter Guilday, The Life and Times of John England, vol. I (New York: America, 1927), 144-46; Patrick W. Carey, People, Priests, and Prelates: Ecclesiastical Democracy and the Tensions of Trusteeism (Notre Dame, IN: University of Notre Dame, 1987), 218-19.

[9]U.S. Census-1850, M-432, Roll 850, 126, 149, 263, NARA-P; "Moore, Anna," Community Register, ASCOLM; "Interview with Moore," John Moore File, 130.1, ASSJ; J.H. Bagget, ed., Directory of the City of Charleston for the Year 1852 (Charleston, SC: Edward C. Councell, 1851), 90-91; "Mary Agnes Moore," March 26, 1865, "William Moore," Jan. 19, 1866, "Mary Anne Moore," Aug. 9, 1866, St. Patrick's Baptismal Register, 1839-1956, ADC;

*U.S. Catholic Miscellany*, March 17, 1849, March 15, 21, 1851.
When Thomas Moore, John's older brother, died at age fifty in
1877, the notation in the cemetery book said that he had resided at
16 Spring Street since 1848. Therefore, this is where he was when
the 1850 Census was taken, along with the rest of the family. The
building is no longer extant. At its location is now (as of 2003)
a lot for U-Haul Rentals and the Piggly-Wiggly Grocery Store.
"Thomas Moore," Jan. 28, 1877, St. Lawrence Cemetery Burial
Records, 1852-1918, ADC.
[10]*U.S. Catholic Miscellany*, May 30, 1857.

## *Chapter 2*

[1]U.S. Census - 1850, M-432, Roll 850, p. 149; Joseph White,
The Diocesan Seminary in the United States: A History from the
1780s to the Present (Note Dame, IN: University of Notre Dame,
1989), 51; "Interview with Bishop John Moore," *The Catholic School
& Home Magazine*, c. 1892, John Moore File, 130.1, ASSJ; Richard
J. Purcell, "Moore, John" in Dictionary of American Biography,
Vol. 13 (New York: Charles Scribner's Sons, 1934), 131; Michael J.
McNally, "James A. Corcoran and St. Charles Borromeo Seminary
- Overbrook, 1871-1907," *American Catholic Studies* 110 (Spring-
Winter 1999): 54; OCD-1849, 104. The seminary's student
records were destroyed in the Fire of 1861, so we have no record of
Moore's student performance at St. John the Baptist Seminary.
[2]General Regulations for the Ecclesiastical Seminary of St.
John the Baptist, Charleston, South Carolina, 1850, 2(x)-A-13,
ADSA. This seminary handbook was the only artifact from
Moore's youth preserved in any archives. He brought the booklet
with him to St. Augustine and preserved it, which suggests that
it had some special meaning for him, especially since he was
disinclined to preserve correspondence from student days or from
Charleston or from his family.
[3]*U.S. Catholic Miscellany*, Aug. 3, 1850; May 3, June 28, July 12,
Aug. 30, Nov. 8, 22, 1851, July 3, 1852, March 10, 1855; Scott J.
Buchanan, A Brief History of the Diocese of Charleston, South
Carolina, 1520-2000," unpublished manuscript, c. 2000, pp. 64-66,
ADC; Richcard C. Madden, Catholics in South Carolina: A
Record (Lanham, MD: University Press of America, 1985), 63.
Reynolds was born in Bardstown, KY, August 22, 1798. After
attending St. Thomas Seminary, Bardstown, and St. Mary's

Seminary, Baltimore, he was ordained in 1823 in Baltimore. After being on the faculty at St. Joseph College and the Bardstown seminary, he became pastor of St. Joseph's, Bardstown, in 1830. He was named the Vicar General of the Diocese of Louisville in 1840, then the Bishop of Charleston in December 1843 and consecrated on March 19, 1844. His funeral was at the Cathedral in Charleston on March 7, 1855. *U.S. Catholic Miscellany*, March 10, 1855.

[4]"Interview with Moore," John Moore File, 130.1, ASSJ; Purcell, "Moore," 131. Some secondary sources corrupt the name of the school's name to "Courbre" or "Combrie," but the correct spelling is "Combrée," with an accent on the first "e." 1859-60 Grade Report for Mr. Flynn, College of Combrée, 25-K-4, ADC.

[5]Buchanan, "A Brief History," 72-73; General Regulations for the Ecclesiastical Seminary of St. John the Baptist, Charleston, South Carolina, 1850, 2(x)-A-13, ADSA.

[6]1859-60 Grade Report for Mr. Flynn, College of Combrée, 25-K-4, ADC; Moore to Mother Lazarus, April 13, Aug. 26, 1885, Bishop Moore File, 130.1, ASSJ. Moore's student records from Combrée are no longer extant.

[7]*Congressi: America Centrale*, vol. 17, fol. 585, rv.-586 r., APF at AUND; Thomas J. Peterman, The Cutting Edge: The Life of Thomas Andrew Becker (Devon, PA: William T. Cooke Publisher, 1982), 21. Moore and Becker certainly got to know one another during the long voyage to Italy and during their studies in Rome, but it is difficult to determine whether friendship continued after they returned to the States. Becker was not part of the New York priests which whom Moore was friendly. Although Becker became the Bishop of Savannah in 1886 until his death in July of 1899, there is no evidence that they visited or wrote one another. There are no letters to Moore from Becker in the Diocese of St. Augustine Archives. The Savannah Archives was destroyed by a fire in February of 1898, so we have no letters from Moore to Becker, if they ever existed. However, it is likely that they saw one another since Becker was a temperance man like Moore and Moore usually traveled to Savannah by train to take a steamer to New York.

[8]"Propaganda, Sacred Congregation of" The Catholic Encyclopedia, 1911 ed., s.v., 458-60.; John Tracy Ellis, "The Formation of the American Priest: An Historical Perspective" in The Catholic Priest in the United States: Historical Investigations,

ed. by John Tracy Ellis (Collegeville, MN: St. John's University, 1971), 22.

⁹J.H. Newman to Richard Stanton, Feb. 21, 1847, quoted in Ellis, "Formation," 24.

¹⁰Lord Acton to Richard Simpson, October 6, 1862, quoted in Thomas Michael Loome, <u>Liberal Catholicism, Reformed Catholicism, Modernism: A Contribution to a New Orientation in Modernist Research</u> (Mainz, Germany: Matthias-Grunewald-Verlag, 1979), 361.

¹¹Manahan's remarks are cited in: <u>The Diary of Richard L. Burtsell, Priest of New York: The Early Years, 1865-1868</u> (New York: Arno Press, 1978), July 26, 1865, 117.

¹²Barry quoted in Ellis, "Formation," 25.

¹³Janssen is quoted in Marvin R. O'Connell, <u>Critics on Trial: An Introduction to the Catholic Modernist Crisis</u> (Washington, DC: The Catholic University of America, 1994), 28.

¹⁴Mark Schoof, O.P., <u>A Survey of Catholic Theology, 1800-1970</u>, trans. by N.D. Smith (Paramus, NJ: Paulist Neuman, 1970), 35-39.

¹⁵At a dinner party given by Father Richard Burtsell on the Feast of St. Ann, July 26, 1865, Father Manahan told an audience of Urban College graduates, including James A. Corcoran and Edward McGlynn, that too much Canon Law was taught in Rome and too much was said about rights but not about duties. Later Burtsell and McGlynn, along with members of New York's Second Accademia, the Ecclesiastical Society (organized by Father Thomas Farrell), also questioned the quality of their Roman training. <u>Burtsell Diary</u>, July 26, 1865, Sept. 10, 1866, Jan. 25, 1867, AANY; Robert Emmett Curran, SJ, "Prelude to Americanism: The New York *Accademia* and Clerical Radicalism in the Late Nineteenth Century," *Church History* 47 (1978): 50-51.

¹⁶Peterman, Becker, 23-24; Robert F. McNamara, <u>The American College in Rome, 1855-1955</u> (New York: Christopher Press, 1956), 101-02.

¹⁷*Esame, 1850-60; Distirbutio Praemiorum, 1839-68; Laureati,* 1831-1909, AUC at AUND; McNamara, <u>North American College</u>, 99, 102; Peterman, <u>Becker</u>, 33; Purcell, "Moore," 131.

¹⁸Peterman, <u>Becker</u>, 22; McNamara, <u>North American College</u>, 63, 97-99; Claudian Northrop to His Brothers, March 5, 1860, 25-A-6, ADC.

[19]Peterman, <u>Becker</u>, 22-23; McNamara, <u>North American College</u>, 95-99.

[20]Peterman, <u>Becker</u>, 22-23; McNamara, <u>North American College</u>, 94-103.

[21]Peterman, <u>Becker</u>, 22; Ellis, "Formation of the American Priest," 25; *Civilta Cattolica*, Sept. 7, 1855; April 25, June 27, Sept.12, 1857; Jan. 9., April 10, 24, Dec. 11, 1858; Jan. 29, Feb. 26, April 30, July 9, 1859; Claudian Northrop to Harry Northrop, April 14, 1860, 25-D-1, ADC.

[22]White, <u>The Diocesan Seminary</u>, 91-97; McNamara, <u>North American College</u>, 63-65, 89, 90-91.

[23]Moore to Lynch, July 3, 1860, 25-H-4, ADC.

[24]*U.S. Catholic Miscellany*, May 30, 1857; St. Lawrence Cemetery Register, "Mary Moore - 1857," ADC; Marriage Records, St. Patrick's Church, Charleston, ADC.

[25]*Civilta Cattolica*, Sept. 10, 1859; W.A. Merriwether to Lynch, March 24, 1860, 25-C-4, ADC; Stephen Bell, <u>Rebel Priest and Prophet</u> (New York: Devin-Adiar, 1937), 6-9. Other contemporaries of Moore's in Rome included: Patrick F. McSweeney, James Nilan, and Robert Seton (New York), Francis J. Friel (Brooklyn), P. Cannon (Buffalo), Stephen Barrett and William Bowman (Pittsburgh), Thomas Killeen (Newark), James McGovern (Chicago). Henry A. Brann, <u>History of the American College, Rome</u> (New York: Benziger Bros., 1910), 417-20; McNamara, <u>North American College</u>, 809, 828, 834.

[26]Barnabo to Lynch, June 30, 1860, 25-M-2; Moore to Lynch, July 3, 1860, 25-H-4, ADC; *Lettre e Decreti*, vol. 351, fol. 426 r., APF at AUND.

## *Chapter 3*

[1]Moore to Propaganda, July 22, 1862, *Congressi America Centrale*, vol. 19, fols. 853 r.-855 v., APF at AUND; <u>OCD-1861</u>, 79-80.

[2]John A. Garraty, <u>A Short History of the American Nation</u>, 3rd ed. (New York: Harper & Row, 1981), 243-46; Maury Klein, <u>Days of Defiance: Sumter, Secession, and the Coming of the Civil War</u> (New York: Alfred A. Knoph, 1997), 429; E. Milby Burton, <u>The Siege of Charleston</u>, 1861-1865 (Columbia, SC: University of South Carolina, 1994), 48-53, 84-88, 250.

[3]Robert N. S. Whitelaw and Alice F. Levkoff, Charleston Come Hell or High Water: A History in Photographs, 23; Burton, Siege, xv-xvi, 251-54. See also: Joseph Kelly, America's Longest Siege: Charleston, Slavery, and the Slow March Toward Civil War (New York: Overlook Press, 2012); John B. Marchand, Charleston Blockade: The Journals of John B. Marchand, U.S. Navy, 1861-62, ed. by Craig L. Symonds (Newport, RI: Naval War College Press, 1976).

[4]James C. McDonald to Moore, March 16, 1864, 30-K-6, ADC; *U.S. Catholic Miscellany*, Nov. 16, 1861; Burton, Siege, 257-64; Robert N. Rosen, Confederate Charleston: An Illustrated History of the City and People During the Civil War (Columbia, SC: University of South Carolina, 1994), 119-21, 131. It is unclear whether Verot actually published the 1862 Ordo. He did publish a Lenten Pastoral Letter in February of 1862 and what he called a *Peace Pastoral* in November of 1863. Michael V. Gannon, Rebel Bishop: The Life and Era of Augustine Verot (Milwaukee, WI: Bruce, 1964), 65-66, 72-73.

[5]Rosen, Confederate Charleston, 138-40; Burton, Siege, 310-13, 317-25; Whitelaw and Levkoff, Charleston in Photographs, 10.

[6]*U.S. Catholic Miscellany*, Nov. 3, 1860; *Charleston Catholic Miscellany*, Sept. 21, 1861.

[7]*Charleston Catholic Miscellany*, March 23, 1861.

[8]Whitelaw and Levkoff, Charleston in Photographs, 29; Richard C. Madden, Catholics in South Carolina: A Record (Lantham, MD: University Press of America 1985), 83; Burton, Siege, 80-84; *Charleston Catholic Miscellany*, Dec. 14, 1861; *Charleston Daily Courier*, Oct. 1, 1866. For a first-person account of the Fire of 1861, see: Emma Holmes, The Diary of Miss Emma Holmes, ed. by John F. Marszalek (Baton Rouge, LA: Louisiana State University, 1994), 105-111. E. Milby Burton states that the Cathedral's insurance policy lapsed the week before the fire (p. 80), however, David Heisser, an expert on Bishop Patrick Lynch, maintains that there was in fact no insurance taken out on the building (Letter, Heisser to author, July 14, 2004). Father James A. Corcoran, editor of the *Miscellany*, expunged the "U.S." from the title of the paper and changed its name for patriotic reasons to the *Charleston Catholic Miscellany* in the December 29, 1860 edition.

[9]Madden, Catholics in S.C., 84, 86-87; Moore to Propaganda, July 22, 1862, *Congressi America Centrale*, vol. 19, fols. 853r.-855v., APF at AUND.

John Moore

[10]*Charleston Mercury*, Nov. 14, 1863; Burton, <u>Siege</u>, 257-60; Rosen, <u>Confederate Charleston</u>, 119-21, 131; Father J. J. O'Connell to the Propagation of the Faith, Rome, Dec. 30, 1863, vol. 19, fols. 853 r. to 855 v., APF at AUND.

[11]Sister Anne Francis Campbell, OLM, "Bishop England's Sisterhood, 1829-1929" (Ph.D. diss., St. Louis University, 1968), 148, 156; Lynch to P.J. Benjamin, Secretary of State, C.S.A., March 3, 1864, 30-K-1; Lynch to William H. Seward, Secretary of State, U.S.A., June 24, 1865, 32-Q-5A; Spalding to Lynch, Aug. 11, 1865, 32-Q-14, ADC; Lynch to Moore, April 10, 1864, 2-A-13; Spalding to Moore, Sept. 16, 1865, 2-A-20, ADSA; Madden, <u>Catholics in S.C.</u>, 91-92, 99. After the War in 1866, Moore interpreted Lynch's ambassadorial purpose as "to obtain the interference of European governments to get better terms for the South when forced to give in." Burtsell Diary, Nov. 15, 1866, AANY. For more on Lynch, see: Robert Emmett Curran, "'Storming Heaven for Charleston': The Lynch Family and the Civil War," *U.S. Catholic Historian* 35 (Spring 2017), 1-26; David C. R. Heisser and Stephen J. White, Sister, <u>Patrick N. Lynch, 1817-1882: Third Catholic Bishop of Charleston</u> (Columbia, SC: University of South Carolina Press, 2015).

[12]J.J. O'Connell, O.S.B., <u>Catholicity in the Carolinas and Georgia</u> (New York: D. & J. Sadlier, 1879), 151-52; Madden, <u>Catholics in S.C.</u>, 94, 97-98; Spalding to Moore, May 29, 1865, 2-A-15, ADSA; *Banner of the South*, Feb. 5, 19,1870

[13]Vincent de Paul McMurray, "The Catholic Church during Reconstruction, 1865-1877" (M.A. thesis, The Catholic University of America, 1950), 92-93; Moore to Spalding, March 30, 1865, 35-J-2, Spalding Papers; Moore to Spalding, April 21, 1865, 35-J-3, Spalding Papers; Moore to Spalding, April 28, 1865, 35-J-4, Spalding Papers, AAB at AASMU; Spalding to Moore, May 8, 1865, 2-A-14, ADSA; Moore to Spalding, May 20, 1865, 35-J-5, Spalding Papers, AAB at AASMU; *Charleston Courier*, May 6, 1865.

[14]Moore to Spalding, March 30, 1865, 35-J-2, Spalding Papers; Moore to Spalding, April 21, 1865, 35-J-3, Spalding Papers; Moore to Spalding, April 28, 1865, 35-J-4, Spalding Papers; Moore to Leonard Perry, Adjutant General, June 22, 1865, June 22, 1865, 35-J-6, Spalding Papers, AAB at AASMU; Madden, <u>Catholics in S.C.</u>, 87.

[15]Moore to Lynch, April 28, 1865, 32-K-2, ADC; Moore to Spalding, April 28, 1865, 35-J-4, Spalding Papers; Moore to Spalding, May 20, 1865, 35-J-5, Spalding Papers, AAB at AASMU; Moore to Lynch, Aug. 18, 1865, 32-S-7, ADC; Moore to Spalding, Sept. 16, 1865, 35-J-13, Spalding Papers; Moore to Spalding, Oct.4, 1865, 35-J-14, Spalding Papers, AAB at AASMU.

[16]Moore to Lynch, April 28, 1865, 32-K-2, ADC.

[17]Spalding to Moore, May 29, 1865, 2-A-15, ADSA; Moore to Spalding, June 23, 1865, 35-J-7, Spalding Papers; Moore to Spalding, July 12, 1865, 35-J-8, Spalding Papers; Moore to Spalding, July 28, 1865, 35-J-9, Spalding Papers; Moore to Spalding, Aug. 17, 1865, 35-J-10, Spalding Papers; Moore to Spalding, Aug. 26, 1865, 35-J-12, Spalding Papers; Moore to Spalding, Sept. 16, 1865, 35-J-13, Spalding Papers; Moore to Spalding, Oct. 4, 1865, 35-J-14, Spalding Papers, AAB at AASMU. See also: Louis-Hippolyte Gache, SJ, A Frenchman, A Chaplain, A Rebel: The War Letters of Pere Louis-Hippolyte Gache, SJ, trans. by Cornelius M. Buckley, SJ, (Chicago, IL: Loyola University, 1981).

[18]Corcoran to Lynch, Aug. 6, 1865, 32-R-6, ADC; Spalding to Moore, May 8, 1865, 2-A-14, ADSA; Moore to Spalding, May 20, 1865, 35-J-5, Spalding Papers; Moore to Spalding, July 12, 1865, 35-J-8, Spalding Papers; Moore to Spalding, July 12, 1865, 35-J-8, Spalding Papers; Moore to Spalding, Aug. 26, 1865, 35-J-12, Spalding Papers, AAB at AASMU; Campbell, "England's Sisterhood," 154.

[19]Moore to Spalding, Aug. 26, 1865, 35-J-12, Spalding Papers, AAB at AASMU.

[20]Moore to Spalding, Sept. 16, 1865, 35-J-13, Spalding Papers, AAB at AASMU.

[21]Moore to Leonard Perry, June 22, 1865, 35-J-6, Spalding Papers, AAB at AASMU; Spalding to Gillmore, May 29, 1865, quoted in Thomas Spalding, Martin John Spalding (Washington, DC: Catholic University of America, 1973), 167.

[22]Charleston Daily Courier, July 31, 1901; Moore to Lynch, March11, 1873, 54-S-7, ADC; Richard J. Purcell, "Moore, John," Dictionary of American Biography, vol. 13, ed. by Dumas Malone (New York: Charles Scribner's, 1934), 131.

[23]David T. Gleeson, The Irish in the South, 1815-1877 (Chapel Hill, NC: University of North Carolina, 2001), 137,158-60.

[24]Moore to Spalding, Oct. 14, 1865, 36B-G-11, Spalding Papers, AAB at AASMU; Spalding, Martin Spalding, 170-72.

[25]Lynch to the Propagation of the Faith, Lyons, France, September 7, 1865, 32-W-2, ADC; Buchanan, "Brief History," 80; Michael J. McNally, "A Peculiar Institution: A History of Parish Life in the Southeast (1850-1980)" in The American Catholic Parish: A History from 1850 to the Present, vol. 1, ed. by Jay P. Dolan (New York: Paulist, 1987), 133.

## *Chapter 4*

[1]St. Patrick's Church File, Item #1- History, Box 602, ADC. Parishioners contributed $1,533.31, whereas $2,785.91 was collected by the bishop. Although there were thirty-six pews in the church at its dedication, $700 was still needed to complete the interior furnishings, including an organ. *U.S. Catholic Miscellany*, Dec. 29, 1838.

[2]St. Patrick's Church File, A Chronicle History of St. Patrick's, 1837-1937, Box 602, ADC; J.J. O'Connell, OSB, Catholicity in the Carolinas and Georgia (New York: D. & J. Sadlier, 1879), 151-53, 187; Richard C. Madden, Catholics in South Carolina: A Record (Lanham, MD: University Press of America, 1985), 94. See also: Michael J. McNally, "Reconstruction and Parish Life in Charleston, SC, 1865-1877: A Pastor's Perspective," *American Catholic Studies* 117 (Spring 2006): 45-67.

[3]Moore to Spalding, March 30, 1865, 35-J-2, Spalding Papers, AAB at AASMU; Moore to Lynch, Feb.10, 1866, 34-N-5, ADC.

[4]Moore to Lynch, May 5, 1866, 35-N-6, ADC.

[5]Bermingham to Lynch, Jan. 12, 1866, 34-A-3; Moore to Lynch, March 1, 1866, 34-T-7; Moore to Lynch, June 23, 1866, 36-D-1; Moore to Lynch, Nov. 6, 1866, 37-T-3, ADC.

[6]Moore to Lynch, Nov. 6, 1866, 37-T-3, ADC; Burtsell Diary, Nov. 14, Dec. 17, 1866, AANY.

[7]Moore to Lynch, Oct. 8, 1866, 37-N-1; Moore to Lynch, Oct. 11, 1866, 37-N-5; Moore, at New York, to Lynch, Nov. 22, 1866, 38-A-1, ADC; Burtsell Diary, Nov. 14, 1866, AANY.

[8]Moore, at New York, to Lynch, Nov. 22, 1866, 38-A-1, ADC; Burtsell Diary, Nov. 14, Dec. 17, 1866, AANY.

[9]Moore, at New York, to Lynch, Dec. 20, 1866, 38-E-7, ADC; Burtsell Diary, Dec. 10, 17, 21, 1866, AANY.

[10]Burtsell Diary, Dec. 25, 1866, AANY.

[11]Burtsell Diary, Nov. 20, 26, 1866, Jan. 8, 9, 15, 25, Feb. 5, 1867, AANY; *Catholic World*, 1867-70. See also: Robert Emmett Curran, SJ, "Prelude to Americanism: The New York *Accademia* and Clerical Radicalism in the late Nineteenth Century" *Church History* 47 (1978): 48-65.

[12]Moore, at New York, to Lynch, Jan. 28, 1867, 38-W-7, ADC.

[13]St. Patrick's Church File, A Chronicle History of St. Patrick's, 1837-1937, Box 602, ADC; Construction Contract with Henry Oliver, builder, May 3, 1867, 40-D-8; Moore to Lynch, April 13, 1869, 46-H-2; Moore to Lynch, June 29, 1867, 40-Y-1; Moore to Lynch, March 19, 1868, 42-Y-1, ADC; *Catholic Mirror*, Sept. 19, 1868; Moore to Propaganda, June 16, 1876, *Congressi America Centrale*, vol. 27, fol. 412 rv., APF at AUND; OCD-1869, 140-42; OCD-1870, 145-47. In December 1885 the wooden St. Patrick's Church was moved across the street so that the new brick church could be built on the spot. The cornerstone of the 700 seat $60,000 edifice was laid on March 17, 1886, and was consecrated by Bp, H.P. Northrop on May 15, 1887. Bishop Moore was present, although Bishop Thomas Becker preached the sermon on the occasion. Madden, Catholics in South Carolina, 142.

[14]Moore to Lynch, June 29, 1867, 40-Y-1, ADC.

[15]Moore to Lynch, March 19, 1868, 42-Y-1; Moore to Lynch, Nov. 9, 1872, 53-W-7, ADC.

[16]Madden, Catholics in South Carolina, 123.

[17]*Banner of the South*, Oct. 2, 1869.

[18]Moore to W. J. Magrath, March 27, 1868, 43-A-2, ADC.

[19]*Banner of the South*, June 18, 1870.

[20]Moore to Lynch, June 29, 1867, 40-Y-1, ADC; *Banner of the South*, March 19, June 18, 1870; *Catholic Standard and Times*, Aug. 3, 1901; Timothy Walch, "Temperance Movement and American Catholics" in The Encyclopedia of American Catholic History ed. by Michael Glazier and Thomas J. Shelley (Collegeville, MN: The Liturgical Press, 1997), 1372-73.

[21]Moore to Lynch, March 1, 1866, 34-T-7; Moore to Lynch, April 13, 1869, 46-H-2, ADC; Moore to Propaganda, June 16, 1876, *Congressi America Centrale*, vol. 27, fol. 412 rv., APF at AUND; *Catholic Standard and Times*, Aug. 3, 1901.

[22]*Banner of the South*, March 21, April 11, 1868; March 27, Jan. 30, March 13, 1869; June 18, 1870; *Freeman's Journal*, July 3, 1873; Quigley to Lynch, June 30, 1873, 55-L-3, ADC; Michael J. McNally, "A Peculiar Institution: A History of Catholic Parish

Life in the Southeast (1850-1980)" in <u>The American Catholic Parish: A History from 1850 to the Present</u>, vol. 1, ed. by Jay P. Dolan (New York: Paulist, 1987), 134-35; Jay P. Dolan, <u>Catholic Revivalism: The American Experience, 1830-1900</u> (Notre Dame, IN: University of Notre Dame, 1978), xvi-xviii, 12-21; Andrew Skeabeck, CSSR, "The Most Reverend William Gross: Missionary Bishop of the South," *Researches of the Catholic Historical Society of Philadelphia* 65 (Dec. 1954): 217-18; Joseph McSorley, <u>Father Hecker and His Friends: Studies and Reminiscences</u> (St. Louis, MO: B. Herder, 1952), 35-37, 41-48.

[23]St. Patrick's Baptism Records, 1850-1876, ADC.

[24]*Banner of the South*, May 22, 1869; St. Patrick's Baptism Records, 1850-1876, ADC; St. Lawrence Cemetery Record Book, 1852-1918, ADC.

[25]"Oh! Blessed rage for order..." from a poem by Wallace Stevens, "The Idea of Order at Key West" (1936) in <u>The Collected Poems of Wallace Stevens</u> (New York: Alfred A. Knopf, 1968), 128-30.

[26]Moore to Lynch, June 29, 1867, 40-Y-1, ADC.

[27]*Charleston Daily Courier,* May 13, 1877.

[28]Moore, at Sweet Chalybeate Springs, VA, to Lynch, Aug. 26, 1871, 51-A-4, ADC; *Charleston Catholic Miscellany*, Dec. 14, 1861.

[29]St. Patrick's Baptism Records, 1850-1876, Aug. 9, 1866, Sept. 6, 1872, July 19, 1874.

[30]St. Lawrence Cemetery Account Book; St. Lawrence Cemetery Record Book, 1852-1918, ADC.

[31]Moore to POF, April 7, 1866, *America Centrale*, vol.21, fols. 205 rv., 206 rv., APF at AUND.

[32]Moore to POF, April 7, 1868, *America Centrale*, vol. 22, fols. 168 r., 169 rv., APF at AUND.

[33]Moore to POF, April 8, 1870, *America Centrale*, vol. 23, fols. 248 rv., 249 r., APF at AUND.

[34]Lynch, at New York, to POF, May 26, 1870 [1871], *America Centrale*, vol.23, fols. 1098rv., 1099 rv., APF at AUND. Although Lynch dated this letter "1870," internal evidence suggests that he wrote it in 1871. Simon Carew, whom Lynch must have met in Rome during Vatican Council I and whom he mentions as coming to Charleston, was not ordained until the summer of 1871.

[35]Moore to POF, March 21, 1872, *Udienze di Nostro Signore*, vol. 171, fols. 421 rv, APF at AUND.

[36]On this topic see: George A. Aschenbrenner, SJ, Quickening the Fire in Our Midst: The Challenge of Diocesan Priesthood (Chicago, IL: Loyola Press, 2002); Donald B. Cozzens, ed., The Spirituality of the Diocesan Priest (Collegeville, MN: Liturgical Press, 1997).

[37]Moore to POF, March 21, 1874, *America Centrale*, vol. 25, fol. 213 rv., APF at AUND.

[38]Moore to POF, June 16, 1876, *America Centrale*, vol. 27, fol. 412 rv., APF at AUND.

## *Chapter 5*

[1]OCD-1867, 232-33; OCD-1870, 145-47; OCD-1871, 320-21; OCD-1877, 214-15; *Banner of the South*, Oct. 2, 1869.

[2]*Banner of the South*, March 21, 1868, March 26, 1870; *Charleston Daily News*, Feb. 20, March 1, 11, 13, 17, 18, 1873.

[3]*Charleston Daily News*, March 15, 18, 1873.

[4]St. Patrick's Benevolent Society File; St. Patrick's Benevolent Society Minutes, May 1857 - June 1878, ADC; *Banner of the South*, March 21, 1868, March 26, 1870.

[5]*Charleston Daily Courier*, Feb. 20, 1873.

[6]*Charleston Daily Courier*, March 5, 1873.

[7]*Charleston Daily Courier*, March 7, 1873.

[8]Moore to Lynch, March 7, 1873, 54-S-3; Sister DeSales, OLM, to Lynch, March 10, 1873, 54-S-4, ADC.

[9]Moore to Lynch, March 11, 1873, 54-S-7, ADC; *Charleston Daily Courier*, March 10, 1873. Moore waits until 1873 to become a citizen. It could be due to the treatment he received by the Union Army during the War. He had firsthand experience of the Union bombardment. At the War's end, his ministrations to the sick and wounded were interfered with by occupying Union officials and they compelled him to take an oath of allegiance to the U.S. Moore rebuffed the coercion, refusing to take the oath. As a result, his mail was held up and inspected both going and coming. It was only when he was named Vicar General did he feel it prudent to become an American citizen on March 11, 1873. *Charleston News & Courier*, July 31, 1901.

[10]*Charleston Daily Courier*, March 11, 1873.

[11]Scott J. Buchanan, "A Brief History of the Diocese of Charleston, South Carolina, 1520-2000" (unpublished manuscript, 2000), 74, ADC; Richard C. Madden, Catholics in South Carolina:

A Record (Lanham, MD: University Press of America, 1985), 119-
21, 137; Moore to Lynch, Aug. 4, 1872, 53-K-1; D.J. Quigley File;
Quigley to Lynch, Nov. 3, 1874, 57-N-7; Quigley to Lynch, Jan.
19, 1875, 58-A-7; Quigley to Lynch, Feb. 3, 1875, 58-C-1, ADC.
In January 1886 Quigley became the first Monsignor (a Domestic
Prelate), the first one in the South. Quigley died in 1903.

[12]William May, History of the New England Society of
Charleston, S.C, 1819-1919 (Charleston, SC: New England
Society of Charleston, 1920), 156-59; Walter J. Fraser, Jr.,
Charleston! Charleston! The History of a Southern City
(Columbia, SC: University of South Carolina, 1989), 292-93, 300.

[13]Moore to Lynch, Oct. 8, 1866, 37-N-1; Moore to Lynch, Oct.
11, 1866, 37-N-5, ADC.

[14]Walsh to Lynch, Oct. 31, 1866, 37-R-2; Walsh to Lynch, Jan.
3, 1867, 38-M-4, ADC.

[15]Walsh to Lynch, April 27, 1867, 40-C-4; Walsh to Lynch,
May 30, 1867, 40-P-6; Walsh to Lynch, May 28, 1868, 43-R-7,
ADC.

[16]OCD-1871, 320; OCD-1872, 338; OCD-1873, 152-3;
Bermingham to Lynch, Sept. 3, 1871, 51-B-2; Moore to Lynch,
Aug.14, 1872, 53-K-1, ADC; Obituary, John Schachte, Charleston
News & Courier, Oct. 4, 1897 (also found in 82-M-3, ADC).

[17]Moore to Lynch, Feb. 16, 1873, 54-P-1; Moore to Lynch, Feb.
27, 1873, 54-R-2; Moore to Lynch, March 7, 1873, 54-S-3, ADC.

[18]Carew to Propaganda, Nov. 10, 1871, America Centrale, vol. 23,
fols. 1430r., 1431 r., APF at AUND; Bermingham to Lynch, Sept.
3, 1871, 51-B-2; Schachte to Lynch, Sept. 4, 1872, 53-N-2, ADC.

[19]Elizabeth M. Wynne to Lynch, May 31, 1873, 55-E-5, ADC.

[20]Sister DeSales to Lynch, June 3, 1873, 55-E-7; Carew to
Lynch, June 15, 1873, 55-G-6, ADC.

[21]Carew to Lynch, July 13, 1873, 55-M-4; Sister Agatha, St.
Agnes Hospital, to Lynch, July 15, 1873, 55-M-5; Carew to Lynch,
Aug. 18, 1873, 55-P-7; Carew to Lynch, Sept. 12, 1873, 55-S-7;
Carew to Lynch, Oct. 14, 1873, 55-W-4; Carew to Lynch, June 29,
1874, 57-A-2, ADC; OCD-1877, 255; OCD-1878, 175, 204, 347;
OCD-1885, 354; OCD-1886, 258; OCD-1887, 259; OCD-1888,
269; OCD-1889, 28.

[22]Moore to Lynch, July 28, 1874, 57-C-3; Moore to Lynch, Feb.
6, 1875, 58-C-4; Moore to Lynch, Sept. 27, 1875, 58-T-7; Moore
to Lynch, March 20, 1876, 59-T-4, ADC.

[23]Moore to Lynch, July 28, 1874, 57-C-3, ADC.

[24]Quigley to Lynch, Nov. 13, 1874, 57-P-6; Moore to Lynch, Nov. 24, 1874, 57-S-2, ADC.

[25]Moore to Lynch, Feb. 6, 1875, 58-C-4; Moore to Lynch, Sept. 27, 1875, 58-T-7; Moore to Lynch, Nov. 21, 1876, 61-N-7, ADC; OCD-1867, 232-33; OCD-1876, 394-95.

[26]Society of St. John the Baptist Minutes, 1867-77, July 5, 1873; Moore to Lynch, Aug. 14, 1872, 53-K-1; Moore to Lynch, Aug. 24, 1872, 53-M-2; Moore to Lynch, Aug. 28, 1872, 53-M-3, ADC; Sister M. Anne Francis Campbell, OLM, "Bishop England's Sisterhood, 1829-1929" (Ph.D. diss., St. Louis University, 1968), 197-98.

[27]Moore to Lynch, Oct. 31, 1873, 55-Y-6, ADC; OCD-1870, 145-47.

[28]Campbell, "England's Sisterhood," 68, 81; Interview with Sister Anne Francis Campbell, OLM, Charleston, SC, June 27, 1996.

[29]Sister Mary DeSales Brennan, Membership Register, ASCOLM; *Charleston Miscellany*, Dec. 14, 1861; Madden, Catholics in South Carolina, 83-84; Campbell, "England's Sisterhood," 96-98, 101, 104-07; Ellen Ryan Jolly, Nuns of the Battlefield (Providence, RI: Providence Visitor Press, 1927), 287-98; Gerald P. Fogarty, SJ, Commonwealth Catholicism: A History of the Catholic Church in Virginia (Notre Dame, IN: University of Notre Dame, 2001), 170-76. See also: Dorothy H. Bodell, Montgomery White Sulphur Springs: A History of the Resort, Hospital, Cemeteries, Markers, and Monument (Blacksburg, VA: Pocahontas Press, 1993); Mary Denis Maher, To Bind Up Wounds: Catholic Sister Nurses in the U.S. Civil War (Baton Rouge, LA: Louisiana State University, 1999); C. Keith Wilbur, Civil War Medicine (Old Saybrook, CT: Glove Pequot, 1998); Harold Elk Straubing, In Hospital and Camp: The War through the Eyes of Its Doctors and Nurses (Harrisburg, PA: Stackpole, 1993); H. H. Cunningham, Doctors in Gray: The Confederate Medical Service (Baton Rouge, LA: Louisiana State University, 1993).

[30]Campbell, "England's Sisterhood,"154.

[31]*Ibid.*,112, 137-38.

[32]Madden, Catholics in South Carolina, 118; Campbell, "England's Sisterhood," 199.

[33]Sister DeSales to Lynch, Aug. 31, 1868, 44-W-2; Moore, at Sweet Chalybeate Springs, VA, to Lynch, Aug. 6, 1871, 51-A-4; Sister DeSales to Lynch, Oct. 15, 1871, 51-G-6; Sister Alphonsa

to Lynch, telegram, Oct. 16, 1871, 51-H-3, ADC; Campbell, "England's Sisterhood," 204.

[34]Campbell, "England's Sisterhood," 205-07; Sister DeSales, at Glencary, WV, to Lynch, Oct. 19, 1876, 61-H-5; Sister DeSales, at San Antonio, TX, to Lynch, Dec. 17, 1876, 61-S-2; Sister DeSales, at San Antonio, TX, to Lynch, Jan. 21, 1877, 62-C-4; Sister DeSales, at New Orleans, LA, to Lynch, Oct. 1, 1877, 64-A-6; Sister DeSales, at Pittsburgh, PA, to Lynch, Jan. 28, 1878, 64-Y-7; Sister DeSales, at White Sulphur Springs, VA, to Lynch, Jan.4, 1879, 67-E-4; Sister DeSales, at Charlotte, NC, to Lynch, Jan. 11, 1879, 67-G-5; Sister DeSales, at Baltimore, MD, to Lynch, May 3, 1880, 70-N-4; Sister DeSales, at Montreal, Canada, to Lynch, June 14, 1880, 70-S-6; Sister DeSales, at Montreal, Canada, to Lynch, May 29, 1881, 72-Y-5; Sister DeSales, at Boloeil, Canada, to Lynch, Feb. 11, 1882, 74-H-3, ADC.

[35]Sister DeSales, to Lynch, June 8, 1872, 53-B-2; Sister DeSales to Moore, June 2, 1873, 55-E-6; Sister DeSales to Lynch, June 3, 1873, 55-E-7; Sister DeSales to Lynch, April 5, 1877, 62-R-3, ADC.

[36]Moore to Lynch, Jan. 6, 1877, 62-A-4, ADC.

[37]Michael J. McNally, "Lynch, Patrick Neison" in American National Biography ed. by John Garraty" and Mark C. Carnes (New York: Oxford, 1999): 169-70: Heisser, 546-47; Edward Lofton, "Lynch, Patrick Neison," in The Encyclopedia of American Catholic History, ed. by Glazier and Shelly (Collegeville, MN: Liturgical Press, 1997), 828-29.

[38]Charleston Catholic Miscellany, April 20, May 4, 11, 18, 1861; St. Paul's German Catholic Church File; Petition from Members to St. Paul's German Catholic Church to Lynch, April 30, 1867, 40-D-2, ADC.

[39]Lynch to the President and Members of the Propagation of the Faith, Lyons, France, Sept. (n.d.) 1865, Verot Papers, 1(y)-B-8, ADSA. Since a copy of Lynch's letter was found in the Archives of the diocese of St. Augustine, Bishop Lynch must have sent a copy of it to Bishop Verot, whose situation immediately after the Civil War was as desperate as Lynch's.

[40]Charleston Catholic Miscellany, May 4, 1861; Madden, Catholics in South Carolina, 120-21; Vincent de Paul McMurray, "The Catholic Church during Reconstruction, 1865-1877" (M.A. thesis, The Catholic University of America, 1950), 65, 78, 80; Wood to Lynch, Jan. 30, 1866, 34-G-6, ADC; McCloskey to

Lynch, Jan. 29, 1866, 34-G-1, ADC; *Banner of the South*, April 11, 1868, Oct. 2, Dec. 4, 1869; *Charleston Daily News & Courier*, Feb. 1, 3, 1873.

[41]McMurray, "Catholic Reconstruction," 126; Lynch to Quigley, Nov. (n.d.) 1876, 61-P-5; Lynch to Quigley, March 3, 1877, 62-M-3, ADC.

[42]Moore to Spalding, March 30, 1865, 35-J-2, Spalding Papers; Lynch to Spalding, May 15, 1869, Spalding Papers, 36A-M-8; Lynch to Spalding, May 29, 1869, Spalding Papers, 36A-M-9, AAB at AASMSU.

[43]Madden, Catholics in South Carolina, 101; Bermingham, at New Orleans, to Lynch, June 28, 1866, 36-D-6; Bermingham, at New Orleans, to Lynch, Aug. 6, 1866, 36-S-5; Bermingham, at New Orleans, to Lynch, Aug. 14, 1866 (telegram), 36-W-5, ADC.

[44]Madden, Catholics in South Carolina, 103-04, 169; *Charleston Daily Courier*, Oct. 1, 1866. The Pro-Cathedral building was used as the Cathedral Grammar School up to the late 1950s. It was finally razed in 1965. Pro-Cathedral File, ADC.

[45]Madden, Catholics in South Carolina, 104, 111; OCD-1868, 133-34; Lynch to the Propagation of the Faith, Lyons, France, Sept. (n.d.) 1865, 1(y)-B-8, Verot Papers, ADSA; St Peter's - Wentworth Street Box,"100th Anniversary Booklet," ADC. The Mill Hill Fathers first came to the U.S. in 1871 to St. Francis Xavier Parish in Baltimore. In the U.S. they were renamed and refounded as the Josephite Fathers in 1892 in Baltimore.

[46]McMurray, "Catholic Reconstruction," 209, 21-13; Lynch to Spalding, Jan. 26, 1866, 39B-G-10, Spalding Papers, AAB at AASMSU; Spalding to Lynch, Jan. 19, 1866, 34-B-7; Gen. O.O. Howard to Lynch, Feb. 1, 1866, 34-H-2, ADC.

[47]Madden, Catholics in South Carolina, 112-13; *Banner of the South*, Dec. 5, 1868.

[48]*Acta Episcopalia* of Cardinal Gibbons, Feb. 26, 1882, AAB at AASMSU; OCD-1870, 145-147; OCD-1871, 320-21; Banner of the South, Oct 2, 1869; *Charleston News and Courier*, March 2, 1882; Buchanan, "History of the Diocese of Charleston," 81-82; Madden, Catholics in South Carolina, 135-36.

[49]Lynch to Bayley, July 3, 1876, 40-K-10, Bayley Papers, AAB at AASMSU; Lynch to Bayley, (n.d.) 1876 (copy), 61-Y-1, ADC.

[50]Bishop John Kain, at Wheeling, WV, to Propaganda, Oct. 4, 1876, *Cong. Generali*, vol. 1006, fols. 5rv.,6r, APF at AUND.

[51]*Acta - Sac Cong*, POF, Jan. 2, 1877, vol. 245, fols. 1rv., 2rv., 3r., APF at AUND.

[52]*Lettere,* POF Decree, Feb. 5, 1877, vol. 373, fol. 112; *Lettere,* POF Decree, March 8, 1877, vol. 373, fols. 153 r., 154 r., APF at AUND.

[53]Moore to Bayley, March 27, 1877, 40-L-16, Bayley Papers, AAB at AASMSU.

[54]Moore to Bayley, March 27, 1877, 40-L-16, Bayley Papers; *Acta Episcopalia* of Cardinal Gibbons, May 13, 1877, AAB at AASMSU.

[55]Moore to Gibbons, April 6, 1877, 73-A-15, Gibbons Papers; *Acta Episcopalia* of Cardinal Gibbons, May 13, 1877, AAB at AASMSU; *Charleston Daily Courier,* May 13, 1877; *Charleston News & Courier,* May 14, 1877; Catholic Standard, May 26, 1877.

[56]*St. Augustine Press,* May 26, 1877; *Freeman's Journal and Catholic Register,* May 22, 1877; Moore to Alesandro Cardinal Franchi, POF, May 23, 1877, Congressi: America Centrale, vol. 28, fol. 94 rv., APF at AUND.

## *Chapter 6*

[1]Michael V. Gannon, *The Cross in the Sand: The Early Catholic Church in Florida, 1513-1870,* 2nd ed. (1983 reprint, Gainesville, FL: University Press of Florida, 1989), 1-3, 20-30, 36-83; Randolph J. Widmer, The Evolution of the Calusa: A Nonagricultural Chiefdom on the Southwest Florida Coast (Tuscaloosa, AL: University of Alabama, 1988), 2-7, 272-75; Jerald T. Milanich, Florida Indians and the Invasion from Europe (Gainesville, FL; University Press of Florida, 1995), 17-97; Milanich, Florida's Indians from Ancient Times to the Present (Gainesville, FL: University Press of Florida, 1998), 1-12, 175; John H. Hann, "Summary Guide to Spanish Florida Missions and *Visitas* with Churches in the Sixteenth and Seventeenth Centuries" (unpublished manuscript for the Bureau of Archaeological Research of the Florida Department of State, 1988). See also: Bonnie G. McEwan, ed., The Spanish Missions of La Florida (Gainesville, FL: University Press of Florida, 1993).

[2]Milanich, Florida Indians, 177-88. See also: John K. Mahon, History of the Second Seminole War, 1835-1842, rev. ed. (Gainesville, FL: University of Florida Press, 1991); C. S. Monaco, The Second Seminole War and the Limits of American

Aggression (Baltimore, MD: Johns Hopkins University Press, 2018).

³Charlton Tebeau, A History of Florida (Coral Gables, FL: University of Miami, 1971), 181-87; Julia Floyd Smith, Slavery and Plantation Growth in Antebellum Florida, 1821-1860 (Gainesville, FL: University of Florida, 1973), 27, 29, 153-70; Larry Eugene Rivers, Slavery in Florida: Territorial Days to Emancipation (Gainesville, FL: University Press of Florida, 2000), 1-84, 153.

⁴Robert A. Taylor, "Florida Goes to War," *Florida Humanities Council Forum* XXXIV (Spring 2010): 4-9; Tebeau, Florida, 199-220, 232-33. See also: William H. Nulty, Confederate Florida: The Road to Olustee (Tuscaloosa, AL: University of Alabama, 1990); Lewis N. Wynne and Robert A. Taylor, Florida in the Civil War (Charleston, SC: Arcadia Publishing, 2004).

⁵Michael V. Gannon, Rebel Bishop: The Life and Era of Augustin Verot (Milwaukee, WI: Bruce, 1964), 66, 145-47.

⁶Gannon, Rebel Bishop, 120-21, 127, 131-33, 136; Michael J. McNally, Catholicism in South Florida, 1868-1968 (Gainesville, FL: University Presses of Florida, 1984), 20-21, 34.

⁷Gannon, Rebel Bishop, 152-57.

⁸*Ibid.*, 145-46, 157.

⁹*Ibid.*, 1, 251.

¹⁰Anne H. Shermyen, ed., 1989 Florida Statistical Abstract (Gainesville, FL: University Press of Florida, 1989), 3; Walter C. Maloney, A Sketch of the History of Key West, Florida, Facsimile Reproduction of the 1876 Edition (Gainesville, FL: University of Florida Press, 1968), iv; T. Frederick Davis, History of Jacksonville and Vicinity, 1513-1924 (St. Augustine, FL: Florida Historical Society, 1925), 500; Hampton Dunn, Yesterday's Tampa (Miami, FL: E.A.Seemann, 1972), 21, 74; Gary R. Mormino and Anthony P. Pizzo, Tampa: The Treasure City (Tulsa, OK: Continental Heritage, 1983), 130; Raymond Arsenault and Gary R. Mormino, "From Dixie to Dreamland: Demographic and Cultural Change in Florida, 1880-1980," in Shades of the Sunbelt: Essays on Ethnicity, Race, and the Urban South, ed. by Randall M. Miller and George E. Pozzetta (Boca Raton, FL: Florida Atlantic University, 1989), 163.

¹¹Arsenault and Mormino, "From Dixie to Dreamland," 166-67, 171.

¹²OCD-1878, 376-79.

[13]Gary R. Mormino, "Tampa: From Hell Hole to the Good Life," in Sunbelt Cities: Politics and Growth Since World War II, ed. by Richard M. Bernard and Bradley R. Rice (Austin, TX: University of Texas, 1983), 139; Raymond Arsenault, St. Petersburg and the Florida Dream, 1888-1950 (Norfolk/Virginia Beach, VA: Donning, 1988), 49; David Leon Chandler, Henry Flagler: The Astonishing Life and Times of the Visionary Robber Baron Who Founded Florida (New York: Macmillan, 1986), 126-27; Thomas Graham, Mr. Flagler's St. Augustine (Gainesville, FL: University Press of Florida, 2014); Canter Brown, Jr., Florida's Peace River Frontier (Orlando, FL: University of Central Florida, 1991), 277-91; Edward C. Williamson, Florida Politics in the Gilded Age, 1877-1893 (Gainesville, FL: University Presses of Florida, 1976), 78-79; Dudley S. Johnson, "Henry Bradley Plant and Florida," Florida Historical Quarterly 45 (Oct. 1966): 118-32; Canter Brown, Jr., "Tampa and the Coming of the Railroad,1853-1884," Sunland Tribune 17 (Nov. 1991): 13-18. See also: G. Hutchinson Smyth, The Life of Henry Bradley Plant (New York: G.P. Putnam's Sons, 1898). See also: James C. Cobb, Industrialization & Southern Society, 1877-1984 (Lexington, KY: University Press of Kentucky, 1984; Richard White, The Republic for Which It Stands: The United States During Reconstruction and the Gilded Age, 1865-1896, The Oxford History of the United States, gen. ed. David Kennedy (New York: Oxford, 2017).

[14]Edward N. Akin, Flagler: Rockefeller Partner and Florida Baron (Kent, OH: Kent State University, 1988), 2-6.

[15]Ibid., 12-19.

[16]Ibid., 8, 26-27.

[17]Ibid., 98-103,108-09.

[18]Chandler, Flagler, 85-89.

[19]Ibid., 90, 95-98; Flagler to Anderson, Nov. 27, 1885, quoted in Akin, Flagler, 116.

[20]Chandler, Flagler, 100-04.

[21]Jacksonville News Herald interview of 1887, quoted in Les Standiford, The Last Train to Paradise: Henry Flagler and the Spectacular Rise and Fall of the Railroad that Crossed an Ocean (New York: Three Rivers, 2002), 47.

[22]Graham, Flagler, 396-98,493-94; Akin, Flagler, 148-51; Chandler, Flagler, 105-06, 110-15.

[23]Chandler, Flagler, 119-23,135.

[24]Ibid., 123-27.

[25] *Ibid.*, 128-32.

[26] *Ibid.*, 135-41. See also: Charles W. Pierce, <u>Pioneer Life in Southeast Florida</u>, ed. by Donald Walter Curl (Coral Gables, FL: University of Miami, 1970); Donald W. Curl, <u>Palm Beach County: An Illustrated History</u> (Northridge, CA: Windsor, 1986), 8-57.

[27] Chandler, <u>Flagler,</u> 158-86; Standiford, <u>The Last Train</u>, 99, 201-03. See also: Thelma Peters, <u>Biscayne Country, 1870-1926</u> (Miami, FL: Banyan Books, 1981).

[28] Standiford, <u>The Last Train</u>, 95-96.

[29] Williamson, <u>Florida Politics in the Gilded Age</u>, 72-78; Tebeau, <u>History of Florida</u>, 278-81; Arsenault, <u>St. Petersburg</u>, 46-48.

[30] Lucille Rieley Rights, <u>A Portrait of St. Lucie County, Florida</u> (Virginia Beach, VA: Donning Company, 1994), 44-49.

[31] Jack E. Davis, <u>The Gulf: The Making of an American Sea</u> (New York: Liveright Publishing, 2018), 153-166. According to Izaak Walton's <u>The Compleat Angler</u> (1653), an "angler" was primarily a person from higher social standing. Such was the case with Florida's late nineteenth sports fishermen and women. *Ibid.*, 157-58.

[32] Louis A. Perez, Jr., "Between Encounter and Experience: Florida in the Cuban Imagination," *Florida Historical Quarterly* 82 (Fall 2003):174; Standiford, <u>The Last Train</u>, 72, 194, 197; Tebeau, <u>Florida</u>, 148; Maloney, <u>Key West</u>, iv, 26. See also: Gerald E. Poyo, "Key West and the Cuban Ten Years War," *Florida Historical Quarterly* 57 (Jan. 1979): 289-307.

[33] Davis, <u>Jacksonville</u>, 358-66.

[34] *Ibid.*, 324, 341-50, 500.

[35] Shermyen, <u>1989 Florida Abstract</u>, 3; Rodney E. Dillon, Jr., "South Florida in 1860," *Florida Historical Quarterly* 60 (April 1982): 442-50.

[36] Gary R. Mormino and George E. Pozzetta, <u>The Immigrant World of Ybor City: Italians and Their Latin Neighbors in Tampa, 1885-1985</u> (Chicago, IL: University of Illinois, 1987), 50-55, 64-68, 72-73.

[37] Tabeau, <u>Florida</u>, 285-86.

[38] Arsenault, <u>St. Petersburg</u>, 60-66, 79-89.

[39] McNally, <u>Catholicism in South Florida</u>, 29; Thelma Peters, <u>Miami 1909</u> (Miami, FL: Banyon Books, 1985), 63; Tebeau, <u>Florida</u>, 287; Chandler, Flagler, 136-37; Federal Writers' Project, <u>The WPA Guide to Florida: The Federal Writers' Project Guide</u>

to 1930s Florida, 1939 Reprint (New York: Pantheon, 1984), 213, 230.

[40]Michael J. McNally, Catholic Parish Life on Florida's West Coast, 1860-1968 (St. Petersburg, FL: Catholic Media Ministries, 1996), 152-53; Michael V. Gannon, Florida: A Short History (Gainesville, FL: University Press of Florida, 1996), 59.

[41]McNally, Catholic Parish Life, 51-52, 148-151.

[42]Ibid., 39; Michael J. McNally, "Catholic Parish Life in the Antebellum South: Columbus, Georgia, 1830-1960," American Catholic Studies 113 (Spring-Summer 2002): 24-25.

[43]McNally, Catholic Parish Life, 11; Aresenault, St. Petersburg, 86 (picture of a cracker homestead, c. 1897). For more on the Florida frontier of the period, see: Brown, Florida's Peace River Frontier; Michel Oesterreicher, Pioneer Family: Life on Florida's Twentieth Century Frontier (Tuscaloosa. AL: University of Alabama, 1996); Pat S. Lane, "Florida is a Blessed Country: Letters to Iowa from a Florida Settler [Port Charlotte, 1885-87]," Florida Historical Quarterly 64 (April 1986): 432-45.

[44]Jay Barnes, Florida's Hurricane History (Chapel Hill, NC: University of North Carolina, 1998), 70-82; Thomas Graham, "The Flagler Era, 1865-1913" in The Oldest City: St. Augustine Saga of Survival, ed. by Jean Parker Waterbury (St. Augustine, FL: St. Augustine Historical Society, 1983), 204.

[45]Graham, "Flagler Era," 204; Chandler, Flagler, 144-45, 167-72; 180-81.

[46]Wilbur Downs, "Yellow Fever," Encyclopedia Americana, vol. 29, 1982 ed., 661-63; Maloney, Key West, 82; Graham, "Flagler Era," 198-99; Francois Delaporte, The History of Yellow Fever: An Essay on the Birth of Tropical Medicine, trans. by Arthur Goldhammer (Cambridge, MA: Massachusetts Institute of Technology, 1991), 1, 4, 7, 15-16, 19-29. See also: Margaret Humphreys, Yellow Fever and the South (Baltimore, MD: Johns Hopkins University, 1999).

[47]Graham, "Flagler Era," 203.

[48]Mormino and Pozzetta, Ybor City, 97-174; McNally, Catholic Parish Life, 72-73.

[49]McNally, Catholic Parish Life, 72; Chandler, Flagler, 179-80; Standiford, The Last Train, 67.

[50]Davis, Jacksonville, 219-27, 401.

[51]Tabeau, Florida, 4, 311-12.

[52]McNally, Catholic Parish Life, 64-66.

<sup>53</sup>Tebeau, <u>Florida</u>, 312-13; McNally, <u>Catholic Parish Life</u>, 66.

<sup>54</sup>Ivan Musicant, <u>Empire By Default: The Spanish-American War and the Dawn of the American Century</u> (New York: Henry Holt, 1998), 263, 267-74; Tebeau, <u>Florida</u>, 314-19; McNally, <u>Catholic Parish Life</u>, 66-67.

<sup>55</sup>Tebeau, <u>Florida</u>, 320; Davis, <u>Jacksonville</u>, 209-15; McNally, <u>Catholicism in South Florida</u>, 49.

<sup>56</sup>Tebeau, <u>Florida</u>, 320-21.

<sup>57</sup>*Ibid.*, 321-23.

<sup>58</sup>Musicant, <u>Empire</u>, 589, 597; Tebeau, <u>Florida</u>, 324-26; McNally, <u>Catholic Parish Life</u>, 68.

<sup>59</sup>Chronicles, Tampa, May 3, 4, June 4, 6, 7, July 3, 31, Aug. 1, 1898, L-5, ASNJM.

<sup>60</sup>Moore to Corrigan, July 11, 1898, G-25-Folder M-N; Moore to Corrigan, July 27, 1898, G-25-Folder M-N, AANY.

## *Chapter 7*

<sup>1</sup><u>Sadlier's Catholic Directory-1878</u> (New York: D & J Sadlier, 1878), 376-79, hereafter called <u>OCD</u>; Moore to Cardinal Alessandro Franchi, Prefect of POF, Aug. 23, 1877, *Scritt.*, vol. 28, fols. 445r-446r, APF at AUND.

<sup>2</sup>Moore to Gibbons, Nov. 8, 1877, 73-H-12, AAB at AASMSU; Moore to Magnien, Oct. 8, Dec. 4, 1878, May 2, Aug. 5, 1879, April 26, 28, Aug. 31, 1880, St. Augustine File, RG-38; Student Personnel Files, RG-49, SA at AASMSU; Bishop Moore's *Ad limina* Report to Rome-1885, ASSJ.

<sup>3</sup><u>OCD-1881</u>, 36; <u>OCD-1882</u>, 47; <u>OCD-1883</u>, 52; Moore to Gibbons, Nov. 20, 1877, 73-I-7, AAB at AASMSU; Moore to Propagation of the Faith (Paris), Sept. 2, 1879, #6259; June 30, 1880, #6263, ADSA.

<sup>4</sup>Moore to O'Connell, July 21, Aug. 31, Sept. 17, 28, 1886, MDRI, Reel 12; Moore to O'Connell, Feb. 22, 1888, MDRI, Reel 4, ADR at AUND; Robert Reardon to Moore, Jan. 8, 1888, 2(x)-C-18, ADSA. Moore did not want to repeat what he considered the errors of Bishop Lynch in Charleston whom he felt was indiscriminate in accepting troubled priests into the diocese of Charleston. Moore to Lynch, June 1, 1877, 63-C-4, ADC.

<sup>5</sup>Moore to Gibbons, July 5, 1883, Gibbons Papers, 77-I-2, AAB at AASMSU; Moore's 1885 *Ad limina* Report to Rome, ASSJ.

[6]OCD-1901, 480-83; OCD-1902, 465-96; OCD-1969, 716-18. For more on Irish priests in the U.S. see: Edmund M. Hogan, The Irish Missionary Movement: A Historical Survey, 1830-1980 (Dublin: Gill and Macmillan, 1990); William L. Smith, Irish Priests in the United States: A Vanishing Subculture (Langham, MD: University Press of America, 2004).

[7]Margaret Humphreys, Yellow Fever and the South (Baltimore: Johns Hopkins Univ., 1999), 5.

[8]Ibid., 4-13, 27-31.

[9]Moore to Gibbons, Oct. 9, 1877, 73-F-8; Nov. 8, 1877, 73-H-12; Nov. 20, 1877, 73-I-7, AAB, at AASMSU.

[10]Oct. 5-31, 1887, Academy of the Holy Names, Tampa Chronicles, 1881-1913, L-5, ASNJM; Clavreul to Moore, Dec. 7, 1887, 2(a)-G-6; Dec. 8, 1887, 2(a)-G-8, ADSA; Humphreys, Yellow Fever, 119-20; T. Frederick Davis, History of Jacksonville and Vicinity, 1513-1924 (St. Augustine, FL: Florida Historical Society, 1925), 176.

[11]Michael J. McNally, Catholic Parish Life on Florida's West Coast, 1860-1968 (St. Petersburg, FL: Catholic Media Ministries, 1996), 32.

[12]Personnel File, Swembergh, n.d., 2(x)-C-22, Clavreul to Moore, Dec. 8, 1887; 2(a)-G-8, ADSA; OCD-1888, 327-28; Michael V. Gannon, Rebel Bishop: The Life and Era of Augustin Verot (Milwaukee: Bruce, 1964), 27-29; McNally, Parish Life, 87.

[13]Moore to Pace, Sept. 12, 1888, 2-P-15, ADSA; OCD-1888, 327-28; OCD-1889, 371-73; McNally, Parish Life, 87-88.

[14]Moore to Pace, Sept., 12, 1888, 2-P-15; Renwick to Moore, Nov. 3, 1888, 2-P-16, ADSA; Moore to Gibbons, Dec. 3, 1888, 85-K-4, AAB at AASMSU; Humphreys, Yellow Fever, 5, 120-21; Davis, Jacksonville, 180-88; Charles S. Adams, ed., Report of the Jacksonville Auxiliary Sanitary Association of Jacksonville, Florida - Covering the Work of the Association during the Yellow Fever Epidemic, 1888 (Jacksonville, FL: Executive Committee of the Association, 1889); Margaret C. Fairlie, "The Yellow Fever Epidemic of 1888 in Jacksonville," Florida Historical Quarterly 19 (Oct. 1940): 95-108. Kenny was born in Delhi, NY, on Jan. 12, 1852. He studied at St. Bonaventure College, Bonaventure, NY, and was ordained by Moore on Jan. 15, 1879. After starting as an Assistant Pastor at Immaculate Conception, Jacksonville, he was named Pastor of St. Monica's, Palatka in 1881, and in 1884 he came to Jacksonville as Pastor of Immaculate Conception. In

May of 1901 a Jacksonville fire burned the church, rectory and St. Mary's Orphanage. Kenny spearheaded a successful city-wide fund drive that eventually in 1910 rebuilt those institutions. He was Moore's Vicar General from 1889 to 1901. In 1902 he succeeded Moore as the third bishop of St. Augustine, until his death on Oct. 24, 1913. OCD-1879 to 1901; McNally, Parish Life, 101.

[15]Moore to POF, Paris, Dec. 7, 1882, POF #6275, ADSA; William Dayton, "Pasco Pioneers: Catholic Settlements in San Antonio, St. Leo, and Vicinity" *Tampa Bay History* 1 (Fall/Winter 1979): 33-35; Edmund F. Dunne, Our American Sicily (San Antonio, FL: San Antonio Colony, 1883).

[16]Moore to Gibbons, Dec. 3, 1888, 85-K-4, AAB at AASMSU; Thomas H. Clancy, SJ., Our Friends (Second Edition; New Orleans: Jesuit Provincial Residence, 1989), 21, 121; Clancy, "Jesuits in the South: The Last 150 Years," The Southern Jesuits 2 (Aug. 1982): 13; McNally, Parish Life 4, 90. See also: John T. McGreevy, American Jesuits and the World: How an Embattled Religious Order Made Modern Catholicism Global (Princeton, NJ: Princeton University, 2016).

[17]Academy of the Holy Names, Chronicles 1881-1913, Oct. 17, 1888, Oct. 5, 1894, L-5, ASNJM; Supplement to House Records, Tampa, vol. I, 1888-1921, "Memoirs of de Carriere" (written Sept. 21, 1899); de Carriere "Note for the Record," Feb. 28, 1908; de Carriere to Thomas Slevin, May 15, 1908, ANOPSJ; "Memoirs of de Carriere," Oct. 4, 1894, Ybor City Missions, 1891-1944, Scrapbook, ASSJ; McNally, Parish Life, 88-89. See also: Michael J. McNally, "Father Philippe de Carriere: Jesuit Pioneer on Florida's West Coast, 1888-1902" *Tampa Bay History* 17 (Fall/Winter, 1995): 35-46.

[18]McNally, Parish Life, 14-15; T. Frederick Davis, "The Disston Land Purchase," *Florida Historical Quarterly* 17 (Jan. 1939): 200-10; Canter Brown, Jr., *Florida's Peace River Frontier* (Gainesville, FL: University of Florida Presses), 261-62, 268, 273.

[19]McNally, Parish Life, 15-16.; G. Hutchinson Smyth, The Life of Henry Bradley Plant (New York: G.P. Putnam's Sons, 1898); Dudley S. Johnson, "Henry Bradley Plant and Florida," *Florida Historical Quarterly* 45 (Oct. 1966): 118-32; Canter Brown, Jr., "Tampa and the Coming of the Railroad," *Sunland Tribune* 17 (Nov. 1991): 13-18.

[20]Gary R. Mormino and George E. Pozzetta, The Immigrant World of Ybor City: Italians and Their Latin Neighbors in Tampa,

1885-1985 (Chicago: University of Illinois, 1987), 47, 50, 53-54, 63-73; McNally, Parish Life, 16-17; Gary R. Mormino, "Tampa: From Hell Hole to the Good Life" in Sunbelt Cities: Politics and Growth Since World War II , ed. by Richard M. Bernard and Bradley R. Rice (Austin, TX: University of Texas, 1983), 139; Gerard E. Poyo, "Cuban Patriots in Key West, 1878-1886: Guardians at the Separatist Ideals," Florida Historical Quarterly 61 (July 1982): 20-36; L. Glenn Westfall, "Latin Entrepreneurs and the Birth of Ybor City," Tampa Bay History 7 (Fall/Winter 1985): 5-21.

[21]Sacred Heart Church, Tampa, Sacramental Records, 1860 to Present; de Carriere to Father Richard White, SJ, June 19, 1902, Supplement to house Records, vol. I, de Carriere to T. Slevin, March 15, 1908, Varia File, Box-Historical Items, Tampa, 1910-1930, ANOPSJ. Irish-born John O'Shanahan was Superior of the New Orleans Jesuits from April 22, 1888, until Nov. 14, 1891, when he was removed from his office because of alcoholism. He died on June 6, 1913. Notebook on Provincials, ANOPSJ; Clancy, Our Friends, 123.

[22]Clancy, "Jesuits in the South," 9-13; McGreevy, American Jesuits, 10-25, 104-41.

[23]"History of the Church in Florida, 1889-1921," Cabinet 18, Drawer 2, ADSP; Supplement to House Records, Tampa, vol. I, "Florida Counties Which Belong to the Jesuits of Louisiana," AR-49; Moore to O'Shanahan, Oct. 15, 1889; "Agreement between Moore and O'Shanahan," Sept. 3, 1891, ANOPSJ; McNally, Parish Life, 103.

[24]Supplement to House Records, Tampa, vol. I, 1888-1921, de Carriere Journal, April 20-June 5, 1889, Varia File, de Carriere to T. Sleven, May 15, 1908, ANOPSJ; McNally, Parish Life, 95, 104.

[25]McNally, Parish Life, 93-94.

[26]Ibid., 95-96. Tyrell returned to Tampa in 1909. From 1909-11 he served as an excurr., then from 1911 to 1924, he served as the first pastor of Our Lady of Mercy, Ybor City. Ibid.,104.

[27]House Diary, Tampa, April 20, 24, May 8, July 11, 12, 1898, ANOPSJ; William Tyrell, SJ, "With the Soldiers in Tampa," Woodstock Letters 28 (1899): 25,27, 29-31, 33-34; McNally, Parish Life, 67-68, 97-98.

[28]Supplement to House Records, Tampa, vol. 1, Nov. 25, 1890; Sept. 11, Oct. 7, Nov. 19, Dec. 15, 1892; Jan. 19, 26, Feb. 14, April

2, 7, 10, 24, March 13, 27, 1893; April 20, 1894, ANOSPSJ; Clancy, Our Friends, 19, 124.

[29]Supplement to House Records, Tampa, vol. 1, Feb. 18, 1890 - Nov. 15, 1895; House Diary, Aug. 25, 1892; March 5, 1896 - June 28, 1901; July 30, 1901 [misdated July 27], ANOPSJ; Moore to Pace, Aug. 2, 1887, 2-N-23, ADSA; Academy of the Holy Names, Tampa, Chronicles 1881-1913, L-5, June 1, 1900, ASNJM.

[30]Moore to POF, Paris, Dec. 7, 1882, POF #6275, ADSA; Edmund F. Dunne, Our American Sicily (San Antonio, FL: San Antonio Colony, 1883); *Tampa Tribune,* Jan. 7, 1990; James J. Horgan, Pioneer College: The Centennial History of Saint Leo College, Saint Leo Abbey, and Holy Name Priory (St. Leo, FL: St. Leo College, 1989), 6-33, 44-50, 62-63; William Dayton, "Pasco Pioneers: Catholic Settlements in San Antonio, St. Leo, and Vicinity," *Tampa Bay History* 1 (Fall/Winter 1979): 33-35.

[31]Wimmer to Moore, March 21, 1887, 2-A-9; Roman Agreement, Benedictines to Moore, June 1, 1887, 2-A-11, ADSA; OCD-1887, 317-19; OCD-1892, 430-32; *Tampa Tribune,* Jan. 7, 1990; Horgan, Pioneer College, 2, 18, 21-27, 31-33, 40, 44-45. Perhaps seeing the error of his former ways, Father O'Boyle later developed warm relations with the Florida Benedictines, often taking his annual retreat at St. Leo's. With his death in 1927, he was buried in the McCabe family plot (his in-laws) in St. Anthony Parish Cemetery. Horgan, Pioneer College, 28.

[32]Horgan, Pioneer College, 49, 61-68. For more on Abbot Haid, see; Dom Paschal Baumstein,OSB, My Lord of Belmont: A Biography of Leo Haid (Belmont, NC: Herald House, 1985).

[33]Horgan, Pioneer College, 68-86.

[34]Mohr to Moore, Dec. 5, 1890, 2-B-6; Mohr to Moore, Oct. 12, 1894, 2-D-1; Mohr to Moore, "School Report - St. Leo's College - 1897," 2-D-4, ADSA; Horgan, Pioneer College, 183-203; Baumstein, My Lord of Belmont, 130-31.

[35]McNally, Parish Life, 105-06.

[36]Horgan, Pioneer College, 263-65.

[37]Quoted in *Ibid.*, 265. Unfortunately, I was unable to access St. Leo's archival sources, so information about the monks' pastoral work comes from secondary sources. Dayton, "Pasco Pioneers," 32-58.

[38]McNally, Parish Life, 36.

[39]Parish Committee (Canning, Andreau, Leonardi, Bell), Tampa, to Moore, Oct. 18, 1880, 2(A)-D-9; Lynch to Moore,

Oct. 26, 1880, 2(A)-D-10; Lynch to Moore, Nov. 8, 1880, 2(A)-D-11, ADSA; McNally, Parish Life, 26-27; Thomas W. Spalding, "Frontier Catholicism" *Catholic Historical Review* 77 (July 1991): 470-84.

[40]Moore to St. Louis Committee, Nov. 18, 1880, 2(A)-D-12, ADSA; Academy of the Holy Names, Tampa, Chronicles, 1881-1913, July 18, 1881, L-5, ASNJM; OCD-1884, 443; McNally, Parish Life, 29-32.

[41]O'Boyle, *Notitiae -1890,* for the Missions of Volusia and Brevard, 2(A)-T-1, ADSA; Moore to Propagation of the Faith, Rome, *Ad limina, relatio* 1885-1895, New Series, 119/621-37, APF at AUND (trans. by Msgr. Christopher J. Schreck).

[42]OCD-1877, 317-18; OCD-1888, 327-28; Promissory Note for $500, Father Joseph Creed, May 5, 1891 (Creed's check bounced, Aug. 6, 1891, but Moore pays off note with the 10 percent per annum interest on July 20, 1891), 2(z)-B-13; St. Mary Star of the Sea, *Notitiae-1878,* 2(y)-B-2; William Cotter to Moore, July 28, 1891, 2(y)-E-14; Cotter to Moore, Aug. 3, 1891, 2(y)-E-16; L.P. Lawrence to Moore, Sept. 5, 1891, 2(y)-E-18; Trustees of All Souls Church, Sanford, to Moore, Dec. 20, 1891, 2(y)-E-20; Michael Fox to Moore, n.d. (c. Feb. 1893), 2(y)-E-21; Kilcoyne to Moore, Aug. 19, 1891, 2(A)-H-20, ASDA; Moore to Gibbons, Nov. 5, 1891, 89-C-3, Gibbons Papers, AAB at AASMSU.

[43]Gannon, Rebel Bishop, 149, 230; Hugon to the Church Building Association (Tallahassee), Feb. 7, 1897, 2(x)-D-4; Hugon, "History of Catholicism in Tallahassee," (n.d. - c.1897), 2(x)-D-12, ADSA; OCD-1881, 423.

[44]*Notitiae-1878, St. Mary Star of the Sea* (the new expenditure policy is printed on the bottom of the form), 2(y)-B-12, ADSA.

[45]"Report on Mater Dolorosa, Tallahassee," Hugon to Moore, n.d. (1895), 2(A)-P-2; Hugon to the Church Building Association, Feb. 7, 1897, 2(x)-D-4, ADSA.

[46]Hugon to the Catholic Church Building Association, Feb. 7, 1897, 2(x)-D-4, ADSA.

[47]Catholic Church Building Association, Tallahassee, to Moore, Feb. 10, 1897, 2(x)-D-7, ADSA.

[48]Hugon to Catholic Church Building Association, Tallahassee, March 11, 1897, 2(x)-D-8, ADSA. We have no extant copies of correspondence from Moore to Hugon or from Moore to the Building Association.

⁴⁹Catholic Building Association, Tallahassee, to Moore, March 13, 1897, 2(x)-D-9; Catholic Building Association, Tallahassee, April 1, 1897, 2(x)-D-11, ADSA. Moore never went to Tallahassee for Confirmation as parishioners requested. <u>Register of Confirmations, 1871-1905</u>, ADSA. On the other hand, the Building Association never took their case to the Cardinal Gibbons (since there is no evidence in Baltimore Archdiocesan Archives of this), which suggests some accommodation was made to the satisfaction of the lay board.

⁵⁰<u>OCD-1901</u>, 480-82.

⁵¹Supplement to House Records, Tampa, vol. I, Sept. 17, Oct. 3, Oct. 4, 1894; House Diary, Tampa, Sept. 17, Oct. 3, Oct. 4, 1894, ASNJM.

⁵²Ghione to Moore, Sept. 19, 1887, 2(A)-C-8; Ghione to Moore, n.d. (c. early 1879), 2(y)-B-10; Ghione to Moore, n.d. (c. early 1879), 2(y)-B-11; Ghione to Moore, n.d. (c. 1880), 2(y)-8-15; Ghione to Moore, Dec. 20, 1897, 2(y)-C-23; St. Mary, Star of the Sea, *Notitiae-1899*, 2(y)-C-24; "St Ambrose Accounts for the Year 1884," (not on the *Notitiae* form), 2(y)-D-6; Moore to Hugon, April 10, 1891, 2(a)-K-5, ADSA.

⁵³2-P-17, Moore to Pace, Mary 10, 1889, ADSA; Moore to Sadlier, June 28, 1889, John Gilmary Shea Correspondence, I-M File, Box 13, MC51, PAHRC.

⁵⁴Moore to Gibbons, Nov. 2, 1880, 75-M-2, AAB at AASMSU; Moore to O'Connell, July 21, Oct. 30, 1886, MDRI, Reel 12, ADR at AUND; Moore to Pace, Feb. 10, 1887, 2-N-14; Moore to Pace, April 25, 1887, 2-N-15, ADSA; Moore to O'Connell, Feb. 22, 1888, MDRI, Reel 4, ADR at AUND; "An Inventory of Edward Aloysius Pace Papers," Biographical Note, ACUA. Moore had several Vicar Generals during his episcopacy: Peter Dufau (whom he inherited from Verot), 1877-1880; S. Langlade, 1881; there is no record as to who was V.G. from 1882-84; Henry Clavreul, 1885-87; Edward Pace, 1887-88; William Kenny, 1889-1901; <u>OCD-1888-1902</u>.

## *Chapter 8*

¹Council of Baltimore III, 1884, 2(x)-A-1, ADSA; Thomas W. Spalding, <u>The Premier See: A History of the Archdiocese of Baltimore, 1789-1989</u> (Baltimore: Johns Hopkins University,

1989), 237-38; The Catholic Directory-1901 (Milwaukee: M. Wiltzius & Co., 1901), 482; Michael J. McNally, Parish Life on Florida's West Coast, 1860-1968 (St. Petersburg, FL: Catholic Media Ministries, 1996), 154, 182; Michael J. McNally, Catholicism in South Florida, 1868-1968 (Gainesville, FL: University Presses of Florida, 1984), 21-22, 26, 67.

[2]Phelan to Moore, Feb. 4. 1889, 2(A)-G-20; Phelan to Gerard, OSB, Feb. 4, 1889, 2(A)-G-21; Kaufmann, to "Whom it May Concern" (a letter of recommendation for the four Sisters), Feb. 23, 1889, 2(A)-G-22; Sister M. Dolorosa, OSB, to Moore, Feb. 25, 1889, 2(A)-G-23, ADSA; Sister Margaret Dunne, OSB, "San Antonio School Memories of the First Hundred Years" in Saint Anthony School Centennial, 1884-1984 (Dade City, FL: Quality Impressions, 1984); McNally, Parish Life, 81-83.

[3]Moore to Pace, Dec. 31, 1889, Secret Archives, 1865-1940, ADSA; James J. Horgan, Pioneer College: The Centennial History of St. Leo College, St. Leo Abbey, and Holy Name Priory (St. Leo, FL: St. Leo College Press, 1989), 46, 50-52. Father Pilz died at Mary Help Abbey, Belmont, N.C., on Sept. 20, 1891, at the age of fifty-six. Ibid., 46.

[4]St. Anthony School Centennial; Horgan, Pioneer College, 52; McNally, Parish Life, 149. See also: "St. Anthony of Padua Catholic School, San Antonio, FL, - History" at www. stanthonyschoolfl.org.

[5]Horgan, Pioneer College, 53-55; McNally, Parish Life, 150.

[6]Horgan, Pioneer College, 276-77. Horgan quotes Moore's letter to Haid on page 277.

[7]Ibid., 278. Horgan quotes Roth.

[8]Moore to Mother Katharine, Oct. 29, 1897, H-110, Agreements Files, Ybor City File, 1897-1900, ASBS.

[9]Mother Boniface to Moore, Aug. 4, 1898, 2(A)-R-10; Mother Boniface to Moore, Aug. 15, 1898, 2(A)-R-11; Muhr, OSB, to Moore, Aug. 15, 1898, 2(A)-R-12, ADSA; Horgan, Pioneer College, 279. Horgan quotes the Moore to Menges letter.

[10]Verot to Bishop Bouger of Montreal (quoted), Feb. 27, 1868, Introduction to the Key West Chronicles (translation), ASNJM. Since the Sisters were at the time a diocesan community and remained so until 1877, Bishop Verot needed the permission of their bishop in Montreal to come to Key West. Father Allard acted as the novice master for the Sisters beginning in November 1843. He became pastor in Key West in 1867, recruited by Verot.

Key West Chronicles (translation), Oct. 15, 1868, ASNJM. After departing from Montreal the Sisters made their way to New York City, then by boat to Key West, hence enhancing the one Sister's first impressions of Key West, which was no comparison to New York. Introduction to the Key West Chronicles (translation), Oct. 24, 1868, ASNJM; Michael V. Gannon, <u>Cross in the Sand: The Early Church in Florida, 1513-1870</u> (Gainesville, FL: University Presses of Florida, 1965), 185; McNally, <u>Catholicism in South Florida,</u> 21.

[11]Mallory deeded the barracks and land to Bishop Verot on Dec. 8, 1868. Key West Chronicles (translation), Oct. 24, Dec. 8, 1868, ASNJM. Gerald E. Poyo, "Cuban Patriots in Key West, 1878-1886: Guardians at the Separatist Ideals," *Florida Historical Quarterly* 61 (July 1982): 20-36; Gerald E. Poyo, "Key West and the Cuban Ten Years War" *Florida Historical Quarterly* 57 (Jan. 1979): 289-307.

[12]*Morning Star and Catholic Messenger* (photostat), June 20, 1875, 1(x)-H-14, ADSA; Moore to Gibbons, March 12, 1886, 80-P-4, AAB at AASMSU.

[13]McNally, <u>Parish Life</u>, 16; McNally, <u>Catholicism in South Florida,</u> 31.

[14]Key West Chronicles (translation), Oct. 3, 1873, Sept. 2, 1878, ASNJM; La Rocque to Verot, March 29, 1875, 1-A-2; Sisters of the Holy Names to Moore, June (n.d.) 1877, 2(y)-D-1, ADSA.

[15]Sisters of the Holy Names to Moore, June 1877, 2(y)-D-1; St. Mary Star of the Sea, Key West, *Notitiae-1888*, ADSA; School Reports, Key West, 1887-88, ASNJM.

[16]Sister M. Theophilus, SNJM, to Moore, Dec. 8, 1890, 2(A)-H-9, ADSA; McNally, <u>Parish Life</u>, 47-51, 94, 159-62.

[17]McNally, <u>Catholicism in South Florida</u>, 26, Table 2.3.

[18]McNally, <u>Parish Life</u>, 149-50, Table 7.1.

[19]*Ibid.*, 157.

[20]*Ibid.*, 46.

[21]Sister Thomas Joseph McGoldrick, SSJ, <u>Beyond the Call: The Legacy of the Sisters of St. Joseph of St. Augustine, Florida</u> (Bloomington, IN: Xlibris, 2008), 25-31; Patricia Byrne, CSJ, "Sisters of St. Joseph, Americanization of the French Tradition" *U.S. Catholic Historian* 5 (Summer/Fall 1986): 243.

[22]"St. Joseph's Academy," St. Augustine, Annual Report - 1881," 2-M-5; "St. Joseph's Academy, St. Augustine, Annual

Report-1882," 2-M-8, ADSA; McGoldrick, Beyond the Call, 38-68, 82, 130-32, 180, 257; Gannon, Cross in the Sand, 183-84.

[23]McGoldrick, Beyond the Call, 278-79; Moore, Memo to Self - SSJ Finances in St. Augustine, Feb. n.d., 1896, 2-R-6, ADSA. Another example of Moore's financial help for the SSJ's was in 1881 when he donated $500 to St. Joseph's Academy, St. Augustine, which represented 13.5 percent of their total receipts that year. "St. Joseph's Academy, St. Augustine, Annual Report - 1881," 2-M-5, ADSA.

[24]Various Annual School Reports 1900-01, ADSA; McGoldrick, Beyond the Call, 378-79.

[25]McGoldrick, Beyond the Call, 301, 311; McNally, Parish Life, 162-63. To point to the poverty of their existence in Ybor City, one Sister assigned to St. Joseph's Academy there wrote, "'We would have starved, but for the sale of our lace.'" Quoted in Byrne, "Americanization," 261.

[26]"Circular to Priests," Jan. 4, 1895, 2-D-10, ADSA.

[27]Byrne, "Americanization," 241, 244, 249, 250.

[28]Ibid., 250, 252-262, 271; Elisabeth C. Davis, "The Disappearance of Mother Agnes Spencer: The Centralization Controversy and the Antebellum Catholic Church," American Catholic Studies 130 (Summer 2019): 31-52. Davis stresses that most of the Sisters of St. Joseph in the U.S. had broken ties with France by 1860. They either centralized authority around their foundation house, as with the Carondelet's, or within their diocese around their local bishop.

[29]Sister Mary Albert Lussier, SSJ, "Data for an Article Concerning the Sisters of St. Joseph of St. Augustine," 502.01, ASSJ; Sister L. Antonia, SSJ, to Moore, Dec. 6, 1890, "Report on St. Joseph's Convent, Fernandina" (written in French), 1(A)-H-8, ADSA; McGoldrick, Beyond the Call, 275-77, 316, 373. A "List of SSJ Superiors" was supplied by Sister Catherine Bitzer, SSJ, archivist for the ADSA and ASSJ.

[30]This letter is quoted in: McGoldrick, Beyond the Call, 317-18. This letter is not to be found in Moore's Papers, since he very rarely made copies of his correspondence.

[31]Sister Pelegie Boyer, SSJ, Superior General to Moore, Dec. 14, 1899 [translated by Sister Mary Albert Lussier, SSJ], 2(A)-R-24, ADSA. Neither the Bishop of Le Puy nor the SSJ General Superior wanted to get stuck paying the transportation costs for

Sisters returning to France. They both preferred putting that financial burden on Moore's shoulders.

[32]This letter is quoted in: McGoldrick, <u>Beyond the Call</u>, 319-21.

[33]Moore to Mother Lazarus, April 1, 1885, Bishop Moore File, 130.1, ASSJ; Moore to Gibbons, March 17, 1885, 79-G-6, AAB at AASMSU; McGoldrick, <u>Beyond the Call</u>, 338-39, 343-44, 363, 371-73; McNally, <u>Parish Life</u>, 163-64; Bitzer, "List of SSJ Superiors," ADSA.

[34]This letter from Mother Lazarus to the General Superior, Le Puy, Sept. 28, 1908, is quoted in its entirety in: McGoldrick, <u>Beyond the Call</u>, 321-25

[35]Moore to Sister Lazarus, Feb. 13, 1885; April 1, 13, 26; Aug. 26, 1885; Aug. 1, 12, 1889; June 5, 1890, Bishop Moore File, 130.1, ASSJ; McGoldrick, <u>Beyond the Call</u>, 335-37, 339-42, 344-49.

[36]*Quemadmodum*, decreed by Pope Leo XIII on December 14, 1890, and attested to by I. Cardinal Verga, Prefect of the Congregation of Bishops and Regulars, and promulgated by M. Carinal Ledochowski, Secretary of State, December 17, 1890, in *Leonis XIII, Pontificis Maximi Acta*, vol. VIII-X (Graz, Austria: Adademischke Druck - University of Verlagsanstalt, 1971), 353-58 (translation by Msgr. Christopher J. Schreck); "The Custom of Telling Faults to the Superior," Mother Magdalen's Annals, 1891-92, vol. 4, 267-68, ASBS.

[37]"Recruiting in Canada," St. Augustine Academy Chronicles, 1890, 1894, 1895, 1897, ASSJ; Byrne, "Americanization," 241-72; McGoldrick, <u>Beyond the Call</u>, 275-77, 363; McNally, <u>Parish Life</u>, 110.

[38]Moore to Rev. Mother [Pélagie Boyer], Jan. 31, 1900, quoted in Byrne, "Americanization," 259; also quoted in McGoldrick, <u>Beyond the Call</u>, 319-21.

[39]Moore [from Chicago] to Mother Lazarus, June 5, 1890, ASSJ; McNally, <u>Parish Life</u>, 100; McGoldrick, <u>Beyond the Call</u>, 326; Interview, Sister Thomas Joseph, McGoldrick, SSJ, St. Augustine, FL, January 20, 2003.

[40]Register of Confirmations, 1871-1905, Entries for 1899-1900, ADSA. The late Michael Gannon also shared the theory of Moore's mental debility from mid-1900, although he never offered any proof of the theory. Interview, Very Rev. Thomas Willis, rector of the Cathedral, St. Augustine, FL, with the author, June 19, 2019.

John Moore

## Chapter 9

[1]Michael J. McNally, <u>Parish Life on Florida's West Coast,</u> <u>1860-1968</u> (St. Petersburg, FL: Catholic Media Ministries, 1996), 11.

[2]*Ibid.*, 11-12. The quote is taken from the diary of Augusta Gallie Floyd, September 17, 1872, as cited in St. Ambrose Centennial Committee, <u>The Branches: Springs of Living Water,</u> Second Edition (St. Augustine, FL: Standard Printing, 1988).

[3]McNally, <u>Parish Life</u>, 26, 118, 148.

[4]*Ibid.* 170-71.

[5]Tyrell to Moore, Jan. 9, 1893, 2(A)-M-11, ADSA.

[6]Supplement to House Records, Sept. 11, 25, 29, Oct. 4, 1891; House Diary, June 30, Oct. 17, 1896; Oct. 4, 15, 1897, ANOPSJ; Chronicles, May 16, 25, 1896; March 12, 1897, L-5, ASNJM; Journal of St. Joseph Convent, Ybor City, 1891, 1897-98, ASSJ; Sister Roselina O'Neill, SNJM, "History of the Contribution of the Sisters of the Holy Names of Jesus and Mary to the Cause of Education in Florida" (M.A. Thesis, Fordham University, n.d. [ c. 1938], 50-53; McNally, <u>Parish Life</u>, 152-53,184.

[7]Bernier to Moore, June 27, 1877, 2(A)-C-4, ADSA; McNally, <u>Parish Life</u>, 38-39.

[8]St. Anthony Parish, *Notitiae,* Jan. 1, 1887 - Jan. 1, 1888, 2(y)-D-14, ADSA; Michael J. McNally, <u>Catholicism in South Florida,</u> <u>1868-1968</u> (Gainesville, FL: University Presses of Florida, 1984), 25; McNally, <u>Parish Life</u>, 126-28.

[9]McNally, <u>Parish Life</u>, 112.

[10]We know that All Souls Parish in Sanford was one of those that did have trustees. Trustees, All Souls Church, to Moore, Dec. 20 1891, 2(x)-E-20, ADSA. The Cathedral parish had trustees or wardens that went back into the early nineteenth century and reaffirmed by Bishop Verot in 1859. The wardens only transferred the Cathedral property to the ownership of the bishop (Joseph P. Hurley) on March 28, 1943. Mary-Cabrini Durkin, <u>The Cathedral-Basilica of St. Augustine and Its History, 1565-2003</u>, rev. ed. (Strasbourg, FR: *Editions du Signe,* 2003), 16.

[11]Dunne to Moore, Jan. 14, 1884, 2(A)-E-5; St Anthony Society "Report of Disaffected Colonists" to Dunne, n.d., 2(A)-E-6, ADSA.

[12]Dunne's Memorandum to Moore, Jan. 24, 1884, 1(A)-E-7, ADSA; Dallas to Clarke, March 7, 1884, Calendared Collection,

I-2-N; Dallas to Hudson, April 24, 1885, Calendared Collection, X-2-O; Dallas to Hudson, May 23, 1885, Calendared Collection, X-2-0; Dallas to Hudson, April 9, 1886, Calendared Collection, X-3-b, AUND; McNally, Parish Life, 81-84, 166.

[13]Ocala People's Petition to Msgr. A. Satollli, Oct. 21, 1893, 2(A)-21; St. Philip Neri, Ocala, *Notitiae* - Jan. 1, 1895, 2(A)-16, ADSA.

[14]Moore to Pace, July 29, 1887, 1-N-22, ADSA; Thomas Graham, Mr. Flagler's St. Augustine (Gainesville, FL: University Press of Florida, 2014), 106.

[15]Graham, Flagler's St. Augustine, 42, 81, 135; Thomas Graham, "The Flagler Era, 1865-1913" in The Oldest City: St. Augustine's Saga of Survival, ed. by Jean Parker Waterbury (St. Augustine, FL: St. Augustine Historical Society, 1983), 189-90, 193-97, 242.

[16]Graham, "Flagler Era," 105-06; McNally, Parish Life, 142.

[17]McNally, Parish Life, 94, 136-37, 142; Sister Thomas Joseph McGoldrick, SSJ, Beyond the Call: The Legacy of the Sisters of St. Joseph of St. Augustine, Florida (Bloomington, IN: Xlibris, 2008), 309. Some of the other benefactors of St. Ann Church in West Palm Beach included: J. J. O'Donohue of New York ($1,500, the altar and sanctuary furniture, the organ, the statues of St. Ann and the Blessed Virgin Mary made in Munich), John D. Crimmons of New York ($1,500 and Sacred Vessels), John McDonald, architect for Flagler's hotels, $100 and plans for the church pro bono. There were also other donors who gave smaller amounts, most were Northern visitors to Royal Poinciana Hotel in Palm Beach. St. Ann's, West Palm Beach, 1896 - File, 2(A)-P-8, ADSA.

[18]Graham, Flagler's St. Augustine, 106.

[19]Les Standiford, The Last Train to Paradise: Henry Flagler and the Spectacular Rise and Fall of the Railroad that Crossed the Sea (New York: Three Rivers Press, 2002), 97-98, 220-22; John Keegan, The Mask of Command (New York: Penguin Books, 1988), 10-11.

[20]Moore to Gibbons, March 25, 1893, 91-H-9, AAB at AASMSU.

[21]Moore to POF, Nov. 4, 1881, POF Files - Lyons, France, File L-78, #3425; James Willcox to Moore, April 2, 1883, 2-A-1; Moore to Pace, Aug. 17, 1887, 2-N-25, ADSA; James Willcox to Moore, June 25, 1883, 77-H-9, AAB at AASMSU.

[22]McNally, Parish Life, 142.

[23]*Ibid.*, 142-43, 173; McGoldrick, Beyond the Call, 272, 309-10. At Bishop Moore's request, Mother Katharine Drexel donated $2,000 to St. Peter Claver School in Tampa, founded in 1894, and taught by two Sisters of the Holy Names. In 1904 she visited St. Peter Claver (Tampa) and St. Benedict the Moor (Ybor City), since she was a benefactor for both institutions. McNally, Parish Life, 188-89.

[24]1886 *Ad limina* Report, Sept. 3, 1886, (handwritten in Italian), 2-N-11; 1892 *Ad limina* Report, Dec. 16,1892, 2-P-24, ADSA.

## *Chapter 10*

[1]Moore to Gibbons, July 5, 1883, 77-I-2, AAB at AASMSU.

[2]All Reporting Parishes, *Notitiae*, Jan.1, 1878, 2(A)-D-1 through 2(A)-D-4; *Notitiae* for all parishes of the diocese - 1877-1901, ADSA; Sadlier's Directory-1879, 382-84; Thomas W. Spalding, The Premier See: A History of the Archdiocese of Baltimore, 1789-1989 (Baltimore: Johns Hopkins University, 1989), 210. Father Hugon, who came to Tallahassee in 1876, made his financial grievances public with an open letter to his parishioners criticizing Moore in 1897. He claims that the bishop owed him $746.45 in unpaid salary (priests were given $200 a year salary, taken out of parish accounts, if the parish could afford it; if it could not the bishop was supposed to supply it). Hugon also charged Moore with not releasing $1,000 he held for the parish from the sale of the old church. Hugon to the Church Building Assoc., Feb. 7, 1897, 2(x)-D-4; Fannie Perkins to Moore, Feb. 10, 1897, 2(x)-D-8; Hugon to Building Assoc., March 11, 1897, 2(x)-D-8; Building Assoc. to Moore, March 13, 1897, 2(x)-D-9; John Winthrop to Moore, April 1, 1897, 2(x)-D-11; Hugon, "History of Catholics in Tallahassee," n.d. (c. 1897), 2(x)-D-12, ADSA. We know that Moore wrote the Building Association at least once on Feb. 17, but we do not have that letter or any others he may have sent. Moore, refusing to make a personal appearance, sent Father William Kenny, his Vicar General, to the parish to resolve the issue. Kenny said that the diocese has no money and is in debt, so Hugon's demand for money cannot be met. The strategy was to get Hugon to retire, offering him an annual pension of $200. Hugon remained in Tallahassee throughout Moore's episcopacy. Hugon, "Report on Mater Dolorosa, Tallahassee," n.d., 2(A)-P-2, ADSA.

³St. Mary, Star of the Sea, *Notitiae,* Jan. 1, 1879, 2(y)-B-12; Immaculate Conception, *Notitiae,* Jan. 1, 1881, 2(y)-D-3; Various Parishes, *Notitiae,* Jan. 1, 1878 - Jan. 1, 1881, ADSA.

⁴Daniel Hughes to Moore, Aug. 5, 1898, 2(x)-D-13; James Veale to Moore, April 9, 1899, 2(x)-E-4, ADSA; OCD-1901, 480-83; OCD-1902, 495-96; Michael J. McNally, Parish Life on Florida's West Coast, 1860-1968 (St. Petersburg, FL: Catholic Media Ministries, 1996), 102, 212-15, 222, 241, 248-49.

⁵Moore to Pace, Feb. 7, 1887, 2-N-13; Moore to Pace Feb. 10, 1887, 2-N-14; Moore to Pace, April 25, 1887, 2-N-15; Moore to Pace, May 10, 1887, 2-N-18; Register of Confirmations, 1871-1905, ADSA.

⁶Walter M. Abbott, SJ, gen. ed., The Documents of Vatican II (New York: America Press, 1966), 300, quoted from the footnote.

⁷McNally, Parish Life, 85-87, 133-35.

⁸Moore to Pace, May 10, 1889, 2-P-17, ADSA.

⁹Moore to Gibbons, Jan. 4, 1883, 22-A-3, AAB at AASMSU.

¹⁰Moore to Gibbons, Nov. 2, 1880, 75-M-2, AAB at ASSMSU; Nelson J. Callahan, ed., The Diary of Richard L. Burtsell, Priest of New York: The Early Years, 1865-1868 (New York: Arno Press, 1978), viii-ix.

¹¹John Gilmary Shea Correspondence, I-M File, Box 3, MC-51, PAHRC; Bishop Moore File, 130.1, ASSJ; Callahan, ed., Diary of Burtsell, x-xiv; Burtsell Diary, Jan. 3-10, 1887, AANY; Moore to Pace, May 14, 1887, 2-N-18; Moore to Pace, July 23, 1887, 2-N-20; Moore to Pace, Nov. 14, 1887, 2-N-30, ADSA.

¹²Msgr. Michael McGuire, "The Case of Edward McGlynn" (July 1981), G-102-Folder #1, AANY; *St. Augustine Record,* April 13, 1887; *Jacksonville Times-Union,* April 13, 1887; *The Catholic Standard,* April 30, 1887; *Charleston News and Courier,* April 13, 1887; Thomas Graham, Mr. Flagler's St. Augustine (Gainesville, FL: University Press of Florida, 2014), 105-06.

¹³Moore to Pace, May 11, 1887, 2-N-17; Moore, "Cathedral Building Fund Drive Account Book," April 15, 1887 to June 30, 1899 (162 pp.); Cathedral, *Notitiae-1887,* Jan. 1, 1888, 2-P-1, ADSA.

¹⁴Moore to Pace, July 23, 1887, 2-N-20; Moore to Pace, Aug. 2, 1887, 2-N-23; Moore to Pace, Aug. 9, 1887, 2-N-24; Moore to Pace, Aug. 17, 1887, 2-N-25; Moore to Pace, n.d. (c. Aug. 11, 1887), 2-P-2, ADSA; Sadlier's Directory-1888, 117-128.

[15]Secretary of War [signature undecipherable] to Moore, Sept. 18, 1883, 2-M-14; Moore to Pace, May 14, 1887, 2-N-18; Moore to Pace, June 6, 1887, 2-N-19; Moore to Pace, n.d. (July 29, 1887), 2-N-22; Moore to Pace, Aug. 9, 1887, 2-N-24; Moore to Pace, Aug. 27, 1887, 2-N-26; Moore to Pace, Sept. 2, 1887, 2-N-28, ADSA.

[16]Tampa Chronicles, Sept. 8, 1899; Feb. 2, 1900; July 30, Aug. 1, 1901, L-5, ASNJM; Moore to Pace, Jan. 17, 1888, 2-P-3; Moore to Pace, Jan. 24, 1888, 2-P-4; Moore to Pace, Feb. 2, 1888, 2-P-5; Moore to Pace, March 8, 1888, 2-P-6; Moore to Pace, March 13, 1888, 2-P-7; Moore to Pace, March 19, 1888, 2-P-8; Moore, Memo to Himself, Dec. 27, 1897, 2-R-18; Sister M. Theophilus, SNJM, to Moore, Dec. 8, 1890, 2(A)-H-9; Moore, "Cathedral Building Fund Drive Account Book," Jan. 28, 1888 through March 23, 1888, ADSA; Moore to O'Connell, Feb. 22, 1888; Moore to O'Connell, May 19, 1892; Moore to O'Connell, Sept. 20, 1893, MDRI, Reel 12, ADR at AUND.

[17]Moore to Pace, July 2, 1888, 2-P-10, ADSA.

[18]Moore to Pace, Nov. 14, 1887, 2-N-30; Cotter to Renwick, Aug. 27, 1888, 2-P-11; Renwick to Cotter [typed], Sept. 10, 1888, 2-P-13; Renwick to Moore, Sept. 10, 1888, 2-P-14; Renwick to Moore, Nov. 3, 1888, 2-P-16, ADSA.

[19]Moore to Gibbons, Dec. 3, 1888, 85-K-4, AAB at AASMSU; Moore to Pace, May 10, 1889, 2-P-17, ADSA.

[20]Moore to Pace, Dec. 26, 1890, 2-P-20, ADSA; George E. Buker, Jacksonville: Riverport - Seaport (Columbia, SC: University of South Carolina Press,1992), 137-39.

[21]Contract - BVM Altar - Draddy Bros., New York, to Moore, Sept. 7, 1893, 2(A)-M-20; Contract - St. Joseph Altar - Draddy Bros. to Moore, June 4, 1896, 2-R-16; Receipt - Renwick, Aspinwall, & Owen, architects, to Moore Oct. 1, 1897, 2-R-14; Receipt for BVM Altar - Moore to Draddy Bros., Dec. 22, 1897, 2-R-15 (this is one of the rare pieces of his correspondence that he kept); Moore, Memo to Self on Cathedral Fair, Feb. 25, 1900, 2-S-2; J. Massey Rhind, marble artist, to Renwick, et al.,Oct. 1, 1900 (copy sent to Moore), 2-E-6; Renwick, et al., to Moore, Oct. 10, 1900, 2-E-4; Renwick, et al., to Moore, June 28, 1900, 2-E-1; Renwick, et al., to Moore, October 15, 1900, 2-E-7; Contract with Rhind dated Oct. 20, 1900 - Renwick, et al., to Moore Oct. 23, 1900, 2-E-9; R.A. Owen to Moore, Dec. 8, 1900, 2-E-13; Renwick, et al., to Moore, Dec. 8, 1900, 2-E-13; Renwick, et al.

to Moore, March 30, 1901, 2-E-18, ADSA; "Jacksonville, FL," Wikipedia.

22POF Files (Jammes Project translation), Lyons, France, L-78, #3413-15; Paris, France, #6292, ADSA.

23F. J. Sheen, "Propagation of the Faith, Society for the," New Catholic Encyclopedia, vol. 11 (N.Y.: McGraw-Hill, 1967), 844-46; Joseph Freri, "Propagation of the Faith, Society for the," The Catholic Encyclopedia, vol. XII (N.Y.: Appleton, 1911), 461-62; Edward John Hickey, The Society for the Propagation of the Faith: It's Foundation, Organization, and Success (1822-1922) (Washington, D.C.: Catholic University of America, 1922), 30-31.

24POF Files, Lyons, France, L-78, #3414-17; Paris, France, #6254, #6277; POF, Lyons, to Moore, June 15, 1885, 2-N-4, ADSA.

25POF Files, Lyons, France, L-78, #3434, #3435, #3437; Paris, France, #6288, #6289, #6293, #6294, ADSA.

26Commission for Catholic Missions among Colored People and Indians, to Moore, Jan. (n.d.) 1893, 2(x)-A-14, ADSA; Ludwig Missionary Association, Reel 5, Ministry to Germans of Pasco County, Florida, AUND.

27Moore to Pace, Jan. 17, 1888, 2-P-3, ADSA; *Acta Episopalia* of Cardinal Gibbons, Oct. 30, 1886, AAB at AASMSU.

28First National Bank, St. Augustine, Promissory Note, June 2, 1888, 2(z)-B-2; Dec. 4, 1889, 2(z)-B-5; Jan. 6, 1890, 2(z)-B-8; Jan. 27, 1890, 2(z)-B-9; Sept. 20, 1890, 2(z)-B-10; Oct. 27, 1890, 2(z)-B-11; Dec. 3, 1890, 2(z)-B-12; June 20, 1891, 2(z)-B-14; Dec. 14, 1891, 2(z)-B-15; March 18, 1893, 2(z)-B-17; April 27, 1893, 2(z)-B-18; March 23, 1895, 2(z)-B-20; April 20, 1895, 2(z)-B-21; Dec. 4, 1895, 2(z)-B-23; The Germania Bank, Savannah, GA, Promissory Note, April 19, 1892, 2(z)-B-16; State Savings Bank of Tallahassee, Promissory Note, Jan. 31, 1898, 2(z)-B-25; Jan. 29, 1900, 2(z)-B-26; Southern Savings & Trust Co., Jacksonville, FL, Promissory Note, Oct. 3, 1899, 2(z)-B-27; Oct. 17, 1899, 2(z)-B-28, ADSA.

29Moore to Gibbons, Jan. 13, 1892, 89-J-3, AAB at AASMSU; ABishop Gibbons, Promissory Note, March 1, 1889, 2(z)-B-3; Matthew Hays, Promissory Note, April 19, 1889, 2(z)-B-4; M.R. Cooper, Promissory Note, Dec. 27, 1889, 2(z)-B-6 and 2(z)-B-7; Jan. 7, 1898, 2(z)-B-24; Dr. E.T. Sabal, Promissory Note, Jan. 20, 1894, 2(z)-B-19; Henry Flagler, Promissory Note, July 31, 1895, 2(z)-B-22, ADSA.

[30]Quigley to Moore, Aug. 17, 1878, 2(A)-C-10; Quigley to Moore, Oct. 7, 1879, 2(A)-C-11; Leonard J. Tormey, stockbroker, to Moore, Nov. 1, 1879, 2(A)-C-12; Tormey to Moore, May 6, 1881, 2(A)-C-16; Tormey to Moore, Nov. 10, 1881, 2(A)-C-17; Tormey to Moore, Nov. 22, 1881, 2(A)-C-18; Tormey to Moore, Memo, n.d., (c. 1882), 2(A)-C-21; Tormey to Moore, June 25, 1883, 2(A)-C-25, ADSA.

[31]Various Deeds, 1878-1892, 2-B-9 through17; Tax Bills 1885-97, 2-G-1 through 30; 2-H-1 through 30; 2-K-1 through 27; William L Jones, lawyer, Buffalo, NY, (about property in Quincy) to Moore, Feb. 11, 1892, 2(A)-K-13; Father Charles Mohr, OSB, to Moore, Jan. 20, 1898, 2-D-5; Moore, handwritten, "Estimated Value of Un-taxable Church Property in the Diocese of St. Augustine," Jan. (n.d.) 1892, 2(A)-M-3; W.D. Wilson, city tax collector, St. Augustine, to Moore, July 9, 1897, 2-R-11, ADSA.

[32]Moore to Msgr. William Preston, V.G. of the Archdiocese of New York, March 1, 1886, MC 51, Shea, John Gilmary Correspondence, I-M File, Box 3, PAHRC; éRemigio Toscano, Havana, to Moore, Feb. 19, 1885, 2(A)-E-16; Thomas D. Sariol, Havana, to Moore, Nov. 4, 1887, 2(A)-G-9; Oct. 21, 1896, 2(A)-P-9 through 12; March 10, 1900 through April 3, 1901, 2(A)-S-14 through 18; April 15, 1901, 2(A)-T-10; Unknown Author (perhaps Kenny), "History of Havana Rents Question," n.d. (c. early 1902), 2(A)-M-13 through 15, ADSA.

[33]Moore Papers, Financial Matters Box; "Cathedral Building Fund Drive," Account Book (in Moore's hand), April 15, 1887 to June 30, 1899, ADSA.

## Chapter 11

[1]Chronicles, St. Augustine Academy, 1877-1900, ASSJ; Moore to Pace, Jan. 3, 1886, 2-N-8; Moore to Pace, Jan. 17, 1888, 2-P-3; Moore to POF, Lyons, France, Dec. 1, 1886, POF Files, File L-78, #3433, ADSA; Hoffman's Catholic Directory-1889, 373; Thomas Graham, "The Flagler Era, 1865-1913," in The Oldest City: St. Augustine's Saga of Survival, ed. by Jean Parker Waterbury (St. Augustine, FL: St. Augustine Historical Society, 1983), 189-91; Sister Thomas Joseph McGoldrick, SSJ, Beyond the Call: The Legacy of the Sisters of St. Joseph of St. Augustine, Florida (Bloomington, IN: Xlibris Corp., 2008), 286-87.

[2]Father Henry Clavreul to POF, Lyons, France, Aug. 19, 1872, 1(x)-H-2; Moore to POF, Lyons, France, Sept. 3, 1886, 2-N-11, ADSA; *St. Augustine Examiner,* April 1, 1872; Michael V. Gannon, Rebel Bishop: The Life and Era of Augustin Verot (Milwaukee, WI: Bruce, 1964), 238-40; Arva Moore Parks, "Miami in 1876," *Tequesta* 35 (1975): 89-145; Margot Ammidown, "The Wagner Family: Pioneer Life on the Miami River," *Tequesta* 42 (1982): 5-37.

[3]*Notitiae-1890,* Jan. 1, 1891, "Missions of Volusia and Brevard Counties," 2(A)-H-13; A.I. Dallas, Orlando, to Moore, Jan. 7, 1891, 2-B-7, ADSA; Hoffman's Catholic Directory-1892, 430-32; Hoffman's Catholic Directory-1893, 444-46.

[4]Moore to Mother Katharine Drexel, SBS, Jan. 6, 1894, ASBS; Michael J. McNally, Parish Life on Florida's West Coast, 1860-1968 (St. Petersburg, FL: Catholic Media Ministries, 1996), 107.

[5]Michael J. McNally, Catholicism in South Florida, 1868-1968 (Gainesville, FL: University Presses of Florida, 1984), 31.

[6]Moore to William Preston, March 1, 1886, MC51, John Gilmary Shea Correspondence, 17-M File, Box 3, PAHRC; Moore to Gibbons, March 12, 1886, 80-P-4, AAB at ASSMSU; Hoffman's Catholic Directory-1896, 463.

[7]*Notitiae-1878,* Jan. 1, 1879, St. Mary, Star of the Sea, 2(y)-B-12, ADSA; McNally, Catholicism in South Florida, 32-33; McNally, Parish Life, 95.

[8]Ghione to Moore, Jan. 18, 1888, 2(y)-C-9; Ghione to Moore, n.d., "Census of Catholics of Key West - 1890," 2(y)-C-12; *Notitiae-1888,* Jan. 1, 1889, St. Mary, Star of the Sea, 2(y)-C-10, ADSA.

[9]*Notitiae-1894,* Jan. 1, 1895, St. Mary, Star of the Sea, 2(y)-C-18, ADSA.

[10]McNally, Catholicism in South Florida, 31, 37; McNally, Parish Life, 95.

[11]McNally, Parish Life, 68-73. See also: Gary R. Mormino and George E. Pozzetta, The Immigrant World of Ybor City: Italians and Their Latin Neighbors in Tampa (Urbana, IL: University of Illinois, 1987).

[12]McNally, Parish Life, 103-06; 177.

[13]*Ibid.,* 95; 176-77.

[14]*Ibid.,* 176-182.

[15]*Ibid.,* Table 7.2, 150; 183-84.

[16]*Ibid.,* 182-84.

[17]Thomas W. Spalding, The Premier See: A History of the Archdiocese of Baltimore, 1789-1989 (Baltimore: Johns Hopkins University, 1989), 195-96, 244.

[18]Kathleen Deegan and Darcie MacMahon, Fort Mose: Colonial America's Black Fortress of Freedom (Gainesville, FL: University Press of Florida, 1995).

[19]Sister Marie Sidonie, SSJ, to Father Superior, Le Puy, Dec. 18, 1872, ASSJ; Bishop Moore, "Numbers of Whites and Blacks by County, Aug. 1890" (written in Moore's hand), 2-B-3; School Statistics, 1900-01, 2(A)-S-24, 2(A)-S-11, 2-S-10, 2-S-11, 2(y)-M-3, 2(y)-K-12 through16, ADSA; Kenny to E.R. Dyer, Secretary to the Commission of Catholic Missions Among the Colored People and Indians, Sept. 15, 1903, RG-10, Box 13, Sulpician Archives at AASMSU; Gannon, Rebel Bishop, 243; McNally, Parish Life, 185-87.

[20]Supplement to House Records, vol. I, Jan. 23, Feb. 2, 14, 17, Oct. 2, 8, 1894, ANOPSJ; Parish Histories, St. Peter Claver, Tampa, Cabinet 9, Drawer 3, ADSP; Moore to Mother Katharine Drexel, SBS, March 13, 1894, Moore, Bishop John File, NMK-10, Box 39, #5, ASBS; McNally, Parish Life, 187-89, 216.

[21]Michael V. Gannon, The Cross in the Sand: The Early Catholic Church in Florida, 1513-1870 (Gainesville, FL: University of Florida Press,1965), 110.

[22]Sadlier's Catholic Directory-1878, 377-78.

[23]Agreement Files, Ybor City File, 1897-1900, H-110, ASBS; C. Vann Woodward, The Strange Career of Jim Crow: Commemorative Edition (New York: Oxford University Press, 2002; first published 1955); Howard N. Rabinowitz, Race Relations in the Urban South, 1865-1890, Urban Life in American Series, gen. ed. Richard C. Wade (New York: Oxford, 1978.

[24]Moore to Mother Katharine, Jan. 6, March 13, April 13, April 19, 1894, Moore, Bishop, John File, MMK-10, Box 39, #5, ASBS.

[25]Moore to Mother Katharine, May 14, June 9, 1895, Moore, Bishop John File, NMK-10, Box 39, #5, ASBS.

[26]Moore to Mother Katharine, Oct. 29, 1897; Moore to Mother Katharine, March 2, June 17, 1899; Moore to Mother Katharine, April 17, June 2, Aug. 2, 31, 1900, Ybor City File, 1897-1900, Agreements File, H-110, ASBS.

[27]Moore to Mother Katharine, June 2, 1899, Ybor City File, 1897-1900, Agreements File, H-110; Agreement, June 17,

1899, St. Augustine & Old Town File, 1898-1899; Writings
of M. K. Drexel, 1885-1907, Promise Book, 3203, 147, ASBS;
*Notitiae-1900*, St. Michael's, Fernandina, Jan. 1, 1901, 2(A)-T-4,
ADSA.

[28]McGoldrick, Beyond the Call, 37-38, 58, 61-65; 130-32;
151-52; 271-72.

[29]Moore to Pace, July 23, 1887, 2-N-20; Moore to Pace, Sept. 2,
1887, 2-N -28, ADSA; Moore to Gibbons, Feb. 13, 1890, 87-D-9,
AAB at AASMSU; Moore to Mother Katharine, Oct. 29, Dec. 20,
1897, Ybor City File, 1897-1900, Agreements Files, H-110, ASBS;
Nelson J. Callahan, ed., Diary of Richard L. Burtsell: The Early
Years, 1865-1868 (New York, Arno, 1978), vii-viii; Joseph Bernard
Code, Dictionary of the American Hierarchy, 1789-1964 (New
York: Joseph F Wagner, 1964), 222.

[30]Moore to Mother Katharine, March 2, 9, 1898, Ybor City
File, 1897-1900, Agreements Files, H-110; Writings of M.K.
Drexel, Promise Book, 1885-1907, #3203, 125, ASBS; Mother
Katharine to Moore, Agreement on St. Benedict the Moor School,
March 9, 1898, 2-D-6; Mother Katharine to Moore, June 14, 1899,
2-D-7, ADSA.

[31]Moore to Mother Katharine, March 29, 1898, Jan. 18, March
2, 1899, Ybor City File, 1897-1900, Agreements File, HK-110;
Moore to Mother Katharine, April 19, 1898, Sept. 16, 1900,
Moore File, NMK-10, Box 39, #5; Writings of M.K. Drexel,
Promise Book, 1885-1907, #3203, 26, ASBS.

[32]Moore to Dyer, April 14, Nov. 24, 1893, July 20, Oct. 25,
1894, July 6, Oct. 30, 1895, April 22, Nov. 20, 1896, March 27,
Nov. 22, 1897, American Missionary Commission, Dyer File -
Mon-Mor, RG-10, Box 13, Sulpician Archives at AASMSU.

[33]Moore to Gibbons, Sept. 2, Nov. 3, 1898; Moore to Dyer, Nov.
12, 1898, June 19, Nov. 20, 1899, Feb. 23, Oct. 10, Nov. 17, 1900,
American Missionary Commission, Dyer File - Mon-Mor, RG-10,
Box 13; (no author given),"Mission Work Among the Negroes
and Indians," c. 1900, Unlabeled File, RG-10, Box 4, Sulpician
Archives at AASMSU.

[34]Agreement with Bishop Kenny July 6, 1903, Agreements File,
Jacksonville File; Agreement with Bishop Barry, March 14, 1927,
Tampa File, Agreements Files, H-110, ASBS; McNally, Parish
Life, 189, 190-91, 278-79.

## Chapter 12

[1]Walter M. Abbott, S.J., gen. ed., The Documents of Vatican II (New York: America Press, 1966), Decree on the Bishops' Pastoral Office in the Church, para. 3, 399-400.

[2]Patricia Byrne, CSJ, "American Ultramontism," *Theological Studies* 56 (June 1995): 302-06.

[3]John W. O'Malley, Vatican I: The Council and the Making of the Ultramontane Church (Cambridge, MA: Belknap Press of Harvard University Press, 2018), 133-35; Roger Aubert, The Church in a Secularized Society in The Christian Centuries, vol. 5, ed. by Roger Aubert, trans. by Peter Ludlow (New York: Paulist, 1978), 61-66; Frederick J. Zwierlein, The Life and Letters of Bishop McQuaid, vol. II (Rome: Desclee, 1926), 59-63. McQuaid's quotation is from a sermon about Vatican I that he delivered in his Cathedral on August 28, 1870. See also: Michael V. Gannon, Rebel Bishop: The Life and Era of Augustin Verot (Milwaukee, WI: Bruce, 1964), 192-227.

[4]Byrne, "American Ultramontism," 306-10; Aubert, The Church in a Secularized Society, 67-68; [No author's name given], A History of the Third Plenary Council of Baltimore (Baltimore, MD: Baltimore Publishing Co., 1885), 73. See also: Ann Taves, The Household of Faith: Roman Catholic Devotions in Mid-Nineteenth-Century America (Notre Dame, IN: University of Notre Dame Press, 1986); Jay P. Dolan, Catholic Revivalism: The American Experience, 1830-1900 (Notre Dame, IN: University of Notre Dame Press, 1978).

[5]Byrne, "American Ultramontanism," 313; Gerald P. Forgarty, S.J., "The Catholic Hierarchy in the United States Between the Third Plenary Council and the Condemnation of Americanism," *U.S. Catholic Historian* 11 (Summer 1993): 19-21.

[6]Moore to Gibbons, April 7, 1884, 77-T-11, ADSA; Gerald P. Fogarty. S.J., The Vatican and the American Hierarchy from 1870 to 1965 (Wilmington, DL: Michael Glazier, 1985), 32-34; [No Author's Name Given], History of Third Baltimore, 75; Joseph F. Martino, "A Study of Certain Aspects of the Episcopate of Patrick A. Ryan, Archbishop of Philadelphia, 1884-1911" (H.E.D. diss.,Gregorian University at Rome, 1982), 32.

[7]Fogarty, Vatican and Hierarchy, 34-35; David Jacquet, "Bishop Gilmour and the Third Plenary Council of Baltimore," *St. Meinrad Essays* 12 (May 1959): 52-53. Gilmour was born in Glasgow,

Scotland, in 1824 of Presbyterian parents, who immigrated to
Nova Scotia in 1829, then to Pennsylvania, to Schuykill County
and the village of Cumbola, where friends there introduced him to
Catholicism. He and his friend Bernard Quinn walked five miles
to Mass in Pottsville on Sundays. Gilmour was baptized at St.
Francis Church in Philadelphia in 1842 and entered the seminary
in 1843, eventually was ordained for the Diocese of Cincinnati in
1852. From 1852 to 1872 he did pastoral work in Ohio. While
pastor of St. Patrick's in Cincinnati from 1857, he translated
from the French a work which came to be known as <u>Gilmour's
Illustrated Bible History</u>, a parochial school text for sixty years. He
also edited the <u>National Catholic Series of Readers</u>, later known
as <u>Gilmour's Readers</u>, which were in use in Catholic schools for
forty years. He became the Bishop of Cleveland in 1872. Due
to declining health, he was advised to travel to Florida and had
arrived in St. Augustine on March 19, 1891, back once again with
his collaborator in Rome in 1885. He died in St. Augustine on
April 13, 1891. He was buried in Cleveland. Michael J. Hymes,
<u>History of the Diocese of Cleveland: Origin and Growth, 1847-
1952</u> (Cleveland, OH: Diocese of Cleveland, 1953), 113-97.

[8]Martino, "Ryan," 29-30.

[9]Robert Emmett Curran, <u>Michael Augustine Corrigan and
the Shaping of Conservative Catholicism in America, 1878-1902</u>
(New York: Arno Press, 1978), 127; Jacquet, "Gilmour," 53;
Zwierlein, <u>McQuaid</u>, vol. II, 345-47.

[10]Zwierlein, <u>McQuaid</u>, vol II., 347-51. McQuaid and Gilmour
were not the only ones uncomfortable with Dwenger on the team
in Rome. Fogarty cites a letter from "Bishop John Ireland to
Gibbons dated April 20, 1885, stating: "I do not expect, I must say,
much good from Bishop Dwenger's presence in Rome: he does
not like some of the decrees, & it is in his character to bring things
down to his own liking." Gerald P Fogarty, S.J., <u>The Vatican and
the Americanism Crisis: Denis J. O'Connell, American Agent in
Rome, 1885-1903</u> (Rome: Gregorian University, 1974), 53, fn. 52.

[11]Zwierlein, <u>McQuaid</u>, vol. II, 352-54; Jacquet, "Gilmour," 54.

[12]Curran, <u>Corrigan</u>, 134-36.

[13]Zwierlein, <u>McQuaid</u>, vol. II, 355-56.

[14]Moore to Gibbons, March 17, 1885, 79-G-6; April 1,
1885,79-I-2, AAB at AASMSU; Moore to Mother Lazarus, April
1, 1885, Bishop, Moore File, 130.1, ASSJ.

[15]Moore to Mother Lazarus, April 13, 1885, Bishop Moore File, 130.1, ASSJ.

[16]Moore to Mother Lazarus, Feb. 13, 1885, Bishop Moore File, 130.1, ASSJ; Moore to Gibbons, June 15, 1885, 79-M-14; Moore to Gibbons, June 22, 1885, 79-O-2, AAB at AASMSU; Forgarty, O'Connell, 55-56.

[17]Moore to Gibbons, June 22, 1885 (an *addendum* of July 2), 79-O-2; Moore to Gibbons, July 6, 1885, 79-O-5, AAB at AASMSU; Fogarty, O'Connell, 56-57.

[18]Moore to Gibbons, July 15, 1885, 79-O-11, AAB at AASMSU. O'Connell veered clear of any entanglement in the divisions among the episcopal team. He also was less engaged in the process of getting the decrees passed, focusing more on being an agent and reporter for Gibbons. At the end of July, he left Rome for the villa at Grottaferrata in the Alban Hills, where the North American College students were spending their summer break. Fogarty, O'Connell, 58-60.

[19]Moore to Gibbons, Aug. 23, 1885, 79-Q-9, AAB at AASMSU.

[20]Moore, Dwenger, Gilmour to Gibbons, August 29, 1885, 79-Q-17, AAB at AASMSU,

[21]Moore to Gibbons, Sept. 9, 1885, 79-R-7; Moore and Gilmour to Gibbons, Oct. 3, 1885, 79-T-2; Moore to Gibbons, Dec. 18, 1885, 79-W-13, AAB at AASMSU; Jacquet, "Gilmour," 56. Unfortunately, Ellis' monumental work on Gibbons does not shed any light on Gibbons' telegram. John Tracy Ellis, The Life of James Cardinal Gibbons, Archbishop of Baltimore, 1834-1921, vol. I (Westminster, MD: Christian Classics, 1987 (replica edition first published 1952), 259-61.

[22]Gilmour to McQuaid, Nov. 5, 1885, quoted in Zwierlein, McQuaid, vol. II, 355.

[23]Fogarty, O'Connell, 61-62.

[24]Moore to Mother Lazarus, April 1, 1885, Bishop Moore File, 130.1, ASSJ; Moore to Gibbons, March 17, 1885, 79-G-6, AAB at AASMSU; Sister Thomas Joseph McGoldrick, SSJ, Beyond the Call: The Legacy of the Sisters of St. Joseph of St. Augustine, Florida (Bloomington, IN: Xlibris, 2007), 277.

[25]Moore to Gibbons, July 6, 1885, 79-O-5, AAB at AASMSU; "Moore's 1885 *Ad limina*," Bishop Moore File, 130.1, ASSJ; "Moore's *Relatio* (*Ad limina*), August 25, 1895," New Series, 74/938-39, 119/621-37, APF at AUND.

[26]Moore to Mother Lazarus, April 13, Aug. 26, 1885, Bishop Moore File, 130.1, ASSJ; Moore to Gibbons, Aug. 23, 1885, 79-Q-9, AAB at AASMSU; "Text of William Moore's Headstone," Gretta Connell to Peter Dolan, November 19, 2018 (courtesy of Peter Dolan).

[27]Muleahy to Lynch, Nov. 26, 1878, 67-B-2, ADC.

[28]Lynch to Msgr. Robert Seton, April 27, 1881, Calendared Collections, II-1-b, AUND; "Bishop Northrop Consecration," undated, newspaper article (c. Jan. 12, 1882, from a Baltimore paper), ADC; "Bishop Lynch Funeral," *Charleston News & Courier*, March 2, 1882. For more on Lynch, see: David C.R. Heisser and Stephen J. White, <u>Patrick N. Lynch, 1817-1882: Third Catholic Bishop of Charleston</u> (Columbia, SC: University of South Carolina Press, 2015).

[29]*Charleston Daily Courier*, March 22, 1882; Sept. 21, 1882; March 12, 1883; Richard C. Madden, <u>Catholics in South Carolina: A Record</u> (Lanham, MD: University Press of America, 1985), 139, 142, 153.

[30]Moore to Gibbons, July 18, 1877, 73-D-7; Moore to Gibbons, Oct. 16, 1877, 73-F-12; Moore to Gibbons, April 3, 1882, AAB at AASMSU; William Elder, Coadjutor Bishop of Cincinnati to Francis Leray, Coadjutor Bishop of New Orleans, May 4, 1880, Calendar Collections, VI-3-b, AUND; Gerald P. Fogarty, SJ, <u>Commonwealth Catholicism: A History of the Catholic Church in Virginia</u> (Notre Dame, IN: University of Notre Dame, 2001), 259-60; Madden, <u>Catholics in S.C.</u>, 138; Thomas W. Spalding, "Gibbons, James," in Michael Glazier and Thomas J. Shelly, eds., <u>The Encyclopedia of American Catholic History</u> (Collegeville, MN: Liturgical Press, 1997), 584-88.

[31]Moore to Gibbons, July 5, 1883, 77-H-9; Moore to Gibbons, June 12, 1886, 81-E-2; *Acta Episcopalia* (diary) of Cardinal Gibbons, July 1, 1888; AAB at AASMSU; Moore to Pace, July 2, 1888, 2-P-10, ADSA; Martino, "Ryan," 13, 15-16, 19.

[32]Hymes, <u>Diocese of Cleveland</u>, 196-97. Vogel, a Catholic, was from Charleston, SC. Moore may have known him from there. During the Civil War, Vogel first entered the CSA Army as an artilleryman in 1861, but then transferred to the CSA Navy, serving on several ships. After the War, he was in the merchant marine, moving to St. Augustine in 1886 and becoming a member of St. Augustine Cathedral. No doubt Moore asked Vogel to put up Gilmour in his house, along with his traveling companions.

Internet Resource, *Find a Grave*, San Lorenzo Cemetery, St. Augustine, "Leopold Ramie Vogel."

[33]Thomas J. Peterman, The Cutting Edge: The Life of Thomas Andrew Becker (Devon, PA: William T. Cooke Publishing, 1982), 21, 29-31, 118, 235-36, 261, 289; Thomas J. Peterman, "Becker, Thomas Andrew," in Michael Glazier and Thomas J. Shelly, eds., The Encyclopedia of American Catholic History (Collegeville, MN: Liturgical Press, 1997), 131-33.

[34]Curran, Corrigan, 137. The literature on these late nineteenth century controversies in the American Catholic Church is quite extensive. Among the works about these topics are: Curran, Corrigan; Fogarty, O'Connell; Forgarty, The Vatican and the American Hierarchy; Fogarty, The Vatican and Americanism; Ellis, Gibbons, vols. I & II; Zwierlein, McQuaid, vols. I-III; Zwierlein, Letters of Archbishop Corrigan to Bishop McQuaid and Allied Documents (Rochester, NY: Art Print Shop, 1946); John Ireland, The Church in Modern Society: Lectures and Addresses, vols. I & II (St. Paul, MN: Pioneer, 1905); David Francis Sweeney, OFM, The Life of John Lancaster Spalding: First Bishop of Peoria, 1840-1916 (New York: Herder and Herder, 1965); Colman J. Barry, OSB, The Catholic Church and German Americans (Milwaukee, WI: Bruce, 1953); Philip Gleason, Conservative Reformers: German American Catholics and the Social Order (Notre Dame, IN: University of Notre Dame, 1968); Thomas W. Spalding, The Premier See: A History of the Archdiocese of Baltimore, 1789-1989 (Baltimore and London: Johns Hopkins University Press, 1989); Marvin R. O'Connell, John Ireland and the American Catholic Church (St. Paul, MN: Minnesota Historical Society, 1988); "The Americanist Controversy: Recent Historical and Theological Perspectives," *U.S. Catholic Historian*, vol. 11 (Summer 1993), entire issue. Moore's following national ecclesiastical events is testified by copies the Archbishop's Annual Meeting Minutes found in his papers: Booklet, Bishop Francis Satolli, "For the Settling of the School Question and the Giving of Religious Education" (1892), 2(x)-A-1; "Third Annual Conference of Archbishops - Minutes, Nov, 16-19, 1892," 2(x)-A-3; "Fourth Annual Conference of Archbishops - Minutes, Sept. 12-13, 1893", 2(x)-A-5; "Fifth Annual Conference of Archbishops - Minutes, Oct. 10, 1893" 2(x)-A-7; "Eleventh Annual Conference of Archbishops, Oct. 12, 1899" and their "Response to *Testem Benevolencia*," 2(x)-A-11, ADSA.

³⁵Moore to Gibbons, Aug. 20, 1886, 81-S-2, AAB at AASMSU.

³⁶Moore to Gibbons, Aug. 20, 1886, 81-S-2; Moore to Gibbons, Dec. 19, 1886, 82-H-6; Moore to Gibbons, Jan. 15, 1887, 82-L-10, AAB at AASMSU; Moore to O'Connell, Aug. 31, 1886; Oct. 30, 1886, MDRI, Reel 12, ADR at AUND; Ellis, <u>Gibbons</u>, vol. I, 600-20.

³⁷Ellis, <u>Gibbons</u>, vol. I, 621-23.

³⁸*Ibid.*, 623-33; Moore to O'Connell, Sept. 20, 1893, MDRI, Reel 12, ADR at AUND.

³⁹Moore to Gibbons, Aug. 20, 1892, 90-D-5/1, AAB at AASMSU; O'Boyle to Moore, Jan, 16, 1895, 2(A)-N-18; Newspaper article, n.d., no attribution (glued on inside flap of the book), "Account Book - Cathedral Building Fund Drive, 1887-1899," ADSA; Ellis, <u>Gibbons</u>, vol. I, 465.

⁴⁰*The Diocesan Record* (Scranton), Oct. 7, 1899; Hymes, <u>Diocese of Cleveland</u>, 113-14. John F. Quinn, "'The Nation's Guest?': The Battle between Catholics and Abolitionists to Manage Father Theobald Mathew's American Tour, 1849-1851," *U.S. Catholic Historian* 22 (Summer 2004): 19-40.

⁴¹*The Catholic Standard* (Philadelphia), Aug. 13, 1887; *The Diocesan Record* (Scranton), Sept. 30, 1899. The CTAU faded from existence with the ratification of the 18th Amendment prohibiting Athe manufacture, sale or transportation of intoxicating liquors within... the United States." It was ratified in 1919 and implemented from 1920 to 1933. Robert A. Rosenbaum, ed., <u>The Penguin Encyclopedia of American History</u> (New York: Penguin Putnam, 2003), 301.

## Chapter 13

¹Richard L.Burtsell, <u>The Diary of Richard L. Burtsell, Priest of New York: The Early Years, 1865-1868</u>, ed. by Nelson J. Callahan (New York: Arno Press, 1980), March 2, 30, May 5, Sept. 14, 15, 23, 26, 1865; April 17, 1866; Jan. 25, May 7, Nov. 20, 1867; Alfred Isacsson, O.Carm., <u>The Determined Doctor: The Story of Edward McGlynn</u> (Tarrytown, NY: Vestigium Press, 1998), 31-33; Margaret Reher, <u>Catholic Intellectual Life in America: A Historical Study of Persons and Movements</u> (New York: Macmillan, 1989), 51-52; Michael V. Gannon, "Before and After Modernism" in John Tracy Ellis, ed., <u>The Catholic Priest in the</u>

United States: Historical Investigations (Collegeville, MN: St. John's University Press, 1971), 305.

[2]Gannon, "Before and After Modernism," 311-312; Robert Emmett Curran, SJ, "Prelude to Americanism: The New York *Accademia* and Clerical Radicalism in the Late Nineteenth Century," *Church History* 47 (1978): 51.

[3]Robert Emmett Curran, SJ, Michael Augustine Corrigan and the Shaping of Conservative Catholicism in America, 1878-1902 (New York: Arno Press, 1978), 2-4; Robert Trisco, "Bishops and Their Priests in the United States" in John Tracy Ellis, ed., The Catholic Priest in the United States: Historical Investigations (Collegeville, MN: St. John's University Press, 1971), 140-41.

[4]Curran, "Clerical Radicalism," 48-50. See also: Edwin G. Burows and Mike Wallace, Gotham: A History of New York (New York: Oxford, 1999).

[5]Isacsson, McGlynn, 2-3, fn. #3, 14; Anthony D. Andreassi, "Burtsell, Richard," in The Encyclopedia of American Catholic History, ed. by Michael Glazier and Thomas J. Shelly (Collegeville, MN: Liturgical Press, 1997), 176.

[6]Burtsell, Diary, ix; Florence D. Cohalan, A Popular History of the Archdiocese of New York (Yonkers, NY: U.S. Catholic Historical Society, 1983), 121; Frederick J. Zwierlein, The Life and Letters of Bishop McQuaid, vol. III (Rochester, NY: The Art Print Shop, 1927), 60.

[7]Trisco, "Bishops and Priests," 197-206; Curran, Corrigan, 4-6.

[8]Joseph F. Martino, "A Study of Certain Aspects of the Episcopate of Patrick J. Ryan, Archbishop of Philadelphia, 1884-1911" (H.E.D. diss., Gregorian Pontifical University, Rome, 1982), 290-308.

[9]*New York Freeman's Journal and Catholic Register*, May 10, 1873; Joseph F. Mooney, Memorial of the Most Reverend Michael Augustine Corrigan, D.D. (New York: Cathedral Library Association, 1902), 48-49, 158-59; Isacsson, McGlynn, 9-10; Curran, Corrigan, 23-62.

[10]Curran, Corrigan, v-vii.

[11]Zwierlein, McQuaid, vol. I, 293-99, 310; Joseph Bernard Code, Dictionary of the American Hierarchy (1789-1964) (New York: Joseph F. Wagner, Inc., 1964), 198.

[12]Stephen Bell, Rebel Priest & Prophet: A Biography of Doctor Edward McGlynn (New York: Devin-Adaire, 1937), 31-32; Code,

Hierarchy, 185-86; Zwierlein, McQuaid, vol. III, 29-30; Isacsson, McGlynn, 15.

[13]Bruce Kupelnick, "Edes, Ella B." in The Encyclopedia of American Catholic History ed. by Michael Glazier and Thomas J. Shelly (Collegeville, MN: Liturgical Press, 1997), 478-79.

[14]Curran, "Clerical Radicalism," 51; Anthony D. Andreassi, "Preston, Thomas Scott," in The Encyclopedia of American Catholic History ed. by Michael Glazier and Thomas J. Shelley (Collegeville, MN: Liturgical Press, 1997), 169-70. Ultramontism in the U.S. provided security, stability, and identity amidst rapid social change from the 1840s to the end of the century. This perspective was characterized by personal identification and devotion to the Pope; Roman centralization, including at the diocesan level; the establishment of an Apostolic Delegation in Washington, DC; the increase of devotional life - an anti-intellectual, sentimental, affective spirituality, Marian devotions, as well as devotions to the Sacred Heart and the Holy Family. Patricia Byrne, CSJ, "American Ultramontism," Theological Studies 56 (June 1995): 301-26.

[15]Msgr. Florence D. Cohalan, A Popular History of the Archdiocese of New York (Yonkers, N.Y.: U.S. Catholic Historical Society, 1983), 122-23; Sylvester L. Malone, Dr. Edward McGlynn (New York: Dr. McGlynn Monument Assoc., 1918), 1-2; Isacsson, McGlynn, 6-14, 17-20.

[16]Msgr. Michael McGuire, "The Case of Edward McGlynn" (July 1981), G-102-Folder #1, AANY; Cohalan, New York, 122-24; Isacsson, McGlynn, 14-15, 24.

[17]Cohalan, New York, 125-26. See also: James J. Green, "American Catholics and the Irish Land League, 1879-1882," CHR 35 (April 1949): 19-42.

[18]Burtsell, Diary, October 1880, AANY; Cohalan, New York, 125-27; Isacsson, McGlynn, 81.

[19]Robert Emmett, Curran, SJ, "The McGlynn Affair and the Shaping of the New Conservatism in American Catholicism, 1886-1894," CHR 66 (April 1980): 185-86; Isacsson, McGlynn, 24-25, 83; Cohalan, New York, 103.

[20]Cohalan, New York, 128-30; Zwierlein, McQuaid, vol. III, 39, 58; Curran, "McGlynn Affair," 186-89.

[21]Curran, "McGlynn Affair," 189-90; Cohalan, New York, 130-32.

[22]Cohalan, New York, 132-34; Malone, McGlynn, 2-4.

[23]McQuaid to Corrigan, Nov. 15, 1889, Calendared Collection, I-1-r, AUND; Zwierlein, McQuaid, vol. III, 37-38, 67, 84-149.

[24]Curran, "Clerical Radicalism," 61-62; Cohalan, New York, 134; Trisco, "Bishops and Their Priests," 257-58.

[25]Gibbons to Cardinal Manning, March 23, 1888, 84-F-5, AAB at AASMSU; Zwierlein, McQuaid, vol. III, 66-67; Curran, "McGlynn Affair," 196-97.

[26]Feb. 9, 1892, *Acta Episcopalia* of Cardinal Gibbons (Diary), AAB at AASMSU; Curran, "McGlynn Affair," 199-204; Curran, Corrigan, 477; Malone, McGlynn, 7-8; Zwierlein, McQuaid, vol. III, 81-82.

[27]Moore to Lynch, Dec. 20, 1866, 38-E-7, ADC. Moore kept up his intellectual interests throughout his life, purchasing Scripture commentaries and subscriptions to ecclesiastical journals. Moore to Patrick Hickey, April 29, 1887, Calendared Collection, I-1-d, AUND; Moore to Pace, July 2, 1888, 2-P-10, ADSA; Moore to John G. Shea, July 13, 1889, Shea, John Gilmary Correspondence, Box 3, I-M File, MC-51; Moore to Martin J. Griffin, July 31, 1891, Martin Griffin Collection, Box 3, RG 8-8-3; Moore to Herman J. Heuser, June 30, 1897, Herman Heuser Collection MC-1, PAHRC.

[28]Moore to Gibbons, Nov. 2, 1880, 75-M-2, AAB at ASSMSU; Burtsell Diary, Oct. 6, 1880; Sept. 7, 1882, Nov. 1884, AANY; Burtsell, Diary, ix AANY.

[29]Burtsell, Diary, Jan. 3-10, 1887, AANY.

[30]Moore to Gibbons, Jan. 15, 1887, 82-L-10, AAB at AASMSU.

[31]Gibbons to Corrigan, Jan. 20, 1887, AANY; Burtsell Diary, Jan. 28, 1887, AANY.

[32]Isacsson, McGlynn, 154, fn. #2.

[33]Burtsell, Diary, Feb. 3, 1887, AANY.

[34]Burtsell, Diary, May 21, 23, 25, 26, 27, 29, 31, June 7, AANY.

[35]Moore to Simeoni, June 27, 1887 (cablegram in Latin), 82-V-9; Moore to Simeoni, June 28, 1887, 82-W-3; Moore to Gibbons, June 29, 1887, 82-W-5, AAB at AASMSU.

[36]Gibbons to Moore, July (n.d.) 1887, 83-D-13, AAB at AASMSU.

[37]Burtsell, Diary, July 10, 14, 15, 16, 1887, AANY; *Catholic Mirror* (Baltimore), June 11, 1887.

[38]Burtsell, Diary, Aug. 10, 12, 13, 17, Sept. 3, 1887, AANY; Moore to Gibbons, Aug. 17, 1887, 83-G-12; Burtsell to Moore,

Sept. 3, 1887, 83-K-4; Moore to Gibbons, Sept. 5, 1887, 83-K-9, AAB at AASMSU.

[39]Burtsell, <u>Diary</u>, Sept. 19, 20, 22, 23, 1887, AANY.

[40]Burtsell, <u>Diary</u>, Sept. 23, 1887, AANY; Moore to Pace, n.d. (c. Sept. 22, 1887), 2-P-2, ADSA.

[41]Zwierlein, <u>McQuaid</u>, vol. III, 47, 58; McQuaid to Corrigan, Nov. 6, 1887 (photostat), Calendared Collection, I-1-I, AUND.

[42]Burtsell, <u>Diary</u>, March 19, 20, 21, 1888, AANY.

[43]Burtsell, <u>Diary</u>, Sept. 27, 29, 30, Oct. 4, 14, 24, Nov. 14, 1890, AANY.

[44]McGlynn to Moore, March 29, 1892; Moore to Ireland, March 31, 1892, AASP-M; Moore to Ledochowski, April 3, 1892; Moore to Pope Leo XIII, April 3, 1892, New Series 194/28, 29, 30, APF at AUND; Moore to O'Connell, March 31, 1892, May 19, 1892, ADR at AUND; Marvin R. O'Connell, <u>John Ireland and the American Catholic Church</u> (St. Paul, MN: Minnesota Historical Society Press, 1988), 361.

[45]O'Connell, <u>Ireland</u>, 361-62; Callahan, <u>Diary of Burtsell</u>, xiii-xiv.

[46]Moore to Gibbons, March 25, 1893, 91-H-9, AAB at AASMSU; Corrigan to Connelly, March 2, 12, 1893, G-77-Folder #6, AANY; Isaccson, <u>McGlynn</u>, 341, 350-51; Zwierlein, McQuaid, Vol. III, 81; Thomas Graham, <u>Mr. Flagler's St. Augustine</u> (Gainesville, FL: University Press of Florida, 2014), 286.

[47]Isaccson, <u>McGlynn</u>, 350-51, 354-57; Bell, <u>Rebel Priest</u>, 246-50.

[48]Moore to Gibbons, March 29, 1893, 91-H-9, AAB at AASMSU; Moore to O'Connell, Nov. 4, 1893, ADR at AUND; Isaccson, <u>McGlynn</u>, 366, 372.

[49]Isaccson, <u>McGlynn</u>, 378-81; Bell, <u>Rebel Priest</u>, 253-55.

[50]Curran, <u>Corrigan</u>, 476; Isaccson, <u>McGlynn</u>, 390-91, 394-95.

## *Chapter 14*

[1]Moore's Will of Sept. 1, 1881, 2-M-6; Moore's Will of Nov. 5, 1891, 2-P-21; Prior Charles, OSB, of St. Leo's, to Moore, Aug. 15, 1898, 2(A)-R-12; Renwick, Aspinwill, & Owen to Moore, June 28, 1900, 2-E-1; Renwick to Moore, Feb. 23, 1901, 2-E-14, 2-E-17, ADSA; *Catholic Standard & Times* (Philadelphia), Sept. 9, 23, 1899, June 9, 1900; *Diocesan Record* (Scranton), Sept. 16, 1899; Moore to O'Connell, Dec. 12, 1899, ADR at AUND; Moore to

Mother Katharine, June 2, 1900, H-110, Agreements Files, Ybor City File, 1897-1900; Moore to Mother Katharine, Sept. 16, 1900, NMK-10, Box 39, #5, Moore, Bishop John File, ASBS; *Charleston Daily Courier*, July 31, 1901; *Florida Times-Union & Citizen* (Jacksonville), July 31, 1901. See also Chapter 10, fn. #20.

[2]*Florida Times-Union and Citizen*, Aug. 10, 1901; *The Tampa Weekly Tribune*, Aug. 8, 1901; *Catholic Mirror* (Baltimore), Aug. 10, 1901.

[3]Gregory of Naziansus, <u>Concerning Himself and the Bishops</u>, trans. by Denis Molaise Meehan, O.S.B., in <u>The Fathers of the Church</u>, vol. 75 (Washington, DC: The Catholic University of America, 1987), para. 775, 73.

[4]*Ibid.*, para. 750-60, 72.

[5]*Acta*, Sacred Congregation of the Propagation of the Faith, Jan. 2, 1877, vol. 245, fols. 1rv, 2rv, 3r, APF at AUND; [Unknown Author], "Memoriam to Moore," *Pascua Florida*, III (1898-1903), Oct. 13, 1901, ASSJ; Richard J. Purcell, "Moore, John" in <u>Dictionary of American Biography</u>, ed. by Dumas Malone, vol. 12 (New York: Charles Scribner's Sons, 1934), 131-32.

[6]*Florida Times-Union & Citizen* (Jacksonville), July 31, 1901; *Catholic Mirror* (Baltimore), Aug. 3, 1901; *Charleston News & Courier*, July 31, 1901; <u>OCD-1879</u>, 382-84; <u>OCD-1900</u>, 480-82.

[7]Two recent examples are: Stanley McCrystal (retired four-star general), <u>Leaders: Myth and Reality</u> (New York: Portfolio/Penguin, 2018) analyzes thirteen examples of leadership and Doris Kearns Goodwin, <u>Leadership in Turbulent Times</u> (New York: Simon & Schuster, 2018) examines the challenges of Abraham Lincoln, Theodore Roosevelt, Franklin D. Roosevelt, and Lyndon B. Johnson. There are also some recent books on leadership in the Church, including: Notker Wolf and Enrica Rosanna, <u>The Art of Leadership</u>, trans. by Gerlinde Buchinger-Schmid and ed. by Sue Bollans (Collegeville, MN: Liturgical Press, 2013) and Walter Cardinal Kasper, <u>Leadership in the Church: How Traditional Roles Can Serve the Christian Church Today</u>, trans. by Brian McNeil (New York: Crossroad Publishing Co., 2003).

[8]John Keegan, <u>The Mask of Command</u> (New York: Penguin, 1987), 2, 11, 89, 316-18.

[9][Unknown author], "Memoriam to Moore," *Pascua Florida*, III (1898-1903), Oct. 15, 1901, 3-5, ASSJ.

[10]*Ibid.*, 3-5, ASSJ.

[11]Renwick to Moore, Nov. 3, 1888, 2-P-16, ADSA.

# *Abbreviations*

ASMS  St. Mary's Seminary Archives

AASPM  Archives of the Archdiocese of St. Paul and Minneapolis, St. Paul, MN

ABA  Archives of Belmont Abbey, Belmont Abbey, NC

ACHRC  The American Catholic History Research Center, Washington DC (Catholic University of America Archives)

ADB  Archives of the Diocese of Buffalo, Buffalo, NY

ADC  Archives of the Diocese of Charleston, Charleston, SC

ADR  Archives of the Diocese of Richmond, Richmond, VA

ADS  Archives of the Diocese of Scranton, Scranton, PA

ADSa  Archives of the Diocese of Savannah, Savannah, GA

ADSA  Archives of the Diocese of St. Augustine, Jacksonville, FL

AHF  Archives of Henry Flagler, Palm Beach, FL

ANOPSJ  Archives of the New Orleans Province of the Society of Jesus, New Orleans, LA

ASBS  Archives of the Sisters of the Blessed Sacrament, Bensalem, PA

ASCOLM  Archives of the Sisters of Charity of Our Lady of Mercy, Charleston, SC

ASNJM  Archives of the Sisters of the Holy Names of Jesus and Mary, Albany, NY

ASSJ  Archives of the Sisters of St. Joseph, St. Augustine, FL

ASSJ-LP Archives of the Sisters of St. Joseph, Le Puy, France

AUC  Archives of the Urban College, Vatican City State

AUND Notre Dame University Archives, Notre Dame, IN
Propagation of the Faith Archives, Lyon and Paris
Congregation of the Propagation of the Faith, Vatican City
University of Notre Dame Archives
Collection from the Archdiocese of Philadelphia
Archives of the Diocese of Richmond
Archives of the Ludwig-Mission Association

CHR  *Catholic Historical Review*

CPL  Charleston Public Library, Charleston, SC

FDL   Francis A. Drexel Library, St. Joseph's University, Philadelphia, PA

JCBARC  Joseph Cardinal Bernardin Archives & Records Center, Chicago, IL (Archdiocese of Chicago Archives)

NARA-P  National Archives & Records Administration Mid-Atlantic Regional Repository, Philadelphia, PA

OCD   The Official Catholic Directory
      From 1878 to 1890 - Sadlier's Catholic Directory
      From 1891to 1899 - Hoffman's Catholic Directory
      From 1900 to 1902 - The Catholic Directory

PAHRC  Philadelphia Archdiocesan Historical Research Center, Wynnewood, PA

RML   Ryan Memorial Library at St. Charles Boromeo Seminary, Wynnewood, PA

TLPC  Father Timothy Lindensfelder Private Collection of Pictures, St. Augustine, FL

VUL   Villanova University Library, Villanova, PA

# *Bibliography*

## Archival Records and Manuscript Sources

American Catholic History Research Center, Washington, DC
      The Catholic University of America Archives
Archives of the Academy of the Holy Names, Tampa, FL
Archives of the Archdiocese of New York, Yonkers, NY
Associated Archives at St. Mary's Seminary and University, Roland
      Park, MD
      Archives of the Archdiocese of Baltimore
      Sulpician Archives
      St. Mary's Seminary Archives
Archives of the Archdiocese of St. Paul and Minneapolis, St. Paul,
      MN
Archives of Belmont Abbey, Belmont Abbey, NC
Archives of the Diocese of Buffalo, Buffalo, NY
Archives of the Diocese of Charleston, Charleston, SC
Archives of the Diocese of Savannah, Savannah, GA
Archives of the Diocese of Scranton, Scranton, PA
Archives of the Diocese of St. Augustine, St. Augustine, FL
Archives of Henry Flagler, Palm Beach, FL
Archives of the New Orleans Province of the Society of Jesus, New
      Orleans, LA
Archives of the Sisters of the Blessed Sacrament, Bensalem, PA
Archives of the Sisters of Charity of Our Lady of Mercy,
      Charleston, SC
Archives of the Sisters of the Holy Names of Jesus and Mary,
      Albany, NY
Archives of the Sisters of St. Joseph, St. Augustine, FL
Archives of the Sisters of St. Joseph, Le Puy, FR
Archives of the Urban College, Vatican City State
Archives of the University of Notre Dame
      Archives of the Propagation of the Faith, Lyon and Paris
      Archives of the Congregation of the Propagation of Faith
Archival Collection from the Archdiocese of Philadelphia
Archives of the Diocese of Richmond
Archives of the Ludwig-Mission Association
Charleston Public Library, Charleston, SC
Francis A. Drexel Library, St. Joseph's University, Philadelphia, PA

Bibliography

Joseph Cardinal Bernadin Archives and Records Center, Chicago,
    IL
Archives of the Archdiocese of Chicago
National Archives and Records Administration - Mid-Atlantic
    Regional Repository, Philadelphia, PA
Father Timothy Lindensfelder Private Collection of Historical
    Pictures, St. Augustine, FL
Villanova University Library, Villanova, PA


# Newspapers

*Banner of the South*, Augusta, GA
*Catholic Mirror*, Baltimore, MD
*Catholic Standard & Times*, Philadelphia, PA
*Charleston Catholic Miscellany*, Charleston, SC
*Charleston Daily Courier*, Charleston, SC
*Charleston News and Courier*, Charleston, SC
*Civiltà Cattolica*, Rome
*Diocesan Record*, Scranton, PA
*Florida Times-Union & Citizen*, Jacksonville, FL
*Jacksonville News Herald*, Jacksonville, FL
*Jacksonville Times-Union*, Jacksonville, FL
*New York Freeman's Journal and Catholic Register*, New York
*St. Augustine Record*, St. Augustine, FL
*U.S. Catholic Miscellany*, Charleston, SC


# Books and Articles

Abbott, Walter M., SJ, gen. ed. The Documents of Vatican II.
    New York: America Press, 1966.
*Acta et decreta concilii plenarii Baltimorensis tertii*. Baltimore, MD:
    John Murphy and Company, 1886.
Adams, Charles S., ed. "Report of the Jacksonville Auxiliary
    Sanitary Association of Jacksonville Florida Covering
    the Work of the Association during the Yellow Fever
    Epidemic, 1888." Jacksonville, FL: Executive
    Committee of the Association, 1889.
Ahern, Patrick Henry. The Life of John J. Keane: Educator and
    Archbishop, 1839-1918. Milwaukee, WI: Bruce, 1955.
Akin, Edward N. Flagler: Rockefeller Partner and Florida Baron.

411

Kent OH: Kent State University, 1988.

Alerding, H. J. The Diocese of Fort Wayne, 1669-1907. Fort Wayne, IN: Archer Printing, 1907.

Ammidown, Margot. "The Wagner Family: Pioneer Life on the Miami River." *Tequesta* 42 (1982): 5-37.

Andreassi Anthony D. "Burtsell, Richard." In The Encyclopedia of American Catholic History, edited by Michael Glazier and Thomas J. Shelly, 176-79. Collegeville, MN: Liturgical Press, 1997.

_____. "Preston, Thomas Scott." In The Encyclopedia of American Catholic History, edited by Michael Glazier and Thomas J. Shelly, 1169-70. Collegeville, MN: Liturgical Press, 1997.

Annals of the Propagation of the Faith. Baltimore, MD: St. Mary's Seminary, Nov.-Dec. 1899.

Arsenault, Raymond. St. Petersburg and the Florida Dream, 1888-1950. Norfolk/Virginia Beach, VA: Donning, 1988.

Arsenault, Raymond and Gary R. Mormino. "From Dixie to Dreamland: Demographic and Cultural Change in Florida, 1880-1980." In Shades of the Sunbelt: Essays on Ethnicity, Race, and the Urban South, edited by Randall M. Miller and George E. Pozzetta, 161-91. Boca Raton, FL: Florida Atlantic University, 1989.

Aubert, Roger. The Church in a Secularized Society. In The Christian Centuries, vol. 5, ed. by Roger Aubert. New York: Paulist, 1978.

Bagget, J. H., ed. Directory of the City of Charleston for the Year 1852. Charleston, SC: Edward C. Councell, 1851.

Barnes, Jay. Florida's Hurricane History. Chapel Hill, NC: University of North Carolina, 1998.

Barry, Colman J., OSB. The Catholic Church and German Americans. Milwaukee, WI: Bruce, 1953.

Baumstein, Dom Paschal, OSB. My Lord of Belmont: A Biography of Leo Haid. Belmont, NC: Herald House, 1985.

Bell, Stephen. Rebel Priest and Prophet: A Biography of Doctor Edward McGlynn. New York: Devin-Adaire, 1937.

Bernreuter, Bob J. Star of the Sea: A History of the Basilica St. Mary Star of the Sea. Key West, FL: Key West Publications, 2012.

Benigni, Urban. "Propaganda, Sacred Congregation of." The Catholic Encyclopedia. 1911 ed. s.v., vol. XII, 456-61.

Bodell, Dorothy H. Montgomery White Sulphur Springs: A History of the Resort, Hospital, Cemeteries, Markers, and Monuments. Blacksburg, VA: Pocahontas Press, 1993.

Brann, Henry A. A History of the American College, Rome. New York: Benziger Bros., 1910.

Brassard, Gerard. Biographical and Heraldic Dictionary of the Catholic Bishops of America. Vol. 1. Worchester, MA: Stobbs Press, 1962.

Brown, Canter, Jr. Florida's Peace River Frontier. Orlando, FL: University of Central Florida, 1991.

_____. "Tampa and the Coming of the Railroad, 1853-1884." Sunland Tribune 17 (Nov. 1991): 13-18.

Buchanan, Scott J. "A Brief History of the Diocese of Charleston, South Carolina, 1520-2000." Book manuscript, ADC, 2000.

Buker, George E. Jacksonville: Riverport -Seaport. Columbia, SC: University of South Carolina Press, 1992.

Burrows, Edwin G. and Mike Wallace. Gotham: A History of New York to 1898. New York: Oxford, 1999.

Burton, E. Milby. The Siege of Charleston, 1861-1865. 2d ed. Columbia, SC: University of South Carolina Press, 1994.

Byrne, Patricia, CSJ. "Sisters of St. Joseph, Americanization of the French Tradition." U.S. Catholic Historian 5 (Summer/Fall 1986): 241-72.

_____. "American Ultramontism." Theological Studies 56 (June 1995): 301-26.

Callahan, Nelson J., ed. The Diary of Richard L. Burtsell - Priest of New York: The Early Years, 1965-1868. New York: Arno, 1978.

Campbell, Sister Anne Francis, OLM. "Bishop England's Sisterhood, 1829-1929." Ph.D. diss., St. Louis University, 1968.

Chandler, David Leon. Henry Flagler: The Astonishing Life and Times of the Visionary Robber Barron Who Founded Florida. New York: Macmillan, 1986.

Childers, R. Wayne. "Historic Notes and Documents: Life in Miami and the Keys - Two Reports and a Map from the Monaco-Alaña Mission, 1743." Florida Historical Quarterly 82 (Summer 2003): 59-82.

Clancy, Thomas H., SJ. "Jesuits in the South: The Last 150 Years."
    *The Southern Jesuits* 2 (Aug. 1982): 9-30.
_____. Our Friends. 2d ed. New Orleans, LA: Jesuit Provincial
    Residence, 1989.
Cobb, James C. Industrialization & Southern Society, 1877-1984.
    Lexington, KY: University Press of Kentucky, 1984.
    Code, Joseph Bernard. Dictionary of the American
    Hierarchy (1789-1964). New York: Joseph F. Wagner,
    1964.
Code, Joseph Bernard. Dictionary of the American Hierarchy
    (1789-1964). New York: Joseph F. Wagner, 1964
Coffey, Michael, ed. The Irish in America. New York: Hyperion,
    1997.
Cohalan, Florence D. A Popular History of the Archdiocese of
    New York. Yonkers, NY: U.S. Catholic Historical Society,
    1983.
Congress of Colored Catholics of the U.S. Three Catholic Afro-
    American Congresses. Cincinnati, OH: American Catholic
    Tribune, 1893.
Crews, Clyde F. "American Catholic Authoritarianism: The
    Episcopacy of William George McCloskey, 1868-1909."
    *Catholic Historical Review* 70 (Oct. 1984): 560-80.
Cross, Robert D. The Emergence of Liberal Catholicism in
    America. Cambridge, MA: Harvard University Press, 1958.
Cunningham, H. H. Doctors in Gray: The Confederate Medical
    Service. Baton Rouge, LA: Louisiana State University
    Press, 1993.
Curl, Donald W. Palm Beach County: An Illustrated History.
    Northridge, CA: Windsor, 1986.
Curran, Olive C., compiler and ed. History of the Diocese of
    Meath, 1860-1993. Mullingar, Westmeath, IR: Diocese of
    Meath, 1995.
Curran, Robert Emmett, SJ. "The McGlynn Affair and
    the Shaping of the New Conservatism in American
    Catholicism, 1886-1894." *Catholic Historical Review* 66
    (April 1980): 184-204.
_____. Michael Augustine Corrigan and the Shaping of
    Conservative Catholicism in America, 1878-1902. New
    York: Arno, 1978.
_____. "Prelude to 'Americanism': The New York *Accademia* and
    Clerical Radicalism in the Late Nineteenth Century."

*Church History* 47 (March 1978): 48-65.

D'Agostino, Peter R. <u>Rome in America: Transnational Catholic Ideology from *Risorgimento* to Fascism</u>. Chapel Hill, NC: University of North Carolina Press, 2004.

Davis, Elisabeth C. "The Disappearance of Mother Agnes Spencer: The Centralization Controversy and the Antebellum Catholic Church." *American Catholic Studies* 130 (Summer 2019): 31-52.

Davis, Jack E. <u>The Gulf: The Making of an American Sea</u>. New York: Liveright, 2018.

Davis, T. Frederick. <u>History of Jacksonville and Vicinity, 1513-1924</u>. St. Augustine, FL: Florida Historical Society, 1925.

Dayton, William. "Pasco Pioneers: Catholic Settlements in San Antonio, St. Leo, and Vicinity." *Tampa Bay History* 1 (Fall/Winter 1979): 33-58.

Deegan, Kathleen, and Darcie MacMahon. <u>Fort Moses: Colonial America's Black Fortress of Freedom</u>. Gainesville, FL: University Press of Florida, 1995.

de la Coua, Antonio Rafael. "Fernandina Filibuster Fiasco: Birth of the 1895 Cuban War of Independence." *Florida Historical Quarterly* 82 (Summer 2003): 16-42.

Delaporte, Francois. <u>The History of Yellow Fever: An Essay on the Birth of Tropical Medicine</u>. Translated by Arthur Goldhammer. Cambridge, MA: Massachusetts Institute of Technology Press, 1991.

Dillon, Rodney E. "South Florida in 1860." *Florida Historical Quarterly* 60 (April 1982): 440-54.

Dolan, Jay P. <u>Catholic Revivalism: The American Experience, 1830-1900</u>. Notre Dame, IN: University of Notre Dame Press, 1978.

Duffy, Patrick. "Westmeath, County." In <u>The Encyclopedia of Ireland</u>, edited by Brian Lalor. New Haven, CT: Yale, 2003.

Dunn, Hampton. <u>Yesterday's Tampa</u>. Miami, FL: E. A. Seeman, 1972.

Dunne, Edmund F. <u>Our American Sicily</u>. San Antonio, FL: San Antonio Colony, 1883.

Durkin, Mary-Cabrini. <u>The Cathedral-Basilica of St. Augustine and Its History, 1565-2003</u>. Revised. Strasbourg, FR: *Éditions du Signe*, 2003.

Egan, Maurice F. <u>The Hierarchy of the Roman Catholic Church in the United States</u>. Vol. I. Philadelphia: George Barre

Publisher, 1888.

Ellis, John Tracy. "The Formation of the American Priest: An Historical Perspective." In The Catholic Priest in the United State: Historical Investigations, edited by John Tracy Ellis, 3-110. Collegeville, MN: St. John's University Press, 1971.

_____. The Life of James Cardinal Gibbons, Archbishop of Baltimore, 1834-1921. Vol. I. 1952. Replica Edition, Westminster, MD: Christian Classics, 1987.

Fairlie, Margaret C. "The Yellow Fever Epidemic of 1888 in Jacksonville." *Florida Historical Quarterly* 19 (Oct. 1940): 95-108.

Federal Writers' Project. The WPA Guide to Florida: the Federal Writers' Project Guide to 1930s Florida. 1939. Reprint, New York: Pantheon, 1984.

Finlay, James C. The Liberal Who Failed. Washington, DC: Corpus Books, 1968.

Fogarty, Gerald P., SJ. "The Catholic Hierarchy in the United states between the Third Plenary Council and the Condemnation of Americanism." *U.S. Catholic Historian* 11 (Summer 1993): 19-35.

_____. Commonwealth Catholicism: A History of the Catholic Church in Virginia. Notre Dame, IN: University of Notre Dame Press, 2001.

_____. The Vatican and the American Hierarchy from 1870 to 1965. Wilmington, DL: Michael Glazier, 1985.

_____. The Vatican and the Americanist Crisis: Denis J. O'Connell, American Agent in Rome, 1885-1903. Rome: Gregorian University Press, 1974.

Fraser, Walter J., Jr. Charleston! Charleston!: The History of a Southern City. Columbia, SC: University of South Carolina Press, 1989.

Freri, Joseph. "Propagation of the Faith, Society for the." The Catholic Encyclopedia, 1911 ed. s.v., vol. XII, 461-62.

Gannon, Michael V. "Before and After Modernism." In The Catholic Priest in the United States: Historical Investigations, edited by John Tracy Ellis, 293-383. Collegeville, MN: St. John's University Press, 1971.

_____. The Cross in the Sand: The Early Catholic Church in Florida, 1513-1870. Second Edition. 1965 Reprint, Gainesville, FL: University Press of Florida, 1989.

_____. Florida: A Short History. Gainesville, FL: University Press of Florida, 1996.

_____. Rebel Bishop: The Life and Era of Augustin Verot. Milwaukee, WI: Bruce, 1964.

Garrity, John A. A Short History of the American Nation. 3rd ed. New York: Harper and Row, 1981.

George, Henry, Jr. Life of Henry George. Toronto: Poole, 1900.

Glazier, Ira A., ed. The Famine Immigrants. Vols. II & III. Baltimore, MD: Genealogical Publications, 1983.

Glazier, Michael and Thomas J. Shelly., eds. The Encyclopedia of American Catholic History. Collegeville, MN: Liturgical Press, 1997.

Gleason, Philip. Conservative Reformers: German American Catholics and the Social Order. Notre Dame, IN: University of Notre Dame Press, 1968.

Gleeson, David T. The Irish in the South, 1815-1877. Chapel Hill, NC: University of North Carolina Press, 2001.

Graham, Thomas. "The Flagler Era, 1865-1913." In The Oldest City: St. Augustine's Saga of Survival. Edited by Jean Parker Waterbury, 181-210. St. Augustine, FL: St. Augustine Historical Society, 1983.

_____. Mr. Flagler's St. Augustine. Gainesville, FL: University Press of Florida, 2014.

Green James J. "American Catholics and the Irish Land League, 1879-1882." Catholic Historical Review 35 (April 1949): 19-42.

Gregory of Nazianzus. Three Poems. Trans. by Denis Molaise Meehan, OSB. In The Fathers of the Church, Vol. 75. Edited by Thomas P. Halton. Washington, DC: The Catholic University of America Press, 1987.

Grehan, Ida. The Dictionary of Irish Family Names Boulder, CO: Roberts Rinehart, 1997.

Guilday, Peter. A History of the Councils of Baltimore (1871-1884). New York: Macmillan, 1932.

_____. The Life and Times of John England. Vols. I & II. New York: America Pres, 1927.

Hann, John H. "Summary Guide to Spanish Florida Missions and Visitas with Churches in the Sixteenth and Seventeenth Centuries." Department of State of Florida, Archeological Research of Florida, 1988. Photocopy.

Heisser, David C. R. "Lynch, Patrick Neison." In The

Encyclopedia of the Irish in America edited by Michael
Glazier, 546-47. Notre Dame, IN: University of Notre
Dame Press, 1999.

_____. Patrick N. Lynch, 1817-1882: Third Catholic Bishop of
Charleston. Columbia, SC: University of South Carolina
Press, 2015.

Hickey, Edward John. The Society for the Propagation of the
Faith: Its Foundation, Organization and Success (1822-
1922). Washington, DC: The Catholic University of
America Press, 1922.

A History of the Third Plenary Council of Baltimore. Baltimore,
MD: Baltimore Publishing, 1885.

Hogan, Edmund M. The Irish Missionary Movement: A
Historical Survey, 1830-1980. Dublin: Gill and Macmillan,
1990.

Holmes, Emma. The Diary of Miss Emma Holmes. Edited by
John F. Marszalek. Baton Rouge, LA: Louisiana State
University Press, 1994.

Honour, John H., ed. Directory of the City of Charleston and
Neck for 1849. Charleston, SC: A. J. Burke, 1849.

Horgan, James J. Pioneer College: The Centennial History of St.
Leo College, St. Leo Abbey, and Holy Name Priory. St.
Leo, FL: St. Leo College Press, 1989.

Humphreys, Margaret. Yellow Fever and the South. Baltimore,
MD: Johns Hopkins University Press, 1999.

Hymes, Michael J. History of the Diocese of Cleveland, Origin
and Growth, 1847-1952. Cleveland, OH: Chancery Office,
1953.

Ireland, John. The Church in Modern Society; Lectures and
Addresses. Vols. I & II. St. Paul, MN: Pioneer, 1905.

Isacsson, Alfred, O.Carm. The Determined Doctor: The Story of
Edward McGlynn. Tarrytown, NY: Vestigium Press, 1998.

_____. "McGlynn, Edward." In Encyclopedia of American
Catholic History edited by Michael Glazier and Thomas
Shelly, 882-85. Collegeville, MN: Liturgical Press, 1997.

Jacquet, David. "Bishop Gilmour and the Third Plenary Council of
Baltimore." St. Meinrad Essays 12 (May 1959): 40-59.

Johnson, Dudley S. "Henry Bradley Plant and Florida." Florida
Historical Quarterly 45 (Oct. 1966): 118-32.

Jolly, Ellen Ryan. Nuns of the Battlefield. Providence, RI:
Providence Visitor Press, 1927.

Joyce, P. W. <u>Atlas and Cyclopedia of Ireland</u>. Part I. New York: Murphy & McCarthy, 1902.

Junior League of Charleston. <u>Historic Charleston Guidebook</u>. Charleston, SC: Nelson's Southern Printing, 1975.

Kasper, Walter Cardinal. <u>Leadership in the Church: How Traditional Roles Can Serve the Christian Community Today</u>. Translated by Brian McNeil. New York: Crossroad, 2003.

Kauffman, Christopher J., ed. "The Americanist Controversy: Recent Historical and Theological Perspectives." *U.S. Catholic Historian* 11 (Summer 1993), 1-124 - entire issue.

Keegan, John. <u>The Mask of Command</u>. New York: Penguin, 1987.

Kelly, Joseph. <u>America's Longest Siege: Charleston, Slavery, and the Slow March Toward Civil War</u>. New York: Overlook Press, 2013.

Kelly, Liam. <u>The Diocese of Kilmore, c. 1100-1800</u>. Dublin: Columbia Press, 2017.

Kennedy, Liam and Paul S. Ell, E. M. Crawford, L. A. Clarkson. <u>Mapping the Great Irish Famine: A Survey of the Famine Decades</u>. Dublin: Four Courts Press, 1999.

Kinealy, Christine. <u>The Great Calamity: The Irish Famine, 1845-52</u>. Boulder, CO: Roberts Rinehart, 1995.

Klein, Maury. <u>Days of Defiance: Sumter, Secession, and the Coming of the Civil War</u>. New York: Alfred A. Knoph, 1997.

Lane, Pat S. "Florida is a Blessed Country: Letters from a Florida Settler [Port Charlotte, 1885-87]." *Florida Historical Quarterly* 64 (April 1986): 432-45.

Laxton, Edward. <u>The Famine Ships: The Irish Exodus to America, 1846-1851</u>. New York: Henry Holt, 1997.

Loome, Thomas Michael. <u>Liberal Catholicism, Reformed Catholicism, Modernism: A Contribution to a New Orientation in Modernist Research</u>. Mainz: Matthias-Grünewald-Verlag, 1979.

Madden, Richard C. <u>Catholics in South Carolina: A Record</u>. Lanham, MD: University Press of America, 1985.

Maher, Mary Denis. <u>To Bind Up Wounds: Catholic Sister Nurses in the U.S. Civil War</u>. Baron Rouge, LA: Louisiana State University Press, 1999.

Mahon, John K. <u>History of the Second Seminole War, 1835-1842</u>. Rev. ed. Gainesville, FL: University of Florida Press, 1991.

Malone, Sylvester L. <u>Dr. Edward McGlynn</u>. New York: Dr. McGlynn Monument Association, 1918.

Maloney, Walter C. <u>A Sketch of the History of Key West, Florida</u>. 1876. Facsimile reproduction, Gainesville, FL: University of Florida Press, 1968.

Marchand, John B. <u>Charleston Blockade: The Journals of John B. Marchand, U.S. Navy, 1861-62</u>. Edited by Craig L. Symonds. Newport, RI: Naval War College, Press, 1976.

Martino, Joseph F. "A Study of Certain Aspects of the Episcopate of Patrick J. Ryan, Archbishop of Philadelphia, 1884-1911." H.E.D. diss., Gregorian Pontifical University, 1982.

Mason, Georgina. <u>The Companion Guide to Rome</u>. Revised by Tim Jepson. Rochester, NY: Companion Guides, 1998.

May, William. <u>History of the New England Society of Charleston, SC, 1819-1919</u>. Charleston, SC: New England Society of Charleston, 1920.

McCool, Gerald A. <u>Catholic Theology in the Nineteenth Century: The Quest for a Unitary Method</u>. New York: Crossroad/Seabury, 1977.

McEwan, Bonnie G., ed. <u>The Spanish Missions of *La Florida*</u>. Gainesville, FL: University Press of Florida, 1993.

McGoldrick, Sr, Thomas Joseph, SSJ. <u>Beyond the Call; The Legacy of the Sisters of St. Joseph of Saint Augustine, Florida</u>. Bloomington, IN: Xlibris, 2008.

McGeevy, John T. <u>American Jesuits and the World: How an Embattled Religious Order Made Modern Catholicism Global</u>. Princeton, NJ: Princeton University Press, 2016.

McMurray, Vincent de Paul. "The Church during Reconstruction, 1865-1877." M.A. thesis, The Catholic University of America, 1950.

√ McNally, Michael J. <u>Catholicism in South Florida 1868-1968</u>. Gainesville, FL: University Presses of Florida, 1984.

_____. "Catholic Parish Life in the Antebellum South: Columbus, Georgia, 1830-1960." *American Catholic Studies* 113 (Spring-Summer 2002): 1-30.

√_____. <u>Catholic Parish Life on Florida's West Coast, 1860-1968</u>. St. Petersburg, FL: Catholic Media Ministries, 1996.

_____. "Father Philippe de Carriere: Jesuit Pioneer on Florida's West Coast, 1888-1902." *Tampa Bay History* 17 (Fall/Winter 1995): 35-46.

_____. "James A. Corcoran and St. Charles Borromeo Seminary -Overbrook, 1871-1907." *American Catholic Studies* 110 (Spring-Winter 1999): 49-69.

_____. "Lynch, Patrick Neison." In <u>American National Biography</u>, edited by John Garraty and Mark Carnes, vol. 14, 169-70. New York: Oxford, 1999.

_____. Moore, John." In <u>American National Biography</u>, edited by John Garraty and Mark Carnes, vol. 15, 762-63. New York: Oxford, 1999.

_____. "A Peculiar Institution: A History of Catholic Parish Life in the Southeast (1850-1980)." In <u>The American Catholic Parish: A History from 1850 to the Present</u>, edited by Jay P. Dolan, vol. 1, 117-234. New York: Paulist, 1987.

_____. "Reconstruction and Parish Life in Charleston, SC, 1865-1877: A Pastor's Perspective. *American Catholic Studies* 117 (Spring 2006): 45-67.

McNamara, Robert F. <u>The American College in Rome, 1855-1955</u>. Rochester, NY: Christopher Press, 1956.

_____. <u>Catholic Sunday Preaching: The American Guidelines</u>. Washington, DC: Word of God Institute, 1975.

Milanich, Jerald T. <u>Florida Indians and the Invasion from Europe</u>. Gainesville, FL: University Press of Florida, 1995.

_____. <u>Florida's Indians from Ancient Times to the Present</u>. Gainesville, FL: University Press of Florida, 1998.

Miller, David W. "Irish Catholicism and the Great Famine" Journal of Social History 9 (Sept. 1975): 81-98.

Miller, Kerby A. <u>Emigrants and Exiles: Ireland and the Irish Exodus to North America</u>. New York: Oxford, 1985.

Monaco, C. S. <u>The Second Seminole War and the Limits of American Aggression</u>. Baltimore, MD: Johns Hopkins University Press, 2018.

Mooney, Joseph F. <u>Memorial of the Most Reverend Michael Augustine Corrigan, DD</u>. New York: Cathedral Library Association, 1902.

Moren, Peter, CSP. "Dr. Edward McGlynn." *Commonweal* 27 (Feb. 4, 1938): 408-09.

Mormino, Gary R. "Tampa: from Hell Hole to the Good Life." In <u>Sunbelt Cities: Politics and Growth since World War II</u>, edited by Richard M. Bernard and Bradley R. Rice. Austin, TX: University of Texas Press, 1983.

Mormino, Gary R. and Anthony Pizzo. <u>Tampa: The Treasure City</u>.

Tulsa, OK: Centennial Heritage, 1983.

Mormino, Gary R. and George E. Pozzetta. The Immigrant World of Ybor City: Italians and Their Latin Neighbors in Tampa, 1885-1985. Chicago, IL: University of Illinois Press, 1987.

Musicant, Ivan. Empire by Default: The Spanish-American War and the Dawn of the American Century. New York: Henry Holt, 1998.

National Archives and Records Administration - Mid-Atlantic Region (Philadelphia). U.S. Census, 1850. M-432, Roll 850.

Nulty, William H. Confederate Florida: The Road to Olustee. Tuscaloosa, AL: University of Alabama Press, 1990.

O'Brien, Michael J. "The Irish in Charleston, South Carolina." Journal of the American-Irish Historical Society 25 (1926): 134-46.

O'Conlain, Michael, ed. A Partial List of Some Memorials in Westmeath Church Yards. Vol. 5. Clonmellon Parish. Millingar, Ireland: Millingar Library, n.d.

O'Connell, J. J., OSB. Catholicity in the Carolinas and Georgia. New York: D. & J. Sadlier, 1879.

O'Connell, Marvin R. Critics on Trial: An Introduction to the Catholic Modernist Crisis. Washington, DC: The Catholic University of America Press, 1994.

_____. John Ireland and the American Catholic Church. St. Paul, MN: Minnesota Historical Society Press, 1988.

Oesterreicher, Michel. Pioneer Family: Life on Florida's Twentieth Century Frontier. Tuscaloosa, AL: University of Alabama Press, 1996.

O'Malley, John W. Vatican I: The Council and the Making of the Ultramontaine Church. Cambridge, MA: The Belknap Press of Harvard University, 2018.

O'Murchadha, Ciarán. The Great Famine: Ireland's Agony, 1845-1852. London: Continuum, 2011.

O'Neill, Sister Rosalina, SNJM. "History of the Contribution of the Sisters of the Holy Names of Jesus and Mary to the Cause of Education in Florida." M.A. thesis, Fordham University, n.d. [c. 1938].

Parks, Arva Moore. "Miami in 1876." Tequesta 35 (1975): 89-145.

Peréz, Louis A., Jr. "Between Encounter and Experience: Florida in the Cuban Imagination." Florida Historical Quarterly 82 (Fall 2003): 170-90.

Peterman, Thomas J. "Becker, Thomas Andrew." In The
    Encyclopedia of American Catholic History, edited by
    Michael Glazier and Thomas J. Shelly, 131-33. Collegeville,
    MN: Liturgical Press, 1997.
_____. The Cutting Edge: The Life of Thomas Andrew Becker.
    Devon, PA: William T. Cooke Publisher, 1982.
Peters, Thelma. Biscayne Country, 1870-1926. Miami, FL:
    Banyon Books, 1981.
_____. Miami 1909. Miami, FL: Banyon Books, 1985.
Pierce, Charles W. Pioneer Life in Southeast Florida. Edited
    by Donald Walter Curl. Coral Gables, FL: University of
    Miami Press, 1970.
Poyo, Gerald E. "Cuban Patriots in Key West, 1878-1886:
    Guardians at the Separatist Ideals." *Florida Historical
    Quarterly* 61 (July 1982): 20-36.
_____. "Key West and the Cuban Ten Years War." *Florida
    Historical Quarterly* 57 (Jan. 1979): 289-307.
Preston, Thomas S. "American Catholicity." *American Catholic
    Quarterly Review* 16 (1891): 396-408.
Purcell, Richard J. "Moore, John." In Dictionary of American
    Biography, edited by Dumas Malone, vol. 13, 131-31. New
    York: Charles Scribner's Sons, 1934.
Quinn, John F. "'The Nation's Guest?': The Battle between
    Catholics and Abolitionists to Manage Father Theobald
    Mathew's American Tour, 1849-1851." *U.S. Catholic
    Historian* 22 (Summer 2004): 19-40.
Rabinowitz, Howard N. Race Relations in the Urban South,
    1865-1890. Urban Life in America Series, gen. ed. Richard
    C. Wade. New York: Oxford, 1978.
Reher, Margaret. Catholic Intellectual Life in America: A
    Historical Study of Persons and Movements. New York:
    Macmillan, 1989.
Rights, Lucille Rieley. A Portrait of St. Lucie County, Florida.
    Virginia Beach, VA: Donning, 1994.
Rivers, Larry Eugene. Slavery in Florida: Territorial Days to
    Emancipation. Gainesville, FL: University Press of Florida,
    2000.
Rosen, Robert N. Confederate Charleston: An Illustrated
    History of the City and the People During the Civil War.
    Columbia, SC: University of South Carolina Press, 1994.
Rosenbaum, Robert A., ed. The Penguin Encyclopedia of

American History. New York: Penguin Putnam, 2003.

St. Ambrose Centennial Committee. The Branches: Springs of Living Water. 2d. ed. St. Augustine, FL: Standard Printing, 1988.

Saint Anthony School Centennial, 1884-1984. Dade City, FL: Quality Impressions, 1984.

Schoof, T. M. A Survey of Catholic Theology, 1800-1970 Trans. by N. D. Smith. Paramus, NJ.: Paulist, 1970.

Shea, John Gilmary. The Hierarchy of the Catholic Church in the U.S. New York: Office of Publications, 1886.

Sheen, F. J. "Propagation of the Faith, Society for the." In The New Catholic Encyclopedia, vol. 11, 844-46. New York: McGraw-Hill, 1967.

Shermyen, Anned H., ed. 1989 Florida Statistical Abstract. Gainesville, FL: University Press of Florida, 1989.

Skeabeck, Andrewe, CSSR. "The Most Reverend William Gross: Missionary Bishop of the South." Researches of the Catholic Historical Society of Philadelphia 65 (Dec. 1954): 217-18.

Smith, Julia Floyd. Slavery and Plantation Growth in Antebellum Florida, 1821-1860. Gainesville, FL: University Press of Florida, 1973.

Smith, William L. Irish Priests in the United States: A Vanishing Subculture. Lanham, MD: University Press of America, 2004.

Smyth, G. Hutchinson. The Life of Henry Bradley Plant. New York: G. P. Putnam's Sons, 1898.

Spalding, Thomas W. "Frontier Catholicism." Catholic Historical Review 77 (July 1991): 470-84.

_____. Martin John Spalding: American Churchman. Washington, DC: The Catholic University of America Press 1973.

_____. The Premier See: A History of the Archdiocese of Baltimore, 1789-1989. Baltimore, MD: Johns Hopkins University Press, 1989.

Standiford, Les. Last Train to Paradise: Henry Flagler and the Spectacular Rise and Fall of the Railroad that Crossed an Ocean. New York: Three Rivers Press, 2002.

Steele, John Carson Hay, Sr. and Robert Pinckney Rhett. Charleston: Then and Now. Orangeburg, SC: Sandlapper Publishing, 2001.

Straubing, Harold Elk. In Hospital and Camp: The Civil War

through the Eyes of Its Doctors and Nurses. Harrisburg,
PA: Stackpole, 1993.

Sweeney, David Francis, OFM. The Life of John Lancaster
Spalding: First Bishop of Peoria, 1840-1916. New York:
Herder, 1965.

Taves, Ann. The Household of Faith: Roman Catholic Devotions
in Mid-Nineteenth Century America. Notre Dame, IN:
University of Notre Dame Press, 1986.

Taylor, Robert A. "Florida Goes to War." *Florida Humanities
Council* XXXIV (Spring 2010): 4-9.

Tebeau, Charlton. A History of Florida. Coral Gables, FL:
University of Miami Press, 1971.

Toíbin, Colm and Diarmaid Ferriter. The Irish Famine: A
Documentary. London: Profile Books, 1999.

Trisco, Robert. "Bishops and Their Priests in the United States."
In The Catholic Priest in the United States: Historical
Investigations, edited by John Tracy Ellis, 111-292.
Collegeville, MN: St. John's University Press, 1971.

Tyrell, William, SJ. "With the Soldiers in Tampa." *Woodstock
Letters* 28 (1899): 24-34.

Walsh, Timothy. "Temperance Movement and American
Catholics." In The Encyclopedia of American Catholic
History, edited by Michael Glazier and Thomas J. Shelley,
1372-73. Collegeville, MN: Liturgical Press, 1997.

Waterbury, Jean Parker, ed. The Oldest City: St. Augustine Saga
of Survival. St. Augustine, FL: St. Augustine Historical
Society, 1983.

White, Joseph M. The Diocesan Seminary in the United States: A
History from the 1780s to the Present. Notre Dame, IN:
University of Notre Dame Press, 1989.

White, Richard. The Republic for Which It Stands: The United
States During Reconstruction and the Gilded Age,
1865-1896. The Oxford History of the United States, gen.
ed. David M. Kennedy. New York: Oxford, 2017.

Whitelaw, Robert N. S. And Alice F. Leukoff. Charleston
Come Hell or High Water: A History in Photographs.
Charleston, SC: Privately Published, 1976.

Widmer, Randolph J. The Evolution of the Calusa: A
Nonagricultural Chiefdom on the Southwest Florida Coast.
Tuscaloosa, AL: University of Alabama Press, 1988.

Wilber, C. Keith. Civil War Medicine. Old Saybrook, CT: Globe

Pequot, 1998.

Williamson, Edward C. Florida Politics in the Gilded Age, 1877-1893. Gainesville, FL: University Presses of Florida, 1976.

Wilson, David A. United Irishmen, United States: Immigrant Radicals in the Early Republic. Ithaca, NY: Cornell University Press, 1998.

Wolf, Notker and Enrica Rosanna. The Art of Leadership. Translated by Gerlinde Büchinger-Schmid and edited by Sue Bollans. Collegeville, MN: Liturgical Press, 2013.

Woodward, C. Vann. The Strange Career of Jim Crow: Commemorative Edition. 1955. New York: Oxford University Press, 2002.

Wynne, Lewis N. and Robert A. Taylor. Florida in the Civil War. Charleston, SC: Arcadia, 2004.

U.S. Department of the Interior. The Eleventh Census of the United States, 1890. 10 vols. Washington, DC: Government Printing Office, 1892-94.

Zwierlein, Frederick J. The Life and Letters of Bishop McQuaid. 3 vols. Rochester, NY: Art Print Shop, 1925-27.

_____. Letters of Archbishop Corrigan to Bishop McQuaid and Allied Documents. Rochester, NY: Art Print Shop, 1946.

## Interviews

Campbell, Sister Anne Francis, OLM. Interview with the author. Charleston, SC, June 27, 1996.

McGoldrick, Sister Thomas Joseph, SSJ. Interview with the author. St. Augustine, FL, January 20, 2003.

Willis, Very Reverend Thomas. Interview with the author. St. Augustine, FL, June 19, 2019.

## Websites

Collège et Lycées Catholiques, Combrée, Father  http://combree.free.fr.

St. Anthony of Padua Catholic School, San Antonio, FL. www.stanthonyschoolfl.org

# Index

## W

Walsh, Patrick  72
Wayrich CSSR, William  94-95
Westmeath  7–14, 8–10, 289, 345
West Palm Beach  121
Widman, Conrad  152, 154, 249
Willcox, Jr. James W.  223

## Y

Ybor City  108, 127, 146, 182, 211,
    221, 249
Ybor, Vincente Martinez  108, 119,
    120, 145, 146, 148, 181
yellow fever  126, 139, 139–142,
    238; Fernandina; Jacksonville
    140; Tampa  140

## About the Author

Michael J. McNally is a priest of the Diocese of Palm Beach. He was ordained in 1973, receiving a B.A., a M.Div., and a M.Th. from St. Vincent DePaul Regional Seminary, Boynton Beach, FL. After two pastoral assignments in Miami, was assigned to the faculty of St. John Vianney College Seminary, Miami, FL, from 1975 to 1979. He was then sent away for graduate studies at the University of Notre Dame, where he received an M.A.(1980) and a Ph.D.(1983).

He taught Church History and served on the faculty of St. Vincent de Paul Regional Seminary from 1982 to 1993 and of St. Charles Borromeo Seminary, Philadelphia, PA, from 1993 to 2005. He was appointed the pastor of St. Mark the Evangelist Catholic Church, Fort Pierce, FL, from 2005 to 2018, after which he retired his pastorate. Since retirement, he is the Chaplain to the Poor Clare Nuns at San Damiano Monastery, Fort Myers Beach, FL.

He is the author of <u>Catholic Parish Life on Florida's West Coast, 1860-1968</u> (St. Petersburg, FL; Catholic Media Ministries 1996) and <u>Catholicism in South Florida, 1868-1968</u> (Gainesville, FL; University of Florida 1984).